D1481989

THE BOSTON MASSACRE

Also by Hiller B. Zobel

LEGAL PAPERS OF JOHN ADAMS (*with L. Kinvin Wroth*)

THE
BOSTON MASSACRE

BY HILLER B. ZOBEL

W · W · NORTON & COMPANY · INC · New York

Copyright © 1970 by Hiller B. Zobel

First Edition

Library of Congress Catalog Card No. 79-77413

SBN 393-05376-8

All Rights Reserved

Published simultaneously in Canada by
George J. McLeod Limited, Toronto

PRINTED IN THE UNITED STATES OF AMERICA

1 2 3 4 5 6 7 8 9 0

For
E.J.B. and H.Z.

CONTENTS

*Illustrations appear between pages 100 and 101
and 196 and 197.*

ACKNOWLEDGMENTS

Over the four years that preparation of this book required, many individuals and organizations freely gave assistance, which I would like here to acknowledge with gratitude. None of them, of course, bears any responsibility for the book's factual or interpretive content.

The late Professor Mark DeWolfe Howe of Harvard, Professor Bernard Bailyn of Harvard, Frederick Bernays Wiener, Esq., and Judge Charles E. Wyzanski, Jr., gave encouragement to the entire project, which the American Council of Learned Societies supported with a generous grant-in-aid.

Lyman H. Butterfield was kind enough to read the full manuscript and to save me from many errors and overstatements: he is not liable for any which may remain.

My long-time colleague, Professor L. Kinvin Wroth, of the University of Maine Law School, frequently let me rely on his knowledge and historical judgment.

Hon. Erwin N. Griswold, as Dean of the Harvard Law School, was, with Professor Howe and Mr. Butterfield, responsible for giving Kinvin Wroth and me the opportunity to edit John Adams's legal papers. The present work depends so much upon the earlier one that Dean Griswold can justly be called the godfather of both.

A study based upon documents, as this one is, depends greatly on the assistance of depository curators. I wish especially to thank the following: John E. Alden of the Boston Public Library, bookman extraordinary; Mrs. Ropes Cabot of the Bostonian Society; Miss Edith G. Henderson of the Harvard Law School's Treasure Room; Miss Carolyn Jakeman of the Houghton Library, Harvard; Hon. John E. Powers, Clerk of the Supreme Judicial Court for Suffolk County, Boston, and his staff, particularly Miss Eileen Kennedy and Miss Virginia Lynch; P. Fellows and Michael Lea of the Public Record Office; Leo Flaherty of the Massachusetts State Archives, Boston; H. S. Cobb, of the House of Lords Records Office, London; Howard H. Peckham of the William L. Clements Library, University of Michigan; Alexander P. Clark of the Princeton University Library; Walter M. Whitehill of the Boston Athenaeum; A. W. H. Pearsall and Miss J. Milan of the National Maritime Museum, Greenwich, England. (Crown Copyright material is printed by permission of the Controller of Her Majesty's Stationery Office.)

Stephen T. Riley, Director of the Massachusetts Historical Society, smoothed an inordinate number of documentary wrinkles. I owe special thanks to him and to the Society's John D. Cushing, Malcolm Freiberg, and Miss Winifred Collins. The Council of the Society liberally allowed me the privilege of quoting freely from countless papers in its collections.

The staffs of various libraries gave unfailing courteous assistance: Bapst Library, Boston College (particularly the Director, Rev. Brendan J. Connolly, S.J.); Boston College Law School Library; Cary Memorial Library, Lexington, Massachusetts; Harvard College Library (Houghton, Lamont, and Widener); Harvard Law School Library.

Work on this book began while I was still in active practice. My then-senior, Robert J. Hallisey, Esq., encouraged my research and writing and arranged for me to be assigned to temporary duty in London, thus to combine workdays at the law with days off in the various British archives.

Rev. Robert F. Drinan, S.J., Dean of the Boston College Law School, a man for all scholars, and the School's Administrative Assistant, Mrs. Louis Bonelli, made my life easier in many ways during the preparation of the book.

John W. Bethell, my father-in-law, unfailing in his interest and hospitality, furnished a summer haven for my family in his home at South Essex, Massachusetts, where much of the book was written.

At various times, many people lent hands when hands were badly needed: John T. Bethell; Thomas N. Bethell; John Carr of Boston's Hayden Planetarium; Marcus McCorison, Director of the American Antiquarian Society; Jules D. Prown, Director of the Paul Mellon Center for British Art and British Studies, New Haven; Clifford K. Shipton, University Archivist, Harvard; John H. Zobel; Charles

Capace, Charles Gibbons, Alfred Konefsky, Thomas Maffei, and Mrs. Michael Putziger, all students at the Boston College Law School; Joseph H. B. Edwards, Esq.; David H. Zobel; Jane Baird; Gregg Benjamin; Francis B. McNamara, Jr., Esq.; and Professor Sanford J. Fox of Boston College Law School.

Mrs. Judith D. Burton, Mrs. Richard Lippman, and Miss Jane Washek typed various drafts and corrections; Mrs. Neil Sommer typed the entire difficult manuscript in final. Mrs. Frank Newell, Jr. and Miss Jane Crimlisk rendered vital secretarial support.

Mrs. Carl Pitha prepared a complicated index under strenuous conditions, promptly, accurately, and with unfailing good humor.

Donald S. Lamm and Eric P. Swenson of W. W. Norton and Company were everything an author could ask: publishers, editors, friends.

Deborah B. Zobel ends the list, but only because wives traditionally do. She and I both know why she should really be first.

Boston
September, 1969

THE BOSTON MASSACRE

CHAPTER 1

HIS MAJESTY'S PROVINCE
OF MASSACHUSETTS BAY

It is an old friend among the historical residue that we all carry; a familiar story that each of us has known since first we realized that our country's freedom grew from bloodshed. The picture has always been with us: the hated Redcoats tramping through the peaceful town of Boston; the honest citizens quietly going about their evening business; a few schoolboys harmlessly taunting the soldiers; the troops forming a battle line, loading with military precision, fixing bayonets, aiming carefully, and, on direct order deliberately given, firing a deadly volley at the helpless civilians. Death is everywhere; Crispus Attucks, the first American to die for liberty, lies an innocent martyr at the feet of his butchers; the soldiers grin through the musket smoke at the other victims sprawled in the gutter, shoulder their weapons, and march off. Five years before Lexington, Concord, and Bunker Hill, the Revolution has begun.

To this basic scenario, some of us learn a sequel. It might be called The Birth of American Justice, or (because every eighteenth-century play needs a subtitle) Even the Guilty Deserve a Fair Trial. This drama differs sharply from the Massacre itself. The characters (except for Crispus Attucks) lack definition or even names. Here the star is John Adams, whose future will include signing the Declaration of Independence and serving as our second president. We are not sure of the details, but we know that purely from a sense of duty, at great risk to his own popularity, lawyer Adams took the impossible case, and somehow convinced an implacably hostile jury to acquit his clients.

The Boston Massacre, in short, is a part, not only of our national history, but of our national mythology. It represents the first tragic culmination of that British policy which provoked independence; it represents the physical sacrifice required to achieve independence; it represents the concept of Boston as Cradle of Liberty. And in its aftermath, it represents that nobility of soul and loftiness of purpose which we like to associate with the Founding Fathers. The Boston Massacre, or more accurately, what we think of when we refer to the Boston Massacre, thus fills a need in our national historic memory. Not the least of the Massacre's attractions as an object of historic contemplation is the speed with which the men of 1770 (on both sides of the Atlantic and both sides of the political fence) recognized the mythological value of what happened in King Street.

One would be unduly cynical to say that if the Massacre had not occurred, it would have been necessary to invent it. But no one leafing the pages of the Boston *Gazette* for 1770 or reading the bloody-shirt–waving tirades which until 1784 commemorated the anniversaries of the "Bloody Tragedy" can doubt that the patriot propagandists knew a good potboiler when they saw one. And no one examining the correspondence between General Gage and Lieutenant Colonel Dalrymple (the commanding officer in Boston), or the various comments of Acting Governor Hutchinson and Judge Peter Oliver could doubt that the royalists knew that an explosion between soldiers and civilians was inevitable.

To understand why both sets of impressions are correct, it is essential to realize that troops had been garrisoned in Boston since the fall of 1768, not for any military purpose, but purely and simply as conservators of the peace, and, as John Adams was later to note, "wretched" ones, at that.

If the occurrence of the Massacre can be blamed on the presence of the soldiers, the presence of the soldiers can in turn be traced to those two prime sources of evil and corruption: money and power.

This is not the place to undertake an analysis of the causes of the American Revolution, nor even a descriptive list of the events which underlay those causes. An ample, if somewhat indecisive, literature has arisen around the origins of the struggle for independence, some of the major items of which have been set out in the chapter notes. The present work will have little to add. At the same time, one has to realize that the Massacre did not, like a classic tragedy, arise, take place, and end all on March 5, 1770. The forces which pointed the muskets on King Street swirled out of the entire American colonial experience, and particularly out of the actions and reactions of Massachusetts and England in the years immediately preceding.

The keys to comprehension of history come from humble metal. You will of course appreciate the dimensions of the Revolutionary prologue better if the taxation-representation arguments of the pamphleteers are current in your mind. But you will not understand the jockeying which preceded the trials of Captain Preston and the soldiers unless you realize that at certain times of the year four months or more passed between the day a dispatch left Boston for England and the day the answer returned. And you cannot grasp the attitude of the crown and its ministers unless you appreciate that Boston in 1765 had a population of 15,520 (in 1,676 houses); Manchester, England, more than 30,-000; Edinburgh about 50,000; and London more than 700,000, which was well over half the entire population of the continental, non-Canadian colonies. In short, to any member of the English ruling group, Boston was not only distant, it was, municipally speaking, insignificant. And more to the point, it was a colonial town. This placed its inhabitants, and indeed the entire province of which it was the metropolis, in a status different from and lower than the English of England. Colonies existed for the benefit and profit of the mother country. This was a truism generally accepted at all levels in England, and even among thoughtful Americans.[1]

Of course the colonials, while acknowledging their subordinate status, tended to emphasize the American aspects of their relationship with England. Consider the nomenclature of the war whose resolution in 1763 is commonly regarded as the watershed in Anglo-colonial relationships. In England, it was called the Seven Years War, because from 1756 to 1763 the Prussians of Frederick the Great, aided by British gold and Redcoats, battled like cornered foxes against the massive French, Russian, and Austrian armies. The North American phase of this war, however, started in 1754 with a skirmish between Virginia militiamen (commanded by twenty-two-year-old George Washington) and a Franco-Indian detachment in the Pennsylvania wilderness. On this side of the Atlantic, the conflict was and is known as the French and Indian War, a title which carries considerable significance. For the American enemies were the savages who threatened the western settlements (and thus, incidentally, the investments of the seaboard land speculators) and the French whose Canadian bases nourished the Indian menace, siphoned the northern fur trade, and left the threat of an armed invasion always open. To recall the great battles of the war is to underline its significance: Braddock's Defeat (1755), Ticonderoga (1758), and, most important of all, Quebec (1759). All British subjects clearly and immediately recognized the import of Wolfe's

heroic victory: the French no longer counted in North America. The
bonfires and church bells in England found reflections and echoes in
Boston, where the sermons of the ministers (the Reverend Jonathan
Mayhew delivered two on one day) embroidered the happy theme
with a local variation: New England was safe for all time from a
French, Catholic invasion. The conflict would continue for another
two-and-a-half years before the definitive peace treaty; but with respect to what one might call New England's war aims, the struggle was
over.[2]

Massachusetts, like the rest of the Empire, received a new sovereign
on October 25, 1760, the day George II died. More important, during
that same year it received a new royal representative, Francis Bernard,
Esquire. When on December 17, 1760, Bernard for the first time addressed the two houses of the legislature, he and his listeners were still
figuratively aglow from the light of those beacons of 1759 celebrating
what His Excellency was pleased to call "The glorious Conclusion of
the North American War."[3]

A new peace, a new reign, and a new governor. Francis Bernard, a
roast beef of a man with influential connections, arrived in Boston on
August 2, 1760. "We made our entry here last Saturday in a very Magnificent manner," he wrote his wife's cousin, Lord Barrington, the secretary at war. Through Barrington's influence, Bernard had been appointed governor of New Jersey in 1758; that same influence, activated
by the financial needs of his family, had helped promote him to the
chief magistracy of Massachusetts.[4]

This "English gentleman of third-rate abilities," as Edward Channing described him with cruel accuracy, came to America without
training or experience to fit him for the problems he would have to
handle there, particularly in Massachusetts. Born in 1712, he had gone
to Westminster School (where one of his younger contemporaries had
been the future general, Thomas Gage) and thence as a Westminster
Scholar to Christ Church, Oxford. Additional study at the Middle
Temple, culminating in his call to the bar in 1737, had gently launched
the quiet career as a Lincolnshire attorney and civic official (including
the recordership of the original Boston) from which his "interest" with
Barrington rescued him.[5]

After moderate success in the Jerseys, an achievement which his
subsequent problems in Massachusetts were to magnify by contrast,
Bernard tried to tackle the emerging demons to the northward. An accomplished raconteur with a large supply of anecdotes, Bernard arrived full of optimism, for he had been assured (by Thomas Pownall,
his predecessor) "that I may depend upon a quiet and easy administration. I shall have no points of government to dispute about, no

schemes of self-interest to pursue. The People are well disposed to live upon good terms with the Governor and with one another." On the scene, he found "a very fair Prospect of an easy Administration." Certainly Bernard began his administration in popularity, although his initial speech to the legislators did draw some unfavorable comment. "He talks like a weak honest Man," some said; and John Adams scornfully dissected his verbal gaffes. But as Adams himself was willing to admit of the speech, "there are no Marks of Knavery in it: there are marks of good sense I think. Grammatical and Rhetorical Inaccuracies are by no means Proofs of Weakness, or Ignorance. They may be found in Bacon, Lock, Newton, &c." Even the epilepsy which later plagued him so seriously did not seem to interfere with Bernard's satisfactory attention to his duties.[6]

When Harvard dedicated Hollis Hall, a badly needed new dormitory, it was Bernard who named the building. And when, a few days later, a carelessly caused fire gutted Old Harvard Hall during a legislative session held there because of the Boston smallpox, Governor Bernard stood in the snow with President Edward Holyoke and "personally directed the townspeople in the work of rescue." Besides which, when the present Harvard Hall rose on the razed site of its predecessor, the housewrights worked from plans drawn by the governor himself, "a very ingenious architect." [7]

Early in his administration, a legislature not noted for its open-handed attitude in fiscal matters conveyed to the governor, "in consideration of" his "extraordinary services," title to Mount Desert Island, off the Maine coast. His popularity, regrettably, rested on weak footing, for in Bernard's first years he did not face many politically difficult decisions. When pressure increased in the mid-1760's, Bernard's political inexperience, his tendency to dissimulation, his slow mind, and, to be fair about it, his determination to follow orders from England, squeezed what had been patronizing good humor into petulant indecisiveness, and led the once-dutiful populace to salute him with such pleasantries as:

> If such Men are by God appointed
> The Devil may be the Lord's anointed.[8]

Like most difficulties which beset governors (and Governors), Bernard's troubles were neither sudden in their rise nor wholly attributable to forces beyond his control. As early as November 1760, even before he had delivered his homiletic discourse to the General Court, he had badly mishandled one of a governor's most important tasks, the appointment of a chief justice.

The problem was thrust on Bernard by the death, September 11, of Chief Justice Stephen Sewall. Sewall, who presided over the five-man Superior Court of Judicature, the highest common-law court in the province, illustrated and indeed justified the strange tendency of colonial Americans to elevate non-lawyers to high judicial office. A deeply learned academic, Sewall came straight to the bench from Harvard, where he had been librarian and tutor. His reputation for scholarship alone prompted his appointment, a fact which may seem strange to a modern America. Today, judges are rarely appointed for their bookishness, and never in any event from outside the legal profession.[9]

In eighteenth-century Massachusetts, law, like life, was simpler. Labor was cheap and (until the political hurricanes blew) diversions were few. The law, even the law of England, was sufficiently cohesive so that someone like Charles Viner could seriously, and fairly successfully, compass it into a single set of folio volumes. A well-to-do gentleman interested in the subject, with hired men to run his farms and collect his rents, and without the temptations of a daily newspaper or even occasional theater, might well devote his free hours to mastering the law's seamless web.

Theory alone, it is true, does not turn an intelligent man into a lawyer, or even a judge. The Massachusetts judicial system, fortunately, provided ample on-the-job training. Justices of the peace, for example, held regular "courts of record"; most of the probate judges and many of the county inferior court judges were not lawyers. At the time of Sewall's death, only one of his superior court colleagues had had any formal legal training at all. In fact, the complex series of courts required so many judges that the province simply did not contain enough lawyers to fill them. The shortages of talent affected the judiciary itself. Many of the county probate judges held additional offices. Superior Court Judge Chambers Russell (one of the non-lawyers) doubled as judge of the Massachusetts Vice-Admiralty Court.

By the time of Bernard's arrival, the number of lawyers had begun to increase markedly. Within six years, John Adams would say of new attorneys: "They swarm and multiply." The bar was already beginning to organize itself and to regulate the conduct of existing members as well as the admission of new ones. It was starting to oppose the unauthorized practice of law by deputy sheriffs, constables, and "pettifoggers." In short, the bar was beginning to act like a profession. Concomitant with this new self-awareness, the lawyers began to take that kind of pride in their knowledge which, a century and a half earlier, had moved Lord Coke to risk his life by daring to tell James I that the law was so complex a science that none could master it but by lengthy studies—not even the king himself, the fount and source of all law. Or, as John Adams wrote on November 5, 1760: "A man whose Youth and Spirits and Strength, have been spent in Husbandry, Merchandize, Politicks, nay in Science or Literature will never master so immense and involved a science." [10]

Fortunately for Bernard, the Massachusetts bar included some of the most accomplished lawyers in America. Edmund Trowbridge, the attorney general, probably knew more about criminal law and the law of real estate than anybody in the country. Benjamin Prat, although wracked with lifelong pain by an amputation at the hip, was clearly judicial timber. John Adams marveled that his "little body, hung upon two sticks," could "send forth such eloquence and displays of mind." In six months he would be appointed chief justice of New York, where he overcame the natives' hostility by his ability to unravel difficult cases and to speed legal business. The Johnsonian leader of the Boston bar, Jeremiah Gridley, sponsored John Adams and Samuel Quincy for admission to practice. "Gridley has a bold spirited Manner of Speaking," Adams noted in his diary. "His Words seem to pierce and search, have something quick and animating. He is a great Reasoner, and has a very vivid Imagination." "Gridleys Grandeur consists in his great Learning, his great Parts and his majestic Manner." Finally, if Bernard preferred to pick what one of his twentieth-century successors might call a "political judge," there was James Otis, Sr., self-taught old warhorse of the Barnstable and Plymouth bars, who had served a year as attorney general in 1748, and who craved the judgeship mightily. Actually, he expected it, for both of Bernard's predecessors had promised the place to him. Only the lack of a vacancy had prevented their appointing him.[11]

Faced thus with the happy opportunity of filling Sewall's seat by selection of a trained lawyer, albeit perhaps a politician, Bernard instead disregarded the logical choices, and indeed the entire bar. He named Thomas Hutchinson. Hutchinson was not a lawyer. This alone would not have made his selection obnoxious, because his mental capacity was famously large—he had been graduated from Harvard at the age of fifteen—and because he had read much in the law. He had also acquired some practical judicial experience, as a justice of the inferior court for Suffolk County and as the Suffolk County probate judge. He knew something of the executive's problems, too, for he was the province's lieutenant governor, and a member of the governor's council. The trouble with this experience was that Hutchinson valued it too highly. He intended to retain the probate judgeship, the lieutenant governor's commission, and his seat on the council, all the while serving as chief justice. Three additional offices and a blank legal education, as well. It was asking too much of the bar to swallow this, and it was especially asking too much of Otis and his strangely brilliant son. The younger Otis went so far as to declare publicly "that he would do all the mischief he could to the Government," and "would set the whole Province in a flame, though he perished in the attempt." [12]

It is keen irony that Bernard's choice of Hutchinson should be regarded, especially by some of the lawyers, as what the chief justice himself called "an eyesore." For Hutchinson's intelligence and ability to absorb legal details equaled that of all but a very few professionals, and he continued to read law in his free moments. His extensive mercantile experience perfectly prepared him for the mass of rudimentary commercial litigation which came before the superior court. He possessed abundant common sense, a knack (which many of those bred to the law never acquire) of being able to state a case simply and succinctly, and a corresponding desire to simplify matters as much as possible. On one notable occasion, after the learned and pedantic Trowbridge had spun out a verbal cobweb, Hutchinson rebuked him gently and judicially: "Brother Trowbridge, the point is now to remove the difficulties and not to raise them." His few recorded rulings on evidence, especially, are modern and untechnical. [13]

Hutchinson's attitude toward the lawyers practicing before him seems to have been marked by unusual courtesy. At the time of his elevation, young John Adams had been an attorney only two years. When Adams was admitted before the superior court in November 1761, Hutchinson noted that occasional tendency of established lawyers, still visible two centuries later, "to browbeat their Inferiors; so," according to Judge Peter Oliver, "when any of his Seniors took Advantage of him in this Way, [Hutchinson] would, with his usual Humanity, support him, as well as show him other Marks of Respect." It was part of Hutchinson's judicial outlook to encourage the advocates to help the court reach a proper result. "I never presumed to call myself a Lawyer," he wrote years later. "The most I could pretend to was when I heard the Law laid on both sides to judge which was right." In this, he was too modest, for it is precisely the ability to decide where between equally well-urged "sides" the Right lies that is the essence of the craft of judging. [14]

To his new office, Hutchinson brought not merely a wide acquaintance with the ways of merchants, but a lifetime of thinking about grave public problems and, more important, of serving his countrymen in the solution of those problems. It was in fiscal matters, however, that Hutchinson's true genius lay. Even John Adams, whose antipathy to the chief justice's person and character increased annually, explicitly conceded Hutchinson's mastery: "As little as I revere his memory, I will acknowledge that he understood the subject of coin and com-

merce better than any man I ever knew in this country." One hardly
need add that Hutchinson's comprehension of the topic led him to oppose such inflationary projects as the Land Bank and to urge successfully that the province use the British reimbursement of the charges of
the great Louisburg expedition to retire the paper currency which had
then (1747) sunk to half its value. This latter plan made excellent
fiscal sense, but it took more than a year to get the bill through the legislature. After that, the storm exploded. "Mr. H," Hutchinson wrote in
a subsequent third-person memoir, "more than once was threatened
with destruction from some of the people of the town, and his house
taking fire on the top, the Lanthorn [chimney-top] being in a blaze,
some of the lower class cursed him and cried 'Let it burn.'"[15]

That cry, and wide resentment of his monetary views, echoed
through the rest of Hutchinson's life. A deflationary, hard-currency
policy automatically favors creditors over debtors. In the agrarian society of eighteenth-century Massachusetts, the latter substantially out-
numbered the former. Hutchinson was storing up enemies for the future. But the significance to Hutchinson of the popular resentment at
the retirement scheme was small indeed compared to the hornet that
buzzed out of the collapsing Land Bank in the early 1740's. A moving
force and director of the Land Bank had been a small businessman-
politician whose estate (among others) the General Court had ordered
sold for the benefit of the Land Bank's creditors. The politician died
before the sheriff could levy execution, and his son successfully resisted the proceedings over the years until he could consume the estate
himself. This son had taken his M.A. at Harvard in 1743, a formal
honor, granted almost automatically three years after receiving the
first degree. On Commencement Day, 1743, the young man had, as
was customary, prepared a *Quaestio*, or declamation. He did not have
to argue orally, but his topic was printed. We do not know whether
Hutchinson (Class of 1727) rode out to Cambridge on that July day.
But anyone who did attend read that the topic was: "Is it Lawful to
resist the Supreme Magistrate, if the Commonwealth cannot otherwise
be preserved?" The politician's son, Samuel Adams, argued the
affirmative.[16]

CHAPTER 2

IMPERIAL PROLOGUE

When Hutchinson took his seat as chief justice on January 27, 1761, the superior court's regular February term was only a few weeks off. The docket for the second Tuesday of the term, February 24, listed that suit which, captioned innocuously enough *Petition of Lechmere*, has become immortalized as The Writs of Assistance Case.[1]

This landmark of American mythology arose out of the common-sense decision by William Pitt, early in 1760, to draw from the colonies financial sustenance for Britain's still-active European war effort. Pitt did not anticipate that any new legislation would be required. The necessary implements were already forged, in a series of trade and navigation acts a century old. These acts embodied the mercantilist theory of trade: to ensure that English colonies furnished the mother country with raw materials and with markets for finished goods, and to deny those advantages to international commercial rivals. The statutes required trade to and from the colonies to be carried in British or colonial ships; they tightly restricted manufacture in the colonies; they prohibited export of "enumerated" raw materials to any place but Britain or the colonies; and they imposed duties on goods brought to America. The penalties were, as appropriate, forfeiture of goods, forfeiture of the vessel, or default on a surety bond.[2]

That, in broad outline, was the way the system looked. It is apparent from even a casual glance that effective enforcement required, at a minimum, an extensive shoreside bureaucracy to handle the paperwork; a strong naval force to intercept vessels violating the rules; an organization (if not a network) of informers; an effective method of searching for contraband ashore; and an adjudicative body capable of rendering prompt justice. Every one of those requirements was to cause problems for successive administrators. But *Petition of Lechmere* dealt principally with the issue of search.

Like other customs officers, Thomas Lechmere, the surveyor general of the customs in Boston, had been entitled, by writ of the superior court, "in the day Time together with a Constable or other public officer inhabiting near unto the Place to enter and go into any Vaults, Cellars, Warehouses, shops or other Places to search and see, whether any Goods, Wares or Merchandizes, in the same . . . Vaults, Cellars, Warehouses, shops or other Places are or shall be there hid or concealed . . . ; and to open any Trunks, Chests, Boxes, fardells or Packs made up or in Bulk, whatever in which any Goods, Ware, or Merchandizes are suspected to be packed or concealed . . ." The writ ran to "all and singular Justices of the Peace, sherriffs and Constables, and to all other . . . officers and subjects within" Massachusetts; it required not only that its addressees (who included by definition every person in the province) "permit" the unlimited searching, but that they "from Time to Time be aiding and assisting . . . in the Execution of the Premisses in all Things as becometh." [3]

A writ is a command to an officer in the name of the sovereign. In its most common form, the ordinary Massachusetts civil writ directed the sheriff to "attach the goods or estate" of a civil defendant and "have him before" the court on a given day to answer the plaintiff's allegations. (The language of a Massachusetts writ today is identical, but the named sovereign is the Commonwealth of Massachusetts rather than George the Third.) The writs under which Lechmere and his men exercised their broad powers of search were not directed toward initiating civil litigation. They aimed instead to strengthen enforcement of the customs statutes. In short, they were writs of assistance.

Unlike a search warrant, a writ of assistance required no immediate prior application to a court. The searching officer need not describe the premises to be searched nor the objects to be seized; he need not even allege that he had "probable cause" to believe that the suspected premises contained the suspected objects. So long as he operated in the daytime, accompanied by "a Constable or other public officer," a customs officer was free to enter and search anybody's house at will. The only limitation on his activities was some unclear English caselaw (that is, a series of judicial decisions, rather than an act of Parliament) indicating that if the search turned out afterward to be wrongful, not even the "probable cause" argument could save an officer acting under a writ of assistance from civil liability.

Once issued, a writ was good (assuming the recipient lived long enough) until six months after the death of the then-reigning sovereign. George II had died October 25, 1760. The news reached Boston December 27, and the customs officers immediately prepared to petition the superior court for the issuance of new writs. At this point, however, sixty-three Boston merchants petitioned the superior court to "be heard by themselves and counsel upon the Subject of Writs of Assistance." James Otis, Jr., was at that time advocate general, or chief prosecutor, of the Massachusetts Vice-Admiralty Court. Because this position made him an officer of the royal customs, Otis resigned, in order to be able to represent the petitioning merchants.[4]

The cross-petitions came on for hearing before the superior court February 24. Oxenbridge Thacher joined Otis, while the great Jeremiah Gridley opened and closed for the customs officials. In the arguments which ensued, particularly Otis's, "the child Independence was born." The constitutional theories with which Otis bombarded the court during his four-hour speech need not detain us. Of much greater significance to the immediate future history of Boston was the attitude of the new chief justice. Hutchinson saw the issue as basically factual rather than legal: What, he asked, was the English practice?[5] It is typical of Hutchinson, as a judge and as a man, that he sought to resolve the issue by the most direct means. Rather than rely on the lawyers for information, he adjourned the proceedings for nine months and used the time to inquire of a correspondent in London. The answer was simple; the writs were granted so freely there that no affidavit or order of court was necessary; a clerk of the Court of the Exchequer made out the writs "of course." Hutchinson permitted the parties to reargue the case in late November. The proceedings, somewhat tamer than the earlier display, changed nothing. The court unanimously decided to continue issuing the writs.[6]

Those writs that followed did not produce the wholesale ransacking which the merchants apparently feared. At the same time, it was clear that the customs service was in general tightening up its collections. The new attitude replaced several decades of peaceful coexistence between the customs officials and the merchants. During those years everyone had come to realize that the Navigation Acts were as impractical as they were restrictive. It was an excellent application of mercantilist theory to impose so high a duty on molasses from non-English sugar-producing islands as to eliminate all such treacle from the North American trade. Unfortunately, the Parliament which enacted the Sugar Act of 1733, with its sixpence-a-gallon duty, failed to realize that the entire molasses output of all the English "sugar islands" could supply only about 25 per cent of the quantity needed to stoke New England's distilleries. Without illicit molasses, the plants would have shut and the rum ceased to flow. This was a distressing prospect, and not only to the tipplers who patronized those ever-multiplying taverns which young John Adams was trying to restrict. Indian and African bellies, too, warmed to Medford's finest, for rum was the *quid pro quo* in both the fur and slave trades.[7]

Since the source cost of molasses at this period was about sixpence per gallon, and the freight about fourpence halfpenny, effective enforcement of the statutory duty would have increased the "landed" value almost 60 per cent and would have ruined the New England distillers; the several trades which depended on their product; and another profitable aspect of the molasses trade: the carriage to the sugar islands of New England products, principally lumber, provisions, and salt fish.[8]

During the years before the Great War, the customs officers administered the statutes, and especially the Sugar Act, in such a way as to keep alive both the letter of the law and the spirit of North American trade. The *modus vivendi* was called "compounding," an eighteenth-century term for which the nearest modern equivalent is "settling." Some writers have suggested that compounding involved the seizure of a cargo, followed by its release upon payment of a fraction of the amount due. That is a possibility; but such a seizure would almost certainly entail the filing of a libel in the appropriate vice-admiralty court, with the consequence (always embarrassing in matters of this stripe) of having a public record of the initial seizure which would remain forever on the court books, no matter what the subsequent disposition of the case might be. My own feeling is that compounding was handled more adroitly. Instead of paying, say, halfpenny a gallon on an entire cargo, a merchant would be permitted to "enter" [declare] only, say, one-fifteenth of the cargo, and thus pay duty on a small fraction of his cargo's value. Evasion of the law and connivance of the customs officers would still be essential elements of the scheme, but the bookkeeping would be tidier. In either case, the loss to the British Treasury was considerable. With that in mind, Pitt issued a circular letter to all the colonial governors, ordering more stringent application of the trade statutes. Bernard himself, even before he had left New Jersey, received explicit instructions on that score.[9]

The two and a half years following the final argument over the writs saw no popular outburst. The House of Representatives tried to nullify the writs' effect by a statute requiring new applicants to name their informers, but Bernard, having received from the superior court judges an advisory opinion that the bill would neutralize the writs, flatly vetoed it. Bernard looked forward to his vacation at Castle William, the island fortress in the harbor, "the prettiest summer residence I know." Lawyers and the courts generally returned to routine business, and by May 1762, Bernard could fairly report "at this precise time, I am a very popular Governor." Hutchinson, meanwhile, found time to continue the researches he would ultimately refine into his *History of the Colony and Province of Massachusetts-Bay*. On December 30, he and John Adams spent fifteen minutes in a court clerk's office discussing the early colonial courts and the old laws by which adultery "and many other offences were made capital, that are not so now." Even the Otis family had cooled its anti-Bernard passions. The governor contemplated the patronage opportunity afforded him by the lapse of commissions upon George II's death, and shrewdly planned to make James, Sr., chief judge of the Barnstable Inferior Court, as well as probate judge for that county. And James, Jr., duly supported the grant of Mount Desert to Bernard.[10]

Even so, the quiet days were fast ending; the successful termination of the European phase of the war in February 1763 hastened their departure. At the peace, Britain's national debt stood at nearly 123 million pounds. Heavy taxes on land and on various other necessaries of life from silver plate to pear liquor had squeezed all segments of the home public limp if not dry. Pitt's drive to enforce the revenue laws had not noticeably succeeded; neither had a 1762 act "for the further improvement of his Majesty's Revenue of Customs." The men who governed England clearly realized that the nation required large additional revenues. The colonies, on whose behalf the war had been fought (or so many Englishmen found it convenient to reason), were the logical source. This made particular sense to the ministry of George Grenville, which faced the need for maintaining a large military force along the frontiers in the vast new territories which British arms had acquired in North America. What better and fairer method of paying for this protection than by levying on those to whom the protection was afforded?

Under the pressure of the moment, the English tended to forget two important facts. First, the amount the respective colonies had expended during the war surpassed the sum that a then-grateful Parliament had repaid them. Second, the elimination of the French menace and the pacifying of the interior had materially improved the commercial and international situation of Old England. As Bernard had written Barrington, the acquisition of Canada alone "will be worth all the Expences of the War." Besides the great accessions to the north, the war and the treaty had opened limitless western areas, which enticed Englishmen of the highest rank. So quickly did the land speculation pressure develop that to avoid imminent inflammation of the already tender Indian situation, it became necessary to issue a restrictive royal proclamation.[11] Facts, however, do not always displace stereotypes, even in the governing of great empires. And it was an ineradicable myth of English policy that the beneficiaries of the fighting and the treaty should pay the cost of the war and the expenses of maintaining the peace. Like many political myths, this one grew by constant repition, and by its first-glance fairness.

Their attention now fully turned toward America as a source of wherewithal, the English policy makers fell into another delusion of the sort reasonably common to the taxing process. They assumed that the already existing revenue structure was basically sound, needing only tightening of the regulations, inspiriting of the enforcement, and additional duties on the pattern of the old. Ignoring the opportunity to examine the relationship between the colonies and the mother country, together with the related opportunity to establish a realistic imperial commercial and fiscal policy, the Grenville administration concocted the Sugar, or American, Act of 1764. Though his contemporaries esteemed Grenville for his financial acumen, the true nature of the problems he was facing seems to have eluded him, or he to have evaded it. Grenville's preoccupation with economies rather than economics led him to an attitude toward American affairs which began by saving England's pounds and ended by losing her colonies.[12]

Grenville proposed that the Americans pay not only the cost of the customs enforcement, but also the cost of the colonial administration. The Sugar Act lowered the duty on molasses to threepence a gallon, increased the list of "enumerated" goods (which could be shipped only to Britain or a British possession), raised other duties, largely eliminated "drawbacks" (refunds of duties paid in England on foreign goods imported there and thence exported to the colonies), and generally required that the *entire* cargo of a vessel bound for the colonies from England be loaded in England (even if the voyage had commenced, and part of the cargo had originally been loaded, in a non-English port—in which case that part of the cargo had to be discharged in England, and, after duty had been paid, reladen). The number of required bonds and cockets (official cargo lists) was increased, and their use imposed on the intercolonial coasting trade. Finally, the statute specifically authorized the commencement of suits for forfeitures in vice-admiralty courts; it created a single new vice-admiralty court with jurisdiction over offenses committed anywhere in America; it placed the burden of proof of compliance with the law entirely on the claimant of the ship or goods; and it abrogated the common-law rule that successful defense of a customs claim subjected the seizing officer to liability for damages.[13]

Even before the king signed the act (April 5, 1764), rumors of its contents and aims had reached Boston. Discussed orally and in pamphlets and merchants' memorials, the plan of the act terrified the commerce-oriented province. The legislature voted to send Hutchinson as a special agent to England to lay the province's case directly before the ministry. Bernard felt that Hutchinson, as lieutenant-governor, should not go to England without special royal leave. That, combined with his own private affairs, caused Hutchinson to request a few months' delay. When the House considered the request on February 2, Oxenbridge Thacher, who had been absent at the earlier vote, returned to his seat. Having opposed Hutchinson earlier on a complicated currency issue, and having served as counsel for the merchants in the writs of assistance arguments and for the shipowner in an important customs case, Thacher was by this time a vituperative personal opponent of Hutchinson—*"Summa Potestatis"* ("Most Powerful"), he called him, or usually just *"Summa."* It was fixed in Thacher's mind that Hutchinson headed an oligarchical conspiracy which aimed at nothing less than the enslavement of the people. Samuel Adams shared this conviction, as did John Adams a short while later. Thacher, however, seems to have caught the feeling earliest. He told the House, Hutchinson wrote, that "he found fault with the choice, as having a dangerous tendency to the liberties of the people, not only as the lieutenant-governor was the officer of the crown, and improper to be at the same time the agent for the people, but also as he was known to have always been, in principle, a favourer of the prerogative." The House thereupon voted to excuse Hutchinson from the service.[14]

Official news of the Sugar Act did not arrive until shortly before the legislature convened in late May. Boston meanwhile held its usual town meeting on May 15 and appointed a five-man committee to draw up instructions for the four Boston representatives at the impending session of the general court. Chairman of the committee was Richard Dana, attorney and justice of the peace. Portly, beetle-browed, short of temper, and razor-tongued, Dana was at this time essentially a political neutral; as the years passed, he would learn how to use his judicial power—it was the justices of the peace who made the first determination in most criminal matters—for radical ends. Now, however, Dana merely joined three of the other committee members in preserving form. The real strength of the committee, and drafter of the instruction, Samuel Adams, was still so much behind the scenes that he had yet to be elected to a major office.[15]

And we particularly desire you [the committee wrote] carefully to look into the laws of excise [that is, custom duties] that if the virtue of the people is endangered by the multiplicity of oaths therein enjoined, or their trade and business is unreasonably impeded or embarrassed thereby, the grievance may be redressed.

As the preservation of morals, as well as property and right, so much depends upon the impartial distribution of justice agreeable to good and wholesome law, and as the judges of the land do depend upon the free grants of the General Assembly for support, it is incumbent upon you at all times to give your voice for their honorable maintenance so long as they, having in their minds an indifference to all other affairs, shall devote themselves wholly to the duties of their own department and the further study of the law by which their customs, precedents, proceedings, and determinations are adjusted and limited. . . .

[I]f taxes are laid upon us in any shape without our having a legal representation where they are laid, are we not reduced from the character of free subjects to the miserable state of tributary slaves?

These excerpts quite neatly characterized Adam's attitude toward the problems facing Massachusetts, an attitude which, as we shall see, was not to change in any particular throughout the days of the troubles: "Put your adversary in the wrong and keep him there." Note the application of the technique: an insinuation that the revenue laws were not merely bad for trade, but immoral (in this instance because the required oaths tempted perjury); a reminder to all the judges that their salaries depended upon the pleasure of the legislature; a pointed suggestion to Hutchinson that he resign the lieutenant-governor's office, and incidentally a sly reminder that Hutchinson had no formal legal training; and, finally, an equating of customs-paying with slavery.[16]

Adams's voice was not the only one raised against the Sugar Act. Members of all factions realized that the act, if enforced, would stifle not only the molasses-rum trade, but also the carrying trade itself. All other facets aside, the molasses duty was unrealistic. "It was," as Hutchinson said, "very bad policy to keep the duty on molasses so high. Had it been then reduced to a penny, or three-halfpence, it would have been acquiesced in by the merchants." At the rate Hutchinson suggested, paying the duty would have been cheaper and less trouble and risk than smuggling the necessary molasses. Grenville's advisors, however, had calculated that threepence per gallon marked the duty which the traffic would bear, so threepence was the figure adopted. Based on the same data, they estimated that a threepence duty would gross £77,775 annually. Both these projections turned out to be grossly inaccurate. "When the new act was carried into execution, by connivance or indulgence in the officers, the duty paid on molasses seldom exceeded three-halfpence per gallon." The actual figures showed that the amount of molasses passing through customs was about one-eighth of the anticipated quantity, and the average total duties secured came to £8,849.[17] It is clear that even after the establishment of the new vice-admiralty court in Halifax in mid-1764, evasion of duties was a major customs problem. Boston-born, British-educated John Temple, surveyor-general of the customs, uncovered a particularly gross instance at the Salem custom house. From evidence which Temple had gathered directly and through informants, it appeared that James Cockle, the collector there, had on at least one occasion been bribed to overlook a penalty due, had suppressed for his own advantage essential customs intelligence, and had entered into fraudulent compositions of duties due on goods landed at Salem. Cockle had been appointed to this position in 1760, at the behest of Governor Bernard. "The Governor," Hutchinson wrote later, "was very active in promoting seizures for illicit trade, which he made profitable by his share in the forfeitures; . . . the Collector at Salem . . . was the Governor's creature." Temple "envied [Bernard] his profits." His investigations disclosed that the governor and his protégé were using Cockle's office and position to mulct the royal revenue for their own benefit.[18]

Cockle regularly accepted documents indicating that sugar or molasses arriving at Salem had been shipped at the West Indian island of Anguilla. Because Anguilla was a British possession, its produce was not dutiable. But in fact the cargoes which Cockle was accepting were French and the supporting documents were forgeries, as Cockle must have realized. "Although it was known that the island did not grow as many sugar canes as to afford cargo for one vessel, yet [Cockle] had admitted a considerable number of vessels to be entered as coming from Anguilla, and appeared quite satisfied. Some had made more voyages than one in the same way, and others were going into the like practice." [19]

Cockle had also demanded and received of masters of vessels in the Portuguese trade "casks of wine, boxes of fruit, etc., which was a gratuity for suffering their vessels to be entered with [i.e., recorded as having carried] salt or ballast only, and passing over unnoticed such cargoes of wine, fruit, etc., which are prohibited to be imported into his Majesty's plantations. Part of which wine, fruit, etc., the said James Cockle used to share with Governor Bernard." [20]

Cockle had indulged in the procedure, referred to earlier, of "suffering a small part of a cargo only to be entered, [i.e., to be declared and dutied] and the remainder to be landed, or shipped to Boston, without duty or entry. And, though the custom-house books must have shewn that many thousand hogsheads of molasses had been exported from the town of Salem in a year, more than had been imported, yet no notice had been taken." [21]

Finally, Cockle and the merchants had apparently rigged an arrangement whereby instead of declaring cargoes and paying duties outright (which would have gone directly into the king's revenue), the merchants would deliberately not declare all or part of the cargo, and would then "compound" or settle the resultant seizure with Cockle at a figure which would be less than the proper duty and which would in part (as I will shortly explain) be payable directly to Cockle and Bernard.[22]

Cockle's and Bernard's actions, while manifestly illegal, were not likely to provoke the ill-will of the merchants. Unfortunately, the Anguilla sugar farce could not be maintained forever. In late August 1764, Cockle received word, which he promptly transmitted to Bernard, that the documents were indeed forged. Had the collector and the governor been content to accept the inevitable end of a good thing, they might have escaped whole. But like many another speculator, they sought to squeeze the last penny into their profits. In the attempt, they achieved the rare distinction of antagonizing not only the customs establishment, but also the merchants, and of branding themselves as avaricious bunglers.[23]

Under the applicable statutes, if a vessel were caught in the act of smuggling, she and her cargo (or their equivalent value) would, by an admiralty proceeding *in rem* (directly against the things involved), be forfeited, with the proceeds split equally among the "informer" (the individual instituting the action), the governor, and the king, the king's share going to the province after all costs had been deducted. Even if the action were compounded, the settlement sum would be similarly divided. In either event, the owner would lose the value of his ship and cargo, but nothing else. If, however, the proceeding ran not *in rem* against the vessel and goods, but rather *in personam* against the smuggler, the law set the recoverable penalty at three times the value of ship and goods, a principle still echoed in today's "triple damages" for antitrust violations. Cockle and Bernard tried to put this distinction to their own profit. They deliberately withheld the news from Temple, instead conveying full particulars to Robert Auchmuty, the advocate general of the Massachusetts Court of Vice-Admiralty, who obligingly commenced libels *in personam* against the traders involved. Only then, one week after Cockle had been officially informed of the forgeries, did he send the news to Temple.[24]

The surveyor general was of course legitimately concerned at the loss of customs revenue which Cockle's conduct suggested. This latest incident served to confirm the suspicions which his earlier investigations had raised, and he confronted Cockle with the charges. In panic, the collector sought to bribe Temple to keep the whole affair quiet.

Temple summarily dismissed him on September 28, 1764. The Salem merchants gleefully marked the occasion "by Firing Guns, making Bonfires, Entertainments, &c.." Now they plainly saw that whatever favors in specie and kind they had extended to Cockle and Bernard for "protection" had been wasted. All the legal entanglements they had hoped to avoid were imminent. What was worse, they would have to pay thrice the amount of the normal penalty. Small wonder that Temple was "much applauded by the merchants in the Town of Boston for his Good and Spirited Behavior." Cockle, they said, had stalled in order to draw as many into the net as he could. For excuse, he argued that he had delayed only long enough to obtain evidence upon which he might support a prosecution. "This raised a great clamour, a great share of which was against the governor; who, being largely interested in the success of the prosecution, was charged with promoting it to serve his own interest, more than from a regard to the duty to which the law, and his oath, in as strong terms as can be, had obliged him." [25]

Despite the actions which had at first convinced Massachusetts of Bernard's excellence, he was basically a mediocrity, whose principal interest in his office, as his correspondence reveals, was monetary. The facts of the Cockle affair brought home to the populace generally, and to the merchants particularly, that Bernard had come to Massachusetts to make his fortune at their expense. This image was not likely to command Yankee affection and respect. Bernard, who attributed the whole affair to Temple's "haughty jealousy," nonetheless candidly admitted the "conniving at foreign sugar & molasses, & Portugal wines & fruit" in which the customs officers engaged. "Incorruption in the best of them," he admitted, "must be considered, not as a positive, but comparative term." Hutchinson suggested that Bernard's own incorruption ought to be measured relatively. "Whether he ever took any improper steps will be determined in England," he wrote a British correspondent. "I do not know that he has done more than all his predecessors used to do." [26]

That the Sugar Act and its attendant machinery failed to produce the desired revenue did not make its provisions any more palatable to Massachusetts. Even before September 29, its effective date in the colonies, a business recession had deepened into a full-scale depression, culminating in the January 1765 bankruptcy of the large mercantile house of Nathaniel Wheelwright; by Wheelwright's collapse, "a great number of people will suffer," said Boston merchant John Rowe. Hutchinson himself wrote to England protesting the unfairness of the revenue scheme. He also took a more public position. In October, Bernard, at the request of Otis and some others, including the rest of the

Boston delegation, called a special session of the legislature, ostensibly for the purpose of devising a self-imposed scheme of taxation which would be acceptable to Parliament. When the session convened on October 18, however, Otis, Thacher, and nine others were appointed a committee to prepare an address, or protest, to the king, lords, and commons. Thacher, in fact, arrived at the session with a draft address in hand. This document closely paralleled the Adams-written instructions of the town of Boston to its representatives (of whom Thacher was one). Explicitly condemning taxation without representation, the address received a prompt favorable House vote, only to draw the council's nonconcurrence. After considerable procedural scuffling between the two bodies, a joint conference committee was established "to consider of a more proper form." Allowing the conferees to wrangle fruitlessly for over a week, Hutchinson, the chairman, then presented a draft which, with some small changes, was ultimately accepted. Its central position represented a triumph for Hutchinson over Adams, for it was directed solely to the House of Commons, and it eliminated any claim of *right* to taxation only upon representation. But in gaining the victory Hutchinson had prepared the way for a later costly defeat. Tucked into the address he had drafted was a condemnation of the vice-admiralty courts for depriving "the Colonies of one of the most valuable of English liberties, trials by juries." In an unguarded future moment, Hutchinson was to urge the "abridgement of what are called English Liberties," and his countrymen, remembering his earlier words, would call him a "cool, thinking, deliberate Villain, malicious, and vindictive, as well as ambitious and avaricious." [27]

CHAPTER 3

VIOLENCE OVER STAMPS

The Sugar Act duties, onerous though they might be in the enforcement, were really only preludes to a more direct and insupportable method of revenue raising. The possibility of Britain's imposing on America a scheme of "internal" taxation, divorced from the customs or the regulation of trade, had existed even before the Sugar Act. In the Parliamentary discussions which preceded enactment of that measure, Grenville had clearly stated the possibility of "certain Stamp Duties" in America. The House, by resolution only, had approved the idea in principle; but for about a year the proposal remained inert, while Grenville listened halfheartedly to assorted American suggestions for raising the money which England needed. It is immaterial whether Grenville gave sincere consideration to the possibility of the Americans' taxing themselves an equivalent of the expected revenue, or whether his offer to receive an alternate system to the stamp duties "had never been made in good faith." The fact is that Grenville did put a stamp bill to the House of Commons in February. After a spirited debate, during which Colonel Isaac Barre, veteran of the Canadian war and a friend of the colonies, first introduced the phrase "Sons of Liberty," the bill passed the Commons on February 27, the Lords on March 8, and received the sovereign's approval on March 22. But it was not the young king who signed the bill into law. Illness or madness (neither doctors nor historians have ever settled the question definitely) incapacitated him temporarily; a specially appointed group of commissioners affixed the royal assent.[1]

News of the Parliamentary debates, and hence of the imminence of the Stamp Act, reached Massachusetts in April. By May 27, the 117 sections of the statute itself had arrived. On and after November 1, taxes of up to £10 would have to be paid for pre-stamped paper, the only sheets on which the following documents could be printed, engrossed, or written: "fifteen classes of documents used in court proceedings (including the licenses of attorneys), the papers used in clearing ships from harbors, college diplomas, appointments to public office, bonds, grants and deeds for land, mortgages, indentures, leases, contracts, bills of sale, articles of apprenticeship, liquor licenses, . . . pamphlets, newspapers (and advertisements in them), and almanacs." Admissions to the Bar (£10), playing cards (one shilling per pack), and dice (ten shillings the pair) also came under the act; criminal matters did not.[2]

From this summary catalogue, it is obvious that the Grenville ministry was quite literally forcing its stamp on every aspect of American life. The individual taxes were not large, and the total sum to be taken out of America was not excessive, especially in comparison with the crushing taxation and serious economic unrest that were afflicting the mother country in 1764 and 1765. What seems to have caused the most grief in the colonies was the all-pervading nature of the duties, the requirement that the underlying blank paper be purchased ready-stamped (from ministerially selected "distributors" to whom the privilege would be worth at least £300 annually), and the enforcement provisions authorizing prosecutions before the juryless courts of vice-admiralty.[3]

The initial Massachusetts reaction was peaceable. At the first proposal of the stamp duties, in 1764, a rudimentary nonimportation association had been formed. This plan, forerunner of a special type of violent nonviolence which would not fully flower for another three years, bound its subscribers (who included some members of both legislative chambers) "to forbear the importation, or consumption, of English goods; and particularly to break off from the custom of wearing black clothes, or other mourning (it being generally of British manufacture) upon the death of relations." The first funeral "agreeable to the New Mode" took place September 17. The association assumed a gastronomic aspect in early 1765, when "a great proportion of the inhabitants of Boston" agreed to eat no lamb during the year, "in order to increase the growth, and, of course, the manufacture of wool in the province." [4]

Neither of these boycotts met particular success. Another Massachusetts suggestion found a readier reception. On June 8, only twelve days after official news of the act's passage reached Boston, the House resolved to write to every colonial assembly, urging that all "consult together on the present circumstances of the colonies, and the difficulties to which they are and must be reduced, by the operations of the acts of parliament for laying duties and taxes on the colonies." By October 7, eight colonies had accepted the invitation, and the Stamp Act Congress convened in New York City.[5]

Meanwhile, in Boston, the pressure rose with the New England summer temperature. On July 2, the radical Boston *Gazette* published the resolves which the Virginia House of Burgesses had passed in late May. These had sprung from the heated brain of Patrick Henry, whose zeal in their support had driven him to rank his king with Caesar and Charles I. They flatly insisted that the Virginians (and by extension all Americans) "enjoyed the inestimable right of" internal self-government and self-taxation. Just as the Speaker of the Burgesses had admonished Henry for his words, so did the amazed Bostonians. James Otis even went so far as to say, before a group of interested listeners on King Street, that the resolves were downright treasonable. But whatever spirit of moderation greeted the Virginia manifesto upon its first appearance soon vanished. At Harvard commencement on July 17, Elbridge Gerry, a young candidate for the master's degree, entertained his audience by arguing the affirmative of the *Quaestio*: "Can the new Prohibitary Duties, which make it useless for the People to engage in Commerce, be evaded by them as Faithful Subjects?" A week later, ironically, Gerry learned that H.M.S. *Niger* had taken one of his merchant father's "schooners out of the Harbour of St. Peters," Nova Scotia, presumably on suspicion of violating the customs laws.[6]

The time of purely verbal resistance had almost ended. In Boston, a secret group calling itself the Loyal Nine began meeting to plan active opposition to the Stamp Act and to the men who would effectuate it. From the start, the Loyal Nine seems to have decided on physical intimidation as the most effective means of resisting the Stamp Act. In this, they were only following Massachusetts tradition. No matter how peaceably and humbly the men of Massachusetts might phrase their petitions to the king and his government, when it came to dealing on this side of the water with their grievances, they had always resorted to the direct approach. In the 1740's, for instance, the Bostonians had staged three full-scale riots; the last, in 1747, arose out of objections to impressment of seamen by the Royal Navy, and lasted three days. Actually, rioting in Boston was almost a ritual. Every November 5 (or November 6 if November 5 fell on a Sunday), the town celebrated the anniversary of the infamous Gunpowder Plot, also known as Guy Fawkes Day, with a North End–South End battle royal. It is significant that the Bostonians called November 5 Pope's Day, and used the occasion to refuel their already warm anti-Catholic sentiments. This particular strain of bigotry, with its related anti-Irish and anti-Scottish biases, underlay much of the tension which later developed.[7]

To the Loyal Nine and other opponents of English policy, the value of Boston's mobbish tradition lay in the immediate availability of a corps of husky, willing bully-boys and, more important, of a leadership cadre accustomed to the difficult job of directing and channeling the mob's energies. Chief of the South End mob, and by force of personality and arms head of the combined mob, was a twenty-eight-year-old shoemaker named Ebenezer Mackintosh. Born in Boston, Mackintosh lived in the South End's Ward Twelve (whose territory included the town gallows on Boston Neck). A volunteer in General James Abercromby's abortive Ticonderoga expedition of 1758, he had become a member of Engine Number Nine, one of the semiformal brigades which were Boston's only organized fire protection; oddly enough, the "master" of Number Nine, the man who had specially selected Mackintosh for inclusion in the Engine, was Stephen Greenleaf, the sheriff of Suffolk County.[8]

In the Pope's Day fracas of 1764, a boy was killed, "many were hurt & bruised on both sides," with "several thousand people following" the participants, "hallowing &c . . ." Mackintosh and others were arrested and charged; after a lengthy delay, they were on February 7, 1765, "tryed [i.e., made the subjects of a probable-cause hearing] before Mr Justice Dana & Justice Storey for the 5th of Nov. affair." Later, a superior court grand jury indicted them, although they were never tried. Mackintosh, already called "Captain," had established himself as a mob chieftain. This reputation did him no harm with the "Caucas Clubb," that informal political association which met in the garret of Thomas Dawes. There, Dawes, Samuel Adams, and an inchoate group of their friends "smoke tobacco till you cannot see from one End of the Garrett to the other. There they drink Phlip," John Adams supposed, "and there they choose a Moderator, who puts Questions to the Vote regularly, and select Men, Assessors, Collectors, Wardens, Fire Wards, and Representatives are Regularly chosen before they are chosen in the Town." At such a "Caucas," some time before the town meeting of March 12, 1765, Mackintosh was named "sealer of leather," a minor regulatory position. The meeting confirmed the Caucas choice, and did so again in 1766, 1767, and 1768. Patronage, artfully wielded, had bound Mackintosh's interest to that of the nascent Sons of Liberty.[9]

When the Loyal Nine allied itself with Boston's mob, opposition to the English colonial policy passed a watershed. Before, disagreement tended to be expressed abstractly, by petitions, newspaper screeds, private letters, even actions at law. In a very real sense, the issue of Britain's relationship with her colonies was being thrashed out, debated.

The decision to use the mobs to achieve political ends represented a conscious conclusion that American words could not, alone or even combined with the words of English friends, reach the ears of those who counted, those who could change the revenue policy. As Bernard Bailyn has written, "Force had been introduced into the Revolutionary movement in a form long familiar but now newly empowered by widely shared principles and beliefs. It would never thereafter be absent." [10] The force which Samuel Adams and the Loyal Nine summoned into the argument destroyed the possibility of accommodation. When the Boston mob was permitted to roar its way into the Stamp Act controversy, the effect was frightening. Indeed, that was precisely what those who summoned the mob had in mind. Their object was simple: compel repeal of the Stamp Act by putting those who were to administer and enforce it in fear of their lives. The radicals sought a political goal by physical means, and they achieved it, as they were to achieve other such goals in the immediate and distant future. But in doing so at such an early stage in the dispute, they ensured that the future course of the disagreement could never be resolved without force.

It is not really an answer to argue, as some have done, that in fact the Boston mob did not cause wholesale or even retail slaughter, and that compared to the Paris rabble in 1789 the Bostonians acted decently and decorously. The essential characteristic of the mobs in pre-Revolutionary Boston, as of mobs anywhere at any time, was the impression they gave of unpredictability. He whom the mob threatened never knew just how far the crowd would go. He knew only that he faced a crew of bullies, rough, loud, frequently intoxicated. In some cases, the mob demanded of its victim that he do something—resign an office, swear not to import British goods. Here the mob's purpose, or rather the purpose of those who summoned up the mob, was to convey to the victim in the most explicit simple terms the frightening alternatives: Do what the mob asks, or the mob will destroy your property and perhaps destroy you. Sometimes, the mob's aim was entirely destructive. It did not seek to compel action by the victim; it reserved the action for itself, action like destruction of a house or tarring and feathering. To the victim, the purpose was really immaterial; the threat of physical harm, brutally and unreasoningly administered, lay behind the whistles and the shouts.

It is a paradox of the violence in Boston during the years from 1765 to 1770 that although the rioters seemed uncontrolled and uncontrollable, they were in fact under an almost military discipline. On one notable occasion, according to the Tory Peter Oliver, Mackintosh paraded the Town with a Mob of 2,000 Men in two Files, & passed by the Stadthouse, when the general Assembly were sitting, to display his Power: if a Whisper was heard among his Followers, the holding up of his Finger hushed it in a Moment: & when he had fully displayed his Authority, he marched his Men to the first Rendevouz, & Order'd them to retire peacably to their several Homes; & was punctually obeyed.

The Boston mob's ardor, there is little doubt, could be turned on or off to suit the policies of its directors. It was a shaped political instrument, consciously used as such. The occasional excesses in which the mob indulged only emphasized its ususal discipline; under stress of combat, even veteran troops sometimes temporarily get out of hand.

The Boston mob, as a political weapon, first came to life on the evening of August 14, 1765, "when the noble Ardour of Liberty" (or so the patriots were later to describe it) "burst thro' its long Concealment, o'erleap'd the Barriers of Oppression, and lifted its awful Crest amid the Group of lowering Dastards, haughty Tyrants, and merciless Paracides." The object of this o'erleaping ardour was Andrew Oliver, secretary of the province, brother to Judge Peter Oliver of the superior court, and stamp distributor-designate. A wealthy merchant and landowner, Oliver made no secret of his appointment; a little while earlier, when Jared Ingersoll landed at Boston from England, bearing his own commission as Connecticut's stamp master, Oliver had joined with other dignitaries in rendering him honors, and in escorting him on the first part of his journey south. The Boston *Gazette* flayed Oliver for his part in the ceremonies, and the night of August 13, the Loyal Nine prepared him a special treat. The next morning, "A Great Number of people assembled at Deacon Elliot's Corner" (at what is today the intersection of Essex and Washington Streets) "to see the Stamp Officer hung in Effigy with a Libel [i.e., label] on the Breast, on Deacon Elliot's tree." Oliver's figure remained all day high on the Liberty Tree—it was already called that—and within a month someone would nail a copper name-plate to its trunk: "The Tree of Liberty." Passers-by stopped to stare; word spread throughout Boston and even to some of the nearby towns; people came from all over. Samuel Adams was there; when someone asked him who and what the effigy was, Adams "said he did not know, he could not tell. He wanted to enquire." Bernard convened the council while Sheriff Greenleaf reconnoitered and wisely or perhaps designedly "forebore any attempt to remove the image." The governor and the council debated throughout the day, with most of the councilors urging "that the people were orderly, and if left alone, would take down the image, and bury it without any disturbance; but an attempt to remove it would bring on a riot, the mischief designed to be prevented." [11] In fact, what choice did Bernard have? Boston possessed no police force, only a few Dogberry-Verges constables better equipped to serve court papers than to keep the peace. The nearest regular troops were in New York; neither the militia (if it could be assembled in time) nor the governor's cadets were reliable. And anyway, it was much simpler to believe that with darkness the fun would end, and the crowd would disperse.

But here as on other occasions, Bernard's hopes betrayed him. When night fell, the throng remained intact. The managers of the proceedings cut down the effigy "in Triumph amidst the acclamations of many thousands who were gathered together on that occasion." They proceeded in rowdy procession along what is now Washington Street toward the Town House (which we today call the Old State House) and poured into the building "in the chamber whereof the governor and council were sitting," still searching for a formula to meet the emergency. "Forty or fifty tradesmen, decently dressed," led the crowd, which now numbered "thousands," through the Town House and down along King Street (today's State Street) toward the waterfront. Oliver owned a dock near the foot of King Street where he had recently put up a small frame building. Assuming that this was to be stamp headquarters, the mob laid it "flat to the ground in a few minutes." A little to the southward, on a street which then as now was called Oliver, stood Oliver's opulent town house, furnished in the genteel, expensive style to which wealthy Bostonians were accustomed. The back gardens of the house ran to the slopes of a commanding eminence called Fort Hill (leveled in the nineteenth century). It was the mob's intention to burn Oliver's effigy atop the hill, and burned it was. But passing Oliver's house, some of them "endeavoured to force themselves into it, and being opposed, broke the windows, beat down the doors, entered, and destroyed part of his furniture." Hutchinson, who had been at the council meeting, had apparently raced the mob to Oliver's home, for he was there when it was assaulted. He tried to obtain help from the sheriff and the colonel of the militia, but neither the civil nor the military powers, nor Hutchinson himself, could stop the mob. By the time peace restored itself, "the blind, undistinguishing Rage of the Rabble," as John Adams called it the next day, had left Oliver's "Garden torn in Pieces, his House broken open, his furniture destroyed and his whole family thrown into Confusion and Terror." It was indeed "a very attrocious Violation of the Peace and of dangerous Tendency and Consequence." [12]

"Attrocious" though they may have been, the mob's actions bore immediate results. Oliver "came to a sudden resolution to resign his office before another night" and agreed in writing to submit his resignation to London forthwith. The news, which Oliver took pains to disseminate widely and promptly, occasioned great joy, another mob, and a second bonfire on Fort Hill, "not to insult the distributor, but to give him thanks." Few onlookers or participants were so shrewd as John Rowe, who noted that Oliver had only "resigned his Commission in Form." Generally, radicals and conservatives alike regarded the event as a "matter of triumph" for the Loyal Nine. Each year thereafter on the anniversary (or the following Monday if the anniversary fell on Sunday) the Sons of Liberty held a huge public celebration; this custom continued even after the Declaration of Independence. Obviously, the patriots realized the significance of the mob's work; destruction of property and bodily harm, threatened and actual, in fact controlled but in appearance unchecked, had proven a successful revolutionary technique.[13]

The force which Mackintosh and the Loyal Nine led through the August night had crushed Oliver. But the real object was not he. In the very essay which deplored the "strange Conduct" toward Oliver, John Adams suggested the true target.

> Has not his Honour the Lieutenant Governor discovered [i.e., revealed] to the People in innumerable Instances, a very ambitious and avaricious Disposition? Has he not grasped four of the most important offices in the Province into his own Hands? . . . Is not this amazing ascendancy of one Family, Foundation sufficient on which to erect a Tyranny? Is it not enough to excite Jealousies among the People? . . . Would it not be Prudence then in those Gentlemen at this alarming Conjuncture, and a Condescention that is due to the present Fears and Distresses of the People, (in some manner consistent with the Dignity of their stations and Characters,) to remove these Jealousies [i.e., fears] from the Minds of the People by giving an easy solution of these Difficulties?

Irate though Adams was, he did not suggest that Hutchinson had supported the Stamp Act; apart from the charge of nepotism, the most damaging indictments he could bring against the lieutenant governor were his watering down of the remonstrance to Parliament in 1764 and his efforts to procure the appointment of Richard Jackson as the province's London agent. Not a word about the Stamp Act; not even a mention of Hutchinson's part in granting the writs of assistance. Nothing about Hutchinson's position against a gold standard in the currency dispute of 1762, which Hutchinson himself conceded had unaccountably raised resentments against him. Adams left all these out, and still considered Hutchinson's guilt large enough to justify the violence against Oliver. And even if he had mentioned them, could he seriously blame Hutchinson in the slightest for the mob's behavior? The answer seems obvious unless this is an example of the technique so well-practiced by the other Adams of putting one's enemy in the wrong and keeping him there.[14]

A more plausible, yet typically unjustified, source of the resentment which was building up and being built up against Hutchinson arose from a set of depositions or affidavits which Bernard had earlier collected and sent to England. Hutchinson was unconnected with any of these except for having sworn one of the deponents. Boston merchant Briggs Hallowell, at the Plantation Office in London, saw the affidavits, noted their contents and attestations. When he returned to Boston in the summer of 1765, he "reported that complaint was made in them of John Rowe, Solomon Davy [Davis], and other merchants, as illicit traders, and that they were sworn to before" Hutchinson. The evening of August 15, a mob surrounded Hutchinson's North End house, inflamed by a further rumor that he "was a favourer of the stamp act, and had encouraged it by letters" to England. Through barred doors and windows, Hutchinson heard the shouts. "After attempting to enter, they called upon him to come into the balcony, and to declare that he had not written in favour of the act, and they would retire quite satisfied." Hutchinson stayed silent; the rabble debated. Finally a neighbor told them Hutchinson had left before dark for his country house in nearby Milton. "Upon this, they dispersed, with only breaking some of the glass" of the windows, each surmounted by the crown of Britain.[15]

It was plain that the mob, and whoever was directing it, controlled Boston. Bernard and the council had been unable to advance any sensible proposal for containing the violence other than to offer a £100 reward for the conviction of the Oliver mobbers. Ordinary people feared the dangers inherent in the mob's power, but, as Hutchinson observed, "would give no aid in discountenancing it, lest they should become obnoxious themselves." On Sunday, August 25, Jonathan Mayhew, cleric and radical pamphleteer, preached from his West Church pulpit a sermon on the text, "I would they were even cut off which trouble you. For, brethren, ye have been called unto liberty . . ." Unfortunately, Mayhew omitted the ensuing clause: "only *use* not liberty for an occasion to the flesh, but by love serve one another." The merchants, irked by the incident of the depositions, now made joint cause with the mob directors. John Rowe, according to Hutchinson, admitted that they proceeded to stir up the mob to attack "the houses of the Custom House officers, the Register of the Admiralty, and the Chief Justice, the last of whom was made the principal object." Rowe's diary for the essential dates is lost; the only documentary evidence so far unearthed to link him so directly with what followed Mayhew's sermon is Hutchinson's bald statement. Circumstantial evidence tying merchants and land speculators to the ensuing events will, however, shortly appear.[16]

There is some indication that Hutchinson's magnificent six-pilastered brick home had been marked for destruction even before Mayhew spoke. Hutchinson, who had arrived with his family from Milton the morning of August 26, heard "whispered" rumors in the late afternoon that "[Customs Surveyor Charles] Paxton's, [Comptroller Benjamin] Hallowell's, & the custom house & admiralty officers' houses would be attacked." But a friend assured him that the window-breaking of August 15 had satisfied the mob, and that he "was become rather popular." He changed his warm suit coat for a thin dressing gown and, in the twilight heat, sat down quietly to supper with his children. Outside, the rumors took violent shape. A bonfire in King Street drew a large crowd which, "well-supplied with strong drink," was easily led to the Hutchinson (now Pearl) Street house (on ground now a part of the Federal Reserve Bank), where the unpopular Paxton had rented lodgings. Paxton was fortunately away for the evening, and his fast-thinking landlord saved the tenant from execution in absentia by standing treat for a barrel of punch. "Hurrah, hurrah," was the response. "He is a clever fellow and no Tory. So come along and we'll drink his health and down with the Stamps." Thirst temporarily slaked, the mob then apparently split up, some members heading for the home and office of Register of the Admiralty William Story on King Street, opposite what is today the Old State House, others for the Hanover Street house of Comptroller Hallowell. The mob at Story's "pulled down the Windows of his Office and burnt all the [vice-admiralty] papers therein . . . broke all the rest of his Windows." This gang moved on to Hallowell's, where another group had already "begun the Destruction. They broke all his Windows, took down some very curious carv'd Work in one of his Rooms," and "plundered his cellars of the wine and spirits in them." Now thoroughly warmed within and without, the mobs converged and thundered into the North End, where Hutchinson, one of the richest men in Boston, worth well over £15,000, still sat at his evening meal, his children around him.[17]

Suddenly, "somebody ran in and said the mob was coming." Hutchinson told his children "to fly to a secure place" and then he "shut up my house as I had done before intending not to quit it." But daughter Sally, having left once,

> repented her leaving me and hastened back and protested she would not quit the house unless I did. I could not stand against this and withdrew with her to a neighbouring house where I had been but a few minutes before the hellish crew fell upon my house with the rage of divels and in a moment with axes split down the door and entred.

My son being in the great entry heard them cry damn him he is upstairs we'll have him. Some ran immediately as high as the top of the
house, others filled the rooms below and cellars and others remained
without the house to be employed there. Messages soon came one
after another to the house where I was to inform me the mob were
coming in Pursuit of me and I was obliged to retire thro yards and
gardens to a house more remote where I remained until 4 o'clock by
which time one of the best finished houses in the Province had nothing remaining but the bare walls and floors. Not contented with tear-
ing off all the wainscot and hangings and splitting the doors to pieces
they beat down the Partition walls and altho that alone cost them near
two hours they cut down the cupola or lanthorn and they began to
take the slate and boards from the roof and were prevented only by
the approaching daylight from a total demolition of the building. The
garden fence was laid flat and all my trees etc. broke down to the
ground . . . Besides my plate and family pictures, household furniture of every kind my own my children and servants apparel they
carried off about £900 sterling in money and emptied the house of
every thing whatsoever except a part of the kitchen furniture not leaving a single book or paper in it and have scattered or destroyed all
the manuscripts and other papers I had been collecting for 30 years
together besides a great number of Publick papers in my custody.[18]

Hutchinson's description does not exaggerate. Joshua Henshaw, no
Tory, wrote his cousin on August 28 "an Account of the base Proceedings of a Mob on Monday Evening, which in short overset all the approved of Measures the other [i.e., the Oliver mob] had taken."

With Respects to the Lieut. Governor's House, where they ended their
vile Transactions [Henshaw continued], such as were never heard of
here before, they had then rais'd a greater Number and were intoxicated with Liquor, broke his Windows, threw all his Furniture out of
his House, stamp'd upon the Chairs, Mahogany Tables, very hand-
some large gilt-framed Pictures, the Peices of which lay in Piles in the
Street, open'd his Beds and let all the Feathers out, took ten thousand
Pounds in Cash, took all his Cloathes, Linnen, Plate and every Thing
he had, cut the Balcony off of the Top of his House, pulled down all
the Fruit-Trees in his Garden, and did him in all £25,000 Damage.

Henshaw's figure is quite exaggerated but there is no reason to doubt
the accuracy of his description otherwise, especially as he "went over
the ruins" the day after the riot. Josiah Quincy, a sadly cross-eyed
young law student only two years out of Harvard, wrote at the same
time that the "Rage-intoxicated Rabble . . . beset the House on all
Sides, and soon destroyed every Thing of Value. . . . The Destruction
was really amazing, for it was equal to the Fury of the Onset." [19]
What reason lay behind this "unparalleled outrage," as Hutchinson

called it? Who were the "demons" who perpetrated it? Hutchinson was admittedly not so "popular" as his friends had suggested, but he was certainly a public figure whose services to the province had been and would continue to be respected and sought after, a man, in John Adams's words, of "great Merit," whose "Countrymen loved, admired, revered, rewarded, nay almost adored him . . . 99 in an 100 of them really thought him, the greatest and best Man in America." Under those circumstances, Hutchinson's friends, although proved by the event to have been tragically misinformed, were not irrational in failing to attend him. Whether their presence would have averted the horrors, no one can say; it may be worth noting that at Philadelphia two months later, when reports formed of a planned assault on the home of Stamp Collector John Hughes, "several Hundreds" of his friends patrolled the streets, causing "the Collection of Rabble . . . to decrease visibly," and ultimately to disperse.[20]

Absent friends, but present enemies. Were their reasons for hating Hutchinson strong enough, valid enough to sanction the gutting of his home? We do not know, because we do not know the reasons themselves. Hutchinson thought the root lay in his unfortunate attestation of the depositions, and that "the merchants, as one of them, Mr. Rowe, acknowledged, stirred up the mob," making his house "the principal object." Samuel Adams offered a characteristic double set of what might properly be called non-explanations. On the one hand, he castigated the rioters as "a Lawless unknown Rabble," and the riot a "Transaction of a truly *mobbish* Nature," the cause of which was "not known publickly—some Persons have suggested their private thoughts of it." But he also cultivated the rumor that the rioters had discovered letters in the house establishing Hutchinson's authorship of the Stamp Act, Adams thus implying that the mob's subsequent destructiveness merely represented its just resentment at the lieutenant governor's perfidy. Since we know that the act was drafted by Thomas Whately of the Treasury Office in London, Adams's insinuations seem almost ridiculous. Far from fearing that his ransacked correspondence would link him to the act, Hutchinson knew that "he had, as far as with propriety he might, used his endeavours to prevent it; and he thought it probable some of his papers to evidence it, might fall into the hands of people who brought the charge against him." In other words, Hutchinson's real worry was that the mob (or whoever was behind it) would destroy the proof of Hutchinson's opposition to the act and would continue to charge him with having favored it.[21]

Hutchinson owned a large mercantile business, and it is possible that here as elsewhere in the colonies the mob's animus was commercial. The "Number of Persons in Disguise with axes Clubbs &c." which stormed the Scarborough, Maine home of Richard King a few months later (after having "talk'd about the Riots in the Prov[ince]"), likewise called themselves "Suns of liburty," but their real aim was the location and destruction of fifty-four notes of hand, three bonds, eight deeds, five executions, and one lease. The private Hutchinson papers which the mob destroyed may well have afforded a rough kind of debtor's relief. In Providence, they had a more facetious explanation. The members of a "Political Clubb" with whom John Adams's friend Daniel Leonard spent an evening, "Thought Hutchinson's History did not shine. Said his House was pulled down, to prevent his writing any more by destroying his Materials." [22]

This gallows humor may have come close to the truth. Among the documents Hutchinson had been collecting as the foundation of his *History* were various papers pertaining to land titles in Maine, at that time part of Massachusetts. This vast area provoked large-scale land and timber speculation, in which Hutchinson's family had participated, some of its claims conflicting with those of other Bostonians. Whether a desire to limit Hutchinson's title search was the ultimate motive behind the riot is still uncertain. Hutchinson's only known reference to the matter is too oblique to be helpful. It comes as a footnote to the posthumously published Volume III of the *History*:

> The lieutenant-colonel of the [Boston militia] regiment, observing two men disguised, with long staves in their hands, who seemed to be directors, expressed his concern at the damage other people, besides the lieutenant-governor, might sustain by the destruction of so many papers. Answer was made, that it had been resolved to destroy every thing in the house; and such resolve should be carried to effect.[23]

Two men disguised. With blackened faces perhaps, and rough clothing? We do not know. We do not even know their names. Indeed few of the rioters escaped the anonymity that prudence, shame, and the nature of a mob imposed on the participants; Hutchinson has provided the only firm identification—Mackintosh. It is a characteristic of mobs that their whole is infinitely more notable than their parts. The crowd becomes an historical entity and later basks in the glare of its own notoriety; the individuals who comprise it remain through the centuries in the shadows which initially encouraged and protected them. Thus it has been with the "hellish crew" who trampled Hutchinson's opulence. In his *History* and his diary Hutchinson labeled Mackintosh as the principal participant; Bernard, some years later, called "one Moore a principal hand"; and Hutchinson's niece, writing more than a half-century afterwards, accused a North Square mason named Atkins of having helped. Other than these, and except for Hutchinson's comment about John Rowe, we have until now no positive indentification of the men who stormed the lieutenant governor's house.[24]

The thick, unexplored files in the office of the Clerk of the Supreme Judicial Court for Suffolk County provide a little more evidence. A jail return, or list of prisoners, dated October 15, 1765, shows that Christopher Barrett, Samuel Taylor, and Stephen Grealy (Greeley) were charged "with being concerned in an Extraordinary Riot in the Evening the 26th day of August last and breaking open and entring the Dwelling house of the Honorable Thos. Hutchinson Esqr. and taking Stealing and Carrying away from thence great sums of his Money and quantitys of his Goods etc." None of these men ever stood trial for the alleged offense; so one cannot say for sure that they were part of the mob. Other evidence in the files, however, circumstantially suggests the makeup of at least a portion of the Boston mob. In early 1765, as a result of the Pope's Day rioting in November 1764, the Suffolk County Grand Jury returned indictments against members of the North End and South End gangs. From the mass of papers, it is possible to state with some certainty the sort of men who were concerned in the 1764 riots. Because we know that a year after the riots, the rival gangs merged under Mackintosh's leadership, it is reasonable to assume that some of the 1764 crowd participated in the 1765 outrages. Other evidence, shortly to be discussed, makes this assumption even more rational.[25]

Mackintosh (spelled McIntosh) was one of the accused, of course. So was another cordwainer, Benjamin Starr, and a leather dresser, Isaac Bowman Apthorp. The others came from various occupations, most involving manual labor. There was a sizable contingent of maritime workers: shipwrights Henry Swift, John Blight, and William Blight, sailmaker Zephaniah Bassett, ship joiner William Bovey, caulker William Larribee, and ropemaker Thomas Rice. Samuel Richardson was a hatter, Ichabod Simpson a housewright, George Hambleton a chaisemaker, John Corbit a distiller, and Benjamin Wheeler a barber. Cornelius Abbot, Henry Gardner, and Thomas Stimpson were bakers; Thomas Smith was simply "laborer." These were apparently young apprentice types. The documents label as "infants," that is, minors, John Blight, Hambleton, Swift, Richardson, Bassett, and Simpson.

Beyond telling us the names, occupations, and (in some cases) ages of the putative mob members, the papers show clearly the people who took an active interest in their fate. This evidence is the most useful of all in connecting the Pope's Day brawlers of 1764 with the more serious rioters of later years. The files contain a number of "recognizances," or surety bonds binding the named individual (defendant or, possibly, witness) to appear at a designated future court session. Since each surety made himself monetarily responsible for the "principal's" appearance, and since provincial Massachusetts lacked anything like a compensated, premium-receiving bail bondsman, one can reasonably assume that a man who stood surety on a recognizance was taking some kind of personal interest in the principal. A surety for Simpson and for Smith was distiller William Speakman, partner of Thomas Chase, one of the Loyal Nine; it was in a "Compting Room" of the Chase & Speakman distillery that the Nine held its meetings. And when the deputy sheriff sought to serve a warrant on Corbit, John "Avarey" "gave his word" that Corbit would appear. John Avery, Harvard 1759, also belonged to the Loyal Nine.[26]

The 1764 rioters, although arraigned, that is, required to plead to the indictments—they all pleaded not guilty except John Blight, whose absence the file does not explain—were never tried. There is no formal indication that the charges were dropped; apparently the matter was permitted merely to die. It is possible that a dearth of evidence forced this development; perhaps it would be fairer to say that the prosecution simply lacked witnesses, at least willing ones. Some time in March 1765, for example, Richardson and Theodore Bliss (whom we shall meet again) "were bro't into Court to give Evidence in behalf of the King." Upon their refusal to be sworn, the court ordered them "committed to his Majesty's goal." The record is bare of any suggestion that Richardson's recalcitrance stemmed from a reluctance to incriminate himself. Indeed, he avoided punishment in an unusual way, one which reinforces the prosposition that a connection existed between Pope's Day 1764 and the Hutchinson riot. He produced a kind of "excuse note," directed to the judges:

> This may certify that about six Weeks ago I was called to visit Samuel Richardson son of Capt. Nathl Richardson. I found his Nerves much disordered with frequent Twitchings and partial Convulsions attended with a Delirium. I bled him largely and gave him several Doses of Physick—upon which the Delirium ceased and his Nerves grew quiet. Upon Enquery I found that He had at Times been liable to Disorders of this Kind from his Childhood.

The note, dated March 21, 1765, bore the signature of Doctor Joseph Warren, Avery's Harvard classmate, and already a rising figure in Samuel Adams's organization. A memorandum in Clerk Samuel Winthrop's hand across the foot of the document records that "upon the above Certificate he was discharged." [27]

Organized though the Hutchinson riot may have been, certainly its cadre went unrecognized. The Reverend Dr. Mayhew, racked by the thought that his flaming eloquence might have lit off the explosion, wrote Hutchinson the day after in shamed apology. "In truth I had rather lose my hand, than be an encourager of such outrages as were committed last Night." But, he went on, "I must beg your Honor not to devulge what I now write, . . . For it could do no good in the present circumstances, . . . and might probably bring their heavy vengeance upon myself." [28]

Actually, Mayhew's fears lacked much basis. The initial popular reaction heartily supported Hutchinson, and the mob's directorate preferred to utilize that reaction as camouflage. By chance, August 27 was the first day of the August term of the superior court. Josiah Quincy attended court, as was his custom, to observe the barristers and to note points of law raised at bench and bar. The chief justice seems to have favored Quincy, and on occasion to have given him legal documents to study. Quincy, even then eager to number himself among "the warmest Lovers of Liberty," had approved the Oliver affair as "a very notable Instance of [Bostonian] Detestation of the . . . unconstitutional Act." But the sight of his mentor in "Court, with a Look big with the greatest Anxiety," still clothed in his garments of the evening before, excited his entire sympathy: "Such a Man, in such a Station, thus habited, with Tears starting from his Eyes, and a Countenance which strongly told the inward Anguish of his Soul." [29]

Hutchinson addressed the court for half an hour, apologized for his appearance, insisted on his opposition to the Stamp Act, and warned against the dangers of rabble-rousing. The court then adjourned until October 15. Later that day, Quincy in his notebook echoed Hutchinson's warning.

> Oh ye Sons of *Popularity:* beware lest a Thirst of *Applause* move you groundlessly to inflame the Minds of the People. . . . Who, that sees the *Fury and Instability* of the Populace, but would seek Protection under the ARM OF POWER? Who that beholds the *Tyranny and Oppression* of arbitrary Power, but would lose his Life in Defence of his LIBERTY? [30]

Upon the adjournment, the Bostonians staged a hasty town meeting in Faneuil Hall, and, according to Hutchinson's wry account, "with one voice expressed their detestation of the disorders the evening preceding, a great number of the actors and promoters being present." Governor Bernard called a council meeting the same day, to which Sheriff Greenleaf was summoned and given a warrant for Mackintosh's arrest. Walking down King Street from the Town House, Greenleaf saw Mackintosh, approached him, and, without apparent resistance, took him into custody. A Tory merchant named Nathaniel Coffin "and several other gentlemen" immediately came over to Greenleaf and told him that plans had been made for a civilian and militia security patrol, to protect the town from a threatened new riot that evening, but that unless Mackintosh was released "not a man would appear." Greenleaf hurried back to the council chamber to report the threat. "And did you release him," Hutchinson asked. "Yes," said Greenleaf. "Then," said the lieutenant-governor in resigned understatement, "you have not done your duty." [31]

Though Mackintosh went free (because, in Hutchinson's opinion, "he could discover [i.e., reveal] who employed him") "six or eight other persons" were apprehended and jailed. What happened there-after is vague. Hutchinson says that "in the dead of night," "several days, if not weeks" later, "a large number of men entered the house of the prison keeper; compelled him to deliver the keys; opened the prison doors; and set every man free who had been committed for this offence [among them, Moore]. They absconded for some months; after which, finding that no authority had taken any notice of the prisoners or of the persons concerned in their rescue, they returned; appeared openly, and were very active in other irregular proceedings." [32]

The escape in fact appears to have taken place around October 1, because on October 2, according to the council records, Greenleaf re-ported the rescue; unfortunately, the affidavits and other materials he submitted at the time have disappeared. At any rate, the council the next day attributed the escape to "the weakness of the Goal," and left it at that. The mystery receives no illumination from the existing court records. As mentioned earlier, the list of prisoners shows that on Octo-ber 15, the day the court resumed its session, Barrett, Taylor, and Grealy were in jail charged with breaking into Hutchinson's house; in addition, one Patrick Murray, another prisoner, was charged with en-tering Hallowell's house "with an intent to Steal some of the goods therein." None of these men ever stood trial, or even faced arraign-ment. The Minute Book notes that each of them was ordered dis-charged, "this grand Jury not having found a Bill against them." In other words, for reasons now unknown, the government was unable to secure an indictment. Time did not improve the chances of a success-ful prosecution, and no other suspects came to book. The popular reac-tion in Hutchinson's favor ultimately led to monetary recompense, under circumstances we will examine later.[33]

During October 1765, men's attention turned to the Stamp Act itself, and to its fast-approaching effective date, November 1. The legal profession, especially, anticipated difficult practical problems. Shortly after the superior court met in October, lawyer Benjamin Kent, repre-senting a prevailing mortgagee, asked the court to waive the statutory two-month grace period and to issue execution twenty-four hours after judgment. If, Kent argued, "Execution did not issue till the Expiration of two Months, the Stamp Act would take Place, and then Execution could not be had at all." This contention carries more significance than its legalistic context might at first suggest. Nothing in the Stamp Act forbade the issuance of an execution—an order to the sheriff to satisfy a judgment out of the property of the losing party; the act merely required that the execution be written on stamped paper. Kent's argument, therefore, could mean only that he and, presumably, the rest of the bar, were convinced that stamped paper would not be available, and that no one would be able to transact legal business after November 1. Note also Kent's unarticulated assumption that the courts would refuse to issue documents unstamped. This assumption was accurate. The popular party's attempt to force the courts to operate in defiance of the act was to provide the radicals with a strong lever for putting Hutchinson in the wrong (at least as they defined it) and keeping him there.[34]

Samuel Adams, meanwhile, was coming out of the semi-obscurity in which he had previously chosen to operate. When the Boston Town Meeting convened on September 27 to select a representative to the legislature in place of the recently deceased Oxenbridge Thacher, Adams won. It is not entirely accidental that his open assumption of power coincided with the decline of Otis. During mid-October, Otis attended the Stamp Act Congress in New York, but "played only a minor role in its deliberations." Upon his return to Boston and afterwards, though he continued to serve the Town in various capacities, mental infirmities had shaken the rod of leadership from his hands. "Otis is fiery and fev'rous," John Adams wrote of him at about this time. "His Imagination flames, his Passions blaze. He is liable to great Inequalities of Temper—sometimes in Despondency, sometimes in a Rage. The Rashnesses and Imprudences, into which his Excess of Zeal have formerly transported him, have made him Enemies, whose malicious watch over him, occasion more Caution, and more Cunning and more inexplicable Passages in his Conduct than formerly." [35]

November 1 drew closer. On October 26, its usual business finished "in Harmony . . . Unanimity and Order," the superior court adjourned its Suffolk County sitting *sine die* until the next regular term, also in Suffolk County, in March 1766. For the time being, the judges and lawyers need not resolve the dilemma that Kent had mentioned. Another, more physical problem took temporary precedence: the reaction of the mob; or more accurately, the use to which the mob would be put. As it happened, during early November the mob and its keepers maintained order, but it was order which carried almost as much terror as open violence. November 1 came and went quietly, marked only by a spate of effigy-hanging on and around Liberty Tree and the town gallows. Four days later, Pope's Day, the North and South End gangs, their respective leaders (Swift and Mackintosh) virtually arm-in-arm, paraded peaceably together, evidently ready to direct their violence jointly as necessary against common enemies. "The liberty party said," according to Hutchinson, "that the disposition of the body of the people was to be judged of from this orderly behaviour; and that the late violence proceeded from a few abandoned, desperate persons. The government party inferred, that this was an evidence of the influence the mob was under, and that they might be let loose, or kept up, just as their keepers thought fit." [36]

November wore on into December amid a suspension of commercial and legal activity. On December 3, some of the merchants entered another rudimentary nonimportation agreement. But still Stamp Act paralysis gripped Boston, with no stamp officer available to distribute the needed stamps, and no public official willing to proceed without them. John Adams described the impasse perfectly:

> The Stamps are in the Castle [i.e., Castle William, the fort on Castle Island]. Mr. Oliver has no Commission. The Governor has no Authority to distribute, or even to unpack the Bales [of stamped paper], the Act has never been proclaimed nor read in the Province; Yet the Probate office is shut, the Custom House is shut, the Courts of Justice are shut, and all Business seems at a Stand. Yesterday and the day before, the two last days of Service for January Term [of the Suffolk Inferior Court], only one Man asked me for a Writ, and he was soon determined to waive his Request. I have not drawn a Writ since 1st. Novr. How long We are to remain in this languid Condition, this passive Obedience to the Stamp Act, is not certain. But such a Pause cannot be lasting. Debtors grow insolent. Creditors grow angry . . . This long Interval of Indolence and Idleness will make a large Chasm in my affairs if it should not reduce me to Distress and incapacitate me to answer the Demands made upon me.

John Adams tended to take things personally. The Stamp Act, "this execrable Project was set on foot for my Ruin as well as that of America in General, and of Great Britain." Political considerations aside, the act was dealing Adams the lowest practical blow a lawyer can receive: it was costing him clients.[37]

But the log jam in affairs as well as in Adams's practice was about to break violently. The day before he wrote those lugubrious thoughts in his Braintree study, the Boston Sons of Liberty made the first move in a scheme designed to force the custom house and the courts to open for business. Since the night of December 15, "a severe Storm" had drenched the Boston area with a "vast Quantity of rain." Monday night, December 16, the Loyal Nine met, wrote, and sent to Oliver a letter demanding that he appear at the Liberty Tree at noon the next day publicly to resign his office as stamp distributor-designate; they also arranged for the printing and distribution (before daybreak) of handbills inviting the public to attend the ceremony.[38]

At the appointed time, the rain still pouring down, Mackintosh personally called for Oliver at his home and accompanied him to the Tree. There lawyer Richard Dana, a justice of the peace, awaited him, as did two thousand of the faithful. It was Dana's duty to administer the oath, and his presence was not without significance. The Loyal Nine had apparently selected Dana especially, in order to stiffen what the Sons felt was his wavering adherence to the Liberty side. If this was the motive, the treatment appears to have met marked success. Dana became a virulent anti-Tory.[39]

Oliver's resignation now having ensured that no one in the province could properly distribute the stamps, and the mob's display of strength having demonstrated the uselessness of resistance, the customs officers easily resolved their doubts: they opened the custom house that very afternoon. Now Samuel Adams and the Loyal Nine could turn their attention to the courts. First, they called a special town meeting for December 18. Next, they pushed through a memorial to the governor and council praying the opening of the courts. Then they arranged for the appointment of a committee to present the memorial, with Adams himself at its head. Finally, they took steps to obtain expert legal advice. On December 18, the rain stopped. Two of the Loyal Nine, Thomas Crafts and Thomas Chase, rode down to Braintree to give John Adams "a particular Account of the Proceedings." An hour later, a constable of Boston brought Adams official notification of his appointment (together with Jeremy Gridley and Otis) as the Town's "Council to appear before his Excellency the Governor in Council, in Support of their Memorial, praying that the Courts of Law in this Province may be opened." To Adams, the coincidence of the appointment and his own "Reflections and Speculations" of the day before was an example of one of the "secret invisible Laws of Nature." He accepted the assignment and spent the next few day consulting, thinking, studying, and ultimately arguing, all to no avail; the government refused to take any affirmative steps. But in the course of one discussion, Samuel Adams found occasion to congratulate John on his selection, "1st. Because he hoped that such an Instance of Respect from the Town of Boston, would make an Impression on my Mind, and secure my Friendship to the Town from Gratitude. 2dly. He was in Hopes such a Distinction from Boston, would be of Service to my Business and Interest." Samuel's hopes, John admitted, "may be well grounded." [40]

Adams, Otis, and Gridley argued the Town's position to the governor and council strongly, almost violently. "The Stamp-Act," Adams insisted, "was made where we are in no Sense represented, therefore no more binding upon us, than an Act which should oblige us to destroy One Half of our Specie. . . . A Parliament of Great Britain can have no more Right to tax the Colonies than a Parliament of Paris." Otis called the "shutting up of the Courts" "an Abdication, a total Dissolution of Government." Even the hyper-dignified Gridley urged that the "Safety of the whole People, the Preservation of all Government is in Issue." All the eloquence was wasted. Bernard's scant legal ability sufficed to allow him to turn the issue over to the judges, citing "the Impropriety of our Intermeddling in a Matter which solely belongs to them to judge of in their Judicial Department." The superior court, it appeared, would stay shut.[41]

With the Suffolk Inferior Court, Samuel Adams fared a little better. Those judges, after all, sat only in Boston. When Adams's man William Molineux "discoursed" them on the subject, they listened attentively, and Molineux was able to report confidently to the town meeting of December 21 that "he had no reason to doubt but that the aforesaid Court would at their next Term proceed to Business as usual." The Suffolk County Court of Probate also required attention. The act bore heavily on the sheaf of documents necessary to the administration of decedents' estates. Besides, unlike the other courts, it sat at no fixed term, its volume of work being set by the local death rate and the energy of the single judge of probate. Bostonian mortality lay beyond the regulation of even the Loyal Nine, but the judge was fair game. His name was Thomas Hutchinson. When Hutchinson flatly refused to hold court or "to suffer any business to be done in the probate office," the Sons of Liberty undertook "to oblige him to conform to the times." His friends frankly told him that if he valued his safety he must either give in, or resign, or "quit the country." So Hutchinson forthwith left his country home at Milton, en route to Boston and to Portsmouth, New Hampshire, where a ship carrying white pine masts for the Royal Navy waited to take him to England. At Boston, Bernard proposed a less radical solution: the appointment of Hutchinson's brother Foster as a temporary replacement, with the understanding that Foster be prepared to conduct the county's probate business, stamps or no stamps. The Town's special counsel, meanwhile, was set to searching the books for appropriate precedents on still another legal question which was beginning to agitate men's consciences. John Adams spent Christmas Day "At Home," looking up the law "Concerning a Compensation to the Sufferers by the late Riots in Boston." [42]

So the year of the Stamp Act waned. When the inferior court opened on January 13, it did indeed hold business as usual and

"rushed upon the thick Bosses of the Buckler and into the thickest of
the Penalties and Forfeitures." John Adams grew closer to the Sons of
Liberty, spending a social evening with the augmented Loyal Nine at
the distillery over "Punch, Wine, Pipes and Tobacco, Bisquit and
Cheese—&c." And Bernard, hoping desperately to be exempted "from
being again exposed to the same Dangers, which I so firmly withstood
and so happily escaped," felt himself "sev'ral Times drove to the very
Brink of Deserting my Post." He made secret arrangements with Rear
Admiral Lord Colvill, commanding on the North American Station, to
send a warship "to receive His Excellency and family, and proceed
with them to Spithead if all other expedients failed." Characteristically, Bernard tried to hedge his bet. "If the Governor was not
forced to quit his government," Colvill wrote the Admiralty, "he
wished that it might not be known that he had had any such
thoughts." [43]

A frigate for Bernard, and possibly a fleet and an army for Boston.
Hutchinson, the Olivers, and Attorney General Trowbridge, among
others, had been predicting that Britain would send military and naval
forces to enforce the act. None actually came. But in New York, Major
General Thomas Gage, commander in chief for North America, was
frankly looking for "a legal pretence to collect all the force I could,
into one body; which might check in some measure the audacious
threats of taking arms, and in case of extremity enable the King's servants, and such as are friends to government, to make a respectable
opposition." Gage, it is clear, was itching for a fight. "No Requisition
has been made of Me for assistance," he wrote his reporting superior,
Secretary at War Lord Barrington, "which I must acknowledge I have
been sorry for, as the disturbances which have happened have been so
much beyond riots, and so like the forerunners of open Rebellion, that
I have wanted a pretence to draw the troops together from every post
they cou'd be taken from, that the Servants of the Crown might be enabled to make a stand in some spot, if matters should be brought to
the Extremitys, that may not without reason be apprehended." Gage
apparently omitted to discuss the problem with Bernard, who complained later in the year to Barrington that he knew nothing about
"designations" of troops to Boston, "and it seems intended that I shall
not." Bernard had other worries, anyway, for he was having difficulty
deciding just which of the available governorships he preferred for his
next assignment. The prospective annual cash return ranked highest in
his table of values, but he considered other factors, too, and rejected
Jamaica and the Leeward Islands "upon account of the Climate; which
I apprehend would not suit my sa[n]guine Complexion." [44]

In England, where the American riots and especially the destruction of Hutchinson's house had received prominent newspaper coverage, the Boston, Philadelphia, and New York nonimportation agreements were likewise bringing home with all the effectiveness of a pocketbook argument the certainty that the stamp tax could never be enforced in America. Fortunately, even before the effective date of the act, the king had concluded that he "would rather see the devil in my closet [i.e., sanctum] than Mr. Grenville" and had brought the Earl of Rockingham to power, thus allowing the formation of a political-mercantile coalition which on March 4, 1766, was able to repeal the Stamp Act (simultaneously passing by unanimous Commons vote a Declaratory Act, in truth a Declaration of Dependence). The transatlantic distance and the rigors of late-winter–early-spring passage kept the good news from Boston until May 16.[45] Because of the delay, tensions increased and reduced the chance of an accommodation. During March, April, and May the superior court was trying to remain shut. The success of that attempt, and the sinuous course the judges adopted to achieve it, tended immediately as well as prospectively to bring the judges into contempt. This in turn could only diminish respect for law generally.

The first incident actually occurred a week before repeal. Bench and bar arrived at Boston for the usual March sitting of the superior court, only to find Hutchinson absent. Judge Peter Oliver said that if "he and his Brethren should proceed in business in defiance of the" Stamp Act, "it would be only for self preservation." All the other judges agreed. "Political finesse," John Adams and Josiah Quincy called it; yet when the court asked "each of the Lawyers singly, whether he desired that the business should proceed, every one of them answered in the Negative; even Mr. Otis himself." But "to quiet the people" a single civil case was tried, and the sitting adjourned for five weeks. (Criminal matters, which did not require stamped paper, went forward as usual.) [46]

Though the Plymouth Inferior Court opened on April 10, when John Adams traveled to Boston five days later he found the superior court (only Hutchinson, C.J., Cushing, and Oliver, JJ., present) determined not to go on. In a burst of what the irate Adams called "Insolence and Impudence, and Chickanery," the court adjourned for two more weeks. At the session of April 29, the "Farce," as Adams accurately described it, reached its nadir. Judges Russell and Oliver did not sit, and the other three desperately fenced with the lawyers. Hutchinson especially "seemed in Tortures." Adams saw the chief justice's convolutions as a hypocritical exercise in demonstrative loyalty, adopted "to lay claim to the Protection of the House of Commons, and to claim a Compensation for his Damages." "I kept an obstinate Silence the whole Time, I said not one Word for, or against the Adjournment. . . . And I had no Disposition to foment an opposition to it, because, an Opposition made with any Warmth might have ended in the Demolition of the Earthly House of His Honours Tabernacle." [47] In other words, Hutchinson's popular standing had sunk so low that the argument of a judge-fighting lawyer might result in his lynching. So Adams thought, at any rate. His possible exaggeration is really immaterial. The indisputable point is that the Stamp Act's legacy to Boston was heightened awareness of the ease with which mobs could be roused to achieve political ends through selective terror. With that awareness came a willingness (which may or may not have been justified by the futility of any other means of protest) to summon up violence. The awareness and the willingness obviously represented a retreat from the rule of law, a retreat which could be checked only by a strong, trusted, and respected judiciary. But the tragic sarabande in which the judges and lawyers participated during the spring of 1766 robbed the bench of strength, trust, and respect. "[C]an we," asked Adams, "be sufficiently amazed at the Chickanery, the Finess, the Prevarication, and Insincerity, the simulation, nay the Lyes and Falsehoods of the Judges of the Superior Court. These are harsh Words, but true. The Times are terrible, and made so at present by Hutchinson C.J." [48]

CHAPTER 4

VIOLENCE OVER
CUSTOMS DUTIES

Definitive news of the Stamp Act's repeal arrived with Captain Shubael Coffin at 11 A.M. on May 16. The tension which had built up in the months since November 1 released itself in a series of festivities unequaled since the days of the Glorious Revolution. "[T]here was scarce a person to be found, even among the officers of the crown, who did not desire the repeal. It freed them, for a time at least, from present certain distress and wretchedness." May 19, the official celebration day, saw Boston lit by "very Grand Illuminations all over the Town. In the Common there was an Obelisk very beautifully Decorated and very grand fire works were displayed." John Adams, defeated that day for election as Braintree's representative in the House, made his way to Plymouth and the superior court, feeling himself "very unfortunate, in running the Gauntlet, through all the Rejoicings." Amid bonfires and booming cannon, nobody seemed to pay any attention to the Declaratory Act.[1]

Freed from the Stamp Act's shackles, the Boston Town Meeting voted on May 26 to instruct its members "for the total abolishing of slavery from among us; that you move for a law, to prohibit the importation and purchasing of slaves for the future." In other counties, slaves began to take the issue to the courts, there to "sue for their freedom," by actions of trespass—to the person—against their putative masters. Resistance to authority pervaded the spirit of the times. At

Harvard, across the Charles in Cambridge, where youthful opposition generally took the individualized form of forbidden pranks, tippling, or wenching, the students that spring, provoked by rancid butter, combined in "the earliest recorded College rebellion." The authorities met the challenge with a directness scarcely to be recognized two centuries later. Led by Governor Bernard himself, the college's governing boards brushed aside written remonstrances and offered the Butter Rebels only two alternatives: apologize or get out. The students apologized.[2]

Samuel Adams, who had taken his first major political office in September 1765 when he was elected to fill Oxenbridge Thacher's unexpired term in the House of Representatives, easily won re-election in May 1766, leading the field with 691 votes out of 746 cast. Adams went on three weeks later to achieve an even more significant victory: by a single vote, he was chosen Clerk of the House. Since the clerk not only voted, but maintained the journals and carried on the correspondence of the Assembly, Adams found himself able directly to influence the politics of the entire province. Indeed, during inter-session recesses, the clerk could continue to send official letters in the name of the House; there were thus times when Adams *de facto* and *de jure* stood for the entire lower legislative branch.[3]

Outside the legislature, Adams was taking special pains to build up his direct-action organization. The Loyal Nine formed the cadre, but others found important roles to play. In 1766, for example, Thomas Young, a first-generation Irish-American from Ulster County, New York, by way of Sharon, Connecticut, moved to Boston and promptly joined the Sons of Liberty. Because the thirty-four-year-old Young practiced "physic and chirurgery" he was called Doctor, despite his lack of formal education. But his major talent lay in newspaper writing, oratory, and other arts of political agitation. Another man soon to become "Famous among the Sons of Liberty," William Molineux, also began to achieve prominence in 1766. Hot, "rash," and prone to drive "matters to an imprudent pitch," Molineux tended to approach problems physically, rather than verbally. His reputation reflected the fears he kindled; as John Rowe said, "Many Things are attributed to him & tis believed he was first Leader of Dirty Matters." Even the liberal John Eliot could find him no more praise than "It's possible he may have been actuated by noble principles." Others tended to dismiss Molineux and Young, too, as "men of no Principles and Infamous Characters." While Molineux and Young were joining the leadership of the radical group, one of its intellectual mainstays was departing. The Reverend Jonathan Mayhew, whose sermon had (inadvertently perhaps) provoked the Hutchinson riot, died of a stroke on July 9, 1766, "much lamented by Great Numbers of people," and was buried two days later after a "very large" funeral in ninety-degree heat.[4]

Later in the month, the government side lost an important man, although his going was only temporary. Charles Paxton, born in Boston in 1708, had been a customs officer since the age of twenty-five. By the 1760's he had become surveyor and searcher of the Port of Boston, as well as marshal of the vice-admiralty courts of Massachusetts, Rhode Island, and New Hampshire. In the former capacity he occupied center stage in the battles over the writs of assistance. Apparently the experience permanently soured his opinion of his townsmen, for by 1766 he was telling John Adams: "This is the lazyest Town upon the Globe —poor, proud and lazy is the Character of this Town." With the repeal of the Stamp Act, Paxton, like others, realized that England would shortly try still again to establish a workable, profitable American customs system. Paxton may have thought to advance himself by an in-person appeal to the treasury board. It had also been suggested that he was "summoned home to advise" the treasury and "for the purpose of assisting in remodelling the American revenue system." This is quite likely, for John Adams once called him "the essence of customs, taxation, and revenue." Certainly he took the occasion to represent his own grievances and those of his friend Governor Bernard, who noted that Paxton's "perfect Knowledge of the Business of the Custom house will make him a fit person to be referred to in Regard to any Complaint that has been or shall be made against me." On July 27, carrying his proposals, his complaints, his ambitions, the governor's letter of introduction, and "the stamped papers that were designed for" Massachusetts, he sailed in H.M.S. *Fortune.*[5]

Whether or not the scope of the duties and the customs rates themselves needed revision, it was clear that only serious measures could ensure the collection of whatever duties were levied. Even writs of assistance, applied full force, could not produce anything but sharp, violent opposition. In Falmouth, Maine (now Portland), not too far from Scarborough, where Richard King's house had been ransacked the year before, customs officers armed with a writ of assistance tried, on August 7, to seize some undutied sugar and molasses in the house of Enoch Ilsley. A mob assembled within a few hours, roughed up the customs officers, kidnapped a deputy sheriff, and rescued, i.e., made off with, the goods. When the news reached Governor Bernard, he issued a reward-offering proclamation, which, he admitted to the Lords of Trade, "is now become a meer farce of Government; since no one dares to discover [i.e., reveal] or prosecute the Offenders, if they were so disposed; & indeed the Offenders are some times, as in this Case, the greatest part of the Town. Formerly a rescue was an accidental or occasional Affair; now, it is the natural & certain Consequences of a seizure, & the Effect of a predetermined Resolution that the Laws of Trade shall not be executed." [6]

Within six weeks Bernard found his prediction fulfilled violently in Boston, almost in his very presence. Acting on information from an anonymous custom house informer, Deputy Collector William Sheaffe and Comptroller Benjamin Hallowell (the same Hallowell whose house had been mobbed in August) went between 8 and 9 A.M. on September 24, 1766, to the North End home of Captain Daniel Malcom, a vessel master and trader, looking for "a Number of Casks of Brandy Wines and other Liquors." Malcom showed Sheaffe and Hallowell all his "Stores and Cellars" save one locked room, which he had rented to a Captain William Mackay. Sheaffe went out and brought Mackay to Malcom's house, only to learn that Mackay did not have the key. When Sheaffe and Hallowell ordered the door opened anyway, Malcom threatened to blow the brains out of anybody who touched the door, donning sword and brace of pistols to underline his determination. The customs officers then tried to persuade Malcom or threaten him (depending upon whose subsequent affidavit one credits) for the better part of the morning, until Malcom ordered them out of the house.[7]

Bernard was just then meeting with the council in the Town House at the head of King Street. Hallowell and Sheaffe hurried to him with their sad tale. Bernard immediately sent for Stephen Greenleaf, the sheriff of Suffolk County, and told him to obtain the aid of the North End justices of the peace, especially Justice John Ruddock, who doubled as captain of a militia company. If further force was needed, Bernard and the council ordered Greenleaf to "Raise his Posse Comitatus," that is, to call on the citizenry to assist the sheriff and the customs officers. Hallowell already held a writ of assistance in the usual form, issued March 22, 1765; to reinforce the legality of his activities, however, he and Sheaffe went to Foster Hutchinson (the lieutenant-governor's brother), who was a judge of the Suffolk Inferior Court, justice of the peace, and a judge of probate, and obtained from him an ordinary search warrant.[8]

Malcom, meanwhile, left his house about noon and walked south to King Street, where at that hour the merchants usually met, weather permitting, "for the genial institution of 'Change [i.e., exchange] . . . to talk shop, ships, and politics for a half-hour or so." There, according to Malcom's later account, Hallowell and Sheaffe "told me they wanted me to compound [i.e., compromise] and open my Door to them, and if there was anything there they would not do me harm." Whether or not the soft approach would have been successful if attempted earlier, plainly the customs officers had no chance of convincing Malcom at this late stage. As his answer to their proposition shows, he realized he had them at a legal and moral disadvantage. "I told them if they had a Right to break open my House they might, but if they persisted in breaking open my House I would take all Legal Methods to have myself righted," which presumably would include unleashing the legal thunderbolts of James Otis, Malcom's lawyer. He "told them I had not anything in their Power, and that they might do what they could but they should never come into my House [except] . . . by breaking open my House." And with that he left Hallowell muttering that the customs officers would need "a Regiment of Soldiers here to assist them in doing their Duty," returned to his house with family and "a few Gentlemen," secured his gate, doors, and windows, and prepared, should the officers break into the house, "to take notice and Witness the same and pursue them according to Law." [9]

Malcom and his friends did not have to wait long. At about 3 P.M., Hallowell, Sheaffe, Sheriff Greenleaf (Sheaffe's Harvard classmate), and two waiters (minor customs officers analogous to modern-day Internal Revenue Service agents) came to Malcom's house. After futilely testing his barred front gate and shouting for him, Greenleaf went around in back, only to find himself similarly shut out and unanswered. Returning to the street, Greenleaf saw a crowd gathering. Although one witness later said of the onlookers that he "never saw People that was going to a Funeral behave more Solemn and concerned than they did, not the least noise nor disturbance no more than if Mr. [George] Whit[e]field had been preaching," Greenleaf thought the crowd looked menacing. Further, a rumor was beginning to circulate that at the first attempt to open Malcom's door, the bell at the nearby Old North Church would be rung, summoning angry citizens into the streets. Hallowell and Sheaffe shared Greenleaf's fears, so the sheriff began canvassing the North End justices of the peace for help. Justice Stoddard pleaded illness; Justice John Tudor agreed to go with Greenleaf to Justice Ruddock; Justice Ruddock "Replied that he was a Very Heavy Man [which was true: when he died six years later he was said to weigh "between 5 and 600 weight"] and Unable to Walk far." [10]

Tudor and Greenleaf went thence to Malcom's, each by a different route. On the way, Tudor heard enough to convince him that any attempt at the house would provoke a riot. Massachusetts at this time possessed a Riot Act, based largely on the English Riot Act. It provided that, in the face of twelve men armed with weapons or clubs, or fifty men armed or not, any civil officer down to constable could call on the crowd, in the king's name, to disperse. This proclamation is what we today inaccurately refer to as "reading the Riot Act." Once an officer could succeed in reading the proclamation, the crowd was required to disperse within an hour. Anyone failing to do so would be liable to forfeiture of all his land and goods to the king, plus a flogging of thirty-nine lashes, plus a year's imprisonment (with thirty-nine stripes every three months). Moreover, once the hour expired, the proclaiming officer was authorized to order citizens to aid in seizing the rioters; should any rioter be injured or killed as a result, neither the officer nor the assisting citizens could suffer civil or criminal liability. The Riot Act gave Tudor and Greenleaf a potent weapon. Why did they not use it? The answer, I think, lies in the common-law definition of riot: "Wherever more than three persons use force or violence in the execution of any design whatever, wherein the law does not allow the use of such force, all who are concerned therein are rioters." Threatening to use force is not the same as using it; no matter how strongly the officers sensed latent violence, in fact the crowd looked peaceful, and plenty of witnesses like "Paul Rivere" were ready to testify that "the people that were gathered there had not any intent to hinder the officers in the discharge of their duty but would have protected them all that lay in their power." So long as the crowd stayed merely sullen, there was no riot, and no ground for invoking the Riot Act. But of course once the sullenness broke into violence, the invocation would do no good.[11]

Greenleaf had one thin hope. As sheriff, he was entitled to call on the bystanders to form a posse to assist him in enforcing the law. Technically, once the sheriff asked the onlookers to join him, they were obliged to do so or face criminal penalties. But as Greenleaf well knew, the street before Malcom's house was no place for technicalities. Any posse would have to be formed by consent, not compulsion. So Greenleaf flatly asked if the crowd would help him. For answer, he received a surprising assent, provided only that the custom house officers would "make Oath who their Informer was." In other words, the aid was refused.[12]

By now, a nearby school had let out, and a crowd of schoolboys augmented the throng physically and vocally. Still baffled, Greenleaf began asking individuals to help him. The answer continued to be No, at least until after Malcom should be secured, for "it was a hundred to one but somebody wou'd be kill'd on the Attempt." Greenleaf gamely replied that "he did not regard that for he cou'd dye but once and it was equal to him which way he dy'd and if he was sure they wou'd fire off ten Pistols right at his Breast, if he was in the execution of his Office he'd do his Duty, and the Person that kill'd him wou'd be hanged." But still he did not move against the house, other than to confer with Tudor and the customs people. In Tudor's words: "Upon the Whole we thought it would be in Vain as Matters Stood to Attempt any thing farther at Present as the Evening was Coming on [and nightfall, after which the writ of assistance would be useless] to all which we All Agreed and I went home." And so did everyone, even the prospective rioters, who, before their departure, received from Malcom "several Buckets of Wine . . . and when they had drank the Wine they hallowed out 'Good Night to You Gentlemen we thank you' —and accordingly they all dispersed." [13]

The schoolboys, meanwhile, "made a talk about the Informer and said it was one Richardson and that they knew where he lived and that they'd goe and give him three Cheers for the great Prize he'd got." They apparently wanted to give him something stronger, for Justice Ruddock later reported hearing "that there was a Number of people at Richardsons the Informers House and threatened him if they Could have got him." Richardson, a man in his mid-forties, originally came from Woburn, a little town about ten miles northwest of Boston. In 1752 he had figured in a messy scandal involving charges that the Reverend Edward Jackson of Woburn had fathered a bastard born to his housekeeper, the widow Keziah Henshaw, Richardson's wife's sister, and later, apparently, his wife. The overtones of that affair, including an insinuation that the child was Richardson's, lasted for almost two decades, culminating in a thunderous slander action between Roland Cotton (Sam Adams's predecessor as Clerk of the House of Representatives) and William Molineux.[14]

Meanwhile, Richardson, on the recommendation of Attorney-General Trowbridge, found employment with Paxton "as a proper person for a Deputation in his Majestys Customs." Richardson received a tidesman's place in the customs, and in his own words, "Gave Information of Siverl breeches of the Acts of Trade and Seizeirs Ware made and the Vessels and Goods Condemned." For this service Richardson, naturally enough, "was thereupon cried out against as an Informer and frequently abused by the people." Still, the customs officers appreciated his talents, and even competed among themselves to obtain them. In December 1760, when Benjamin Barrons, having been suspended as Boston collector, was battling desperately to regain his office, he sought to enlist Richardson in his fight against Paxton (whose accusations of corruption had unseated Barrons), Bernard, and Judge Chambers Russell. "I have a rod in piss for them," Barrons told Richardson, promising him double the fees Paxton was paying if Richardson would join him, and if not, to "ruine [him] Eternally." [15]

After some hesitation, Richardson refused. One cannot know for sure if Richardson's subsequent difficulties stemmed from his having spurned Barrons. Without question, in backing Paxton over Barrons he was not following a winner. The ex-collector, although a former London merchant, had taken pains "to ingratiate himself with the local commercial aristocracy," chiefly by undermining the very revenue he was supposed to collect. In fact, when Richardson chided him for being "frequently in Company with some Merchants that are Concerned in the Illicit trade," Barrons insouciantly replied, "I know they are as well as you," adding with a laugh, "I tell them they must take care." Paxton, on the other hand, a native Bostonian, sought to enforce the customs duties strictly, and was accordingly detested. Naturally, the dislike extended to anyone in Paxton's circle. By the mid-1760's, Richardson had secured a reputation for vileness unmatched in Boston. "If there was even a color of justice in the public opinion," wrote John Adams many years later, "he was the most abandoned wretch in America. Adultery, incest, perjury were reputed to be his ordinary crimes. His life would exhibit an atrocious volume." Samuel Adams, writing soon after the Malcom affair, as usual exceeded his cousin in precise vituperation: Richardson, "a Person of the most infamous Character," a "detestable Person," "has for a long time subsisted by the Business of an Informer & is said to be such an one as was never encouraged under any Administration but such as those [of] Nero or Caligula." [16]

Evil though Richardson might be, on the day of the Malcom fracas he managed to evade the cheering schoolboys and the crowd of "about two hundred people" which the radically inclined John Rowe had estimated demonstrated before Malcom's house. As the evening continued, Bernard and the council apparently prolonged their meeting, trying to fathom what had happened; but, as Rowe noted, "they could make nothing of it." Sheaffe and Hallowell repaired to the Custom House, where they drafted a long, detailed report on the day's frustrations. The next morning, Bernard held another council. Hallowell and Sheaffe appeared, presented their document, and, having been sworn, answered additional questions. Ruddock, Tudor, and four other witnesses followed with statements under oath. Despite the "many Evidences," that is, witnesses, the governor and council, Rowe reported, still "could make nothing of it." [17]

Notwithstanding its bafflement, Bernard's administration plainly intended to extract maximum propaganda value from the affair by sending the affidavits to England. At the Boston Town Meeting of October 8, Samuel Adams took immediate steps to neutralize these efforts. First, he caused the appointment of a nine-man committee (including himself, Otis, Hancock, and Rowe) to ask the governor for copies of the depositions, "that so the Town having Knowledge of their Accusers, and of the nature and design of the Testimonys taken, may have it in their power to rectify mistakes, and counter-work the designs of any who would represent them in a disadvantageous Light to his Majestys Ministers." Then he arranged to make the "Light" a little less disadvantageous by putting the Town on record as favoring relief for the "sufferers" of the August riots. After hearing the victims described as "those Gentlemen who have suffered in a manner that no man ought, especially in a state of civil society," the Town voted "that on application of such Sufferers to the General Assembly in a Parliamentary way, the Representatives of this Town be directed, and they are accordingly directed in their best discretion to use their influence, that such losses be made up as far as may be, in a manner the most loyal and respectful with regard to his Majesty, the most constitutional and safe with regard to our invaluable rights & privileges and the most humane and benevolent with regard to the Sufferers." [18]

Throughout the pre-Revolutionary period, Adams displayed unmatched mastery of the weasel word, the technique of the "intentionally ambiguous statement," which "by equivocal qualification, sucks all the real meaning out of the word to which the hearer or reader has attached significance." The Compensation Resolution, however, stands as his virtuoso performance. Not a phrase in it stands up to be counted; the sum of the phrases weighs less than any of them. You cannot tell from reading it exactly what the Town proposed to do, except that the deed was to be financed not by Boston alone, but by the entire province, because before anything else happened, the "application" would have to be made to the General Assembly.[19]

Having thus soothed the Town's conscience at minimum out-of-pocket cost, Adams took his *ad hoc* committee to the Town House to demand the depositions from Bernard. Typically, Bernard tried to avoid the problem by referring the committee to the council, which in turn passed the question squarely back to the governor, noting that the council had never ordered the depositions kept secret. After Bernard finally agreed to allow the Town to take copies, Adams organized a second committee (including himself, Otis, Hancock, Rowe, and merchant Edward Payne) to interview additional witnesses and take further affidavits. Immediately, the committee began work, and by the next session of the town meeting, two weeks later, the radicals had assembled their version of the affair in nineteen depositions. These they transmitted to the province's London agent, Dennys DeBerdt, with a lengthy apologia for the disturbances since the summer of 1765, signed by Otis but written by Adams.[20]

Bernard had already sent the earlier depositions to Lord Shelburne, secretary of state, possibly by superior court judge Chambers Russell. Russell, Massachusetts' judge of vice-admiralty, left for England October 16 on an unspecified mission. He showed a strong conservative attachment, as befitted a man with two high judicial offices (indeed within a few years John Adams came to regard him as one of "the original Conspirators against the Public Liberty"), and Bernard might logically have selected him as messenger. The depositions reached Shelburne, although Russell died shortly after reaching England. Robert Auchmuty then received the vice-admiralty commission, and Trowbridge went on the superior court. Jeremiah Gridley (the defender of the writs of assistance) replaced Trowbridge as attorney-general. Jonathan Sewall, a close friend of John Adams and a one-time pupil of Russell, had been named vice-admiralty advocate-general to replace Auchmuty; when Gridley died a few months after becoming attorney-general, Sewall was elevated to that place as well.[21]

As fall 1766 turned into winter, still another significant change took place in the structure of customs enforcement. Joseph Harrison, the former Collector of New Haven, an intimate of the Marquis of Rockingham, received his appointment as Collector of Boston on July 11, 1766, less than two weeks before Rockingham lost the ministry. He "was Sworn in the 28th October and entered on the Execution of his Office the 1st of Novemr." The customs service was in many ways a big business, especially for New England, chronically short of hard money and ready cash. In early November, for example, John Adams, stopping at an inn while traveling up to Salem for a court sitting, "saw 5 Boxes of Dollars containing as we were told about 18,000 of them, going in an Horse Cart from Salem Custom House to Boston, in Order to be shipp'd for England. A Guard of Armed Men, with swords, Hangers, Pistols and Musquets, attended it." [22]

Despite the large sums which were going out of the economy, the demise of the Stamp Act more than outweighed the loss, psychologically, if not fiscally. "The Repeal of it was great Joy," one of John Adams's Braintree neighbors told him two days after the dollars incident. The man told Adams he would "be willing to do any Thing in Reason out of Duty to the K[ing]." Repeal, Adams noted pithily, "hushed into silence almost every popular Clamour, and composed every Wave of Popular Disorder into a smooth and peaceful Calm." With this lack of discontent, Samuel Adams faced, for neither the first nor the last time, the problem of percolating public dissatisfaction with the established order. Adams's task, however, was complicated by the need somehow to arrange recompense for the August riot victims along the lines suggested by the Boston Town Meeting's resolution, that is, through recompense by the entire province, not just by Boston.[23]

The General Court convened October 29, and two days later Adams sustained a decisive defeat: restitution was voted down, 44–36. On November 4, despite the recommendations of a committee which included such radicals as Otis, Hancock, Speaker Thomas Cushing, and the firebrand of Western Massachusetts, Joseph Hawley, the House again voted down compensation, 51–43. A majority clearly wished to pin the cost of the riot on Boston, but supporters of the metropolis tried to raise the money elsewhere. "Some proposed a lottery. Others mentioned other schemes for raising money [principally a proportional assessment on the other towns]; but none were approved of." Substantial sums were involved: Hutchinson sought over £3000, Hallowell over £500, including recompense for a "Clock that Chimes that Cost 20 Guineas in London less than two years since, and since ye riot has been in the hands of two of ye best Clockmakers here and Cost considerable, but was quite useless, sometimes Striking 3, 4 & 5 hundred without Stoping." [24]

On November 4, compensation was once again defeated, 54–35. The issue had obviously become broader than the mere justice of restoring riot-gutted property. From the first, Bernard had clearly conveyed to everyone, especially the legislators, the deep concern with which the ministry, Parliament, and even the king regarded the question of recompense. Continued failure to make proper fiscal amends, it was now certain, would embarrass Massachusetts and its English friends and might well provoke the same sort of confrontation crisis which the Stamp Act repeal had only just ended.[25]

At this point, Hawley came forward with a solution. The most successful and prominent lawyer west of Worcester, "violent in his resentments" and well-articulated radical principles, he had little reason or desire to see the riot victims made whole. Indeed, he hated Hutchinson personally, his rancor provoked by a courtroom incident of a few weeks before, an incident which in fact inspired the scheme that Hawley now unfolded. The case had arisen out of a Berkshire County version of the Boston riots, centering about the rescue of a debtor from the custody of a deputy sheriff. Ten of the men had been arrested, indicted at the Berkshire County Court of General Sessions, and in early September, 1766, tried and convicted. We do not know if Hawley represented them in that court. But when one man, Seth Warren, appealed his three-pound fine to the superior court at Springfield later in the month, Hawley not only appeared for him but took direct steps to force Attorney-General Trowbridge to drop the prosecution. This failing, Hawley tried to dismiss the indictment by arguing a technical point of law in open court. But Chief Justice Hutchinson, relying on authority and principle, overruled the exception and ordered the trial to proceed (for in those days, an appeal from the Sessions entailed a trial *de novo*). After a strong summation by Hutchinson, the superior court jury promptly found Warren guilty; the court reimposed the three-pound fine.[26]

Now, six weeks later, Hawley with perfect timing arranged to relieve his client, to vilify Hutchinson publicly and safely, and simultaneously to solve the political crisis. The chief sufferer, he told the representatives (obviously meaning Hutchinson), was "a person of unconstitutional principles, as one day or other he will make appear." As for the Parliamentary suggestion that recompense was due, "the Parliament of Great Britain has no right to legislate for us." Besides, "the rioters who had been in error had a claim to favour as well as the sufferers." Therefore, Hawley proposed, let recompense be granted; but let the statute grant also amnesty and pardon to all persons who had been guilty of any crimes or offenses against law occasioned by the late troubles.[27]

Put into statutory form, Hawley's plan was, after a brief delay to obtain popular approval and a futile effort to eliminate the amnesty provision, voted into law. Because pardon was a clear crown prerogative, Bernard frankly doubted that he was authorized to sign it. But he convinced himself somewhat justifiably that the losses, particularly Hutchinson's, would never otherwise be repaid; "if the act should not be approved in England, all the effect would be the suspending, for three or four months, of prosecutions which, experience had shewn, could not be carried on [a typical overstatement—the ten Berkshire rioters had, after all, been convicted, one of them twice] . . . But, as to the compensation the act would have an immediate effect, and could not be recalled." This was just what happened. "The money was paid out of the Treasury to the sufferers. When the Act was laid before the King it was disapproved; but it had all the effect designed, and nothing more was said about it." Nothing more about the propriety of payment, perhaps. But Samuel Adams kept alive the fact of the compensation, and even sought propaganda advantage from the very step he had once opposed. Three years later, castigating Hutchinson in the Boston *Gazette*, he urged the family to remember "the *unexampled* act of generosity . . . this act of *pure generosity*." [28]

CHAPTER 5

THE CUSTOMS COMMISSIONERS

Although the repeal of the Stamp Act had reduced the inflammation which produced the outrages of 1765, the underlying ailments remained uncured. Development of an effective revenue system still formed the nucleus of Britain's American policy. As the Malcom incident showed, however, the Boston population opposed not merely the concept of effective customs regulation, but, on a more personal level, the characters of the officers charged with customs enforcement. As a truism, "Nobody loves a revenue collector" has few equals; in Boston, the resentment went deeper. Recalling Bernard's connivance with Cockle, Hallowell's domineering manner, and Richardson's foul reputation, the Bostonians seem to have sensed a basic lack of integrity in the customs officers, and hence in the system they sought to enforce. The refusal to help Sheriff Greenleaf (who was after all not a customs official), and perhaps even Greenleaf's easy willingness to forbear, cannot all be laid to Sam Adams. True, he and the Sons poured the salt; but someone else had made the wounds.

The Malcom fiasco emphasized still another pressure operating against orderly acceptance of an effective customs service. Boston, like Massachusetts, America, and even England, lacked a civilian peace-keeping organization. The amateur constables were good for little else but summoning jurors; the sheriff and his deputies merely served writs and attended various ceremonies. Police, as we know them today, or as Britain and America were to know them in the next century, simply did not exist. Theoretically, the civilian authorities could in a serious emergency call upon military assistance. But the only indigenous soldiers, if one can call them that, were the train-bands, militia who met annually and elected their own officers. Springing from the population, they could not be counted on, politically or militarily, to cope with the kind of mob whose leash the Sons of Liberty held.[1]

This left only regular soldiers as potential keepers of the peace. The main body of British troops was stationed at New York, from whence General Gage commanded the entire North American army. Detachments occasionally passed through Boston; the province had erected barracks at Castle William for troop use when needed. But no permanent force had ever been ordered to Boston. Although Gage, as we have seen, was willing to send them, Bernard realized the political dangers inherent in garrisoning Boston. "I have never," he told Barrington, "had any intimation from General Gage that he intended to send Troops into New England. He knows my opinion, which is that they should not be quarter'd in the old Colonies which have been long settled and inhabited, unless call'd for by the Civil Magistrate or Government of the Province, as necessary to preserve the publick peace." [2]

At the very time that Bernard wrote, he was in the middle of handling a ticklish problem caused by the chance landing in Boston of a sizable troop contingent. On November 26, 1766, "A Transport Ship arr'd bound from Halifax to Quebec but could not get up the River. She has seventy people belonging to the Royal Train of Artillery on board, forty-three women & nineteen children." Besides illustrating the extent to which domesticity encumbered the peace-time British army, even on the move and in foreign service, the incident caused Bernard a near-showdown with the Adams-Otis–led House. The General Court having recessed just before the artillerists arrived, to permit popularization of the Indemnity Act, Bernard and the council had put the soldiers and families in the provincial barracks at Castle William and supplied them with provisions, including those required by the recently passed Quartering Act. When the House reconvened a week later, an inquiry commenced into the propriety of Bernard's action. The details do not particularly concern our present purpose, although Bernard, to give him his due, handled the issue neatly, meeting Otis's arrogant legalisms with an explanation unanswerable in its common sense. The incident's real significance lies in its disclosure of the popular sensitivity to the mere suggestion of a quasi-permanent military presence.[3]

The quartering problem, potentially serious though it was, comprised only one facet of the over-all North American question confronting the British government. The others were, in the words of the young Earl of Shelburne, Secretary of State for the Southern Department: "A proper system for the management of the Indians, . . . a reduction of the contingent expenses of the establishment in North America, and the raising an American fund to defray American expenses in part or in the whole." Shelburne, who regarded the fiscal question as "of the greatest consequence," proposed to attack it by revision of the royal land grant system. Others suggested a more direct approach. The idea (which, it will be remembered, affected even Pitt) that the Americans somehow "owed" England a monetary debt, persisted through the years. In 1775, Dr. Samuel Johnson accurately expressed the opinion of many Englishmen, certainly of many members of Parliament, when he wrote: "Those who thus flourish under the protection of our Government should contribute something toward its expense. . . . I should gladly see America return half of what England has expended in her defence." A minority saw the failings of this approach: "If we by taxes increase their expence of living in their own country," ran an anonymous article in the *Annual Register*, "how shall they save money to purchase from us those manufactures, and those utensils [which the colonies had previously imported from Britain]?" [4]

The majority of the House of Commons, however, "wished to raise a colonial revenue, punish the colonies for their ill-behavior after the repeal of the Stamp Act, and exercise the rights to which Parliament laid claim in the Declaratory Act." To this receptive audience now addressed himself Charles Townshend, Chancellor of the Exchequer. Townshend has been aptly described as having "boundless wit and ready eloquence, set off by perfect melody of intonation, but marred by an unexampled lack of judgment and discretion." These characteristics he soon proceeded to demonstrate. Ignoring the exceptional imperial risks which any American revenue scheme entailed, Townshend blandly proposed a comprehensive scheme of legislation "for asserting the Superiority of the Crown, and endeavouring to lay a foundation for such taxation as might in time ease this Country of a considerable burden." As finally drafted, the several Townshend Acts provided: (1) an American import tax on paper, painter's lead, glass, and tea; (2) establishment of an American Board of Commissioners of the Customs to supervise a tightened customs policy; and (3) revision of the system of vice-admiralty courts. While the statutes were being enacted, Townshend died suddenly, but not before casually admitting to the House that the "considerable burden" which the new system would take off the back of the English taxpayer totaled only £40,000 annually. Truly, Townshend's was "a policy imperfectly conceived and foolishly applied"—"men in high positions can be, and often are, fools." [5]

From the first, it seems to have been intended that the five-man American Board sit at Boston. True, Boston was nowhere near the north-south center of the American coastline; but London recognized that much of the colonial irritation commenced or was encouraged in the northern metropolis. "If the laws of trade are enforced in the Massachusetts Government the other Provinces will readily submit—Boston having always taken the lead in trade as well as in politicks." The object of Townshend's plan (if it can fairly be called a plan or said to have an object) was "tightening up the enforcement methods in order to collect the revenue." By virtually inviting a direct clash between the Massachusetts revenue-evaders and the Boston-based customs establishment, Townshend's careless scheme ensured an enforcement crisis.[6]

Even as Townshend was smooth-talking his plans past the administration, events in Massachusetts again began to show that "The Government is as much in the hands of the people as it was in the time of the Stamp Act." Hutchinson, although defeated for election to the council, attempted (with Bernard's support and encouragement) to attend council sessions *ex officio*. Led by Hawley, still smarting from the legal setback at Springfield, the House formally condemned Hutchinson's appearance at the council board as "a new and additional instance of ambition and a lust of power." After Bernard and the House had taken turns yapping inconclusively at one another, Hutchinson voluntarily agreed not to sit with the council. Even this did not satisfy the radicals, and they sponsored a resolution condemning Hutchinson's mere attempt to attend the council deliberations. Within weeks of flaying Hutchinson for his multiple officeholding, the legislature, as he noted sardonically, "added another, though temporary, yet very important post, by electing him the first of three commissioners empowered to adjust and settle" the long-standing New York–Massachusetts boundary dispute.[7]

Hawley, continuing to nurse his personal resentment of Hutchinson, opened a bitter newspaper attack on the chief justice and the entire court. "What shall we do with Hawley?" Hutchinson rhetorically asked puisne judge John Cushing. "I can freely forgive him, but how shall we save the honour of the court?" The answer came in the fall, when the judges disbarred Hawley for his journalistic insolence. Drafting of the order had been assigned to the newest judge, Trowbridge. Immensely learned, particularly in real estate law, criminal procedure (he had been attorney-general for eighteen years), and evidence, Trowbridge added technical strength to a bench otherwise devoid of "bred" lawyers. He also brought a cantankerous and quibbling (one might almost say legalistic) disposition, well known to his contemporaries at the bar. "After a long Wrangle, as usual when Trowbridge is in a Case, . . ." was how John Adams began his report of one court-room incident. With Trowbridge's appointment the superior court resumed its full complement of five judges; but at the May 1767 Barnstable term, where Trowbridge sat for the first time, Judge Lynde opened the court, "the chief Justice not being there, having a paralytic stroke." [8]

The indisposition was only temporary, and by August Hutchinson had returned. His first official act was to charge the Boston Grand Jury on a facet of the common-law rule of self-defense: "[I]f a Man is attacked, upon any Pretence whatever, in his own House, whether it be to treat him contemptuously for the Diversion and Sport of those who assault him, or for whatever other Cause, if the Man who is thus beset kills any one or all of those who thus abuse him, he is only guilty of Manslaughter." Grand jury charges often served as opportunities for the judges to educate the jurors and onlookers and to expand political doctrine. It is not quite clear why Hutchinson chose this particular time to discuss this particular point. Massachusetts had been quiet; nothing indicated any immediate threat of rioting, certainly nothing like the uproars in 1765. Perhaps Hutchinson merely thought the month an appropriate one in which to chastise the Sons of Liberty, who annually celebrated August 14 (the day Oliver was mobbed) with pageantry and alcohol.[9]

News of the Parliamentary activity was beginning to arrive. Hutchinson himself felt that "America was in such a state, that it seems to have been good policy to abstain wholly from further taxes of any kind." But, he realized, once the ministry and Parliament determined to impose the new duties, "it was of the greatest importance to provide, at all events, for effectually enforcing the payment of such taxes." A second riot-caused repeal would be a disaster, one that might very likely lead to independence. As Bernard accurately put it: "If they [i.e., Parliament] should give Way, they may as well at once Repeal all the former Acts of Trade which impose Duties." So Hutchinson, using the dignity of his office through the forum of the grand jury, may have been trying to pre-cool the Boston temper.[10]

Others, though perhaps not so concerned for the welfare of the Americans, shared Hutchinson's belief that vigorous customs enforcement, in other words the elimination of smuggling, must be the linchpin of the American revenue plan. As early as April 1767, Gage had recommended to London that "small detachments of troops [be] posted along the Coast to assist the Custom house Officers in the execution of their Duty." No troops were yet stationed in Boston, the nearest garrisons still being Halifax and New York.[11]

Meanwhile, in England, Parliament passed the act establishing the

American Board of Customs Commissioners. Townshend, Paxton's "dear . . . patron," had secured for him one of the five commissionerships, presumably out of friendship, although years later the celebrated Major Robert Rogers was to suggest to John Adams that "Paxton made his will in favor of Lord Townshend [Charles Townshend's elder brother] and by that manoeuvre got himself made a commissioner." It was said that Lord Townshend, when in America as one of Wolfe's brigadiers at Quebec (he succeeded to the command upon Wolfe's death), "borrowed Money of Paxton . . . to the amount of £500 at least that is not paid yet." The decision to locate the board at Boston rather than at a port nearer the coastal mid-point was ascribed to "Mr. Paxton's Interest with Charles Townshend." But John Temple, another commissioner, also had Boston connections; he had been born there in 1732 and, after living in England, had returned as surveyor general in 1761; in 1767 he had solidified his political and social ties by marrying Elizabeth "Betsey" Bowdoin, daughter of the wealthy radical councilor, James Bowdoin. Paxton, Temple, and their three fellow commissioners were commissioned September 8 and "Gazetted" the same day. The commissioners who were in England at the time, Paxton, Henry Hulton (the First Commissioner, one-time comptroller of the customs in Antigua, formerly in charge of the "Plantations" section in the London commissioners' office) and William Burch (a Norfolk gentleman), promptly embarked for Boston with Samuel Venner, the board's secretary; John Porter, comptroller-general; John Williams, inspector-general; and "a Number of Clerks," including Temple's brother Robert.[12]

They landed at Boston, "a most unwelcome cargo," on a "wet Rainy" November 5, in the midst of the Pope's Day festivities. The celebrants included an effigy of the Devil, conveniently labeled "Charles," which followed Paxton as he walked uptown from the wharf, and "twenty Devils, Popes and Pretenders" bearing labels "Liberty, Property and no Commissioners." The commissioners joined in the laughter, and no further incident occurred. This did not indicate acceptance of the Townshend Acts—indeed a town meeting on October 28 had explicitly resolved to oppose the ministerial policy by nonimportation of English goods and encouragement of American manufactures. Despite their resentment, the Bostonians seemed willing to let the commissioners set up shop peacefully; even Otis publicly disclaimed objection to them as such. On November 17, the three arrivals from England, joined by Temple and John Robinson (who had previously served in the Rhode Island customs), formally "opened" their commission and the next day held their first "board," or meeting, at Deblois' Concert Hall on Hanover Street. The brick Custom House itself stood on the north side of

King Street, near the present site of 50 State Street. Grizzel Apthorp owned it, and charged the commissioners one hundred guineas a year rent.[13]

Two days after the commissioners began work, the new duties took effect. Their bite could be substantial; Captain Blake, arriving with a dutiable cargo just before the deadline, saved his consignees "about three hundred pounds Lawful money." In a single year, duties at Boston and Salem-Marblehead alone took 32,000 ounces of silver out of the hard-money–hungry Massachusetts economy. The commissioners, despite the tensions produced by Temple's immediately "set[ting] himself up in opposition to all the rest . . . ," performed an efficient service. It was a service, however, which tended to produce high personal returns for the officers involved without commensurate effort. The commissioners regularly broke up their meetings at 2 P.M. Yet Hulton made enough to be able to purchase Jeremy Gridley's former house, and eighteen acres of land, in "Brooklyn" (Brookline) which, with subsequent improvements, came to be worth nearly £1300 sterling. He also owned a coach, a "sulkey," a post chaise, and a seat in King's Chapel. Underlings in the customs service did well, too. John Bernard, the governor's son, who occupied the clerk-like position of Naval Officer at Boston (which of course had no connection with the Royal Navy), estimated its worth at £1000 sterling per annum. The patronage possibilities inherent in the customs service are obvious. There was, moreover, a tendency throughout the government to regard a public office, once achieved, as a private interest, and to assume that a man who occupied a position in the colonial service was entitled almost to demand continued employment. Thus when the revisions of 1767 abolished the old district surveyor-generalships, Charles Steuart, of the Eastern-Middle District, was created cashier and paymaster of the American customs. (It is worth noting that bureaucratic inertia and poor communications combined to interpose three months between the abolition of Steuart's old job and his receipt of the news.) [14]

A crowd of officers successfully pressing a more effective revenue service. Well might Josiah Quincy in the Boston *Gazette* compare them to "locusts"; well might Samuel Adams write to provincial agent DeBerdt of his fear that a "host of pensioners, by the arts they may use, may in time become as dangerous to the liberties of the people as an army of soldiers." [15]

Another type of pest had appeared in Boston to plague Adams, this one less a locust than a gadfly. His name was John Mein (pronounced "Mean"). After arriving in Boston from Scotland some years earlier, he had opened the "London Book Shop" and a lending library; one of his patrons was John Adams. Quickly becoming popular, the shop began to gross £80 weekly. Mein was elected a Boston constable, a post he could never have attained without Sam Adams's approval. By late 1767 he felt himself able to undertake publication of a twice-weekly newspaper, the Boston *Chronicle*. Mein sought controversy the way John Hancock sought adulation or Bernard financial security. Because he combined physical and moral courage with Tory leanings, his penchant for combat found a ready outlet in Boston. Well-conceived, well-edited, and above all, well-written, the *Chronicle* soon achieved journalistic pre-eminence. From the start, it became a radical target. The *Chronicle*'s first issue contained a sneering attack on the Earl of Chatham and encomiums on the Marquis of Rockingham. Nothing could be better calculated to rouse the Sons of Liberty: Pitt was their hero, Rockingham anathema. The Adamses, Otis, town clerk William Cooper, and other radicals knew their way around pen, typestick, and composing stone. Indeed, every Saturday, they went down to the Queen Street print shop of Benjamin Edes and John Gill, there to "set the Press" for the Boston *Gazette*, the voice of Massachusetts radicalism. Less than a month after Mein's piece appeared, the *Gazette* printed a bitter open letter signed "Americus," but bearing Otis's stamp, which capped a string of abuse by urging that "Dishonor stain with the blackest Infamy the Jacobite Party." In the light of then-recent history, "Jacobite" rated high on the scale of opprobria. It implied that Mein was not only a contemptible Scot, but a traitor, and perhaps even a Roman Catholic.[16]

Mein collared Edes at the *Gazette* office the day the "Americus" letter ran and tried vainly to learn the author's name. When he returned the next day, he found Edes still adamant, and challenged him on the spot. "I told him I was not to be at every fellow's beck," Edes reported later, "and did not regard him." Mein left, carrying his considerable choler with him. Later that evening, January 19, 1768, Mein came across Gill, who was considerably his inferior physically, and caned him severely, a piece of vengeance which was to cost him a criminal fine and substantial civil damages. But the penalties did not quiet Mein's ire nor his journalism; the *Chronicle* continued to nick the "well-disposed" for almost two years.[17]

CHAPTER 6

THE *LIBERTY* RIOT

With the start of 1768, the ministry created a new position, Secretary of State for the Colonies. To fill it, the administration called on forty-nine-year-old Wills Hill, the Earl of Hillsborough. An Irish peer with two years' experience at the Board of Trade, he must certainly share with Grenville and Townshend the credit (if it can be so termed) of having sponsored the most thoughtless and unimaginative aspects of British colonial policy during the 1760's. Only the impossibility of one man's having lost America saved Hillsborough from that distinction.[1]

"His character is conceit, wrongheadedness, obstinacy, and passion," said Benjamin Franklin, who knew him in England at this time, and whose famous transcription of an interview in 1770 fully supports this estimate. Horace Walpole called him "a pompous composition of ignorance and want of judgment," which latter quality even the king came finally to appreciate. Hillsborough was the kind of man who could, while on holiday in the south of France, arrange for the issuance of admiralty orders to "The Commodore in the Mediterranean, to send a Frigate to Marseilles, to carry Lord Hillsborough & Family to Naples, stopping at Genoa & Leghorn if found necessary." And yet there were those who welcomed his advent to power. "Things are coming apace to a crisis," Barrington wrote Bernard. "My friend Lord Hillsborough will have his hands full, but for the sake of the publick I am glad America is in his hands. He has prudence firmness & temper." "[K]nowing your Lordship's Connexion with that noble Lord, I have

Reason to congratulate myself," was Bernard's reaction to the news.[2]

The first test of Hillsborough's "prudence firmness & temper" began brewing in Boston even before news of his appointment arrived. Anxious to stimulate concerted resistance to the Townshend program, Samuel Adams conceived the idea of inviting the legislatures in other colonies to join Massachusetts in petitioning the king himself for repeal of the acts. Although willing to address the king directly, the House conservatives "prevented for that Time the sending circular Letters to the other Assemblies inviting them to join them, by a Majority of 2 to 1." Adams, patient as always, permitted his opponents to believe that no more legislative business remained. When the conservatives, many of whom came from out-country districts, had departed, Adams managed to assemble a majority which not only forced reconsideration, but ultimately approved what became famous as the Massachusetts Circular Letter of 1768.[3]

The letter safely dispatched, the radicals turned their attention and venom directly on Bernard. Joseph Warren ran a piece in the Boston *Gazette* which, while carefully avoiding mention of the governor by name or title, referred to him unmistakably. "Enmity," "Cruelty," "obstinate Perserverance in the Path of Malice," "manifold Abuses," "diabolical Thirst for Mischief," and "guileful treacherous Man-hater"—all of these and more Warren laid to Bernard's charge. His dignity and the king's massively affronted, Bernard tried futilely to persuade the legislature to condemn the piece; the House instead resolved "to take no further Notice of it." At the March sitting of the superior court, Hutchinson in his charge to the grand jury emphasized the then-viable rule that libel of a public official was an indictable offense. His words apparently found a responsive audience. The jurors called for Attorney-General Sewall and asked him to prepare an indictment against Edes and Gill for the next day. Meanwhile, according to Bernard, "the Faction who conducts that Paper was indefatigable in tampering with the Jury"; the next day the jurors "ignored" the bill, and thus aborted the indictment.[4]

From words, the Sons of Liberty turned during March to action. *Item:* One evening, about one hundred "lads . . . paraded the Town with a Drum & Horns, passed by the Council Chamber," while Bernard was there with the council, went on to Paxton's and "huzzaed." *Item:* About sixty "lusty fellows" went to Commissioner Burch's home and "with Clubs assembled before his Door [a] great Part of the Evening, and he was obliged to send away his Wife & Children by a back Door." As Bernard remarked later, "if it was only a Joke it was a very cruel one." *Item:* A cargo of Madeira wine was landed at night and, duty unpaid, carted through Boston "under a guard of 30 or 40 stout fellows, armed with bludgeons," the deed "as publickly known as if it had been at Noon Day." "The Officers either do not or dare not know where the Goods are carried." *Item:* As Inspector William Woolton was returning to his lodgings one evening, "4 Men passing him, one with a Stick or Bludgeon in his hand accosted him saying, 'Damn your Blood we will be at you to Morrow Night.' " *Item:* The Harvard undergraduates, irked at a tightening of the college rules regarding excused absences, rioted and tossed brickbats through a tutor's window—the seniors compounded the offense by asking for transfers "to the college in Connecticut." [5]

Bernard was justifiably frightened. The commissioners looked to him for protection, and he knew himself to be helpless. They urged him to apply for troops, but this he could not do without first consulting the council, which would "never advise it let the Case be ever so desperate." The commissioners must simply "wait till a violent Opposition is made to their Officers." Bernard perceived plainly that the crescendo of opposition to the Townshend Acts would ultimately lead either to a British retreat—which was unthinkable—or to the forcible, i.e., military, imposition of the duties. But however inevitable the coming of the troops, Bernard dared not hasten it, nor even appear to do so. "I have," he wrote in concluding a report to Barrington on the troubles, "conducted myself so as to be able to say, and swear to, if the Sons of Liberty shall require it, that I have never applied for Troops. And therefore, my Lord, I beg that Nothing I now write may be considered as such an Application." [6]

The very day that Bernard sent Barrington his nonapplication for troops, almost one hundred Boston merchants adopted an agreement not to import "European goods," to encourage American manufactures, and to concert with other merchants as far south as Pennsylvania. Samuel Adams, of course, was no merchant. But the nonimportation principle lay close to the heart of his strategy. His control of the merchants, coupled with his control over the mob, put Boston's economic and physical peace virtually into his sole power. Such a concentration of authority became particularly useful to Adams at this time, for the long-simmering question of his public indebtedness was about to boil over. As tax collector, Adams was, to put a neutral gloss on his behavior, substantially in arrears: £4000, according to a Town committee, including a court judgment of almost £1500. No part of these sums had yet been repaid by March 1768. At the March 14 town meeting, Adams presented a most humble petition praying additional time, and noting without apparent embarrassment that collection had been impeded by the "Stamp Act, and the Confusion consequent thereupon; which in a great Measure interrupted the course of Business of every kind." After some debate, the Town allowed him six additional months. Then, at a second, all-day town meeting eight days later, despite "many Debates about Mr Adams," his "Friends were so warm in his favor that the Gentlemen could not get a Reconsideration of the Vote passed on Monday last." Adams was safe.[7]

It is not too speculative to suggest that the favorable results of the meetings, particularly the second one, stemmed from the Town's realization of the immense power which lay at Adams's command. Consider the events of March 18, midway between the meetings. The second anniversary of the Stamp Act's repeal (and, by agreement, a put-over St. Patrick's Day) dawned to "beating of Drums and firing of Guns . . . and the whole Town was adorned with Ships Colors." Liberty Tree sported two effigies, one marked "C. P." for Paxton, the other "J. W." for John Williams, the same inspector-general of the customs who had landed with Burch, Hulton, and Paxton. As if to show the radical directorate's intention that the celebration be kept raucous but not overly personal, the radicals Thomas Crafts, John Avery, and William Speakman promptly cut down both dummies. That finished, Boston turned to the main business of the day. Tory and Whig alike celebrated at separate multi-toasted dinners, after which "The Company were very cheerful & Gay." As the evening wore on, two mobs of "young fellows & negroes" began to gather in King Street and at the Liberty Tree in the South End. Eight hundred strong, they "made great Noise & Hallooing," passing by Province House, Bernard's official residence. Their yells terrified the governor, who along with Hutchinson and Sheriff Greenleaf was trying to comfort the Burch family, which had moved to the house "for safety" the day before. Confident in its power, the mob headed for Williams's North End home.[8]

Williams, "as sly, secret and cunning a fellow, as need be" had small use for his superiors in the service, and continually boasted that his "consequence," "Connections, and Interest [i.e., influence]" were greater than theirs. Possibly the Sons recognized a potential kindred spirit; they may have been awed by his announced readiness "for their Reception"; or it may be that Sam Adams felt the time inappropriate for a proper mobbing. "We know who have abused us," he had written only four days earlier. "We owe them *Contempt,* and we will treat them with it in full measure: But let not the hair of their scalps be touched. The time is coming, when they shall lick the dust and melt away." At any rate, the crowd stopped outside of Williams's house and "did him no Damage—which the greatest part of the Gentlemen in Town were very glad of." [9]

Glad the "Gentlemen" may have been that the affair turned out "trifling," but they must also have realized that the timetable for scalping and dust-licking (figurative or literal) rested solely in the control of one man. Clearly the commissioners recognized the threat implicit in Adams's ability to impose order. Unable to convince Bernard to apply for troops, they wrote for aid to England and, for immediate naval assistance, to Commodore Samuel Hood, commander in chief on the North American Station. They also asked the Home Government for ships; Hillsborough caused the admiralty to send out a frigate, two sloops, and two cutters. Meanwhile, after some delay, Hood sent down from Halifax H.M.S. *Romney,* 50 guns, Captain John Corner commanding. *Romney* did not reach Boston until May 17. In the interval Lt. Col. William Dalrymple, field commander of the Fourteenth Regiment, arrived in Boston from New York with "several officers." Presumably the group was headed for Halifax, the Fourteenth's station; but the Boston sojourn afforded a fine opportunity to examine the town and its situation through experienced military eyes.[10]

Dalrymple and his party found affairs relatively quiet, although about a week before he arrived a waterfront dispute had briefly threatened to ignite more violence. The center of this short storm had been Hancock, whose brigantine *Lydia* arrived on April 8 after an eight-week run from London. As usual, a pair of customs officers called tidesmen, or tidewaiters, boarded the ship to watch the discharging. This they could lawfully do, provided they remained on deck. The next evening one of them, Owen Richards, was found below in the steerage, his clear purpose a search for dutiable goods. Now it was one thing to detect a shipowner in the act of landing undeclared cargo; it was quite another to rummage through a vessel's contents to discover such goods. The law recognized the distinction, and so did Hancock. As soon as he heard of Richards' capture, he hurried to interrogate the hapless officer, who refused to come out. Having assured himself that Richards lacked any authority to search, Hancock ordered his men to haul the tidesman on deck and keep him there. As *Lydia*'s boatswain and mate hustled Richards topside by his arms and thighs, a group of waterfront bystanders including Captain John Matchet and the ubiquitous Malcom cheered the proceedings on. "Damn him, hand him up," Malcom said. "If it was my vessel, I would knock him down." Rough words and rough treatment, but entirely legal. Indeed when the outraged commissioners pressed Sewall to proceed against Hancock at common law, Sewall replied, in a carefully composed opinion, that no offense had been committed. The commissioners tried to overrule Sewall by sending the file to the treasury with an opinion by their special solicitor, Samuel Fitch, contradicting Sewall's, and a request that London order the prosecution. The commissioners gained nothing by this effort; London denied the request. When Sewall learned of it, he resented the implied rebuke so strongly that in the very next case he allowed his feelings to blunt his professional enthusiasm.[11]

Unfortunately for the commissioners, successful prosecution of that matter required the utmost legal effort, for it was the famous case of the sloop *Liberty*. This vessel, also owned by Hancock, reached Boston from Madeira on May 9 with a cargo of wine, some belonging to Hancock and some "on freight" for other merchants. Her master, Nathaniel Barnard, went to the Custom House the next day and "entered" twenty-five pipes of wine. Since this quantity (only about 3,150 gallons) fell far short of the *Liberty*'s capacity, and since Hancock had previously boasted in front of Comptroller Hallowell that "he would run [i.e., smuggle] her cargo of Wines on Shore," the customs officers were morally certain that dutiable wine had been landed. But as Collector Joseph Harrison put it, they could "get no legal Information." The tidesmen who had gone aboard as soon as the ship reached the wharf May 9 "gave no Information." "They were examined and said there had been no Wine run out of the Ship." Still the rumor of smuggling persisted. It "was the publick talk of the town, and became a common topick." To add to the mystery, Captain John Marshall, master of another Hancock ship, the *London Packet*, died on May 10 at the age of thirty-two. He had, it was said, unloaded his ship the night before, "by which he overheated himself." But because even in eighteenth-century Boston captains did not usually take a physical part in discharging their vessels, the explanation seemed odd.[12]

While these strange events remained very much on the minds of the customs officials, the radicals found a more serious topic. On May 17 H.M.S. *Romney* arrived from Halifax with H.M. Schooner *St. Lawrence*, in belated response to the commissioners' March request. With her fifty guns, *Romney* ranked as only a "fourth rate" ship of the line. But she gave the customs commissioners immediate command of Boston harbor. It was bad enough from the radicals' view to have her swinging from a single anchor in King Roads; on May 23 she moved up to the town and moored within two cable lengths of Hancock"s wharf. *Romney* now was in position to threaten the town itself, as well as the *Liberty*. *Romney*'s presence meant that, for the first time in the dispute, England had brought military force to bear on Boston. Regrettably, *Romney*'s was not a quiet presence; Captain Corner, like any other naval commander on a foreign station in those days of slow travel and primitive medicine, found himself short-handed. He sent *Romney*'s "long Boat, man'd & arm'd with an officer to Cruize in the S.E. Entrance of the Harbour," to stop inbound vessels and impress, i.e., forcibly enlist, needed seamen from their crews. This activity, irritating enough under ordinary circumstances, particularly aroused the

Bostonians. They knew that a sixty-year-old statute, never repealed, prevented impressment of seamen from vessels employed "in any part of America." Notwithstanding the clear statutory prohibition, Corner kept up his long boat patrol and his impressment activity. On June 9 an officer and two midshipmen went with newly pressed Thomas Furlong to the *Boston Packet* to pick up Furlong's gear and wages. A crowd gathered on the wharf, shouted insults at the officers, threatened them with stones, and ultimately "rescued" Furlong. Aboard *Romney*, Corner had the crew exercise "Great Guns and Small arms." [13]

With the town's feelings against Corner and his ship heated to boiling, it required only a small incident to provoke serious trouble. As if acting on cue, the customs officers provided the incident. The morning of June 10, Thomas Kirk, one of the tidesmen who had attended the *Liberty* in May, approached Collector Harrison with a story which Harrison instantly recognized as the "legal Information" he had been seeking. Kirk, it seemed, was entirely retracting his original account. The truth, he now said, was that on the evening the *Liberty* had arrived, the late Captain Marshall "made proposals" to Kirk to permit the surreptitious landing of wine. Kirk "peremptorily refused," upon which Marshall and five or six brawny associates shoved him into the cabin and nailed down the hatch cover. In this impromptu brig he remained three hours, while outside he could hear the ship's tackles and "a Noise as of many people upon Deck at work hoisting out Goods." When the noise ceased, Marshall let Kirk go, after warning him that his life and his property depended on his eternal silence.[14]

Delighted with this evidence, Harrison nonetheless paused long enough to check with Kirk's partner. That man could not corroborate the story because, he said, he had been asleep the entire time. In truth, said Kirk, the fellow had been drunk and had gone home to bed. Satisfied, Harrison had Kirk reduce his story to writing and swear to it. Then he laid the affidavit before the commissioners. Why he did this is not clear, since the Boston officials could take enforcement action without additional authority. The board had Harrison ask their solicitor, David Lisle, for a legal opinion. Lisle did not hesitate. Landing goods without payment of duty rendered the vessel in question liable to seizure, judicial condemnation, and sale. Seize the *Liberty*, he advised.[15]

Seizure was, of course, something easier to advise than to execute. Joseph Warren himself had earlier warned Hallowell that if the *Liberty* were taken, "there would be a great Uproar," adding that he "could not be answerable for the Consequences." Aware of this, Hulton, who was then chairman of the commissioners, suggested that immediately after seizure the officers deliver the *Liberty* into Captain

Corner's charge. Hallowell and Harrison, who would have to make the actual arrest, decided to obtain even greater security. They asked Captain Corner to send a boat to assist in the seizure itself. Shortly before sunset, Harrison, Hallowell, and Harrison's son (who served as a customs clerk) walked to the wharf; the Harrisons "went thro' the necessary forms of seizing the vessel, and met with no Interruption"; *Romney*, meanwhile, sent her "boat man'd and arm'd" to the wharf. The sailors and marines "found a large mob assembled arm'd with stones which they threw," wounding some of *Romney*'s people. Having cast off the sloop's "fast," or mooring, the landing party, still under a heavy rock barrage, brought her to *Romney*'s stern, where she anchored "with a proper officer and men to take Care of her." [16]

Deprived of the ship, the crowd turned on the Harrisons and Hallowell. As they walked home from the wharf a mob attacked them with clubs, stones, and brickbats. Harrison, badly battered about the chest, managed to keep his legs and escape through an alley. Hallowell, although only superficially wounded, was knocked to the ground and left there, covered with blood. Someone floored young Harrison, dragged him along by the hair of his head until some bystanders rescued him. In another part of town, a second mob set upon Customs Inspector Thomas Irwin (or Irving), who had had no part in the seizure, and cuffed him badly. Two of the more moderate rioters helped him to escape through a house.[17]

The mob then surrounded Hallowell's house, breaking windows and trying to force an entry; someone inside called out that Hallowell had almost been killed, but was not at home. Diverted, the rioters moved to Harrison's rented lodgings, again smashing the windows. At the owner's fervent assurances that Harrison was not there, they departed. Still full of sport, they converged on the home of Inspector-General John Williams, who was fortunately out of town. In an orgy of rock-hurling, the crowd shattered a hundred window panes. When a terrified Mrs. Williams appeared and told them that she was alone, they spared the house further damage and departed.

Apparently determined to find something to destroy, the crowd combed the waterfront for *Romney*'s boats. Corner, acting on explicit instructions from Hood, had ordered these back to the ship, so the rioters tailed onto Harrison's pride and joy, a pleasure boat "built by himself in a particular & elegant manner." They took it from the water, dragged it through the streets, and grandly burned it on the Boston Common. Even those flames did not satisfy all of the mob; only after considerable argument, a vote, and the voice of radical leadership booming "To your Tents O Israel," did the throng disperse. The Tories (and probably others) thanked heaven that the mob had resisted breaking into a liquor supply; "if they had procured it in Quantity," Bernard said, "God knows where this Fury would have ended." The terrorizing in March, the radicals had dismissed as "the Diversion of a few Boys, a matter of no Consequence," "the common Effects of Festivity & Rejoicing, & there was no Harm intended." But the crowd on June 10 was, as John Rowe admitted, "a considerable mob." The radical-dominated council agreed that the affair was "criminal, and the actors in it were guilty of a riot." And Sam Adams himself "confess'd there was a Riot on that Evening." If Adams had had his way, perhaps there would have been more than a riot. The next day someone is supposed to have heard him, "trembling and in great agitation," say to a group: "If you are men behave like men; let us take up arms immediately and be free and seize all the King's Officers: we shall have thirty thousand men to join us from the Country." [18]

The commissioners needed no further impetus. Saturday, June 11, "being apprehensive of danger from the Outrageous Behaviour of the populace," they "apply'd for Boats to bring them on Board" *Romney*. "At 6 P.M.," *Romney*'s log reads, "sent three Boats man'd and arm'd,"— the marines with fixed bayonets—"at 7 the Boats Return'd with the Commissioners, their familys, Clerks, Tide waiters &c. to the Numr. of 67 persons." One customs official remained ashore. John Temple, always a dissident member of the board, always more friendly toward the radicals (and in turn more esteemed by them) than the other commissioners, took the occasion to break openly with his colleagues.[19]

During the fevered weekend, the battered Hallowell and Harrison negotiated desperately with Dr. Warren, trying to work out a formula which would relieve the popular pressure, yet preserve the commissioners' authority. The officials were even willing to forego the usual advantages of a seizure. Harrison agreed in writing to release the *Liberty* in return for Hancock's bare word that the ship, or equivalent security, would be produced when required. But when Warren tried to close the deal near midnight on Sunday, he found "that Mr Hancock had taken the Advice of his Council & Friends & wou'd have nothing to do with the Business but wou'd let it take its Course." [20]

The course was to be long and tortuous. As a result of the complicated admiralty proceedings, Hancock lost his vessel, and was plunged into a drawn-out legal battle over his personal liability. It lasted all winter, "a painfull Drudgery" for his lawyers, John Adams and James Otis, and a large drain on Hancock's time, patience, and purse. On the other side, Sewall felt "he could not please the Commissioners of the Customs." He told Bernard he wanted to resign as advocate-general. His prosecution of the case, at best unenthusiastic, could not overcome the shortage of testimony. The more the crown (which is to say, the commissioners) pressed for evidence, the more apparent became the thinness of the case. Quick to appreciate the snare into which the customs officers had stepped, the radicals began circulating accounts of the proceedings for consumption in other colonies. This series, entitled "A Journal of the Times," emphasized "the twin themes of the venality of the Customs Commissioners and the arbitrary injustice of the Court of Admiralty." Doggedly, the prosecution continued until finally, on March 25, 1769, Sewall and the commissioners formally gave up. "The Advocate General prays leave to retract this information and says Our Sovereign Lord the King will prosecute no further hereon." [21]

The attempt to exact criminal penalties against the rioters came to a more humiliating finish. Because the jurors were elected by town meetings, and because the radicals controlled the Boston Town Meeting, the Grand Jury which was to hear the matter included Malcom himself; worse, the attorney-general could produce no one willing to testify. "There had been 2 or 300 people who paraded and did great part of the mischief in the public streets in the Day-time," wrote a frustrated Bernard. "And yet no man could be found who dares to charge any of them." No testimony; a grand jury which would not indict even if the evidence were there; and, should an indictment somehow issue, no possibility of a conviction at trial. Everyone in Boston realized that justice ran only on paths chosen by the radicals. It is understandable that the king and his ministers, pondering events like these, came to regard Massachusetts as "a Colony in which the exercise of all civil power and authority was suspended by the most daring Acts of force and violence." [22]

CHAPTER 7

"A MOST UNEQUAL WAR"

T he commissioners and their entourage stuffed themselves uncomfortably but safely into *Romney,* where they gobbled £75 worth
of Captain Corner's personal stores weekly. Generally, they were "very
genteelly entertained . . . the Captns Lady being on board." Ashore,
Sam Adams took immediate steps to force their permanent removal,
and *Romney's.* Placards all over town called the Sons of Liberty and
anyone else to a meeting Tuesday morning at "Liberty Hall," the area
immediately under Liberty Tree. Despite rain and haze, "Vast numbers of the populace and others, met at the time and place" and "from
thence removed to Faneuil Hall." Why not hold the original meeting
at Faneuil Hall? Here is demagogic genius at work. Liberty Tree and
Faneuil Hall were five-eighths of a mile apart, virtually at opposite ends
of the Main Street. The crowd moving from Tree to Hall would pass
through the center of Boston, past the Province House, the Town
House (where the council sat), and within a block of the Custom
House.[1]

At Faneuil Hall, it was proposed to adjourn briefly, to permit the selectmen to "call" a "Regular" or "legal" town meeting. This was another stroke of skill, since it converted a crowd (or what some might
even call a mob) into an organ of government. Put another way, it
enabled the mob to speak with the recognized voice of the Town.
When the crowd reconvened that afternoon as a town meeting, it
came under Otis's command, for he was moderator. He proposed moving the concourse to the more commodious Old South Meeting House

which lay on the Main Street halfway between Faneuil Hall and Liberty Tree. Thus the radicals enjoyed for a second time parading their strength past the establishment. Once reassembled, the meeting proceeded to approve a previously prepared petition to Bernard and to appoint a twenty-one–man committee to deliver it. John Rowe, one of the committee, called the petition "very smart." If by "smart" Rowe meant what we might call "fresh," he squarely hit the mark. Addressing Bernard as though the situation lay entirely in his control, the petition complained of "an armed force, seizing, impressing, and imprisoning the persons of our fellow-subjects." With a bland assumption that the commissioners had "thought fit, of their own motion, to relinquish the exercise of their commission here," the petition concluded by insisting that Bernard "issue your immediate order to the commander of his majesty's ship *Romney*, to remove from this harbour." Under the existing circumstances, removal of *Romney* would automatically have removed the customs apparatus, but of course the petition did not mention that point.[2]

Bernard received the committee (which included Sam Adams, Hancock, Warren, Young, and Malcom, as well as the more conservative Samuel Quincy), listened "very cordially" to a brief speech by Otis, "spoke very sensibly to some parts of the Speech & Petition & promised an answer in the morning." He "then had wine handed round," and the committee returned to Hancock's in eleven chaises. Bernard's answer, sent the next day, handled the petition rather neatly. He agreed to use his good offices to have *Romney's* impressment activities "regulated so as to avoid all the inconveniences to this Town, which you are apprehensive of"; and in this, he was reasonably successful. He noted his obligation to "protect aid and assist the Commissioners." And of course he disclaimed control, formal or otherwise, over *Romney's* movements. The last was superfluous. Even as the Town committeemen were draining their glasses in the governor's drawing room, *Romney* was swinging to her "Small Bower" anchor just northwest of Castle William, having warped down the harbor that morning. From there, she protected the fort while commanding the harbor. On June 16 and 17 Corner moved her to within one mile of the Castle; meanwhile, he publicly agreed not to impress any more Massachusetts seamen. On June 20, while *Romney* dried her sails after two days of rain, the commissioners and their families, "to the Number of 23 persons," went ashore to the Castle, where the Burch and Hulton families occupied "Apartments . . . rather elegant than commodious." They ate with two of the other commissioners, one of whom returned nightly to the *Romney*. Temple, however, did not associate with the group, though he lodged at the Castle "to save appearances." Harrison, having been "advised by his friends to make his escape," soon joined the party. And it certainly was a party, "rather like one of the Publick water drinking places in England," Hulton's sister said. "We have a great many Visitors comes every day from Boston incog," including such radicals as John Rowe. With "seldom less than twenty at dinner," at their "most Agreeable Summer Retreat," the customs entourage indeed lived "luxuriously." Pleasant though it was, the commissioners knew they could not remain happy exiles for ever. On June 20, even before settling down, they sent Hallowell to London for help.[3]

In Boston, meanwhile, although Bernard's treatment of the petition won Otis's open approval and his interposition with Captain Corner had gained him some brief popularity, his respite was only temporary. The same turbulent town meeting had produced, by a committee whose labor rested principally on John Adams, a set of Instructions for the four-member Boston "seat" in the imminent legislative session. These were really a catalogue of current grievances, designed more for propaganda purposes than for the guidance of the legislators. They clearly indicated that present friction would increase and future difficulties multiply: Resist the customs establishment (they said); protest naval participation in customs enforcement; eliminate impressment (quoting the old statute saving American vessels from the press gang); and ascertain who if anyone had asked for troops, because "every such Person, who shall solicite or promote the importation of Troops at this time, is an Enemy to this Town and Province, and a disturber of the peace and good order of both."[4]

The rumor which had stimulated the last portion of the Instructions rested on solid fact. Bernard, as we know, had indeed solicited and promoted the arrival of soldiers, although he did not dare request them openly. And even before quitting *Romney*, the commissioners had written directly to Gage in New York, vividly depicting their plight, the increase of violence, and the unlikelihood of Bernard's ever receiving council approval to ask for troops. Bernard's reluctance to proceed without that approval may have been based more on political expediency than on reality. He did consider himself "directed to Consult the Council about requiring troops." But as early as 1765, a circular letter from then-Secretary of State Conway to all the governors had enjoined the executive "to use your utmost power for repelling all acts of outrage and violence, and to provide for the maintenance of peace and good order in the province, by such a timely exertion of force, as that occasion may require; for which purpose you will make the proper application to General Gage" or the naval commander. A cognate letter to Gage required him to "concur" in appropriate "timely Exertion of Force."[5]

Certainly Bernard recognized the need for such an Exertion. "Troops," he told Barrington, "are not wanted [i.e., needed] here to quell a Riot or a Tumult, but to rescue the Government out of the hands of a trained mob, & to restore the Activity of the Civil Power, which is now entirely obstructed." But still he would not ask for troops on his own. The War Office had expressly ordered Gage "to take no Step whatever . . . but at the Express Requisition of the Civil Magistrate," including such matters as (1) "Marching, or Quartering the troops"; (2) taking any "Step whatever towards Opposing the Rioters"; and even (3) repelling "Force by Force, Unless in case of Absolute Necessity." So Gage had to tell the commissioners that although his "Inclination would lead [him] to order Troops to march immediately for [their] Protection," he could do nothing until Bernard acted.[6]

Why did Bernard refuse to take the responsibility? Did he fear the physical consequences if the Sons should learn he had requested soldiers? Did he hope that somehow his personality and efforts could encourage a permanent settlement? Or was he simply trying to avert an inevitable explosion long enough to allow Barrington and other friends at home to find him a happier, safer, and more lucrative position? Probably all three contributed to his attitude toward the "very hard Warfare," "a most unequal War" which began to engulf him. But the money question appeared to plague him worst. Forced, he said, to provide for a large family, he felt that the £200 by which his net worth had increased annually since 1760 did not suffice, and was in any event an inadequate reward for the rigors of trying to rule Massachusetts. Even a public official may of course properly concern himself with his family's welfare. Something, however, seems particularly amiss when a royal governor diverts his attention from the acute imperial problems convulsing his province to weigh alternative future assignments, with special regard to the climate of each colony.[7]

Perhaps this is too harsh an indictment of Bernard. The magnitude of the difficulties he faced in the summer of 1768 matched the ferocious ability of the opponents who created and exploited them. Confused, hoping to be relieved of his administrative burden, saddened by the death of his fifteen-year-old son, Bernard lacked the mental resiliency and moral stamina to compete with Warren, Otis, and the Adamses. "Trouble is my portion," he had once said. Without considerations of Freudian wish-fulfillment, we can agree. Besides facing the Sons of Liberty, Bernard also bore the incubus of the British ministry, particularly Lord Hillsborough.[8]

By the kind of mistiming which seemed to characterize and plague Hillsborough's *modus operandi*, in the midst of the *Liberty-Romney* hubbub (June 17), Bernard received from London orders whose exe-

cution he accurately foresaw would ruin him. Now he would "be obliged to act like the Capt. of a fireship, provide for my retreat before I
light the fusee." Tell the legislature, Hillsborough instructed Bernard,
that it must disapprove and rescind the February Circular Letter—or
else. "Else" meant a peremptory dissolving. Hoping with his characteristic irrational and intermittent optimism that the legislators would voluntarily comply, Bernard on June 21 raised the recision issue simply as
a matter of royal "requisition," or request. "The consequence of their
refusal he did not mention to them." Of course they guessed, or knew,
and within three days had forced Bernard to disclose Hillsborough's
threat. The hapless governor managed to salvage a shred of personal
self-respect by refusing to oblige the House in its outrageous demand
for copies of his prior correspondence with Hillsborough. He also
showed decent public spirit, urging the House to finish work on a tax-
relief bill, which dissolution would necessarily kill. But this could not
deter the legislators. Nor did the arrival of Hutchinson, called home
from the superior court's eastern circuit by Bernard's express, influence
them. Emboldened by the support they had received from other colonial legislatures, they vented with oratory and votes the frustrations
imposed by the administration, the commissioners, and *Romney*. "[A]
very full house" refused, by 92 votes to 17, to rescind, and "92" passed
into the Revolution's numerology. Bernard, as his order required, dissolved the General Court; Massachusetts was without a legislature.
The next time one could be elected—in the fall—Adams took care to
link the seventeen rescinders with Popery, "which, to most New Eng-
landers, was synonymous with tyranny, oppression, and every other
abomination." Few retained their seats, then or ever after.[9]

Bad though the crisis was, Bernard had good reason to believe help
might be soon at hand. Gage, relating to Bernard the commissioners'
plea, reiterated his refusal to dispatch troops without a direct request.
The next day, however, he sent Bernard, "in order to save Time" if
need should arise, a letter to the officer in charge at Halifax, Lt. Col.
William Dalrymple of the Fourteenth Regiment. The letter ordered
troops to move. He also wrote directly to Dalrymple. Whenever Bernard might instruct him, Gage said, Dalrymple should proceed with
troops and artillery to Boston, without regard "to the leaving Halifax
without Troops." Occasion, size of force, destination, and the presence
of the artillery were, however, left entirely to the governor's discretion.
Still without orders actually to garrison Boston, Gage felt himself
nonetheless authorized to begin assembling sufficient troops at Halifax
to expedite the movement when the orders did arrive. In response to his
instructions, Dalrymple and Hood started clearing the Nova Scotia
outposts and preparing ships to transport those troops and the Halifax

garrison to Boston. Like Bernard, Gage was unwilling to assume the responsibility of placing soldiers in Boston, because, as Gage's American biographer has observed, "he foresaw that *he* would then be the object of a storm of abuse, both in England and America." Each, if only he knew it, could have saved himself the worry. Two weeks earlier, Lord Hillsborough had sent Gage "Secret and Confidential" instructions "forthwith" to quarter one or (at his discretion) more regiments in Boston under an officer "upon whose Prudence, Resolution and Integrity you can entirely rely." The troops were "to give every legal Assistance to the Civil Magistrate in the Preservation of the Public Peace and to the officers of the Revenue in the Execution of the Laws of Trade & Revenue." Hillsborough wrote on June 8, two days before the *Liberty* riot; for reasons unknown, Gage did not receive the letter until September 7, an unusually long delay in the summer season, even for west-bound ships. Once more, the slowness of communications had negated an attempt by London to control events at Boston.[10]

With Gage's renewed offer of help in hand, Bernard again hoped to provoke the council into "advising" that Boston needed troops. In this it appeared that the mob would, paradoxically, come to his aid. The evening of July 5, a gang of fifty or sixty went out to Roxbury, then a pleasant little village three miles from Boston. Roxbury was Dr. Warren's home town, and the site of Bernard's summer house. Dividing into two groups, they surrounded the rented quarters of Commissioner John Robinson. Robinson had long since fled to the Castle, but perhaps the mob thought he had sneaked back home. After learning of their error, the bully boys stayed anyway, stealing ripe fruit, snapping boughs of fruit trees, flattening fences, and trampling the garden. They left at midnight, cheering all the way back to Boston, where the radicals excused the episode as "a Frolick of a few Boys to eat some Cherries." [11]

Several days later, thirty men revived the *Lydia* and *Liberty* incidents by boarding a schooner which had been seized for failure to pay duties on a cargo of molasses, incarcerating the two customs officers aboard, and landing the molasses. Mindful of the resentment engendered by *Romney*'s part in the *Liberty* seizure, the customs hierarchy had deliberately permitted the molasses ship to lie at the wharf under minimal supervision. They wanted to test the radicals' insistence that the *Liberty* would have been safe enough without *Romney*'s protection. Bernard openly ridiculed the experiment, and now events seemed for once to have justified his prophecy. The next day, however, as if simultaneously to mock the governor, vindicate the town, and show everyone where the real power of government lay, the radicals, simply by threatening the schooner's captain with "the pain of the displeasure of the town," forced the relading of all the molasses. "So we are not without a Government," Bernard commented. "Only it is in the hands of the people of the Town." [12]

Sometimes, however, those hands slipped. During the *Liberty* riot, it will be remembered, Inspector-General Williams had been away from Boston; the mob broke his windows; the next day a placard promised him direct action whenever he should return.[13] Williams's business (or perhaps his discretion) kept him out of town until mid-July. The night of July 15, the ringing of fire bells and cries of "Fire" produced a concourse of people streaming toward Williams's North End home. Breaking into the courtyard, they came face to face with the fully armed inspector-general. A parley ensued, at which the mob demanded that Williams report the next day to Liberty Tree, there to resign his commission, as Oliver had done three years before. Williams refused to do either, but told his visitors he would be "upon the Change" (that is, at the head of King Street) the next day at noon and would be glad then and there to meet them. Temporarily mollified by Williams's reasonableness, or perhaps baffled by his fortitude, the mob dispersed.

The following midday, fifteen hundred people milled around on the Change, waiting for the fun. Williams did not disappoint them; just about noon he made his appearance, not on the street, but upon the second-floor balcony of the Town House overlooking King Street. Coolly surveying the crowd, he told the people that he had come, according to his promise, to answer any questions or objections they might care to put to him. No one answered. For fifteen minutes Williams stood there, waiting. Finally, he repeated his offer. "Again, nothing was said, except by an ignorant Fellow, whose Absurdity created Laughter." In a few moments, the crowd had vanished, and Williams went home "in Peace & Quiet." [14]

Although, as John Rowe noted, Williams's original visitors were the Sons of Liberty, and although the heads of "the faction" were directly pressuring him, the radicals publicly dissociated themselves from the whole affair, "giving it out that the Mob of that Night were not the true Sons of Liberty and acted without Authority." But Williams said he had heard some of the people in King Street asking aloud why "those who set them on did not appear to talk for them." [15]

Tory sentiment generally applauded Williams's courage; but the more cynical conservatives suspected the affair for its patness. These suspicions were reinforced by the way the radicals, although suppressing newspaper discussions, promptly used the incident "to bring an odium upon the Commissioners, who, it was said, if they had remained, would have been in no more danger than the inspector." Talk of the episode was still current when Bernard met the council the morning of July 29. He could use it, naturally, as justification for raising the question of soldiers. The councilors could similarly use it to advise (as they did, unanimously) that troops were unnecessary. Rumors had spread that the meeting concerned the introduction of troops; this "greatly alarmed the Inhabitants." Worse, Bernard had of course laid Gage's offer before the council. Although he first "enjoined the council secrecy upon their oaths," a large number of the councilors belonged to the radical party, or were coming to fear or sympathize with it. Bernard thus gave his enemies proof, whenever they might choose to publish it, that he had in fact been negotiating for the garrisoning of Boston. Simultaneously he gave the Tories proof that he now possessed the power, if only he would use it, to bring military order into what many regarded as mob-controlled chaos. Bernard's continued refusal to use his resources could only dishearten and disgust the loyal faction.[16]

In England, meanwhile, Hallowell had related his version of the *Liberty* riot and the commissioners' flight. Within ten days, Hillsborough had issued his orders: The Sixty-Fourth and Sixty-Fifth Regiments, in Ireland awaiting transfer to North America in the spring of 1769, "should be immediately sent thither," after being "completed by Draughts from the other Regiments in Ireland to Five Hundred men each." The Admiralty was to furnish transports "with the usual Allowance for Women Servants and Baggage," "54 women, 10 servants, and 50 tons for baggage," a frigate for convoy, which would then remain upon the North American station, together with H.M.S. *Rippon,* currently preparing to take a new governor to Virginia. Instructions were to go to all the ships there to support and protect civil and revenue officers, "and for enforcing a due Obedience to the Laws of this Kingdom, the Execution of which has, in several Instances, been unwarrantedly resisted, and their Authority denied." [17]

The letter in which Hillsborough told Bernard of the additional help fairly crackled with the secretary's rage. The entire object of the king's policy, he said, was to induce "a due Obedience to the Law." "No Remissness of Duty will be excusable, upon pretence of Terror and Danger in the Execution of Office." Poor Bernard; it is almost impossible not to feel sympathy for him. His only ambition by now was to quit Massachusetts, preferably with a full purse, but above all with a whole skin. Yet there sat Hillsborough, snug in London, casually (albeit angrily) commanding him to impossibilities: eliminate laggard justices of the peace, particularly radicals; conduct a full inquiry into the late riots and tumults; discover the perpetrators of the violence of June 10;

consider the possibility of sending the wrongdoers to England for trial in the King's Bench under authority of a statute dating from Henry VIII; convene the next legislature outside of Boston, away from the mob's threats; and if the impressment question arises again, remember that in the Government's view impressment in America is legal.[18]

CHAPTER 8

TROOPS TO BOSTON

August, with its ugly memories of Stamp Act riots, was never a pleasant month for the Boston Tories. August 1768 opened with a concerted effort by John Rowe and other merchants to mount an effective nonimportation agreement. The earlier one had failed for inability to obtain concurrence of the New York and Philadelphia merchants. This time, a series of meetings and the attendant pressure produced signatures to the agreement and, in some cases, refusals to sign tempered with undertakings to observe the restrictions. Only thirty-five merchants refused to do either, preferring the risk of being, as Bernard put it, "brought to reason by Mob-Law." [1]

The governor did not exaggerate; the instigators of the nonimportation agreement showed an alarming closeness to the Sons. On August 15, third anniversary of the Oliver riot, radical merchants led the all-day festivities. Following a rally at Liberty Hall, "where there was a variety of Good Musick exhibited & Great Joy appeared in every countenance," over one hundred "Gentlemen," including the selectmen and the Boston representatives in the dissolved legislature, drove to The Greyhound in Roxbury for an outdoor spread and numerous toasts: "Scalping Salvages let loose in Tribes, rather than Legions of Placemen, Pensioners and Walkerizing Dragoons." Among the merry-makers were "some who were immediate actors in the riot which they were celebrating, and that which next succeeded it" (the Hutchinson riot). "In the procession," Bernard reported, "was one Moore, who was a principal hand in pulling down the Lieut. Governor's House, was committed to Goal for it, and rescued from thence by a Number of People in the night." [2]

Nonimportation combinations, raucous celebrations of violence, known rioters like Moore free to join the ceremonies honoring their own crimes—it was too much for the conservatives, especially with the *Gazette* continuing to hammer home its barbs. "Otis and the two Adams," Hutchinson reported, "[Town Clerk William] Cooper & [Dr. Benjamin] Church go regularly every Saturday in the afternoon to set the Press. . . . They all profess a great friendship for me." What John Adams had to say six years later certainly applied now: "The printers are hot indiscreet Men, and they are under the Influence of others as hot, rash and unjudicious as themselves, very often." The Tories badly needed a breather. Auchmuty asked the chief justice to adjourn the forthcoming superior court session. The bar, he said, "are for it," and, anyway, he wanted to attend a wedding in Halifax. Judge Trowbridge suggested sitting just for two or three days to conclude routine business and then adjourning to November. Bernard planned to go to the mineral springs at Brookfield for a month while Mrs. Bernard took the waters there. Problems of arranging for the easy arrival of the soldiers caused Bernard to cancel his journey, but perhaps it was just as well. Boston's radical wrath burned extraterritorially, as Commissioner John Robinson learned. Having left the Castle, he went to Newport, Rhode Island, presumably to look after customs matters there. His presence becoming known, a mob surrounded the tavern where he lodged. When he did not emerge, the rioters ransacked the establishment; but Robinson escaped, returning to the Castle by way of Dorchester. The furies that pursued Robinson to Newport might well have followed Bernard to Brookfield, had he gone.[3]

The governor's game at the moment was an equal combination of hope and caution. Knowing the information he had woven into his correspondence with Hillsborough and Barrington, he could feel reasonably sure the soldiers would arrive by New Year's Day. Yet he had not received definite word, and as the events of July had proved, a propensity to riot still smoldered, although only the Liberty boys could say where the next fire would blaze, or how high it would burn. Bernard could well predict the site of the flame should the radicals ever be able to prove that he had done anything at all to bring in the soldiers. Accordingly, he remained as quiet as possible. Even to Hutchinson, "he protests he does not expect" troops. But of course Hutchinson knew. "The Council have a great secret," the lieutenant governor wrote, and added archly: "So have the Freemasons." Hancock, Otis, Crafts, Warren, Rowe, and Revere all belonged to one or another of the two local lodges; Boston Freemasonry was considered a radical stronghold. Bernard, in short, was fooling nobody except perhaps himself. The radicals had, indeed, passed beyond merely anticipating the arrival of troops and had begun active preparations. In early July the selectmen caused the Town's arms, about four hundred muskets, to be removed from storage in the attic of Faneuil Hall, ostensibly for cleaning. Afterwards, the weapons were permitted to stand on the main floor, where they remained through August and September.[4]

Gage, meanwhile, received orders from London to move the troops. On August 31, he sent Captain William Shirreff (or Sheriff), one of his aides, to Boston "under pretence of private business" to confer with Bernard. The option of one regiment or two, and the futher option of placing "the whole or any part" of the troops in the Castle, Gage left to Bernard's determination. At a secret meeting on September 3, Bernard and Shirreff agreed that two regiments were necessary, one in town, the other at the Castle. If the town-based soldiers "should be insulted and threatened," then the Castle regiment would move to town, leaving a two-company garrison. Bernard and Shirreff also worked out details of housing the new troops at the Castle and of keeping the existing fifty-man provincial garrison there to avoid "giving any umbrage or afford[ing] any Cause of Jealousy to the Province." Finally, Bernard asked for an artillery detachment. Gage had instructed Shirreff that as soon as the governor determined the number of troops needed, the force should be ordered to embark from Halifax forthwith. To save time, Shirreff brought with him a set of orders to Dalrymple with appropriate blank spaces, to be filled in "agreeable to [Bernard's] opinion of the number that will be necessary." Once completed, this would be sent direct from Boston, without waiting for Shirreff's return to New York. To protect Bernard, however, it was necessary to pretend that the governor had taken no part in the arrangements. As a result, there arose the strange spectacle of Bernard, in his report of the conference with Shirreff, suggesting to Gage the phraseology of future military orders. Be sure, he told Gage, to "intimate" that one regiment should be town-quartered, lest the council "advise me to Quarter them all at the Castle."[5]

Secretive though Bernard and Shirreff may have thought themselves, the officer's presence and business soon became well known. A violent piece appeared in the Boston *Gazette*. "Among a certain Set of People, Sir," it said, "I have observed that Mobs are represented as most hideous Things. I confess they ought not to be encouraged; but they have been sometimes useful. In a free Country I am afraid a standing Army rather occasions than prevent[s] them." It caused Bernard to consider seriously for the first time the real possibility of a bloody opposition to the soldiers' arrival. What was it Benjamin Franklin had said three years earlier about soldiers sent to America? "They will not find a rebellion; they may indeed make one." Now Bernard needed to ensure that the military presence in Boston meant peace and security, not bloodshed and insurrection "which would at least fall upon the Crown Officers, if it did not amount to an opposition to the troops." [6]

With typically incomplete reasoning, Bernard calculated that the bad news would most easily be accepted if given in small doses. Incredibly, he "thought it best that the Expectation of [the soldiers] should gradually precede the arrival" so that the radicals "might have time to consider well what they were about, & prudent men opportunity to interpose their advice." Bernard's scheme contained only two basic flaws: conception and execution. Sam Adams consummately used the "time" Bernard so willingly gave him to fan "the Expectation" into a rage that almost led to a pitched battle on the Boston docks. Furthermore, Bernard adopted a singularly clumsy and indeed dishonest way of starting "the Expectation" going. On September 8, several days after his conference with Shirreff and the subsequent letter to Gage, he told "one of the Council" that "I had private advice that troops were ordered hither, but I had no public orders about it myself." The same day, he told John Rowe "in Conversation" that "he had Stav'd off the Introducing Troops as long as he could but could do it no longer." Before night, as Bernard boasted, the news "was thoroughly circulated all over the town." [7]

The result, naturally enough, was a combination of "sullen discontent" and "panic fear." The day before, H.M.S. *Senegal* had left Boston, virtually unnoticed, although in fact she carried the orders to Dalrymple. When, on the day of Bernard's disclosures, a large merchantman sailed for Halifax, her departure produced "an alarm in Boston that she and the Man of War were gone to fetch 3 Regiments." A special town meeting was called for Monday, September 12. On Saturday night, a time in Boston usually remarkable for its quiet, the Sons of Liberty secretly and silently hoisted a barrel filled with turpentine (although some said it was empty) to the top of the beacon that crowned Beacon Hill. The hill in those days stood as high as the top of the present State House dome, and so commanded the countryside for miles. Its beacon had originally been built to allow a quick alarm if an enemy's ships should ever appear. By putting up the barrel, the Sons showed that they considered the anticipated troops "the enemy." They also threatened to oppose that enemy with a swarm of armed farmers as well as the riot-tested Boston mob. At extraordinary Sunday meetings, the council and the Boston selectmen each tried to force the other to accept responsibility for removing the barrel. Not until Thursday, during the dinner hour, did Sheriff Greenleaf lead a half-dozen men quietly up the hill, "and in about ten minutes, luckily as he thought, effected his purpose." [8]

Both before and after the barrel-hoisting, the town seethed. Well-believed rumors had it that at secret meetings Friday and Saturday plans had been made to attack the Castle on Monday, and to oppose the troops in blood upon their landing. Amid the uproar, Otis, Sam Adams, and Warren met quietly at the latter's house to prepare the scenario for the Monday town meeting.[9]

At the meeting, with Otis in the chair, vivid oratory, "inflaming Speeches and Treasonable resolves," filled Faneuil Hall. Plans for investing Castle William died quickly, but no one knew whether because of inherent moderation or the arrival of H.M.S. *Magdalen*, which Corner placed "to cover or annoy the passage to the Castle." Instead, the meeting passed two resolves. One asked Bernard, in substance, to state the basis for his hints that troops were expected. The second requested him to issue precepts for a new legislature. After a final motion appointing a committee to consider and recommend further steps, the meeting adjourned.[10]

Another committee, including Adams and Warren, put the questions to Bernard. He refused to call an assembly. As to the soldiers, he said blandly that his "apprehensions" of their arrival arose "from information of a private nature; I have received no public letters, notifying me the coming of such troops, and requiring quarters for them." In the face of Bernard's correspondence with Gage (not to mention his talks with Shirreff), this was a bald lie. Indeed, within the week, before any soldiers had even arrived, Bernard was asking Gage for "considerable Reinforcements." The committee reported his disclaimer to the town meeting the next day, but one doubts whether anybody believed a word of it.[11]

Ignoring the governor thereafter, the radicals reeled off a succession of fiery speeches which, someone told Bernard, "followed one another in such Order & Method, that it appeared as if they were acting a Play; everything, both as to matter & order, seeming to have been preconcerted before hand." With sulphurous references to an approaching war with France (a war whose possibility lurked solely in the mind of Sam Adams), the speakers, particularly Otis, repeatedly urged the people to use their arms against "the enemy," pointing as they spoke to the four hundred freshly cleaned muskets neatly racked in the middle of Faneuil Hall. Aroused, someone moved from the floor that the pieces be distributed immediately. Even Adams was unwilling to go that far, and the motion was defeated. But Otis kept up the hot words. The people, he shouted, had a right to oppose with arms a military force sent to oblige submission to unconstitutional laws. A voice—probably one of the moderates—asked him to be more explicit. "We understand each other very well," replied Otis, pointing again to the muskets. "There are the Arms; when an attempt is made against your liberties, they will be delivered: Our declaration wants [i.e., needs] no explanation." Stimulated by this display, the meeting followed recommendations of the special committee and voted to defend "at the utmost peril of their lives and fortunes" King George and their own British liberties; to call a "convention" on September 22 on the model of the dissolved general assembly; and to urge Bostonians, because of the French danger, to observe strictly the law requiring each householder to provide himself "with a well-fixed firelock musket, accoutrements, and ammunition." [12]

The oratory and the resolutions fitted well with what Adams had been saying quite openly. One Richard Sylvester was to swear a few months later that about this time Adams publicly declared that lighting the beacon would bring 30,000 countrymen to Boston, "with their knapsacks and bayonets fixed . . . We will destroy every Soldier that dares put his foot on Shore." This sort of tough talk softened considerably a few days after the town meeting. The radicals learned from Agent DeBerdt that London had indeed ordered troops; other letters described the angry English reaction to Hallowell's report, and the subsequent plans "for bringing the Bostoners to Reason." Those plans were said to include carrying fifty of the radicals to England for trial. The last rumor was false—Attorney-General DeGrey and Solicitor-General Dunning had concurred in an opinion that since no overt acts of *treason* had been alleged, the statute of Henry VIII did not apply; but the rumor and the hard news of troops sufficed to impose a temporary quiet on Boston. "Much confusion among the popular party," Captain Corner noted. "Don't like the news but put the best face on the matter." Momentarily subdued though the radicals might be, their out-of-town image continued to bear a menacing aspect. Gage, trying to arrange for a routine movement of the Sixty-second Regiment from St. Augustine, found that the owners of the transports "refuse to proceed, tho their Charter Partys are Signed and Sealed. And give for Reason that they are told the Troops are designed for Boston, and they dare not go there. They have been spoke to and threatened by some of the Chiefs of the discontented, and they are affraid to incurr their Displeasure." Boston's reputation for truculence in effect challenged Britain's naval and military strength, and excited in return that fight-seeking strain which Gage had revealed during the Stamp Act crisis. "If open and declared Rebellion makes its Appearence," he wrote Hillsborough hopefully, "I mean to use all the Powers Lodged in my Hands, to make Head against it." [13]

Meanwhile the long-delayed movement of the troops toward Boston began. Completion of the Irish regiments (the Sixty-fourth and Sixty-fifth) had been retarded by their refusal to accept any new men older that thirty. Lord Townshend, the lord lieutenant of Ireland (brother of Champagne Charlie, and friend to Paxton), put in a hard August week and brought both regiments up to strength, only to find them unable to embark because the transports had not yet arrived. By the morning of September 4, however, that problem had resolved itself, and the troops were safe aboard. Unfortunately, their commanding officer, Major General Alexander Mackay, had still not reported; at 7 A.M., he rode express into Cork, just managing to catch the transport *Raven*. All waste effort. Bad weather delayed the final departure until September 10. Even afterwards, storms continued to pound the transports and their single escort, the 38-gun frigate *Hussar* (commanded, incidentally, by young Hyde Parker, who as Admiral Sir Hyde Parker at the Battle of Copenhagen in 1801 was to hoist the signal which Nelson chose not to see).[14]

At Halifax, where navy war ships rather than chartered transports were to carry the troops, operations went much more smoothly. Receiving his admiralty orders and Gage's letter on a Sunday, Hood immediately set the yard workmen to preparing the warships to accommodate troops. Security had been maintained by clamping an embargo on Halifax port. In a few days Hood had without incident embarked nine companies each of the Fourteenth and Twenty-ninth Regiments, one company of artillery (with five field pieces), and an 84-man detachment from the Fifty-ninth Regiment. On the morning of September 19 he sent them to Boston in a nine-ship squadron commanded by Captain Smith of H.M.S. *Mermaid*. Troop commander was Lieutenant Colonel Dalrymple of the Fourteenth, who embarked with six companies of his regiment in H.M.S. *Launceston*. A member of a distinguished Scots family, "a man of most amiable manners and disposition," Dalrymple was "an officer in whose Prudence, Resolution, and Integrity" Gage felt he had "reason to confide." A later feminine appraisal, colored perhaps by intervening events, found him "proud, haughty, & voluptuous, devoted to self, & self gratification hated in general by those under his Command, & universaly despised." His second-in-command was Maurice Carr, who had purchased his lieutenant colonelcy in the Twenty-ninth two years earlier. We know little about the rank and file, crammed uncomfortably into the men-of-war, on "2/3 Allowance of All Species (except Beer)." Judging from descriptions of deserters published in New Jersey a few years later, the average man in the Twenty-ninth was over thirty, medium tall, and Irish. (Even a man "born in the Regiment" is described as speaking "pretty much of the Irish Accent.") The Twenty-ninth had not been in America for the 1756–63 war, and had apparently not acquired any American recruits after arriving in Canada.[15]

America had no particular objection to Redcoats, per se. About eight thousand Americans had enlisted in the army during the war; regular officers had frequently wintered in Boston. Americans, like Englishmen generally, disliked having to maintain a peace-time standing army. In later years, orators would say that the Boston episode taught chiefly the baleful effect standing armies have on liberty. But the issue in 1768 was really much simpler. Up to then, British soldiers in America had been serving militarily, that is, fighting England's and America's mutual enemies: Frenchmen, Indians, Spaniards. The Redcoats sailing to Boston from Halifax and Cork, on the other hand, were coming explicitly to enforce statutes and to maintain law and order, entirely by threat of physical force. It is true that the statutes were so unpopular and the disorders so severe that without the soldiers there would be neither upholding of the one nor suppression of the other. This merely emphasizes and explains the emotion stired by the very idea of troops. The soldiers in 1768 came solely as policemen.[16]

England's experience in this area was a little different. Throughout the late 1760's riots convulsed the country. "The Weavers' mob, the Seamen's mob, the Taylors' mob, the Coal miners' mob." Even London, Benjamin Franklin reported, "is now a daily scene of lawless riot and confusion. Mobs patrolling the streets at noonday, some knocking all down that will not roar for [John] Wilkes and liberty; courts of justice afraid to give judgment against him." Superficially, the English mob rioting resembled the American. "In being riotous," America's friend Isaac Barre told Parliament, "the Colonies have mimicked the mother country." Barre missed the point. Only in England and in Hillsborough's Ireland had soldiers been used against civilians; in Boston, never. On May 10, 1768, soldiers outside the King's Bench prison had fired on a mob demonstrating for John Wilkes, killing several, including a young boy. The Massacre of St. George's Fields, as Wilkes's supporters on both sides of the ocean called the incident, had no Massachusetts parallel.[17]

Gage came closer than Barre to defining the true relationship between the English and American rioters. "The news of the Tumults and Insurrections which have happened in London and Dublin," he wrote Hillsborough, "and in general every Circumstance, which can involve the Mother Country in Difficulty and Distress, is received by the Factions in America, as Events favorable to their Designs of Independency. Hoping that Confusion and Divisions at home, will render any Designs in Government to oppose their Schemes, ineffectual." As a perceptive modern observer has noted, the English in 1767–1768, absorbed with the Wilkes, "Junius," and East India Company crises, paid small attention to the American news. The tidings, they had learned from the Stamp Act troubles, were likely to be bad anyway.[18]

CHAPTER 9

THE OCCUPATION BEGINS

The official, "public" orders which Bernard had so long disclaimed reached him on September 16, a Friday. The day before, he told Captain Corner that he wished himself "away"; he frankly hoped to depart for England on "discretionary leave" within three weeks. Nonetheless he began, in his bumbling way, to tackle the serious question of quarters. The basic issue, simply put, was whether any of the troops would be barracked in Boston proper, as opposed to Castle William, three miles down the harbor but technically within the town. Arguing interminably, sometimes with the council, sometimes with the selectmen, Bernard made no headway against the net of legalisms they threw at him. For a time, it seemed that the troops might never garrison Boston, even if they should make their way ashore, a possibility which Gage, reading Bernard's fretting account, must have appreciated.[1]

While Bernard and the officials debated technical interpretations of the Quartering Act, the radical-dominated town meeting ordered that a day of fast and prayer be celebrated September 20. At the Hollis Street Church, Reverend Mather Byles, Tory and wit, had his congregation sing the hymn "Whence do our mournful thoughts arise? And Where's our courage fled?" Two days later, the convention began. Called for the implicit purpose of opposing the soldiers, it opened just as the Boston militia was completing two days "under arms exercising and firing." By an additional, perhaps countervailing, irony, the day the convention first sat, September 22, was a minor royal holiday, the seventh anniversary of King George's coronation. Inspired by the first circumstance and at least undeterred by the other, seventy delegates gathered in Faneuil Hall, elected former House Speaker Thomas Cushing as chairman and Samuel Adams as clerk. The convention then temporarily adjourned, partly to allow late-chosen members a chance to arrive, partly to permit Adams to arrange the committee work, and partly because "Mr. Otis in the Country much disconcerts them." Troubled by doubts over the course of events, Otis remained away for the first three days of the convention, and did not sit until the meeting of September 26. In his absence, Bernard and the radicals traded communications, an exchange somewhat restricted on the one hand by Bernard's fear of even seeming to recognize the extralegal convention and its consequently illegal acts, and on the other by the convention's refusal to accept any informal message from him. As if to mock the man-made winds, "strong Gales" battered the coast the 23rd and 24th, giving rise to reports that the Halifax squadron had been sunk or dispersed.[2]

Whether because of the moderation of the western delegates, or because of a general realization that condign retribution was indeed nigh, the convention's ultimate "result" or manifesto, although full of snide fleers at lawyer Bernard's legalisticisms, took a surprisingly mild tone. In this it reflected the entire convention. "Otis, when he joined them, was perfectly tame; and his Colleague Addams when he attempted to launch out in the language used in the House of Representatives, was presently silenced." Still, wrote observant Reverend Andrew Eliot, "if the troops arrive before they break up, I will not be bound for their moderation." Eliot's forebodings never came to a test. At 9 P.M., on Tuesday, the 28th, Captain Corner received "certain accounts" that the squadron was off Boston. He sent *Romney's* sailing master and a pilot out to meet it and at 4 A.M. followed himself, boarding H.M.S. *Mermaid* at 8 A.M., about nine miles off Boston Light. Six ships of the flotilla anchored in Nantasket Roads by noon. Ashore, the convention delegates, in John Mein's famous description, "broke up and rushed out of Town like a herd of scalded hogs." [3]

Bernard meanwhile had himself boated out to Castle Island even before the flotilla came to anchor. Lieutenant Colonel Dalrymple, still woozy from the heavy weather the fleet had encountered, met him there and immediately asked for quarters. Bernard responded with a tedious description of his struggle with the council, culminating in an admission that no quarters were available. This performance convinced Dalrymple (and through him, Gage) that the governor "either had not Power to give any [quarters], or would not exercise it"; and that in any event the military could expect little concrete assistance from the civilian administration. Under the circumstances, this was an unfortunate impression to create, because it tended to reinforce the officers' already evident feeling that the army was in Boston not as the governor's servant, but as his independent savior.[4]

As if to convince Dalrymple of his own helplessness, Bernard called a council meeting the next day. The councilors accordingly were ferried out to the Castle, while the remaining three ships of the storm-scattered flotilla came to port. Bernard had invited Dalrymple and Captain James Smith of *Mermaid* (senior naval officer at Boston) to attend the meeting. Dalrymple told the gathering, "in a very genteel manner," that he had been ordered to quarter one regiment in Boston proper and that he would like to have barracks where, with the men under the eyes of their officers, he could guarantee that they would be kept in good order. He hoped, he said, that he was going among friends, and that his men would on their parts behave as such.[5]

The soft approach failed. "After much Altercation," the council fell back on the technicalities of the Quartering Act, insisting also that since Castle William was "in the Town of Boston," Dalrymple could barrack both regiments there and still keep within his instructions. "This idle and futile Argument" drew from Dalrymple only the contemptuous observation that Boston and the Castle "certainly were distinct in his orders; that he was not used to dispute his Orders but obey them & therefore should most certainly march his Regiment into the Town." If barracks were not provided, "he could not be answerable for the good order of his Men, which it would be impossible to preserve if they were intermixed with the Town people and separated from their Officers." Bernard and the council debated the point with their customary loud futility, "and the Council broke up, resolved to make no Provision for the Troops in Boston, on any Pretence." Dalrymple then tried to "stimulate" Bernard to exert his authority, but Bernard continued to insist that he was powerless. Something more than impatience spurred Dalrymple. The longer the delay in bringing the troops ashore, he felt, the greater the chance that the radicals could organize and effectively oppose the landing whenever it might occur.[6]

Fortunately for both Bernard and Dalrymple, the power of decision was soon taken from them. When Bernard arrived at Castle Island the next day, he found awaiting him Gage's staff engineer, Captain John Montresor. Gage, having received private letters from Boston as well as an account of the town meeting, had decided that "the people in & about Boston had revolted." Perhaps it would be more accurate to say that Gage permitted the intelligence to confirm his preconceptions. At any rate, he dispatched Montresor "to assist the Forces as Engineer & to enable them to recover & maintain the Castle and such other Posts as they could secure." Montresor also carried orders directing Dalrymple to put both the regiments, not merely one, in Boston proper.[7]

Dalrymple prepared immediately to move. The Twenty-ninth, which had tents and field equipment, could temporarily encamp on the Common. Bernard, "with some Persuasion," bypassed the council and gave the orders necessary to turn the province-owned Manufactory House over to the Fourteenth. In the harbor, the ships began moving. By the morning of October 1, the men-of-war had ranged themselves off the wharves on the east side of town. As each ship anchored she put a spring on her cable, "a hawser passed out through a stern port and made fast to the anchor cable, so that by hauling in on the spring with the capstan the ship could be swung even though she was stationary, and her guns trained to sweep a different arc at will." This evolution provoked radical ire; the ships, said Paul Revere, maneuvered "as for a regular Siege." But one really cannot fault Captain Smith for taking precautions; it was not so long since Sam Adams had threatened that a 30,000-man army would charge out of the countryside to blast the regulars into the sea.[8]

Thus at noon on October 1, the moment arrived which so many had dreaded and so many others had hoped for. The troops and the artillery began coming ashore, those from the smaller vessels directly down the brows to Long Wharf, the rest in the boats of the fleet. Perhaps because of the visible overwhelming force, "all the threatnings of Opposition vanished," and the soldiers marched brilliantly up King Street with "Drums beating, Fifes playing, and Colours flying." Each regiment followed two banners, on poles ten feet long: the King's Color (the Union Jack), and the yellow-bordered regimental color six-and-a-half by six feet with the regimental number embroidered on a red shield surrounded by roses and thistles.

The red coats of the soldiers and the yellow jackets of the drummers gleamed in the sunlight. Men "of the battalion," the ordinary infantrymen, wore black, white-laced, three-cornered hats. The grenadiers, the tallest men in the regiments, seemed even taller with their distinctive high, mitre-shaped bearskin caps, fronted red, bearing the House of Hanover's white horse badge and motto: *Nec aspera terrent* ["They fear no difficulty"].

The drummers, many of them blacks, wore white bearskin caps with badge and motto. Grenadier officers wore caps like the men, embroidered in gold and silver; officers of the battalion wore the cocked hats, silver-laced. On the chests of all the officers, crescent-shaped silver gorgets shone in the sunlight. They wore crimson sashes over the shoulder; swords on waist belts; and in the hand, the espontoon, or ceremonial half-pike (the grenadier officers carried fusils, carbine-like light muskets). The sergeants, too, wore silver-laced hats and swords. Their sashes were crimson and buff or (for the Twenty-ninth) crimson and yellow; they carried long-shafted ornamental battle axes called halberds.

Past the Custom House the troops marched, past the Town House, on to Queen Street, past the half-built new court house. There, as the Twenty-ninth was passing, the ranks halted briefly. Captain Ponsonby Molesworth stepped to the roadside and leaned casually against a fence. Like many officers, Molesworth bore noble blood. Through his mother, he was related to the Ponsonbys, the great Irish family that included Lord Ponsonby and the Earl of Bessborough. As Molesworth waited for the march to resume, he looked idly at the house across the street, the residence of William Sheaffe, the collector who had fared so ill in the Malcom matter two years before. Attracted by the sounds of the parade, fifteen-year-old Susanna (Sukey) Sheaffe came out on the second-floor balcony. Struck by her beauty, Molesworth stared for several seconds, "That girl seals my fate," he murmured to another officer.

The march resumed, following Queen Street to its end, then left on Treamount Street and past the Old Granary burial ground. By four in the afternoon, the soldiers "were all paraded on the Common." The whole business, as even Bernard admitted, had been "done not only without opposition, but with tolerable good humour." 9

While the troops were landing and marching through town, Dalrymple quickened his search for quarters. The Manufactory House, which Bernard tried to assign the army for barracks, had been built some years earlier to encourage cloth manufacture by providing space for communal spinning. Popular at first, the idea had soon waned, and by 1768 the province was renting the various rooms to private families. The terms of the tenancy were such that Bernard had acted quite legally in turning the manufactory over to the soldiery. But accomplishing the transfer was another matter. Whether or not possession is really nine points of the law, on October 1 it was enough to keep Dalrymple and his soldiers out. The tenants simply refused to budge. Perhaps in this, they did the military a service. As Dalrymple reported somewhat sourly to Gage, the house was "ruinous and unable to contain half the Number of a Regiment." 10

Turning next to the selectmen, Dalrymple, in his own words, "demanded Quarters" for his men. The selectmen promptly replied that housing of the troops was no "Cognisance" of theirs. So, leaving the Twenty-ninth to pitch its tents on the Common, Dalrymple marched the Fourteenth to Faneuil Hall. There, while the troops stood in Dock Square, Dalrymple and the town officials spent two or three hours "in altercation." Finally, "by Dint of some Address," he managed to have

The Bloody Massacre, engraving by Paul Revere after Henry Pelham; courtesy, The Metropolitan Museum of Art, Gift of Mrs. Russell Sage, 1910.

Action and errors fill this famous propaganda piece. From the fictitious "Butcher's Hall" sign to the inaccurate casualty list (neither Monk nor Clark died of his wounds), hardly a detail is correct. Still, it made for superb propaganda, which is why we all remember it. But where is the eighth musketman? And where is Crispus Attucks?

The Liberty Bowl, by Paul Revere; courtesy, Museum of Fine Arts, Boston.

In February 1768, the Massachusetts House of Representatives addressed a circular letter to other legislatures, inviting them to join in a petition to the king seeking repeal of the Townshend Acts. Enraged, the Home Government ordered Governor Bernard to obtain a recision or to dissolve the legislature. When by a 92–17 vote the House refused to rescind, fifteen Sons of Liberty commissioned Paul Revere to fashion a 45-gill bowl of 45 ounces of silver. The original "Paul Revere bowl" thus celebrates transatlantic resistance to government: Number 45 of John Wilkes's *North Briton Review* had attacked the king and provoked a lengthy series of official reprisals.

Samuel Adams (1722–1803), by John Singleton Copley; courtesy, Museum of Fine Arts, Boston.

Copley began this portrait in 1770, not long after the Massacre. Pointing peremptorily toward the Province charter, the Town's Instructions rolled clublike in his right hand, Adams, having put his opponents in the wrong, prepares to keep them there.

Samuel Hood (1724–1816), mezzotint after Lemuel Francis Abbott; courtesy, National Maritime Museum, Greenwich, England.

Shown here as an Admiral and earl, Hood commanded the North American station as a commodore during 1767–1770. He got on well with the radicals, but it was at his orders that H.M.S. Rose began the impressment cruise that led to violent death aboard the Pitt Packet.

Joseph Warren (1741–1775), by John Singleton Copley; courtesy, Museum of Fine Arts, Boston.

Medical man, radical leader, and polemicist, Warren served the Whig cause brilliantly in all three capacities until he died with a bullet in his brain at Bunker Hill.

John Temple (1732–1798), by John Singleton Copley; courtesy, Dr. Irving Levitt and the Detroit Institute of Arts.

Bostonian by birth, and a long-time revenue officer, Temple was the only one of the five Customs Commissioners to win any local popularity. But although he married a daughter of the radical leader James Bowdoin, Temple did not desert the royal cause. He was later knighted and became the first British Consul General in the United States (1785).

Grenadier private, Twenty-ninth Regiment, 1769, from Everard, *History of . . . 29th [Regiment]*.

Taken from a contemporary drawing, this sketch shows how Corporal Wemms' men looked the night of March 5, 1770, in their high bearskin caps, bayonets fixed on their "Brown Bess" flintlocks.

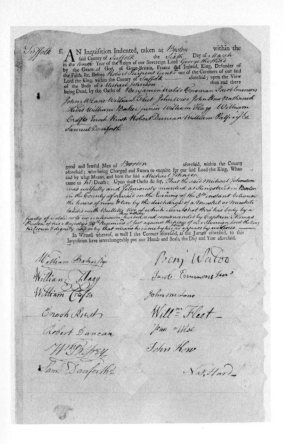

Inquest on a Victim of the Boston Massacre, 1770; courtesy, the Bostonian Society.

It was the coroner's duty, aided by a special "jury," to examine any corpse, hear testimony if necessary, and report the cause of death. The day after the Massacre, even before the soldiers' names were known, a coroner's jury, which included the radicals William Palfrey and Samuel Danforth, viewed the remains of "Michael Johnson" and concluded that he had died from two musket bullets "which were shot thro' his body." Not until some hours later was Michael Johnson identified as Crispus Attucks.

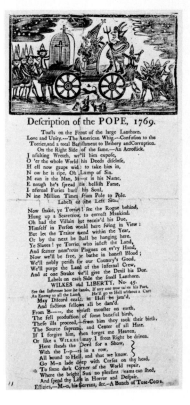

Broadside, 1769; courtesy, New-York Historical Society.

Boston traditionally celebrated November 5 (Guy Fawkes Day) in an orgy of anti-Catholicism and brawling. The central figure was a wheeled effigy, "the Pope," illuminated, surrounded with lesser figures, and covered with appropriate rough verse. The 1769 Pope featured political, rather than religious, sentiment, much of it directed against John Mein, the printer run out of town by a mob the week before.

Corporal, Fourteenth Regiment, 1770, taken from Barnes, *Military Uniforms of Britain & the Empire;* courtesy, Seeley Service & Co. Ltd., London (publishers).

The tricorne hat means that this is a soldier of the battalion, i.e., not a grenadier; he holds the familiar "Brown Bess" flintlock musket (.760-inch bore, 44-inch-long barrel).

James Otis (1725–1783) by Joseph Black-burn; courtesy, Mrs. Carlos P. Hepp.

Jeremiah Gridley and John Adams were better book lawyers than Otis, and Josiah Quincy probably his courtroom superior. But for all-around legal ability, Otis, when his mind was right, had no equal. High-strung and virtually an alcoholic, Otis found fewer and fewer opportunities to display his forensic and literary brilliance. He had threatened to set the Province in a blaze or perish in the attempt. His argument against the Writs of Assistance lit the flame; a lightning bolt ended his manic genius in 1783.

Charles Paxton (1704?–1788), by J. Cornish; courtesy, the American Antiquarian Society.

One of the two Boston-born Customs Commissioners, Paxton drew the anger and contempt of his townsmen. His unswerving devotion to the royal revenue ensured his banishment when the War began. He never lost his affection for Boston, however; in 1779 he told his fellow exile, Thomas Hutchinson, that he would give 100 guineas to be buried near his parents under King's Chapel, Boston.

Graves of the "Martyrs" of 1770 and of Samuel Adams; photograph by Thomas F. Maffei, courtesy, the photographer.

Under one stone in Boston's Old Granary Burial Ground lie Christopher Seider (Snider)—the young victim of Richardson's fear —and the five men who fell in King Street. A few feet away, the same sod covers Samuel Adams, who made of the six corpses more than ever they could have been in life.

John Adams (1735–1826), by Benjamin Blyth; courtesy, the Massachusetts Historical Society.

Short, plump, intelligent, and lawyerlike, John Adams was marked for professional pre-eminence from his first days of practice. By 1766, when this portrait was painted, he was well on his way to the head of the bar, and to leadership in the radical party. The great political-criminal cases of 1768–1770 sped his way to both positions.

Plaque Commemorating the Boston Massacre; photograph by Stephen W. Plimpton, courtesy, the Bostonian Society.

It is one of the many ironies of the Massacre that the tablet supposedly marking its location was until recently fixed firmly to a building across the street from the site of the shooting. Demolition of the structure will permit accurate relocation of the plaque.

Robert Treat Paine (1731–1814), statue by Richard A. Brooks; photograph by Emmet Calvey, courtesy, the photographer.

This twentieth-century statue well captures the Paine John Adams knew: "[A]n impudent, ill-bred, conceited fellow. Yet he has Witt, sense, and Learning, and a great deal of Humour, and has Virtue and Piety except his fretful, peevish, Childish Complaints against the Disposition of Things." After a series of brief careers as schoolkeeper, merchant, whaler, and chaplain, Paine, as he wrote in his diary, "was wedded to a Lady of great birth and parentage; her maiden name was Law." Paine's lackluster performance in the Massacre trials suggests that the marriage was not particularly successful. The independence crisis rescued him from mediocrity: he served in Congress; signed the Declaration; became Massachusetts Attorney-General; and sat on the Commonwealth's Supreme Judicial Court.

one of the doors opened, and began bedding down the Fourteenth. By 9 P.M., all of the men were in the hall. On his first day in garrison, Dalrymple had secured not only the Cradle of Liberty, but the 400 town muskets, still standing on the floor.[11]

Even as temporary quarters, Faneuil Hall was inadequate. The next day, Bernard arranged to make the entire Town House (except for the council chamber) available, and Dalrymple moved the Faneuil Hall overflow there immediately, quartering some of the men in the very room where the House of Representatives usually sat. The sight and sound of soldiers tramping through the center of town on a Sunday to occupy the seat of self-government distressed the people and added to their animosity. In the face of the overwhelming military and naval force they were of course helpless, at least temporarily. But the rage and frustration bubbled. It would take more than the romantics of a Captain Molesworth to overcome their corrosion.[12]

Bernard still remained unable to solve the problem of quarters. He realized, as did everyone, that the Twenty-ninth could not spend a Boston winter in tents on the Common; nor could the Fourteenth long remain on the drafty floors of Faneuil Hall and the Town House. Further, when the Irish regiments arrived, they too would require suitable quarters. The Castle would hold only one regiment at most, "and that, by putting twelve men in a Room of Eighteen Feet Square." Bernard talked of having "a few Companies sent to Salem and Newbury," but that would not really help. Dalrymple, for his part, tried to press the governor and council to action. If the province did not supply quarters, as the military men thought it should, only two choices remained: rent private facilities at the expense of the crown; or commandeer uninhabited houses, outbuildings, barns, or other structures. Naturally reluctant to follow the first course, the officers dreaded the second. The Quartering Act specified bluntly that any officer who took upon himself to quarter soldiers in any way other than provided by the act, or who used "Menace or Compulsion," would, upon conviction before two justices of the peace, "be ipso facto cashiered, and . . . utterly disabled to have or hold any military Employment." Although Gage may have been exaggerating slightly when he complained that in "this Country, where every man studys Law, and interprets the Law as suits his Purposes," an "Officer of Rank and long Service may be cashiered, by the Management of two Justices of the Peace, the best of them a keeper of a paltry Tavern," there was no doubt that any officer trying to quarter troops ran a real risk of losing his commission.[13]

None of these considerations, nor the personal, blunt intervention of Dalrymple himself in the council's deliberations, affected the councilors. The officers, it is true, were beginning to find quarters. Captain

Brabazon O'Hara and Major Jonathan Furlong of the Fourteenth each leased a house from John Rowe; Dalrymple rented lodgings on Green's Lane (south of the present-day intersection of Congress and Milk streets). But the troops remained unhoused. Mischief began to develop. On the night of October 9, "some Villains cut the Frame of the Guard House so as to Render it useless." The men were beginning to desert. Within the first two weeks, Hutchinson reported, seventy men had deserted; Andrew Eliot thought only forty, but added, "no one will betray them." Indeed, some people, it was said, were actively encouraging desertions.

Provocations went in the other direction, too. On the night of October 28, Captain John Wilson of the Fifty-ninth drunkenly accosted a group of Negro slaves. Struck perhaps at the incongruity of slavery in the midst of a populace so outspoken in its love of liberty, Wilson urged the blacks to take direct action. "Go home," he shouted, "and cut your Masters Throats; Ill treat your masters, & come to me to the parade; & I will make you free, & if any person opposeth you, I will run my Sword thro' their Hearts." Drunk or sober, Wilson had touched a tender nerve. In short order he found himself before Justice Richard Dana, who placed him under bond to appear at the March superior court. The selectmen, meanwhile, passed orders to the town watchmen "to see that good Order is observ'd in the Night, and that they take up all Negroes whom they shall find abroad at an unseasonable Hour."

"The present disposition," said Eliot, "is to treat *them, the troops,* with civility, but to provide nothing." This was not universally true. Observing that the soldiers were "destitute of Camp Equipage and unprovided with every requisite for dressing their Provisions," a baker named William Hill arranged to have this service performed for them in his own household. Shortly thereafter, he became the Fourteenth's official baker.[14]

In New York, Gage was growing impatient. He wanted prompt compliance with the law, without what he considered needless technicality. "Considering what is passed," he wrote Bernard, "how short a time it is Since, that a Resolution was taken to rise in Arms in Open Rebellion; I Don't See any cause to be Scrupulous in doing what is Judged Absolutely Necessary for the Service, and for the Security of the King's Government." Even these exhortations induced no progress, and Gage decided to go up to Boston to intervene personally. Arriving with his staff on Saturday, October 15, Gage received a 17-gun salute from the Artillery detachment, and then reviewed the troops; they "were under arms & made a Good Appearance." The following Monday, Bernard called a council meeting and introduced Gage, who shortly demanded in-town quarters for the troops, and then withdrew, leaving Bernard to stay till 8 P.M. ("2 Hours at Dinner time excepted") wrangling with the council. Determined not to furnish quarters, the radical majority pelted Bernard with reasons justifying refusal, before finally agreeing, six votes to five, that the troops could have that same Manufactory House which Bernard had previously been unable to secure for them.[15]

Pleased with his conciliar success and convinced that the law was with him, Bernard sent Sheriff Greenleaf and two deputies to clear the building of its temporary occupants, "the outcasts of the Workhouse and the scum of the Town." Encouraged, perhaps, by the radicals, the tenants still refused to leave. On hearing this, Bernard asked Hutchinson to go back with Greenleaf and try to persuade them to move. Speaking both as lieutenant governor and as chief justice, Hutchinson explained to the tenants that they were legally obliged to leave; they replied that lawyers had advised them the law was otherwise. Greenleaf gave up. A few days later, however, having arranged for some military support, he returned surreptitiously, located an unbarred window, and let himself into the cellar. The tenants soon discovered him, surrounded him, and locked him up. A hasty hand-signal brought the soldiers from the nearby Common, but all they could secure was the yard and Greenleaf's release before they in turn were surrounded by a growing mob. The crowd cursed the soldiers loudly, although offering no physical abuse, and allowed the troops to blockade the building for two days. When it became obvious that the siege was failing, the council disclaimed the use of force; the troops were withdrawn. Modulated popular violence had thus effectively prevented the government from making official use of a government building. Well might Gage, sitting for his portrait before John Copley's easel, conclude that the town was "under a kind of Democratical Despotism" and that as to "Government in Boston," there was "in Truth very little at present." There were also still no customs commissioners. Gage asked them about their return, and received for reply an acknowledgment of the troops' presence and a request to identify the "Civil officer who would undertake to ask the assistance of the Troops, if there shoud be occasion for it." Gage could not say, and neither could Hutchinson or Bernard, both of whom stood silently by. The commissioners, Andrew Eliot agreed, "are so much the objects of popular odium that they will be in actual danger if they go without their guards." Meanwhile, commissioner John Temple felt secure enough to hold his son's christening in Christ Church. This commonplace religious event presented a political paradox, for although young Grenville Temple's maternal grandfather was James Bowdoin, the radical who led the council's refusal to quarter the troops, one of his godfathers was General Gage.[16]

As the October days shortened, Bernard kept up his battle with the council and the Boston justices. Technicality followed evasion, and wrangling succeeded argument, until at last, on October 26, the twenty-eight-day battle ended in "the definitive refusal." Gage had not hung on so long as Bernard. The cold weather was coming fast, and the out-of-barrack troops continued to desert. In an effort to lower the desertion rate, Gage had approved the sentence of a court martial on Private Richard Ames of the Fourteenth. At 7 A.M., on October 31, before both regiments and such of the public as cared to attend, Ames faced a firing squad. Still, the only real way to hold the men was to get them into military quarters. On October 27, the regiments began moving into leased warehouses and stores, and soon were established in a roughly circular area centered on the Custom House. Two companies of the Twenty-ninth, for example, occupied the sugar warehouse on Brattle Street owned by James Murray and James Smith, while some of the regiment's younger officers lived in a nearby house. The artillery detachment and the unit of the Fifty-ninth went into warehouses on Griffin's Wharf (future site of the Boston Tea Party) and Wheelwright's Wharf. Space on this latter, despite Otis's prediction that no one would ever let property to the army, was furnished at £25 sterling per month by William Molineux himself.[17]

Even though the radicals had completely thwarted Bernard's attempt to require provincial compliance with the Quartering Act, they had not finished with him on that issue. When the army began occupying the newly rented quarters, the radicals threatened any officer who put troops in the barracks with the cashiering proviso of the act. To avoid this clause, it was necessary to have a justice of the peace formally certify the appropriateness of hiring private quarters; but no justice would dare risk the popular wrath by attending to this formality. A dangerous impasse loomed, which Bernard resolved by appointing a civilian straw to "place" the troops in the barracks, and thus spare the officers from the legal onus of having done so. The entire bitter experience of the quartering battle had thoroughly alienated Bernard from the council. He devoted quantities of time, paper, and ink to urging Hillsborough that future councilors should be appointed by the crown directly, to hold their offices during the king's pleasure.[18]

Whatever Bernard's private sentiments, he accommodated himself to a situation which, he hoped, might well improve with time. The troops had arrived and been quartered. Although the regiments from Ireland had not arrived, they were expected daily; barracks had been already leased, so that there would be no chance of duplicating the October fiasco. "Everything," Gage wrote Hillsborough, "now has the appearence of Peace and Quiet in this Place." The general and his staff relaxed at a large soiree where the company included, besides Lieutenant Colonels Dalrymple and Carr, Captain Molesworth, Captain Thomas Preston of the Twenty-ninth, conservative merchants Philip Dumaresq and James Forrest, and the radically inclined selectman, John Rowe. The commissioners, however, had not yet made their official reappearance, although Rowe saw John Robinson in town on November 9.[19]

Despite their absence, the commissioners had been able to stimulate commencement of the ill-fated personal proceedings against Hancock, Malcom, and four others concerned in the *Liberty* incident. The sum involved was immense, £9,000 treble damages; Hancock was required to post security of £3,000 sterling. It is sufficient commentary on Hancock's financial standing that he was able to find this amount in hard-money–short Massachusetts. Attacking such a large target boosted Tory morale, though the radicals, and later their English friends, called the prosecution "irregular & groundless." "The Honor of the Crown is like to be in some Measure vindicated," said Bernard. Gage "hoped this Example will encourage the Civil officers of every Degree to do their Duty without Fear, and to curb effectively the Licentious and Seditious Spirit, which has so long prevailed in this Place." It is indicative of the discoordination which characterized British policy-making, and perhaps Hillsborough's own weak grasp of the Boston situation, that when he received Gage's letter, the Earl confessed himself "entirely ignorant of the grounds" of the prosecution and "the names of the persons prosecuted."[20]

Hancock's case highlighted what Bernard had come to realize was a serious sub-problem to the larger issue of law-enforcement. The attorney-general's function included only the drawing up of indictments and the court presentation of criminal matters. It was not his business "to prepare Prosecutions by procuring Informations and Evidence." In other words, he was strictly a litigator, not an investigator. Any investigative services would produce no fee, and "by being unpopular must prejudice him in his other Business." This latter was an important point, since the attorney-generalship was not a full-time, salaried position; the office carried a small emolument, but it was understood that the occupant would maintain his own private practice. Moreover, "what little pittance of Salary or Pay he gets is from the People," which made the attorney-general even less likely to risk investigating popular wrongdoers. Besides, were an attorney-general to try to work up the facts of a case, "he has not the Means to perform it, there being no Fund from which Money can be drawn to pay for private Intelligence, without which Prosecutions of this kind are generally defeated." The customs commissioners, on the other hand, "wanting [i.e., lacking] not Money to go to Work with, have procured a full discovery of some of the late high-handed Breaches of the Laws of Trade," and hoped (vainly, it turned out) to use the evidence to good advantage against Hancock and his associates in the admiralty prosecutions.[21]

As Bernard was perceptive enough to realize, "the Part which the Lawyers take in Disputes concerning civil Rights is of no little Importance to Government." He thought the best way to secure the political affections of the province's outstanding legal talent would be the establishment, by crown payment, of three "standing Council," namely, attorney-general, solicitor-general, and advocate-general. This, he felt, "would have made the principal Lawyers look towards the Crown, whereas now they generally turn towards the People." Bernard had, he said, "private Intimations from Gentlemen of the Law of their Inclination to quit the Cause of the People for that of the Crown; but now the latter is thought the losing Game, the former the winning one." [22]

Bernard did not identify the lawyers, and it may be that he was indulging his penchant for overstatement. Still, we know that the commissioners felt the Hancock prosecution "was not conducted with that Vigor and Spirit which the Service required." When Sewall resigned as advocate-general to accept an absentee-type vice-admiralty judgeship at Halifax, Bernard tried to press the office on John Adams. Adams had just moved from Quincy to a white house in Brattle Square, near the barracks. Although only thirty-three, he was already marked as "likely to make a shining figure at the bar." "He has a large practice," Reverend Andrew Eliot noted, "and I am mistaken if he will not soon be at the head of his profession." By anybody's standards, he was one of what Bernard called the "principal Lawyers." The office now proffered him would, as he realized, be "a sure introduction to the most profitable Business in the Province." But he turned it down, because, as he said, he did not want to lay himself "under any restraints, or Obligations of Gratitude to the Government for any of their favours." [23]

CHAPTER 10

TRUMPETS OF SEDITION

The transports carrying the Sixty-fourth and Sixty-fifth Regiments began arriving on November 10; more came November 13 and 15, although the storm-delayed *Dolphin* did not moor until November 25. Captain Parker's frigate *Hussar* had been blown into New York, while the transport *Raven*, carrying Major General Mackay and more troops, lost her foremast and main topmast, and ran south before the wind as far as the West Indies; she did not reach Boston until April 30, 1769. Disembarkation of the November arrivals proceeded in smooth contrast to the earlier friction. A detachment of the Sixty-fifth took over the Castle, and the rest went quietly into town quarters. The last Halifax troops arrived in early December: "the remains of the 14th, 29th, and part of the 59th Regiments, including a Number of Women &c. belonging to the Army." Some of the married enlisted men rented quarters for their families in private homes. Grenadier James Hartigan of the Twenty-ninth and his wife Elisabeth took lodgings on King Street. Hugh Montgomery, another grenadier in the same regiment, leased space for his wife Isabella and their three children in a North End house owned by radical Councilor Royall Tyler.[1]

On November 13, *Romney* had returned from Halifax, flying Commodore Hood's broad pendant. With *Mermaid*, *Rose*, *Viper*, and *Beaver*, she was "unrigg'd" preparatory to wintering in Boston. Hood, a seasoned naval officer with years of experience on the North American station, had "a great character," i.e., reputation, and, despite the symbolism of his fleet's presence in the harbor, soon established a warm

connection with the Boston Whigs, particularly James Bowdoin. The
day of Hood's arrival, the commissioners and their officers attended
church, their first public appearance. They resumed regular activities,
making no attempt to mollify popular resentment. A month later,
when John Rowe went to see them on business, "their High Mighti-
nesses" insolently kept him waiting "from twelve till almost three." But
Rowe's sputtering rage at "this Behaviour of theirs" did not prevent his
attending the fortnightly Assembly honoring the commissioners. The
Assembly, at which sixty couples danced, was said to be "the best
there is in all America," and forced the Whigs to set up their own ball,
"the Liberty Assembly," "in Opposition." [2]

Generally, as Hutchinson put it, "short quiet succeeded long disturbance." Unused to the troops, afraid of them, and above all, still largely
unaware that the military could not use force until requested by civilian authority, the townspeople remained gloomy, uneasy, but tranquil.
General Gage and his staff left for New York on November 24, satisfied
that Boston was secure. Dispatches from Boston for the rest of the winter continued to describe the town as "quiet" or even "perfectly quiet."
Despite their "raptures at the *cheapness* of spirituous liquors," the
troops, awed by the severe army discipline, behaved themselves. General John Pomeroy and Hood, "prudent, discreet men," kept the situation under good control. But because Boston was not used to a quasi-
permanent garrison, popular discontent grew, encouraged, Bernard
thought, by certain unnamed justices of the peace. These magistrates
granted warrants "against soldiers for obeying orders and doing
their duty" and threatened prosecutions against the military people for
profaning the Sabbath by changing the guard on Sunday. Hutchinson
described the growing tension accurately and perceptively:

> Though the people had been used to answer to the call of the town
> watch in the night, yet they did not like to answer to the frequent
> calls of the centinels posted at the barracks, and at the gates of the
> principal officers, in different quarters of the town; and either a re-
> fusal to answer, or an answer accompanied with irritating language,
> endangered the peace of the town.[3]

Daytime military activities, too, galled Boston. Years later, John
Adams recalled the annoyance of having a body of troops paraded
daily for exercise in Brattle Square outside his house, waking the family with "the Spirit Stirring Drum, and the Earpiercing fife." In an effort to ease the tension, Pomeroy rescheduled the Sunday guard relief
so as not to interfere with church services; and he reduced the number
of challenge points. This last innovation met with enough success to
stimulate a story that no sentry would so much as challenge a house-

breaker seen *in flagrante delictu,* because to raise the alarm might (contrary to orders) deprive a man of his liberty. The navy operated under no such restraint. On December 5, Captain Sir Thomas Rich of H.M. Sloop *Senegal* stirred old feelings when he "pressed all Capt. Dashwood's hands." [4]

The pressure slowly mounted in Boston; in London, the king, lords, and Commons considered ways to end the near-treason. All through December, January, and into February the discussions went on. Finally, on February 13, 1769, both Houses presented an address to the throne recommending that the governor be directed to obtain full information of "all treasons, or misprision of treason" committed in Massachusetts since December 30, 1767, and to transmit the information and the names of the principal offenders to Whitehall, so that a commission could issue under Henry VIII's treason statute and the accused be brought to England for trial. But the same ships which carried the grim news to Boston also brought private correspondence from the radicals' English friends assuring them that the fearsome statute was being held up *in terrorem* only, and that in fact the administration planned no vigorous measures.[5]

Through the winter Boston continued calm. At 10 P.M., the night of January 30, three "notorious thieves" in the new jail on Queen Street (including a soldier named Bryan Donnelly) tried a risky means of escape: they set the prison on fire. "The Fire got to such a height before it was discovered, that the Flames spread rapidly through every Apartment & in a few hours entirely consumed the same, leaving nothing standing but the bare Walls." The conflagration roused townsfolk and garrison. Soldiers and sailors joined the citizens and, in selectman John Rowe's frank opinion, saved the town by their exertions. The next day he personally waited on Pomeroy and Carr to thank them. Even the radical Boston *Gazette* conceded that the army and navy contingents and their officers "were very serviceable in assisting and relieving the inhabitants." [6]

The *Gazette*'s acknowledgment was only a shrub of civility in a desert of journalistic opposition. Starting in mid-October, the radicals had begun "the most sustained effort to spread ideas through news items that was made in the entire twenty years" before the Revolution. Cast in the mold of a daily report, the "Journal of the Times" first appeared in New York. Later it spread to newspapers as far south as Georgia. It even ran in London. Late in December, the Boston papers began to print the items. Composed by Samuel Adams and others, including (Bernard thought) at least one councilor, the "Journal" retailed horrifying accounts of the way the soldiers were supposedly behaving toward the townsfolk. "If the Devil himself were one of the party," moaned Bernard "as he virtually is, there could not have been got together a greater Collection of impudent virulent and seditious Lies, perversions of truth and misrepresentations than are to be found in this publication." Exposing the falsehoods, however, did no good: "If a Lie does but answer the purpose of the day," Bernard said, "they are perfectly unconcerned at the future detection of it; and when the falsity is made apparent, they stand wholly unabashed." "To set about answering these falsities would be a Work like that of Cleansing Augeas's Stables," he concluded, and proposed "bringing in a Stream strong enough to sweep away the Dirt and Collectors of it altogether." [7]

Adams showed his usual shrewdness in starting the "Journal" elsewhere than at Boston. Obviously, as even Bernard could understand, Adams aimed "to raise a general Clamour against His Majesty's Government in England and throughout America as well as in Massachusetts Bay," thus to force removal of the troops and warships. But Adams had a short-range objective also. He crammed the "Journal" with "[e]very little insignificant fact relative to the troops, which was not thought worthy of notice, or made no impression, if known." By the time the original articles returned to Boston for republication, there remained only "a general remembrance of the fact, so as to make the aggravations more easily received. Many false reports, which had been confuted, were mixed with true reports, and some pretended facts of an enormous nature were published, of which so much as the rumour could not be remembered." What use was Hutchinson's warning to his correspondents that "Nine tenths of what you read of the Journal of Occurrences in Boston is either absolutely false or grossly misrepresented"? To what end did Bernard call for the Home Government to punish Edes and Gill, those "trumpeters of sedition"? The paper, as Hutchinson admitted, "had a very great effect. A story of a fictitious quarrel incensed the lower part of the people, and brought on a real quarrel." [8]

The troops, although insulted and harassed individually, in small parties, even while on parade, and figuratively pelted during their off hours by warrants, writs, and indictments, remained nonetheless patiently submissive. Adams, knowing of Bernard's belief that it was the radicals who stirred the cauldron, chided the governor and his party for not being able to "endure the thoughts of not having their own prophecies fulfilled, their misrepresentations successful, and their malevolence gratified." Then, in a characteristic maneuver, he proceeded to enunciate his own brand of self-fulfilling prophecy: "One man has as good reason to affirm, that a few, in calling for a military force under pretence of supporting civil authority, secretly intended to introduce a general massacre, as another has to assert, that a number of loyal subjects, by calling upon one another to be provided with arms, according to law, intended to bring on an insurrection." [9]

The "conspiracy" theory underlay Adams's revolutionary philosophy and to a degree shaped his course of action. "There was," he constantly reminded his Boston readers, "a cursed Cabal, principally residing in this town, who having been disappointed in their expectations of the sweets of the stamp act, were perpetually intriguing to bring about another parliamentary tax act; for no other purpose than that they might feast and fatten themselves upon the spoils and plunder of the people." John Adams, too, believed that a "conspiracy," "regularly formed," had been in execution since 1763. If the Stamp Act and the Townshend duties owed their birth to these greedy plotters—a contention which such incidents as the Bernard-Cockle affair had only strengthened—then clearly the troops had likewise been called in, not merely to serve as peace-enforcers, but to further a calculated attack on Massachusetts' fundamental liberties. [10]

This explanation of the current oppression offered two main propaganda advantages: a visible hate figure; and an underlying truth. It was much easier to whip up rage at a Bernard or (later) a Hutchinson than at the vague and distant "Ministry." By concentrating their fire on Bernard, the radicals avoided having to attack the government and, more important, the king. Further, royal policy in Massachusetts was indeed coming more and more to be executed (and, to the extent that American advices played any part in shaping London's attitudes, formulated) by Bernard's so-called "Cabinet Council": Hutchinson, Secretary Andrew Oliver, and Admiralty Judge Auchmuty. The two advantages coalesced unpleasantly in early April 1769, when, through the assistance of a friendly member of Parliament, the Boston radicals obtained and published copies of six reports Bernard had sent to Lord Hillsborough. "In the Mean time," Bernard complained, "they have been read by the whole Town at the Printers," producing, in John Rowe's words, "great noise & censure." [11]

Here was another brilliant example of putting one's enemy in the wrong and keeping him there. Bernard, after all, was not being pilloried for his perfectly proper consultations with Oliver, Hutchinson, and Auchmuty. The friction now was made to arise from what the radicals insisted was his over-candid reporting of minor items and his abuse of the council. Bowdoin, indeed, seized on Bernard's epistolary style to accuse Bernard of trying to establish himself in the "character" of a "Dictator." [12]

Bernard found all this incomprehensible. He was convinced, and had been since the customs battles of 1761, that the merchants and some of the less reliable revenue officers were trying to cripple the tax laws, and that Adams and the Sons of Liberty were aiming to subvert royal authority generally. Knowing the activities of the Loyal Nine and the controlled mob, can one call him wrong? Perhaps, indeed, it was Adams's design to cover his own plotting by constantly "revealing" Bernard's. Whatever his reasoning, Adams's strategy, added to Bernard's ineptness, combined to rob the governor of his last shreds of effective power. The administration conferred a baronetcy on him, and he did not leave the province until August. But by April 1769, "the Nettleham Baronet," as the Whigs scornfully dubbed him, had ceased to be anything more than an impotent, provocative symbol.[13]

CHAPTER 11

DEATH BEFORE
IMPRESSMENT

Before the weary Bernard could leave (or escape) his soured government, another crisis challenged him. Hood's squadron had "suffered greatly by Desertion in the course of the Winter," and recruiting in England was hampered by the service's inability to compete with the wage scales on merchant ships, East Indiamen, and whalers. The commodore had consequently authorized selective impressment from Boston-bound ships. On April 3, he ordered H.M. Schooner *Hope* and H.M. Frigate *Rose* to "Cruise between Cape Ann & Cape Codd from three to ten Leagues distant from the Light House," thus blockading the entrance to Massachusetts Bay.[1]

> And from every Ship or Vessel from a foreign Port [Hood's orders continued] you will take a good man or two, according to the number on board, sending a man from the *Rose* in the room of each that you take, if it is agreeable to the Master; and when your Compliment is Compleat, and you have raised Ten in Addition, you will send them to me by the *Hope* Schooner.

Well aware of the sensitive business he was about, Hood cautioned restraint and politeness:

> And I recommend it to you not to distress any Ship or Vessel, & to guard your Officers against being in a passion, or making use of Language any ways unbecoming; who on their visiting a Ship or Vessel, are to ask if any men are inclined to enter for the Kings Service, and

if all refuse, I wish the man (or men) to be taken the Master is most willing to part with, rather than a favourite, provided he is not distempered. This the Master of each Ship or Vessel is to be told, and whenever a man is taken without sending another in his room, I would have a note given, that the ship in Nantasket Road may be prevented from taking another from the same Vessel. . . . You will continue upon this service till further orders, & cautiously avoid taking a man belonging to, or married in, this Province.[2]

Rose, a 20-gun frigate, normally carried a complement of 120 officers and seamen, plus 24 marines. Her thirty-year-old captain, Dublin-born Benjamin Caldwell, had held his command since April 19, 1768. An alumnus of the Royal Academy at Portsmouth, which one admiral later called "a sink of vice and abomination," Caldwell owed his present appointment to the Bessborough-Molesworth connection, part of Ponsonby Molesworth's family. Having joined the ship at the Sheerness dockyard, where she was fitting out under the temporary command of her lieutenant (i.e., executive officer), Henry Gibson Panton, Caldwell set about completing the ship's company. He arranged the appointment of another Dubliner, John Forbes, as master-at-arms. Thirty years old, seasoned, and rugged, Forbes seemed well qualified for his role as *Rose*'s chief disciplinarian. Caldwell also caused four "young gentlemen" whom he regarded as being under his special care to be entered on the ship's muster list. They included fourteen-year-old Henry Stanhope, of fashionable Mortimer Street, Cavendish Square, London, a cousin to the famous Lord Chesterfield. Ranging in age from twelve to eighteen, the boys served as midshipmen, although carried on the ship's books as "Master's mate," or even "Captains servant." Because *Rose* was not large enough to rate any commissioned officers besides Caldwell and Panton, it was the young midshipmen and the warrant officers like Forbes who stood the watches and supervised the lower-deck hands. There *Rose* was having problems; on June 28 when she dropped down to the Nore to begin sea victualing, six men deserted.[3]

By August 13, although she could muster only 89 effectives and 22 marines, *Rose* was ready for sea. That afternoon, William Shirley, governor of Massachusetts from 1741 to 1756, his wife, and six servants came aboard for transportation to a new assignment in the Bahamas. *Rose* immediately "weighed and came to sail." But the same storms which had scattered the Boston-bound transports blocked her track; it was not until October 19 that she reached Nassau, and November 27 Boston, with a sprung bowsprit and "other Damage." *Rose* did not put to sea again until 7 A.M. on April 13, when she left Boston harbor under the commodore's blockade-and-impress orders.[4]

Three hours after sailing, *Rose* halted a Boston-bound brig from Bristol, boarded her, and pressed John Eagleson, twenty-eight, of Cape Fear, North Carolina. Later that day, another boarding party pressed an Englishman, Charles Raynsford, twenty-two, of Greenwhich, Kent. And so it went for over a week, *Rose* sailing up and down across the mouth of the bay, stopping what vessels she could, which was not always easy, and impressing men from each, which was not easy, either —when *Rose* bore after a Glasgow-Boston snow, the merchantman's second mate and six crewmen took a boat and rowed successfully away to shore. If *Rose* did find seamen to press, Caldwell usually sent an equivalent number of his own hands "in lieu," as Hood had ordered. But the exchanges were only temporary, designed merely to enable the merchant ship to reach a Massachusetts harbor. That accomplished, the Navy men would leave the merchantman and await transportation back to *Rose*.[5]

Not until April 20 did anything out of the ordinary happen. At 4:30 that morning, Surgeon John Rice died, apparently from illness. Thirty-year-old Robert Brice, the Scottish surgeon's mate, assumed his late chief's duties. On Friday, April 21, at 10 A.M., Caldwell read the burial service over Rice, and at noon read the Articles of War to the assembled ship's company, a necessary preliminary to the administration of punishment. Samuel Stannas received "a Dozen Lashes for Swearing." [6]

All Friday night, *Rose* sailed on a northeasterly course in westerly and fresh northwesterly breezes and clear weather. Around midnight, she passed five or six leagues (about fifteen miles) to the east of Boston light. With the dawn, a sail came in sight a point or so off the starboard bow. *Rose* immediately gave chase. By 7 A.M., she had closed sufficiently to identify the stranger as a brig and to fire a warning swivel. The brig maintained her course, so Caldwell ordered a second swivel shot, and then a shot from one of the forward 12-pounders. By 8 A.M., *Rose* was within hailing distance. In response to instructions which Caldwell shouted through his speaking trumpet, the brig finally came to under the lee of *Rose*'s starboard side, with her head paralleling the warship's.[7]

Quickly Caldwell ordered *Rose*'s cutter cleared and hoisted out. Into her he sent Panton, Midshipmen Stanhope and Peter Bowen (another of Caldwell's "young gentlemen"), and seven seamen, including the recently impressed Raynsford. The oarsmen soon brought the cutter alongside the brig, where the mate tossed them a line. As the boarding party gained the deck, Panton faced three men, a seaman, the mate, and Captain Thomas Power of the brig *Pitt Packet*, owned by Robert Hooper of Marblehead. Known as "King" Hooper to his envious countrymen, Hooper possessed one of the most ample fortunes in Massachusetts, a fortune which Captain Power was then increasing to the extent of a full cargo of Cadiz salt, a small amount of wine and champagne, three kegs of gin, and 600 lemons.[8]

Cargo, however, did not seem to be Lieutenant Panton's chief concern. Although he asked Power for the ship's papers, he took scant notice of the bill of lading and the bill of health which the captain handed him. How many men did Power have on board, Panton asked. Six before the mast, the master replied, besides himself and the mate, not counting James McGlocklin, the cook. Panton paused for a moment, an imposing figure in his blue coat with white lapels and cuffs, and his plain white, gilt-buttoned waistcoat. Then, unbuckling his sword belt and placing belt, scabbard, and sword on the companion leading to Power's cabin, he asked the master to take him and the two midshipmen below.[9]

In the cramped cabin, Bowen and Stanhope watched while Panton demanded first the brig's log book, then writing materials. Carefully copying the names of the crewmen, he told Power to say if he had any particular crewman for whom he wanted a favor done, so that Panton could mark his list and not take the man. Power said that he had one man who was married and that it would be "very hard" to take him. By no means, Panton replied, would he take any such man, for he had orders to take "none that was married." But he did want to be sure that Power had no other hands save those listed. If he found more aboard, it would, he said, be the worse for the captain. Then he went back on deck with the midshipmen.

Hugh Hill, *Pitt Packet*'s mate, had been standing nervously by the companionway while the conference had been proceeding. When Panton emerged he told Hill to call the crew aft, and he ordered *Rose*'s people to begin searching below. Hill said he would send aft what men he could find. He must send them all, Panton said. Stubbornly insisting that he could not have the whole crew aft, Hill went forward. Bowen, whom Panton ordered to follow Hill, heard the mate shout toward the focsle, but no one answered. Hill and Bowen then returned aft, where only John Roney and another crewman stood before Panton.

Glaring at the sailors, Panton shot a "steadfast" look at Hill. "Go, sirrah," he said, "and turn your People up, or I shall take *you*." "Sir," said Hill, "you may use your pleasure." Panton's temper remained cool. "We must search for them," he told Bowen, and ordered him with two of the cutter's crew to look through the main hold, while Stanhope remained on deck to tend the cutter.

Bowen and his men, candles in hand, went carefully through the darkened hold, hearing no sound but their own steps in the salt, seeing nothing but the cargo. Coming out of the main hold and moving forward along the 'tween decks, Gibson, one of Bowen's men, suddenly pointed to a boxlike opening in the deck capped by a wooden cover. This scuttle gave access to the brig's forepeak, a triangular-shaped space separated from the hold by a wooden bulkhead, used for storage and, if necessary, for ballasting adjustments. Bowen ordered Gibson and Churchill, his other seaman, to unlay the scuttle. As soon as Churchill pulled the cover off he could see that the forepeak contained something more than paint pots or ballast. "Here they are," he called to Bowen. The missing seamen had been found.

Peering through the scuttle, Bowen could discern few details in the dimness. Obviously the men were refusing all invitations to leave their refuge. They swore (in both senses of the word) to remain where they were, threatening to cut off the limbs of the first man who dared approach them. This was a threat they were clearly capable of executing. They held up to Bowen's straining gaze a hatchet, a harpoon, a musket, and a nasty two-pronged spear called a fish gig. The midshipman scrambled back topside to tell Panton.

Unsheathing his sword (but leaving scabbard and belt lying on the companion), Panton strode forward and down into the 'tween deck. At the scuttle, Panton first asked the men to come out; they refused, repeating their oaths. Then he said he wished to search the space, and asked them to let him come down into the forepeak. For answer he received the same amputative threat which they had given Bowen, and the same demonstration of willing capability. Again Panton ordered them out, adding that if they refused he would have to "oblige" them. Bring arms, they told him; he would be their "mark" and they would put out his "lamp" first. Realizing his present helplessness, Panton sent Bowen scurrying on deck to have Stanhope man the cutter and return to *Rose* for assistance. To the men in the forepeak he said only: "I have known as stout fellows as you, and by God I will have you out."

While Stanhope and four sailors brought the cutter back to *Rose*, Bowen borrowed the brig's speaking trumpet and told Caldwell what had happened. The captain promptly assembled a strong show of force. Into the cutter he ordered master-at-arms Forbes (with a supply of leg irons), three sailors and marines, and a load of cutlasses, pistols, and muskets. Stanhope was still in charge of the cutter, but to give Panton some seasoned assistance, Caldwell sent over William Peacock, the most experienced of his midshipmen. Laden though it was, the cutter quickly covered the distance between the ships and made fast to the brig with the help of a line tossed by Roney. Over the bulwark the reinforcements poured, led by Forbes with a pistol in one hand and a cutlass in the other. "By Jesus,'" he shouted, "I'll have these dogs out. Where is these buggers?"

Meanwhile, at the scuttle, Panton had obtained a candle from the brig's people, and had resumed his attempt to resolve the crisis peaceably. It was, he said, foolish of them to be obstinate. They told him that even if there were fifty men armed they would not surrender, and that if Panton had any regard for his own life he would let them pass. No, said Panton, it was his duty and he could not do it. They knew, they said, that he was a lieutenant, and they knew his orders; with renewed curses and direct personal threats they again asked him to let them pass. Thinking to try a different strategy, Panton handed down through the scuttle the candle he had been holding, asking the men to let him see what sort of place they were in. One of them took the light and moved it about the forepeak. Panton, saying he could not see, moved to climb down. At that, the atmosphere again chilled. From the forepeak, a sailor named Pierce Fenning pointed a musket at Panton, warning him that it was loaded and primed. Panton remained calm. Taking the candle back he asked, "Aye! Will you shoot me?" cheerfully adding, "I will take a pinch of snuff first." But he sent Bowen topside again to see if the cutter had returned.

As Bowen emerged, he met Forbes and the others, who followed him below, leaving Stanhope in charge on deck. With the armed, excited naval people crowding around the scuttle, Panton again asked the men below if they would surrender. Again they refused. After briefly recapitulating the previous debate for Peacock's benefit, Panton ordered him to take a party into the hold and open the after bulkhead of the forepeak. With the help of the brig's crowbar and adze, which Power had permitted them to use, they set to work on the wooden bulkhead. Forbes gave two strokes. From the other side came threats to shoot the first man to make a hole. One of the sailors brandished the fish gig through the still-open scuttle; another pointed the musket at Panton, only to have Bowen strike it aside with his cutlass. At this, Panton ordered the scuttle cover replaced; one of the boat's crew then stood on it. The two officers went down into the main hold to check Peacock's progress.

Forbes had ripped a small hole through which the naval party, crouched on the bulk salt cargo, could by the light of the candles they carried just make out the quartet in the forepeak. Through the opening, the musket again pointed, this times at Forbes. It was withdrawn, and Forbes immediately used his crowbar to break off a large plank. Panton ordered a halt to the demolition, while he appealed once more to the sailors, pointing out their numerical inferiority and the impossibility of escaping. He also promised them good usage if they would come out voluntarily. Panton might have been talking to deaf men, as they sulphurously told him. Still again the musket was run out, this time with a direct threat to kill Panton if anyone touched the bulkhead. The weapon then pointed at seaman James Sinclair, a Scot who had joined *Rose* just before she sailed; whoever was holding the weapon "snapped" it three times. Marine Private James Silley, clutching a pistol, grabbed the musket barrel with his free hand; but he could not wrest it out of the forepeak. Instantly he presented the pistol, loaded only with powder, and fired it into the half-darkness. The blast bloodied the lip of Michael Corbet. "See what one of your men has done," Corbet shouted to Panton. The lieutenant replied that it was not done by his order, and that when Corbet came aboard *Rose*, Panton would show him the man that did it, presumably to allow Corbet to take his own reparation. While Corbet thought about this, Panton again asked the men if they would come out; again he promised them good usage; and again they refused, with Corbet particularly threatening to kill the first person who might offer to approach them.

Panton ordered the work to continue. The musket poked through again; Silley, having reloaded his pistol, once more tried unsuccessfully to wrestle it out. When he failed, Panton took his pistol away, and explicitly ordered Forbes not to fire. Having halted the work a second time, he again asked the sailors to come out. "Keep clear, Gentlemen, at your peril, for we will not be pressed," they replied. And Corbet added, "You, Lieutenant, stand clear; if you don't, I'll be the death of you." "You may depend upon it," said Panton, "if you kill anyone, you'll be hanged for it." And he added, in an apparent attempt to ease the tension, that he would appreciate their lending him the ax in order the sooner to beat down the bulkhead. "We'll lend it to scalp you," was the answer, accompanied by probing thrusts and dartings of Corbet's harpoon through the ever-widening opening.

Panton sat on the salt opposite, watching the work. Suddenly the harpoon's triangular point struck the left side of his throat. "Peacock," he shouted, "the rascal has stabbed me thro the Jugular vein." Peacock, turning in horror, saw Panton's blood "spout out amazingly." He fired his pistol (which was loaded with ball as well as powder) into the forepeak and rushed to Panton's side; Raynsford joined him instantly, but the handkerchiefs they applied could scarcely staunch the blood from the three-inch long, three-inch deep wound. Bowen and two seamen carried Panton up the hatchway and, with mate Hill's help, to the cabin, while Peacock asked *Rose* "for God's sake to send the doctor."

Caldwell immediately hoisted out the barge, and sent her, manned and armed, with acting-surgeon Brice. Brice did what he could, but within a half-hour, Panton had died. There was other work for Brice.

Peacock's random shot had broken the arm of John Ryan, who had then crawled out of the forepeak, through the hold, and across the water casks, fainting with pain and thirst. As Brice emerged from the cabin where he had been treating Panton, someone asked him to dress Ryan's wound. "Let the rascal bleed and be damn'd," said Brice. "He ought to have a brace of balls drove through his head." So Ryan remained "in his Gore" until he was taken on board *Rose* some time later.

The naval people had other concerns at the moment. Corbet and his two companions remained barricaded in the forepeak, still armed, still defiant, still dangerous enough so that no sailor was willing to resume the assault. The English settled into a waiting siege and an exchange of epithets. Marine Corporal Edward Wilks posted sentries, and when Wilks told the prisoners they ought to behave better, because Panton had died, they refused to believe it. They said they meant no harm to anyone unless he came armed against them. If Wilks would lay down his arms, they added, they would lay down theirs and he would be welcome to eat or drink with them. Wilks indignantly refused.

Patient waiting paid off. A little after noon, Pierce Fenning and William Conner gave themselves up. Guarded by half the boarding party, they were taken quickly aboard *Rose*. It was later rumored that the "drink" which they had invited Wilks to share was more real than imagined, and that alcohol, rather than reason or force, had compelled their surrender. But the various logs do not support this possibility, nor does the record of testimony at the subsequent trial; and the decidedly Tory Boston *Chronicle*, while mentioning the rumor, reports that the men did not appear drunk when brought to the frigate.[10]

Corbet still held out, though the powder blast he had taken from Private Silley's pistol had caused a painful and bloody, albeit not serious, facial wound. At about 3 P.M., he asked Wilks to call the mate and have something brought to stop the bleeding. Hill himself went down and urged Corbet for his own good to come out. Corbet asked Hill's counsel. The mate replied kindly that he would not give Corbet advice to his prejudice. Corbet immediately surrendered.

Brought on deck, Corbet was led past the cabin companion. As he saw Panton's body inside, his eyes watered. "You rascal," he shouted at Silley. "You are the instigation of this gentleman's death." Then he was hustled into the waiting cutter and over to *Rose*. Panton's body remained aboard the brig, while next to his name in *Rose*'s Muster Book went "DD [i.e., discharged, dead] 22 April 69. Kill'd Impressing Seamen."[11]

Now began a three-day beat to Boston. With two-thirds of the brig's hands confined aboard *Rose*, Caldwell sent two seamen and two petty officers to assist her. In the forenoon of April 24, the offshore breeze began to abate. Richard Wells, *Rose's* master (i.e., navigator), came to the brig to search. He carried a custom house "deputation" which he offered to show Power. There was no need, the captain said; the vessel was "all open"; Wells could search. Wells did, but he could find nothing besides the salt, wine, gin, and lemons. For the spirits and fruit he seized the vessel and hacked the king's broad arrow on her mast.[12]

Then followed twenty-four hours of uncertain winds and long calms. During the dog watches, Caldwell noted in his log, "Ship's head round the Compass." In the evening the wind came up again, continuing strong enough during the night to bring *Rose* off Boston harbor by 8 A.M. on April 25. The air lightened; Caldwell, having ordered the boats out to tow, rigged *Rose's* long oars to assist the ship in. Nine of the sweeps broke during the next four hours, but at noon *Rose* anchored in Nantasket Road and the brig, with Panton's body, came up to the town. The next afternoon, Caldwell brought *Rose* into King Road.

April 27, while *Rose's* hands furled her sails, cleaned the ship, and repaired the rigging, Panton's body, attended by Hood and most of the army and navy officers in Boston, was carried for interment to the burial ground of King's Chapel on Tremont Street. On the ship's muster, his servant had already been marked "D [i.e., discharged] by reason of his master's death." [13]

Panton's obsequies completed, the navy and the civilian authorities turned to the problem of dealing with his killer. At 11 A.M. on April 29, Bernard, Hutchinson, Hood, Secretary Oliver (the same who had publicly resigned as stamp master), and Admiralty Judge Auchmuty boarded *Rose* amid a 15-gun salute to the governor "to examine the Prisoners." Besides confronting Corbet and his companions, the group, or someone else, also took testimony from the eyewitnesses. Within a few days, the Boston *Chronicle* ran a full account of the tragedy, based on the depositions of Bowen, Peacock, and Forbes.[14]

For all its apparent simplicity, the Panton tragedy posed subtle, delicate questions of fact, law, and politics. Bernard and his advisors addressed themselves primarily to the latter two categories. The three civilians who accompanied him aboard *Rose* were the "Cabinet Council" on whose advice he had come to rely almost exclusively in his never-ending battle with the Whigs. Moreover, they, along with the governor, Hood, and seven other high government and customs officials from Massachusetts, Rhode Island, and New Hampshire, comprised a special court of admiralty for the trial of "piracy, or robbery or Felony upon the sea." [15]

This court, appointed by standing commission, sat only rarely. It filled a gap in the judicial system caused by the inability of the common-law courts to hear and determine crimes committed at sea. The problem was not new. Indeed, the statute which originally established a similar court in England had been enacted in 1536, the twenty-eighth year of Henry VIII's reign, and was usually referred to in context as "the statute of 28 Henry VIII" or simply "the statute of Henry." By that statute, procedure before the special court included grand jury indictment and trial by jury "in such like manner and form, as if such offences had been committed upon the land." [16]

Because in 1536 England possessed no overseas colonies, the statute only specified trial in England. To remedy the inconvenience that this created as the Empire expanded, Parliament in 1700 provided for trial of marine crimes by commissioners sitting in the colonies. Through fear that colonial jurors might be less likely than English jurors or American commissioners to convict Americans of "piracy, robbery, or felony" committed on, say, Spaniards or Frenchmen in time of peace, the new statute directed trials to proceed "according to the course of the admiralty," that is, without jury. Which statute applied, and which mode of trial, were problems facing the crown officials.

While Bernard and his advisors pondered these questions, the four prisoners, transferred on April 30 from *Rose* to *Romney* and on May 9 from *Romney* to *Rippon,* had managed to retain as counsel John Adams and James Otis. It is a mystery that four obscure Irish seamen found their way to the two most brilliant of the available lawyers (Sewall, the only other man in their class, was already engaged on the crown side as advocate-general). Perhaps Adams's client, "King" Hooper, owner of the brig, provided the link. Or perhaps the radicals, sensing the political importance of the case, attended to the matter. At any rate, Adams and Otis entered the case early, although, according to Adams's recollection a half-century later, Otis's "unhappy distemper was then in one of its unlucid intervals, and I could hardly persuade him to converse with me a few minutes on the subject; and he constantly and finally refused to appear publicly in the cause." Adams's memory was inaccurate. Otis did take an active part in the proceedings. Almost as soon as he was retained, he publicly expressed certainty that the men could obtain a jury trial. Unfortunately, Otis chose the May 1769 sitting of the superior court at Plymouth for his stage, and the judges (including Hutchinson) for his audience. Hutchinson apparently mentioned Otis's boast to Samuel Fitch. Ironically enough, it was the research into which this Tory lawyer immediately plunged which provided a substantial statutory underpinning to Otis's declaration. By "rummaging up Acts of Parliament," Fitch found a 1717 statute which clearly specified that under the act of 1700 the accused "may be tried and judged . . . in such a manner and form as" provided by the Statute of Henry; in other words, by jury. Worse, from the crown's viewpoint, he learned that in 1718, a South Carolina grand jury had been called to indict, and a petty jury to convict, the infamous pirate Stede Bonnet.[17]

Important though the jury-trial issue was, others equally central demanded resolution. Of what, for example, were the men to be accused? And what rules of law should be applied, common-law, or admiralty (that is, civil-law)? The two problems intertwined. As a general proposition, killing in self-defense or even (as a last resort) to resist unlawful restraint was legally justifiable. Whether killing Panton was justifiable depended on what role Panton was filling at the time he died. If he had been acting as a kind of customs inspector, searching for contraband, then any act by Corbet and his friends to impede the search was itself unlawful, and by definition the killing was unlawful. If, on the other hand, Panton and his men had been trying to press the sailors, then the test of justification turned on Panton's motives and on his authority.

From what we now know of Hood's original order to Caldwell, of *Rose's* activity during the earlier part of the cruise, and of the log entry concerning Panton's death, there seems little doubt, even without the evidence of what happened aboard *Pitt Packet,* that Panton went at the head of a press gang. In reporting the incident to the Admiralty, Hood first described the killing as having resulted because the men "would not suffer Lieutenant Panton to make a search as an officer of the Customs for fear of being impressed." But in the next paragraph, the commodore explained that because of "Desertion in the course of the winter I was under a necessity of raising men to enable the Ships to go to sea." And he enclosed a copy of the order to Caldwell. Hood prided himself "that no complaint, or even murmur has arose here, in the course of raising men, from the caution I took not to distress the Trade of the Province." But of course the inbound vessels from whom *Rose* had been taking men must have reported her activities. And a few days before he wrote the Admiralty, Hood ordered Caldwell "to continue all the new raised Men on a Supernumerary List till such time as I may particularly order the Disposal of them." At the same time, orders went to Lieutenant Scott, commanding H.M. Schooner *Halifax,* to take up *Rose's* interrupted patrol and her impressment activities, too.[18]

As the crown officers reviewed this recent history, they must have realized the virtual impossibility of proving Panton's purpose to have been an ordinary search. They must in addition have wondered whether Hood, for all his care, tact, and good relations with the radicals, had not plainly violated a Parliamentary statute of 1707: "No Mariner, or other person who shall serve on board . . . any . . . trading ship or vessel, that shall be imployed in any part of America . . . shall be liable to be impressed or taken away, or shall be impressed or taken away, by any officer or officers, of or belonging to her Majesty's ships of war." Unlike some of the other materials in the case, this statute was not at all obscure. Only the year before, following the *Romney* impressment fracas, the Town of Boston had sent instructions, written by John Adams himself, to its representatives in the legislature, reminding them of the statute and urging its enforcement.[19]

Even if Panton's attempted impressment were illegal, Corbet would not automatically be justified in killing him. Here is where the choice-of-law problem came to the surface. At common law, a killing was murder if it was committed intentionally, unjustifiably, inexcusably, and with malice. In the absence of malice, the killing dropped to manslaughter. There were no degrees of either murder or manslaughter. Each was punishable by death. In the case of manslaughter, however, the guilty party could, if he had never before been convicted, plead benefit of clergy, and escape the noose. At common law, a man indicted for manslaughter and convicted, or even a man indicted for murder but only found guilty of manslaughter, would not be hanged. But the statutes left uncertain whether benefit of clergy was available before the special admiralty court. And unfortunately for the prisoners, if the trial, like ordinary admiralty proceedings, were to be conducted according to the civil law, then the verdict must be either murder or acquittal; the civil law knew nothing of manslaughter.[20]

All the legal issues were of course heightened by the political atmosphere which surrounded the entire incident. Antipathy toward the military apparatus afloat and ashore and the inner circle's reaction to that antipathy were facts of Boston life affecting everything that happened in the metropolis. Thus on May 5, General Mackay, who had only just reached town from the West Indies, received a deputation from the town meeting asking him to move all his troops into the countryside during the forthcoming general election. Pleading lack of power, Mackay politely refused, but agreed to keep the men in the barracks.[21]

Despite the obvious discontent, the authorities decided to push the Corbet prosecution. By May 5 they had pitched on May 23 as the trial date, and had summoned to Boston the members of the special court of admiralty, including John Adams's Harvard classmate, Governor John Wentworth of New Hampshire.[22]

Adams, meanwhile, drew up in his own handwriting on behalf of each client a lengthy plea "demanding juries as a right." "I almost killed myself," he later reported, "by writing, day and night, four of these pleas of enormous length in which a number of acts of parliament were recited at large." For all the verbosity, their point was simple: the standing commission authorized trial by the 1700 statute, without jury; by the statute of 1717, the procedure should have followed the statute of Henry, that is, with a jury. Therefore, concluded Adams, this particular court lacked jurisdiction to try the prisoners, and should not "take any further Cognizance of the Matters and Things charged." Despite the peremptory conclusion, Adams did not really mean that the court lacked the power to hear the case; he meant merely that if the trial were to take place at all, the facts must be found, not by the commissioners, but "by a petit Jury of the said County of Suffolk." [23]

On the morning of Tuesday, May 23, the court, only seven members being present, met in the council chamber in Boston's Town House. The trial itself would be held up the street, in the just-completed Court House (approximately on the site of what until recently was Boston's City Hall Annex); the meeting in the Town House was merely organizational. Here Advocate-General Sewall first disclosed to the judges the fruits of Fitch's "discovery" of the 1717 statute apparently requiring a jury trial—the same statute on which Adams's "pleas" rested. None of the judges wanted a jury, since a panel of Suffolk County farmers and Bostonians would be unlikely to weigh the evidence with anything but an acquittal in mind. But the statutes seemed plain. Bernard, apparently relieved at being legally forced to take a popular position, "was of opinion that there was nothing in them to prevent" a jury trial. Even Hutchinson reluctantly agreed. The entourage moved over to the Court House.[24]

Following the reading of the three statutes and the commission, Bernard announced that the judges "were disposed, if it might be done consistently with law, that the prisoners should be tried by jury," and that they "were considering in what manner to convene a Grand Jury and Petty Jury." Because many procedural problems remained (how, for example, should prospective jurors be selected and summoned?), the trial, Bernard said, would be put over to Thursday, May 25.[25]

The afternoon of May 23, the court, sitting informally in the council chamber, heard Adams, Otis, and Sewall on the jury-trial question. The advocate-general conceded the right, but Hutchinson continued to fret over the mechanics of jury selection. Although Bernard raised the chilling thought that perhaps the only proper course (in light of the statute of Henry) was to ship the men back to England for jury trial there, everyone agreed that local juries would somehow have to be called. To Otis went the task of preparing, for the next day's session in the council chamber, the *venire facias,* the order commanding the sheriff to summon the veniremen (i.e., prospective jurors).[26]

While Otis was drafting a suitable form of order, Hutchinson returned to the basic problem: did trial really have to be by jury? The chief justice possessed a first-rate legal mind, which soon produced a lawyerlike solution. He began by reading the 1717 statute literally. It says an accused "may" be tried by jury. Otis and Adams had argued that "may" meant "shall." The only statute explicitly requiring a jury trial was the statute of Henry; and the jury which that statute contemplated would consist of twelve Englishmen. This suggested two thoughts. First, Bernard, in his bumbling way, may have been correct. The combined effect of the two statutes might require any jury trial to be held in England. Alternatively, perhaps the act of 1717 had merely permitted the use of a jury in American trials without requiring it. Whether or not the Home Government had authorized any given court to proceed with a jury would depend on the language of that court's commission. But, as Hutchinson pointed out to bench and bar the next morning, the present commission, although reciting all three of the statutes, only conferred the powers contained in the jury-denying statute of 1700. It was a neat piece of statute-juggling. While Adams had relied on the clash between that statute and the 1717 act to sustain the jury right, Hutchinson had used it to remove the jury entirely.[27]

Although of course news of Hutchinson's analysis became promptly known, when the court reconvened on May 25 it deferred making any ruling. Otis was permitted to argue against Hutchinson's point; but the court then adjourned until May 29. At that time, Adams formally filed his pleas, and the court again adjourned (until June 14), ostensibly to take the point "under consideration." No one expected the lengthy pause to work any changes. Hood was reported "very ill of a Bilious disorder, to which he is Subject." Bernard would be unwilling to proceed without him. A rumor floated that the jury question would have to be decided by the authorities in England. Most probably, however, the continuance was designed to allow Hutchinson an opportunity to put his thoughts into more polished form.[28] This the chief justice did in his usual thorough way. When court reconvened on June 14, he read, as the commissioners' opinion, a five-page closely reasoned expansion of his earlier thoughts, and the jury-trial issue at last died.[29]

The trial itself was no anticlimax. A capital charge invariably commands interest. Here the crime bore political overtones. The victim had been a uniformed king's officer in pursuit of his duty; the case rubbed the emotions of a garrisoned town. Newspapers had long since published large chunks of the evidence. Because a successful defense depended upon showing that Panton had been exceeding his orders,

saving Corbet's neck would mean embarrassing the Royal Navy. John
Adams probably did not exaggerate when he said a half-century later
that no previous trial "had ever interested the community so much . . .
No trial had drawn together such crowds of auditors from day to day;
they were as numerous as those in the next year, at the trials of Preston and the soldiers." The lawyers prepared intensely, to the exclusion
even of politics. The day before the trial started, the town meeting
elected Otis moderator. But "the Constable not being able to find him,"
the Town chose Richard Dana.[30]

Testimony took over two days. Fitch, who conducted the trial for
the crown, put on Bowen, Stanhope, Peacock, and Forbes to tell what
happened aboard *Pitt Packet*. Cross-examined by the defense counsel
and (as was customary in naval courts-martial) by members of the
court—whose queries were sometimes palpably partial—they insisted
that Panton had done nothing to provoke Corbet. On the question of
Panton's intent, they showed considerably less certainty.

> "Did you [someone asked Forbes] consider yourself as searching
> for Goods, or as one of a Press Gang?"
> "When the Lieutenant said they were well stowed forward, I
> thought there were goods. I am not to be a judge of my officer's busi-
> ness. I imagine it was for seizing Smugglers as well as anything else.
> I am not a judge whether Lieutenant would have pressed them. The
> latter end they behaved so rough and turbulent that the Lieutenant
> I believe would take some of 'em on board the *Rose*."
> "Did you hear Lieutenant say he would press 'em?"
> "I did not that I remember." [31]

> "Did you [Otis inquired of Bowen] consider yourself with Mr.
> Panton as searching for goods, or as a press gang?"
> "As searching for Goods. First I searched for Men and then for
> Goods."

William Pettygrew, a civilian physician, and Surgeon's Mate Brice
testified in grisly detail to the cause of death. The crown's case then
closed with the brief testimony of Private Silley and Seaman Bem-
bridge. Silley's response to a final question emphasized the confusion
in the prosecution's evidence: "I understood that I came on board in
order to help Mr. Panton search for prohibited goods or to impress
men as he gave orders." [32]

Following the usual practice, Fitch summed up his case before the
defense began. Emphasizing that Panton was authorized to search for
goods, he argued that the lieutenant's peaceful manner negated any
claim that the prisoners could reasonably fear his intentions. Self-defense, therefore, was no longer an issue. Having established, as he
thought, the unlawfulness of the killing, Fitch went on to grapple in-

conclusively with the substantive law problem. Despite strenuous mental gymnastics, about all he could say was that whatever law, civil or common, applied, the prisoners were guilty of murder. But if the judges should disagree, then even if they applied the civil law, nothing prevented them from finding manslaughter, and punishing accordingly. All in all, he thought, "no safer Rule can be proceeded by than to proceed by the common Law."

If Adams responded to this point while opening the defense, no record has survived. At this stage, he appears to have been fairly confident. He filled out, and gave to the sheriff for later service, a writ which would commence an action by Ryan against Peacock, alleging damages resulting from the midshipman's pistol. Before that lawsuit could be fairly started, however, it was necessary to win the criminal case. To that end, Adams put on the brig's people: Captain Power, Mate Hill, Seaman Roney, and Cook McGlocklin. They testified in sum that Panton was indeed carrying his sword when he went below, and that at all times he acted like a press gang officer, never once identifying himself in any way as a customs inspector. A little after Panton died, one of the navy people had said that the lieutenant was a custom house officer. Hill remembered the remark particularly, because shortly thereafter, Power asked him if he had seen the shipping book which Panton had taken during their first interview. "No," said Hill and went to ask Bowen and Stanhope. They were equally ignorant, but offered to search Panton's pockets. Hill went with them to the cabin and watched while they removed all Panton's papers. He even shuffled through the documents, looking for the book. It was not there; neither was any kind of parchment or commission.[33]

Surprisingly, Adams also called two of *Rose*'s men. Corporal Wilks had for some reason been broken to private four weeks before the trial. He testified only to the prisoners' insistence after the killing that "they did not mean any Harm to any one without it was them that came armed against them." Charles Raynsford, the young seaman who had been pressed at the start of the fatal cruise and who had come aboard with Panton, denied flatly that he had ever heard the lieutenant say he wanted to search for uncustomed goods.[34]

The prisoners could not testify. It was only in the nineteenth century that the accused in any criminal proceedings received the right to testify in his own behalf; and of course he could never be forced to testify against himself. Quartered aboard *Rippon,* they were apparently brought ashore daily for the proceedings, and returned to the ship afterwards. But as if to offset the enforced silence of his clients, Adams put on a surprise closing witness. Robert Calef testified that on April 30 Bowen had visited him at home. In the course of discussing the unhappy incident, Calef said, Bowen had admitted that Corbet gave Panton "all the fair warning imaginable and it was the lieutenant's own fault." Hearsay or not, this was a telling point, particularly with the in-court evidence so close on the question of Panton's intent.

Adams sought to press his advantage. He rested his evidence and, although it was late in the afternoon, immediately began his closing argument. His prepared notes in hand, the law books containing the supporting authorities on the table before him, the little lawyer went for the heart of the case. First, were impressments, generally, legal? "For if Impresses are always illegal, and Lt. Panton acted as an Impress Officer, Michael Corbet and his Associates had a right to resist him, and if they could not otherwise preserve their Liberty, to take away his Life. His Blood must lye at his own Door, and they be held guiltless. Nay I think that Impresses may be allowed to be legal, and yet Corbet might have a Right to resist." Then Adams planned to hammer the nonimpressment statute; and to close with a demand for exculpation. "I am not contending for the Sentence of Manslaughter, against my Clients," his prepared notes read. "I think they are intituled to an honourable Acquittal."

The argument never finished. Somewhere in the early sentences, Hutchinson interrupted to move an adjournment. This was agreed, and the comissioners left the courtroom. Baffled; annoyed as only a lawyer can be when a judge ignores a finely chiseled argument, particularly an undelivered argument; above all, worried for his clients, Adams spent an anxious night. The next morning the tension increased, but the court remained closeted. So much could be going wrong. Bernard might even be reviving his idea of shipping the men to England and the doubtful mercies of an English jury.[35]

Finally, at 1 P.M., the judges returned. Calling the prisoners to the bar, Bernard turned a solemn, gloomy countenance on the terrified men and the equally frightened audience. He addressed each prisoner by name, and everyone expected the death sentence to follow. But the last surprise of this strange case was happy: "The Court," intoned Bernard, "have considered the evidence in support of the libel [i.e., charge] against you, and are unanimously of opinion that it amounts only to justifiable homicide; you are accordingly acquitted and discharged from your imprisonment." Bernard sat down. The silence continued a moment longer, and then Auchmuty said in loud redundance: "The Court is unanimous in this opinion." [36]

The grounds for the unanimous opinion were not published, although Hutchinson in his subsequent *History* stated them clearly enough: "It appeared that neither the lieutenant nor any of his superior officers were authorized to impress, by any warrant or special authority from the lords of the admiralty; and the court," which, remember, included Hood himself, "was unanimously of opinion that the prisoners had a good right to defend themselves, and, though the fact of killing was fully proved, that they ought to be acquitted of murder, with which they were charged, and that, at common law, the killing would not have amounted to manslaughter." [37]

Adams, characteristically, saw conspiratorial fear as the real motive behind the decision. His prepared argument had been based in part on the anti-impressment act of 1707. The statute book, appropriately dog-eared, had rested in the pile of volumes before him as he argued. Adams believed that Hutchinson recognized the book and the statute. Worried lest the act be disclosed, the chief justice then, according to Adams, forced the adjournment and the acquittal, in order to keep the law secret. This strange idea, a product of Adams's later years, does not make sense. The act of 1707 was well known in Boston, partly because of the Boston Instructions, which Adams himself had written.[38]

A much more plausible explanation for the outcome arises from the evidence itself. The case was too full of reasonable doubt, apart from the propriety of Hood's orders to Caldwell. Why entertain a lengthy heated debate on the legality of impressment generally, and the applicability of the various statutes, including the act of 1707? Why rest the decision on difficult points of law, thus provoking a violent reaction no matter what the decision? The special court, like courts before and since, may well have preferred to pick the narrowest and hence least-assailable ground for decision: that is, by resolving the case on the facts alone. This happy bit of judicial statesmanship avoided knotty issues, saved time, and, incidentally, did Corbet and his friends the justice they clearly deserved.

Yet even such a logical hypothesis does not convince completely. The "cover-up" theory still commands bits of factual support. Bernard never mentioned the incident in his contemporary gubernatorial correspondence. He certainly inundated Lord Hillsborough with enough trivia to make us wonder why this major event—the actual shedding of official blood—went unreported. And why did Hood take such extraordinary pains to force settlement of Ryan's claim against Peacock? The day the trial ended, the sheriff rowed out to *Rose* to serve the writ. At an early point in the litigation, Hood wrote Hooper and Adams, offering Ryan a cook's warrant in the Navy, if he would drop the action. "I am no further interested in this matter," he wrote his radical friend, James Bowdoin, "than for my feelings for both parties, and the desire I have to relieve them." Strange words from a commodore about an Irish merchant seaman and an impoverished, orphaned midshipman. Was Hood truly so altruistic? Or did he realize that Peacock would have to establish, or at least try to establish, that he had acted in the performance of a lawful duty? Was Hood reluctant to have the whole Corbet-Panton affair relitigated? Whatever his motive, Hood's offer was rejected; Ryan made a counterproposal, "on terms not possible to be complied with." Adams said later that Ryan had refused "because he had fallen in love and would be married." But after a few weeks' more negotiating, Ryan settled for £30. We do not know whether Hood supplied the funds. We do know that when the Massachusetts Council refused to pay the expenses of the special court—from pique at having no Massachusetts councilors named in the commission—Hood personally paid the bill. His extraordinary desire to placate everyone may merely mean that the Whiggishly inclined commodore was trying to avoid irritating the Americans. Or he may have had some fear that any re-ignition of the case would highlight and perhaps discredit his active encouragement of impressment.[39]

If his aim was to retain American respect, Hood seems to have been successful. Seventeen years and a war later, when Adams was the first American ambassador to England, Hood, by then Admiral Lord Hood, took advantage of Adams's participation in the case "to make [him] a friendly visit," and incidentally to talk of diplomatic matters.[40]

Adams did not suffer from his representation of Corbet. Within a week, the commissioners of the customs themselves had retained him to argue in favor of a customs officer's power to seize a vessel. True, Sewall had gone to Halifax—oddly enough aboard *Rose*—on business. But there were other, more loyal, counsel whom the commissioners could have briefed. The selection of Adams and his acceptance indicates quite clearly that the Corbet case had left no bitter feelings on either side.[41]

CHAPTER 12

SOLDIERS AND THE LAW

Ａs *Rose* stood down the harbor, she carried passengers even more significant than Sewall and his party. Crammed into every available space aboard the small frigate and her larger convoy, *Rippon*, were the soldiers of the Sixty-fifth Regiment. General Gage was loosening his hold upon Boston.[1]

Although no riots had flared since the army's arrival, it was not a return of normal tranquility which had persuaded the general and the home authorities to reduce the Boston garrison. Life had borne hard on the regiments penned in the bay metropolis. The officers had passed the winter comfortably enough. But the rank-and-file, the real occupying army, met daily hostility. Even for the officers, such gaiety as the small provincial town could afford hardly compensated for the pressures generated by the increasing civilian-military friction. Shortly upon arrival, both Brigadier Pomeroy and Major General Mackay had importuned Gage for transfers; Major Pierce Butler of the Twenty-ninth (a future signer of the United States Constitution) burdened Carr, Mackay, and Gage with desperate pleas for home leave.[2]

The apparent calm of the winter lulled Gage and the government. On June 3, Gage received from Hillsborough discretionary authority to remove the troops. Having reinforced the Twenty-ninth and the Fourteenth with volunteers from the homeward-bound Thirty-fourth, he ordered Mackay to send the Sixty-fifth, the Sixty-fourth, and the artillery to Halifax. Either of the two remaining regiments was to be placed in the Castle, the other in Boston.[3]

Gage also sought Bernard's written opinion as to whether any troops at all need remain in Boston. Bernard, recall orders in hand, saw no reason to invite more trouble. He frankly felt the troops essential, yet he did not want to commit himself, at least in any communication that the Bostonians could reach; Bernard had still not recovered from the shock of seeing his private reports to the ministry printed and distributed in Boston. He therefore dodged Gage's inquiry assiduously, relaying instead the "opinion of All the principal Officers of the Crown & Government that the removal of Troops at this time would probably have very dangerous consequences." Only when Gage guaranteed him American anonymity did he state his views explicitly.[4]

Shortly after the Sixty-fifth departed, Hood and Mackay planned to send four companies of the Sixty-fourth to Halifax in H.M.S. *Launceston*; but the day before the scheduled embarkation, the newspapers carried a set of resolves which Sam Adams had propelled to a unanimous vote in the House of Representatives. Because one of these flatly asserted that "no laws" except those passed by the people's representatives were in any way binding, Mackay and Hood, after consulting the worrying Bernard, stopped the embarkation. This in turn "caused an uneasiness in the town" and prompted Adams to claim blandly that although the resolves had indeed passed unanimously, the publication was premature, and that they could be altered.[5]

Mackay and Hood now proposed to Bernard that the embarkation proceed. Typically, Bernard answered "that to provide for the future was more the Lieut. Governor's business than mine . . . & I would advise with him." Fortunately, Hutchinson, in his role as chief justice, had just returned from the eastern circuit. He saw no reason to detain the troops, and on July 4, the soldiers embarked and sailed. Three weeks later, Hood took the rest to Halifax with him in *Romney* and the sloop *Viper*. Happy that the garrison had been reduced by more than half, Adams changed the offensive resolve. From denial of all Parliamentary rights over Americans, he scaled it down to mere denial of the right to tax, insisting that this meant only internal taxes, not port duties.[6]

Once again Adams had embarrassed Bernard. Mercifully, the governor's agony had almost ended. A few more nasty inconclusive verbal exchanges, a petition for his removal, and it was over. On August 1, Bernard packed himself aboard *Rippon*, and along with 36,563 ounces of Custom House silver, sailed for home, leaving his wife and children to follow. Unfortunately, the winds were light, the passage out-harbor tedious. The townspeople, who would never abandon the conviction that it was Bernard who had caused the troops to come in the first place, celebrated his departure with flags and cannon fire, while "all the bells in town were rung for joy." Even the night did not spare him; as the still-becalmed *Rippon* rocked gently to the Atlantic swells, Bernard could see a monumental bonfire on Fort Hill, near where Andrew Oliver's house had been besieged.[7]

With Bernard and half the garrison gone, Gage wrote about this time to Hillsborough: "I should be glad to relieve the Troops from the oppression they are said to suffer where they are, and save a deal of vexatious trouble, by removing them to places where they would be less obnoxious; amongst people better disposed and less turbulent." But in fact he had not removed the military; he had merely decreased its effectiveness, while maintaining its visibility, presence, and obnoxiousness. Rather than saving "a deal of vexatious trouble" he had ensured more.[8]

After Mackay and Pomeroy left, Lieutenant Colonel Dalrymple once more became Gage's man in Boston. The situation was in fact beyond salvage, but Dalrymple did as well as anyone. Spending his own money to meet military expenses, he fast won Gage's approval. Moreover, he and the other officers, including Lieutenant Colonel Carr, commanding the Twenty-ninth, and Captain Thomas Preston of that regiment, fitted actively into the Boston social scene. Captains Molesworth and French of the Twenty-ninth, both Masons, became officers of Boston's Grand Lodge, an honor they shared with the radical leaders Thomas Crafts, Paul Revere, and Dr. Joseph Warren.[9]

All the dinners and concerts could not conceal the frictions arising between the lower strata of the Boston population and the enlisted men. In January, for example, John Rowe's manservant Cato had "got" a sword from grenadier James Fairchild of the Fourteenth. In June three wigmakers led by John Paymount (Jean Piemont), Hutchinson's own hairdresser, drubbed Private John Timmons of the Twenty-ninth.[10]

When the civilians were not robbing or fighting the soldiers, they were actively enticing them to desert, continuing a practice which had begun in the earliest days of the occupation. One private reported that his would-be seducers wanted him to teach them "the Exercise and Discipline of the Regular troops." Lured, perhaps, by promises of land, the soldiers deserted in groups estimated by the fairly impartial Reverend Andrew Eliot to be as large as six or eight men. To counter this trend, Gage had recommended that Dalrymple "throw out hints amongst them that the King will Reward his Officers and Soldiers with the Estates of the Rebels." But the hints failed. When Dalrymple sent a party to recapture deserters, the country folk turned out a black-faced mob to surround the detachment "in very great numbers" and rescue the prisoner. The officers liked to believe that many of the deserters deplored their new-found freedom and would, if given a chance, return to their units. Whether from fear or contentment, however, the deserters were staying out. "How far we can ever retake them or get them back but by voluntary surrendering is more than I can say," Mackay had lamented.[11]

Personal hostility toward the army and its men, as well as encouragement of deserters, were expected, and hence bearable. More subtly corrosive of spirit and purpose, thus more destructive of peace and order was the double standard of formal justice which the army, from Gage down, believed it faced in Boston. The soldiers, one ought always to remember, went into Boston not as an occupying army but rather as a force of uniformed peace-keepers, or policemen. Their role as even the radicals conceived it was to assist the executive and if necessary the courts to maintain order. The radicals, of course, insisted that good order pre-existed the soldiers' arrival; in refuting arguments for the military's presence, however, they recognized their theoretical basis. The soldiers, the keepers of peace, in turn regarded themselves as allies of the judicial system.

Yet within a very few months after their appearance, the soldiers learned that in the courts and laws they would find only resourceful, implacable enemies. Soldiers had been posted at various guard points around town. A sentry who challenged passers-by too vigorously might find himself facing a criminal charge for assault against the peace. It is of course arguable that the riot protection which the military presence was designed to assure did not require the posting of sentinels and the challenging of civilians. Such activities increased the army's visibility and tended to provoke the civilians without really aiding the maintenance of order. Still, public sentinels were sufficiently a normal part of garrison life so that the soldiers could fairly expect the townspeople to accept them.

Instead, the Bostonians resisted actively. When Private Dukesberry of the Twenty-ninth was brought before the Court of General Sessions of the Peace on criminal charges for challenging a passer-by, the hapless soldier and the two officers attending court as observers heard Justice of the Peace Dana furiously denounce the practice of challenges, openly advising civilians not to submit. On another occasion, Dana was heard to tell a jury to believe "Nothing, or Just what they Pleased, of what was said by the soldiers against [the] Inhabitants; But Every thing in the fullest manner said against the military by the Inhabitants. As they were people with whom they were acquainted [,] the Military Vagabonds they knew nothing of." [12]

"The minds of the people," Mackay had written, "are so poyson'd, " that a grand jury would not indict a civilian, even on clear evidence, for any offense against the troops; and conversely would indict soldiers "without reason Law or Justice" After vainly trying to have the attorney-general represent the soldiers, he advised men with admittedly valid claims against townspeople to drop the charges, "as no redress could be obtained for A Soldier in Boston." Even Otis was moved to say one day in open court that "he was ashamed of the ill usage given to the troops, and that the shameful ill treatment given them by the inhabitants was the cause of all the prosecutions raised against those innocent strangers." [13]

The causeless oppression from the civil magistrates also increased the pressures to desert. But the real vice of the judicial misbehavior caused an even more serious problem. The military developed an abiding contempt for the legal process. "You must not expect," said Gage, "that a Boston Jury will either decide by the rules of Justice, Law, or Equity, or trouble themselves about what is right or Wrong." "You will soon see," he remarked contemptuously on another occasion, "how well those People who talk so much of Law, obey the Laws themselves." Even worse, the military felt itself betrayed by its nominal partner in peace-keeping, the judiciary. "We are in a pleasing Situation," Mackay had written sarcastically, "who are ordered here to Aid & assist the Civill Majistrate in preserving the peace & protecting his Majestys Subjects, when those very majistrates are our Oppressers." [14]

In the summer of 1769, the military began to stumble over another technicality of local law which exacerbated many of the army's sore feelings. In cases of theft, a province statute authorized imposing damages of triple the value of the stolen goods. Unlike an ordinary fine, this would be paid directly to the victim; if the convict lacked the funds, the statute permitted the court to empower the victim to sell the offender's services to the highest bidder. "They have Indented him as a Slave & sold him for a term of years," a horrified Mackay reported to Gage the first time the procedure was enforced against a soldier. He hurried to Hutchinson and Admiralty Judge Auchmuty, only to learn that the law had been correctly applied. Gage responded in loud anger. "I can hardly write with Patience on this more than infamous Affair." He recommended hustling the man aboard one of the transports. If the civil authorities demanded him, Gage said, they should be refused. "Complaints may be sent to me." [15]

Fortunately, the citizen who had bought the soldier's services was willing to accept "a few Guineas" in settlement of the matter, and the soldier went free. Shortly thereafter, however, Private John Moyse (or Moise) of the Fourteenth was convicted of breaking and entering a shop and stealing over £26-worth of goods. Unable to pay the treble damages, Moyse was sold for a three-year term. Mackay in turn found the price too steep for settlement, and reported this dilemma to Gage. Powerless to help, the general exploded with rage. "Such an infamous piece of Tyranny, savours more of the Meridian of Turkey than a British Province. It is a trite Remark, that these Bawlers against Government under the pretence of Liberty, are always the greatest Tyrants. It is not Tyranny they dislike, they only Squabble for the Power to become Tyrants." In fact, the affront to good order and decency was even greater than the sputtering Gage supposed. As he learned from Mackay's next letter, Moyse, far from resisting his involuntary servitude, gloried in it. The whole thing had been "a connivance . . . in order to secure him his Discharge, or in other words a sort of Legall Dismission from the Regiment." "It may be difficult to get him," Gage glumly conceded.[16]

The contempt which the army was developing toward Massachusetts laws and the way they were enforced began to take a more physical form. In the market on July 13, Private John Riley of the Fourteenth traded punches with Cambridge victualer Jonathan Winship. Enraged, Winship stormed over to Justice of the Peace Edmund Quincy and swore out a complaint. Promptly hauled before Quincy, Riley pleaded guilty and was fined five shillings and costs. Quincy allowed Riley a day to raise the money, Riley's sergeant, John Phillips, meanwhile having made himself responsible for payment or for Riley's appearance before the justice. Riley did indeed return the next day, accompanied by Sergeant Phillips and at least two other enlisted men. But because he either would not or could not pay, Justice Quincy sentenced him to jail, and began drawing up the "mittimus," or commitment order.

Meanwhile Riley's captain, Charles Fordyce, tried to help. He asked Lieutenant Alexander Ross of the Fourteenth, a friend of Quincy's, to see if he could "compound" the affair, that is, fix the ticket. Ross agreed, and reached the justice's Dock Square office just as Quincy was completing the mittimus. Despite Ross's urging, Quincy allowed the order to stand. Constable Peter Barbour moved to take Riley into custody.

At this, the matter quickly got out of hand. Reinforced by other soldiers, including some of the Fourteenth's grenadiers, the most powerful men in the regiment, Riley fought off Barbour and a passing civilian named Jeremiah Belknap, who tried to help the constable. Swords drawn, cursing and shouting, the soldiers began pushing Riley toward the door and freedom. "Sir, take care of your men," Quincy begged Ross. "I can do nothing," Ross answered. Someone heard him shout "Go;" someone else thought it was "Don't go." But no one could tell, then or later, whether the former meant "go to jail," as opposed to "go

to the barracks," or whether the latter meant "don't leave," as opposed
to "don't go to jail."

The confusion continued after Riley and his rescuers pushed
through the door, down the stairs, and into the street. Ross was heard
to order the men to the barracks. But the witnesses were not sure if
this was part of the rescue or if "You rascals, to your barracks directly," was merely Ross's effort to prevent the disturbance from becoming even more serious.[17]

One thing was certain: a lawfully held prisoner had been forcibly
and illegally wrested out of the custody of a civilian court. The radicals, having responded with relative mildness to a similar rescue in
Essex County some weeks earlier involving a naval officer named Samuel Fellows, seized eagerly on the propaganda opportunity afforded
them by the Riley-Ross incident. The House of Representatives called
in Barbour and Belknap and after hearing their stories appointed a
special investigating committee to report the facts. Depositions were
taken and printed in the free-wheeling "Journal of the Times," for un-
rebuked distribution in other colonies. To press the advantage among
the radicals' English supporters, an account was rushed to John
Wilkes.[18]

Although patriot nostrils flared at the "daring outrage," justice was
slow to right the wrong. A week after the fracas, Ross, Phillips, and six
soldiers were called for a preliminary hearing before Justices of the
Peace Dana, Hill, and Ruddock. Despite a lobster-baiting tirade by
Dana, Phillips and Ross were released; the others were formally
charged with the riot and rescue and were put under a surety to appear at the forthcoming sitting of the superior court. For some unknown reason, however, charges were not pressed until the November
adjournment. At that time, the grand jury indicted not only five soldiers, but Ross, too. The trial followed a month later. Evidence of the
rescue itself being so clear, the only real issue was whether or not Ross
had participated. His counsel, Admiralty Judge Auchmuty, insisted he
had not. "Mr. Ross's Inactivity," he urged the jury, was "no Proof that
he was guilty of a Riot. Nor Proof that he aided, incouraged, and abet-
ted." Nonetheless, Ross, like four of his men, was convicted. Having
been fined seven pounds each, the soldiers let the matter drop. On
Ross's behalf, Auchmuty, having sought and obtained an arrest of
judgment, next moved for a new trial. The court took the motion under
advisement until the March term. By then, more deadly business had
engrossed the judges. With neither time nor inclination to shape the
technicalities for freeing Ross, the court denied the motion and fined
him twenty pounds. The incident had no adverse effect on his career.
He served as aide-de-camp to Lord Cornwallis at Yorktown, and died

a general.[19]

If the Riley-Ross affair reinforced the disdain with which the soldiers regarded the legal system, and confirmed the townspeople's belief that the army was inherently lawless, the next incident emphasized to both sides the acute physical danger which the military presence was thrusting upon Boston. On October 23, Ensign John Ness of the Fourteenth commanded the so-called Neck Guard, posted about a mile from the Town House at the fortification athwart the narrow isthmus connecting Boston with the mainland. This post in effect controlled land access to and egress from the town. That the army should pre-empt it had caused resentment from the early days of the garrison. Sam Adams insisted that the guardhouse was "erected, upon land belonging to the publick, and it is commonly said, without the leave, or even asking the leave of the publick!"

At about 9 P.M., Suffolk County Coroner Robert Pierpoint pushed into the guardhouse, demanding to see Ness. James Hickman, sergeant of the guard, ordered the sentry to keep Pierpoint out, and told the angry coroner to come back the next day. Pierpoint did leave, threatening to shoot Ness or any of the guard who might pass his house. "I have a brace of pistols loaded for that purpose," he said.

The next morning, a constable appeared with a warrant from Justice Dana against Ness for stealing Pierpoint's wood and for assaulting him. On Ness's promising to go to Dana's as soon as he was relieved, the constable left. But within a few minutes, Pierpoint himself and a large crowd came to the guard room, abusing and pressing in upon the sentries. "Why have you come?" Ness asked. "To give assistance," was the answer; but no one would explain what kind of assistance was needed, nor to whom it would be given. As the push increased, Ness asked the people to disperse and not to press or insult the sentries, lest he be obliged to turn out the guard. At that, the crowd rushed the sentries. A frightened Ness called the guard and drew the soldiers up in front of the guard house with fixed bayonets, ordering them not to meddle with the civilians. But the mob began tossing brickbats and stones, calling the soldiers "bloody back dogs" and saying they had no business there. Still Ness ordered the guard to remain silent. Thus they stayed for about fifteen minutes, until the relief arrived.

As Ness marched his guard back into town, the mob followed, growing as it went along, cursing, throwing stones, and even punching the soldiers. Soon the rowdies had broken into the column. After a brief scuffle, the guard formed again. But as it did, one of the men's muskets discharged, and a bullet whistled into the upper part of blacksmith Richard Gridley's shop. Horrified, for he believed the weapons unloaded, Ness whirled and gave his men positive orders neither to load nor to strike any of the mob. Even so, the crowd kept a greater distance, although the rain of stones continued; a rock caught a soldier in the head, opening a bloody cut.

While the guard was fighting its way back, Captain Molesworth, who happened to be the officer of the day, sat in his home, talking with two other officers. Glancing out the window, he saw Ness's battered band pass by. The three Redcoats raced into the street. Alarmed by the tone of the crowd and the force with which it was again beginning to press toward the soldiers, Molesworth hurried up the street. Just as he reached the soldiers, blacksmith Obadiah Whiston broke into the ranks and punched a soldier full in the face. Stunned and bleeding, the man could not defend himself; only Sergeant Hickman, quickly barring the way with the butt of his halbert, stopped Whiston from a second attack. Immediately, four of the guard fixed bayonets and stood with their muskets at waist level. The crowd, Whiston included, backed off.

Taking command, Molesworth ordered the guard to close up. "Be careful not to strike any of the mob unless obliged to it in your own defense," he said. "But if any man strikes you, put your bayonet through him." Hearing this, the crowd held back. The guard marched safely into the barracks. Ness's prudence and Molesworth's rashness had saved the day.[20]

As he had promised, Ness walked over to Dana's house in Crooked Lane (today Devonshire Street, between State Street and Dock Square). Outside, a mob had gathered. "Here comes the bloody back rascal," someone shouted. "He will be soon in goal. We shall shortly conduct him there." Ness found similar hostility inside. Because Pierpoint had "sworn the peace" against Ness, that is, lodged a formal complaint, Dana could lawfully demand that Ness post security for good behavior pending trial. As soon as Ness came before him, Dana asked if he had brought bail. Shocked, Ness began to protest his innocence and to ask for permission to round up witnesses. "You are not now on your trial," Dana answered, and told Ness that unless he could find one hundred pounds bail, he would be committed.

By this time, several of Ness's fellow officers had joined him. Desperately, he begged them to help him obtain security. They went out, returning in a while with three or four substantial citizens prepared to sign as sureties. For reasons of his own, Dana refused to accept any of them. Shortly thereafter, Captain Brabazon O'Hara of the Fourteenth strode in, carrying one hundred pounds in cash. He thrust it before the justice; but again Dana refused. Ness was growing more and more worried. Pierpoint had been present from the start. Throughout the proceedings, he vented his feelings freely. "Rascal! Scoundrel!" he called Ness, clenching his fist and threatening to knock the officer down. He said he could hardly keep his hands off. "I have a great mind to revenge myself this minute." But when Ness complained, Dana would not help. "I am deaf," he said, "and could not hear that you received any abuse." Finally, the conservative merchant Henry Lloyd offered himself as security and Dana accepted.[21]

Meanwhile, in the street outside, Molesworth was encountering more trouble. He had romantically eloped with Sukey Sheaffe in April, but despite his Masonic connections, he does not seem to have captured Boston's fancy. He appears instead to have been a prototypically arrogant, thoughtless young officer. Soon after his arrival, for example, he and a friend, having rented a horse and "chair" for an outing to nearby Jamaica Plain, ran the horse to Dedham, several miles beyond. They had pushed the beast so hard that he died thirty-six hours later. Then, in midsummer 1769, Molesworth had purchased from Messrs. Cox and Berry, jewelers, a "Pair best Paste Drop Earrings" (hopefully for the new Mrs. Molesworth), but had neglected to pay for them.

Recently, the town had learned of still another escapade, better suited to fashionable London than provincial Boston. One Sunday, while the guard was changing near the Town House, people gathered to hear the band and watch the spectacle. The constables began dispersing the crowd, which included Governor Bernard's second son, John. As Molesworth, the officer of the day, saw John leaving, he invited him to stay. When the constables protested, Molesworth, "in a sneering manner, called upon the musicians to play up the yankee doodle tune."[22]

Now, in the crowd before Dana's, Molesworth's unpopularity began to bear unhappy consequences. As he walked along, the crowd blocked his way. He pushed through, and Gridley the blacksmith followed him, shouting provoking and abusive insults. Aware of the danger of replying, Molesworth said nothing. "Here is the fellow," Gridley yelled, "who threatened to run me through the body. If there is law in Boston, I'll be revenged."[23]

There was indeed law in Boston, as Ness, Molesworth, and Sergeant Hickman were soon to discover. When Ness appeared before the court of general sessions to answer Pierpoint's charge, he found no witnesses against him. Three of the soldiers told Ness that the coroner had offered them two hundred dollars, plus assured escape from the army, if they would testify against Ness. But they had refused, and the case collapsed. Ness was acquitted.[24]

Once again, however, he was brought before the magistrates, this time on the charge of having ordered his men to fire on the civilians; a statute prohibited "the Firing of Guns Charged with Shot" in Boston.

Hickman, too, was "taken up" at the same time, Whiston having complained about his use of the halbert. During the hearing, conducted at the Town House before Justices of the Peace Dana, Ruddock, and Pemberton, the military men received rough treatment. "Who brought you here? Who sent for you?" Dana thundered. "By what authority do you mount guard, or march in the streets with arms? It is contrary to the laws of the Province, and you should be taken up for so offending. We want none of your guards. We have arms of our own, and can protect ourselves." Then he added menacingly: "You are but a handful. Better take care not to provoke us. If you do, you must take the Consequences."

While the witnesses were giving evidence, Pierpoint rose and again threatened to knock down Ness. When Hickman contradicted some of the testimony, someone else called the sergeant "a damn'd rascal." And when Dana raised the question of bail, the crowd rumbled dangerously. "Bail him with a rope," several people cried. After another squabble over sureties, however, both men were released on bond.[25]

Then it was Molesworth's turn. Summoned before Dana and Pemberton, he found himself face to face with Gridley. "The Army is a parcel of blackguard rascals," Gridley shouted. "Don't call names," one of the justices said gently. Then Dana himself exploded. "Do you want to murder the inhabitants?" he asked Molesworth. "If you do, you will find yourselves deceived; they will prove too hard for you."

"You," he said to Molesworth and the officers accompanying him, "have spirited up the soldiers to murder the inhabitants. There is no walking the streets at day or night, for the hourly abuses committed by the soldiers." The officers remained quiet. But Dana was not finished. "The inhabitants of the town acted properly," he insisted. "They had a right not only to strike a man of the guard for firing his gun, but to have dragged him from among the rest of the guard and brought him before a justice."

"Could they legally act so without a warrant?" Molesworth asked.

"You are out of order," the justice roared. "I don't sit here to be taught the law. Yes, the lives of the inhabitants are not to be put in danger." And turning to the bystanders, he said: "You had a right to act as you did."

"If any of the inhabitants," he told Molesworth, "struck any of the guard with only a fist or a stick, and that soldier, in consequence of your orders returned the blow with a bayonet or other weapon which killed him, you would have swung for it."

On the question of bail, Dana was adamant. No military men could stand surety; two civilians were rejected; at last Dana agreed to accept William Sheaffe (Molesworth's father-in-law) and another townsman.

The total bail was two hundred pounds.[26]

Final disposition of the cases awaited superior court action. At the November adjournment, Molesworth and Ness were indicted; Hickman's case seems to have been "nol prossed" (i.e., dropped). At least there is no record of any trial; indeed, he does not appear even to have been indicted. When Ness's case came on, the evidence against him was so thin that the judges unanimously agreed he should be acquitted. Today, his acquittal would have been directed. But in the eighteenth century, judges could only suggest; to the jury remained the final dispositive power. Happily for Ness, his jurors agreed with the court, and he was found not guilty. Molesworth's case was more difficult. The words he had spoken—and no one denied his uttering them—were undoubtedly unlawful. No officer could order bayonet thrusts in retaliation for mere physical blows. True, soldiers, like anyone else, could defend themselves from assaults. They could even, if no other means were available, defend their lives by killing their assailants. But killing in self-defense must literally be the only alternative to giving up one's own life. Under any other circumstances, soldiers could use lethal force on civilians only when ordered to do so by the civilian authorities.[27]

This last point now lay very much in the forefront of the radical strategy. "Surely," Sam Adams had written a little earlier, "no Provincial magistrate could be found so steel'd against the sensations of humanity and justice as wantonly to order troops to fire on an unarm'd populace and (more than) repeat in Boston the tragic scene exhibited in St. George's Field." [28]

Under the circumstances, even Dalrymple felt Molesworth was wrong. "I cannot vindicate Capt. Molesworth's heat of expression," he wrote Gage. The jury shared his view. The same jurors who had acquitted Ness returned a guilty verdict against the captain. Counsel moved to arrest judgment and for a new trial, which motions the court took under advisement. Strangely enough, no final action seems ever to have been taken. Subsequent court records are entirely silent; it does not even appear that the matter was nol prossed.[29]

By the end of 1769 the relative positions of the soldiers, the civilians, and the courts had become hardened. The military men justifiably felt themselves in physical danger. "This is but a prelude to some motion more consequential," wrote Dalrymple. "I am sure something very unpleasant is at hand." [30] The incident at the Neck Guard and the subsequent street battle could easily have degenerated into a fatal skirmish. The townspeople seemed to be acting as though they believed the troops could never, under any circumstances, fire without civilian orders. The conviction of Molesworth, and even the laborious clearing of

Ness, offered a check to the discretion of the officers; fear of the consequences might force a beleaguered subaltern to hold back his men longer than he properly ought.

Finally, and perhaps most significantly, the soldiers felt themselves morally isolated. "The people seem determined to embroil things entirely, to effect which they will leave nothing undone to render the situation of the troops embarrassing, and indeed unsupportable," Dalrymple told Gage. The courts, the supposed impartial dispensers of justice, gave no help. "Galway juries will cease to be proverbial when the behaviour of the late Boston ones are publicly known." (Galway was the original home of lynch law.) Any small incident might trigger a catastrophe. In the early dark of Christmas Day, as Private James McKaan of the Twenty-ninth stood guard at the Neck, a crowd kicking a "football" approached him. Someone booted the ball directly off McKaan's head. He and the rest of the guard restrained their tempers, and the incident passed. But it might easily have taken a more serious turn. The "tyranny of the justices," the performances of Dana, likewise disheartened the soldiers. "The men are rendered desperate by continued injustice," Dalrymple observed. Worse, the highest civil authority, Acting Governor Hutchinson, could do nothing. As the year faded, Boston saw the final public manifestation of the town's contempt for the military and of the establishment's impotence. The Suffolk County Grand Jury, without the assistance of Attorney-General Sewall, who indignantly refused to participate, indicted Bernard, Gage, the commissioners, and some customs officials, for having "grossly misrepresent[ed], vilif[ied], slander[ed], and abuse[d] the citizens and magistrates of Boston." Though the radicals let the indictments die, the soldiers, their officers, and their radical-despising commander-in-chief had received the message.[31]

CHAPTER 13

COFFEE HOUSE BRAWL

Redcoats furnished the radicals a series of highly visible hate-figures. Adams, however, was too skillful a mover of men to rely entirely on civilian antipathy to the military. He took more pleasant and positive steps to stimulate solidarity. August 14, 1769, the Sons of Liberty held a spread in the field next to Robinson's Inn (the Sign of the Liberty Tree) in Dorchester, which 355 people attended. A sailcloth awning kept the rain off the celebrants, while they drank forty-five toasts, enjoyed after-dinner mimicry by the majestic, witty hatter, Nathaniel Balch, and chorused two different versions of the Liberty Song. John Adams, who had an eye for such things, "did not see one Person intoxicated, or near it," and the group rode with dignity back to Boston in a train of 139 carriages, Hancock in the lead, Otis at the rear. Interspersed among the radical cadres bounced such conservatives or middle-roaders as lawyer Andrew Cazneau, Dr. John Jeffries, barrister Samuel Quincy, and artist John Copley. No one knows why they attended, although a cynic might suggest that as professional men, they were hoping to encourage business. Or perhaps they were worried about something else. "I felt as if I ought not to loose this feast, as if it was my Duty to be there," John Adams wrote that evening. "Jealousies arise from little Causes, and many might suspect, that I was not hearty in the Cause, if I had been absent." Whatever his guests' reasons, Sam Adams was glad to have their attendance. As his perceptive cousin noted, such gatherings "tinge the Minds of the People, they impregnate them with the sentiments of Liberty. They render the People fond of their Leaders in the Cause, and averse and bitter against all opposers." [1]

Sam Adams knew other ways to brew aversion and bitterness. Once again he turned to nonimportation. In the early days, the nonimportation movement had been more voluntary than coercive. By mid-1769, however, Adams realized that the success of nonimportation depended directly on the number participating. In fact, because the more radical merchants tended to participate most willingly, while the Tories continued to import, nonimportation might well give the conservatives a permanent commercial advantage. So long as abstentions from the association were tolerated, any subscriber who felt himself unable to resist the economic lure could (as many did) abandon the radicals and resume importing.[2]

Adams therefore encouraged the merchants (1) to make subscriptions to the nonimportation agreement mandatory, (2) to exert pressure against any merchant who might resume importing, and (3) to arrange for the confiscation and storage of any British goods which might somehow be landed. To maximize compliance, Adams bent those Whig propaganda machines, the Boston Town Meeting and the newspapers, to the task of isolating and ostracizing any merchants who resisted. Whoever continued to import, even inadvertently, would, like John Rowe, be called before the committee and given "a pretty tight Lecture." Deliberate violators might meet the fate of Hutchinson's nephew, Nathaniel Rogers: "Twice my house was besmeared, the last time with the Vilest filth of the Vilest Vault." The subscribers agreed not to import until January 1, 1770. Some of the nonsubscribers were nonetheless willing to have their goods stored under committee auspices until the first of the year. But, like many subscribers, they insisted that after New Year's Day the goods need no longer be kept off the market.[3]

Adams's campaign to inspirit resistance toward the revenue system received sharp encouragement about two weeks after Bernard's departure. Through friends with Parliamentary connections, the radicals received another packet of Bernard's reports to the ministry, together with much correspondence of the commissioners of the customs. The latter bore particular interest for Otis. He soon convinced himself that the commissioners, particularly Henry Hulton and John Robinson, had represented him "as inimical to the rights of the Crown, and disaffected to his Majesty," and that the letters were full of "personal abuse and insult." Otis and Sam Adams discussed the matter with Robinson and Hulton. Then Otis met alone with Robinson. Each time Otis came away unsatisfied.[4]

Erratic even at the calmest moments, Otis seemed unusually affected by the strain of events. On September 3, while he, the two Adamses, and others were at work in the *Gazette* office, "Cooking up Paragraphs, Articles Occurrences, &c.—working the political Engine," Otis numbed his companions with his constant chatter. As John Adams put it, "he grows narrative, like an old Man." While in this mood, anything Otis said or wrote was liable to haunt him. Among the articles which he wrote that Sunday evening was an intemperate attack upon all the commissioners but Temple. "Superlative blockheads," he called them. "It is strange considering the frequent conferences & communications between those able lawyers Gov. Hutchinson, Judge Auchmuty, the Attorney-General, Jonathan Philanthrop [i.e., Sewall], and the Commissioners, these have not learnt law enough to know they have no right to scandalize their neighbours." And then he laid his fire directly on Robinson: "'Tis strange that Mr. Robinson, even in his Welch clerkship, could not find out that if he '*officially*' or in any other way misrepresents me, I have a natural right if I can get no other satisfaction to break his head." [5]

The day this appeared in print, Otis once again publicly displayed his instability in "one continued Scene of bullying, bantering, reproaching and ridiculing the Select Men." "There is," John Adams concluded, "no Politeness or Delicacy, no Learning nor Ingenuity, no Taste or Sense in this Kind of Conversation." By his conduct, Otis was giving renewed life to Judge Oliver's bitter aphorism of a few years back: "if Bedlamism is a Talent he has it in Perfection." [6]

The next day, September 5, the "fiery and fev'rous" Otis let his "Inequalities of Temper," his "Rashnesses and Imprudences," his "Excess of Zeal" lead him into near-fatal tragedy. It was obvious that he had been brooding over the way the commissioners had first defamed him and then (as he saw it) denied him satisfaction. He must also have realized that his verbal violence in the *Gazette* might provoke physical retaliation. When Otis heard, that Tuesday morning, that Robinson had purchased a walking stick, he marched into the same shop and demanded "the fellow of it." [7]

About seven o'clock in the evening, carrying his new cane, Otis walked into the British Coffee House, down King Street from the Custom House. Under the most relaxed circumstances, Otis would not be particularly welcome there. The Coffee House was a social rendezvous for army and navy officers, customs officials, and their friends; in short, it was a Tory hangout. This evening was no exception. Among the bystanders who watched Otis as he entered the main room were Captain Brabazon O'Hara of the Fourteenth, Captain Jeremiah French of the Twenty-ninth, Captain Ralph Dundass of H.M. Schooner *St. Lawrence*, the Tory merchant James Forrest (nicknamed "the Irish infant"), and the Boston *Chronicle*'s John Mein. Also, William Browne, of Salem, one of the celebrated seventeen representatives who had voted to rescind the Massachusetts circular letter in 1768. But Otis was looking for the tall figure of Robinson.[8]

Shortly after Otis arrived, the commissioner strode in, a sword at his side. Seeing Otis without a weapon, he went to a back room, laid his own aside, and returned to the public room. A few feet apart, they faced each other tensely.

"I demand satisfaction of you, Sir," roared Otis.

"What satisfaction would you have?" Robinson asked.

"A gentleman's satisfaction." By this, Otis meant fistcuffs, since a statute outlawed dueling.

"I am ready to do it."

"Then come along with me," said Otis, moving toward the King Street doorway. But Robinson, instead of following, reached for Otis's nose. In eighteenth-century Massachusetts, gentlemen considered nose-tweaking an insulting, pain-inflicting (and therefore satisfying), yet nonfatal way of expressing contempt. To spare himself both injury and insult, Otis held off Robinson with his cane. The commissioner lifted his own stick and began swatting at Otis. For about a minute they dueled thus, neither man seeming to gain any advantage. Then the by-standers took away the sticks, and the combatants went at it with fists.[9]

At that, the melee became general. Men held Otis; someone landed a blow on his head that opened a one-and-a-half-inch cut down to the bone of his forehead. Hatless and wigless, Otis bled freely. John Gridley, Jeremiah's nephew, passing by on King Street, pushed his way into the room. Crying, "It is dirty usage to treat a man in that manner," he rushed between Otis and Robinson. Somebody tried to pull him away, but Gridley shook him off. As he grabbed Robinson by the collar, the commissioner's coat split down to the pockets. Someone standing on a bench rapped Gridley's head; someone else gripped his shoulder. Blinded by his own blood, Gridley flailed away with his right arm. A sheathed sword or a stick cracked across his wrist, and Gridley retreated with a fratured ulna. As he left, he heard shouts of "Kill him! Kill him!"[10]

Meanwhile, Thomas Dupee, another passer-by, unable to force his way through the growing crowd at the front door, went to the side entrance and worked his way into the room. Two or three men were holding Otis, whether to break up the fight or to pin him, Dupee could not tell. The lamp had been broken in the melee; through the dimness, Dupee saw Robinson punch Otis's face. Comptroller Benjamin Hallowell managed to get between the combatants and ease Otis out of the room. Gridley, the hand of his broken arm thrust into the front of his coat, came over to Otis and offered to defend him, as far as he was able, from any more abuse. "I am much obliged to you," said Otis, leaving to have his wounds treated.[11]

Although cut on the forehead and generally bruised, Otis was not in danger. Pain and fever oppressed him the first night, but the crisis had passed by the next day. Two weeks after the fight, John Adams reported after spending a social evening with him that his conduct was in some respects improved over what it had been before. "Otis bore his Part very well, conversible eno', but not extravagant, not rough, not sour." Within a month the Town elected him to a committee to consider a suitable response to Governor Bernard's newly revealed official correspondence. On November 13 he was elected moderator of the town meeting, serving as such at two subsequent meetings as well. Yet a rumor persisted that he was delirious and that his standing with the radicals was slipping daily. Even this gave the Tories no comfort. As one of them noted, if Otis was indeed losing ground, "that more pernicious Devil Adams gains it." Otis's decline and the rise of Adams were, true enough, demonstrable facts by late 1769. But the change in their relative positions, as well as Otis's mental deterioration, had long antedated the tavern brawl. The common assertion that Otis "was never the same man afterwards that he had been in his earlier years," is, to the extent that it suggests a causal relation between the fight and the decline, entirely wrong.[12]

Robinson suffered no physical effects from the brawl, and apparently no mental ones from the newspaper war which followed. On October 5, exactly one month after the fight, he married Anne (Nancy) Boutineau, daughter of a Boston attorney and niece of the Peter Faneuil who had donated the Hall. That night and the next, anonymous admirers saluted Robinson and his bride with a shower of stones through the bedroom window. This was nothing new to Robinson. He recalled the raid on his rented Roxbury estate in 1768, which Sam Adams had called the work of mere "liquorish boys."[13]

The radicals took a more serious view of the Robinson-Otis battle. Literally before Otis's fever had subsided, they were stirring up sentiment against the commissioner. Within two weeks, Otis himself was calling the brawl "a premeditated, cowardly and villanous attempt . . . to assassinate me." As early as the day after the fight, John Rowe found "the Inhabitants greatly alarmed at the Usage Mr. Otis met with—tis generally thought he was very Rascally treated." Even Dalrymple admitted privately to Gage that "Mr. Robinson beat the other most excessively." The town, Dalrymple noted, was consequently "in an uproar." No one was sure whether Otis would bring a lawsuit or would, in Dalrymple's elegant phrase, "try the fortune of a second day." [14]

Because the incident had obviously broken the king's peace, criminal sanctions could lie against any of the participants. Some of them reportedly met at Commissioner Paxton's immediately after the brawl, passing "mutual congratulations." They must also have given thought to possible consequences. The next day, Paxton advised the Suffolk County deputy sheriffs not to try to serve process aboard any warship; apparently Captain Dundass feared retaliation. The army, as Dalrymple proudly told Gage, was not the subject of any such warrant.[15]

Unable to touch the naval officer, and lacking any valid charge against the army, the radicals turned toward an easier target, the civilian, Browne. Believing that his had been the blow which disabled Gridley, the people were "more enraged against him than against Robinson." He remained hidden all day (September 6) in an officer's room in the Coffee House. Toward evening the radicals found him and carried him "in triumph" to Faneuil Hall for a preliminary hearing before Justices of the Peace Dana and Pemberton. The crowd of two thousand which followed, filling the hall, was not a friendly throng. When Justice of the Peace James Murray, hastily called to Browne's aid, arrived, the bystanders repeatedly threw him out bodily. Selectman Jonnathan Mason, a Son of Liberty, forgot politics long enough to shout: "For shame, gentlemen, do not behave so rudely!" He then helped Murray into the room. The crowd hissed. Murray bowed. Another round of hisses; another bow; a patter of applause. As Murray finally sat down, Pemberton and Dana invited him to join them, for of course, as a justice of the peace, he, too, was entitled to preside. Murray wisely declined.

After hearing the rest of the evidence, the sitting justices decided to "bind over" Browne, that is, put him under recognizance to appear at the next sitting of the Court of General Sessions, there to answer to the charge of "assaulting, beating, and wounding" Gridley. Looking about for someone to serve as his bail, Browne could find nobody. Finally Murray agreed. Before binding himself, however, he prudently told the justices that his offer was not to be taken as a vindication of what Browne had done.

The formalities completed, Dana and Pemberton told the people to disperse. But the crowd, anticipating more sport, stayed. When Murray pushed out next to Dana, someone pulled the wig from his bald head. Though the mob closed in, trying to trip him, a group of radicals, aided by some of Murray's friends, hustled him through the dark streets. As the party fought its way through the press, Murray's disheveled wig followed behind, borne on a pole. Despite offers of refuge in a nearby house, Murray insisted on going home. Warned by one of the radicals, "No violence, or you'll hurt the cause," the mob suffered Murray and his impromptu escort to escape safely. To make up for the lost sport, the throng then went to John Mein's bookshop near the Coffee House and to the print shop of his Boston *Chronicle* on what is now Washington Street, between Summer and Essex Streets. At each, they left the signs "so besmeared with dirt," outhouse-type dirt, that the boards had to be taken down.[16]

CHAPTER 14

KING STREET SHOWDOWN:
JOHN MEIN

In the fall of 1769, Sam Adams began visibly to increase the pressure and tempo of the nonimportation campaign. Piqued by a verbal counterattack which John Mein had successfully begun, and dissatisfied at the progress of the boycott, Adams had for some time been publicly identifying and castigating the recalcitrants, including Mein, in the Boston *Gazette*. Now he took steps to arouse the town's anger at their expense. The occasion he chose was a special town meeting called "to consider and determine what Steps" ought to be taken to restore the character of Boston, "greatly aspers'd and injured" by the recently unveiled correspondence home of Bernard, Gage, Hood, and the commissioners.[1]

After Clerk William Cooper read selections from the letters, Adams gave a brief pep talk to the "Loyal and Religious people," "really oppress'd and under a Tyrany," victims of an unprecedented amount of "Malice and falsehood." A committee of radicals (including both Adamses and Otis, although he was absent from the meeting) was appointed to "invalidate" the letters. Having thus warmed the people into a satisfactorily antiadministration mood, Adams turned to the real business of the meeting. He produced a list of alleged importers and proposed that they be "stigmatiz'd & declar'd Enemys of the Country," their names to be "recorded in the Town Books as such to the latest [i.e., uttermost] posterity." Radical lawyer Benjamin Kent seconded the proposal with a declaration that "those who dar'd to Import any Goods contrary to the agreement of the Merchants were Guilty of High Treason against the Majesty of the People." Nathaniel Balch, the after-dinner entertainer at the recent Dorchester celebration, pointed out that some of the recalcitrants were now ready to sign. "It is too late in the day," Adams said. "Their previous conduct was so highly blameable that atonement could not be made on this side the Grave. God perhaps might possibly forgive them, but I and the rest of the People never could." Thus inspired, the meeting passed the motion unanimously.[2]

Despite his publicly pious inflexibility, Adams was of course willing and eager to obtain as many supporters as possible. A couple of weeks later, the merchants met in Faneuil Hall and resolved (or re-resolved) neither to import any merchandise nor to deal in any such until all the Townshend duties and "every other kind" were totally abolished. They even agreed, conditionally upon a similar undertaking by New York and Philadelphia, not to import sugar or molasses from the British sugar islands. This new agreement was reported to be achieving only "very indifferent success." But the original agreement was attracting, or more accurately, compelling, additional signatures. The hold-outs, one observer reported, were believed to be "in real danger of their Lives. Their Property was actually unsafe, their Signs, Doors and Windows were daub'd over in the Night time with every kind of Filth, and one of them particularly had his Person treated in the same manner." [3]

Adams was indeed playing a hard game. Although they maintained a certain mystery about their organization, the Sons of Liberty used abrupt methods. Realizing that Ebenezer Mackintosh knew "more of their Secret Transactions than the whole of what they call the Torys put together," the radicals "threatened [him] with Death in case he should inform." The Tories knew that Mackintosh "would be a means of unravelling the whole Scene of Iniquity," but feared that even if he remained alive, his evidence would "weigh but little" in the minds of radical-controlled juries. They hoped, therefore, that the ministry would have him brought to England where his revelations would at least have propaganda value. Meanwhile, the Sons of Liberty hardly concealed their philosophy. Kent had been clear; so were others. "The common Argument they make use of is this: that the people make the King, and that whenever they think it proper to depose him, they act Constitutionally." "A no less worthy person than a Deacon" told the Tory merchant George Mason "that the Revolution principles were gaining ground daily, and that by and bye he did not doubt but we should have a blessed form of Government in which no Tyrants would be allow'd to oppress the People." And yet at this time, Hutchinson was blandly reporting: "The body of the people, I am sure, are convinced that they cannot subsist without the protection of Great Britain . . . And yet they have imbibed principles which make them a distinct independent government. They will sooner or later see the absurdity of such principles & be again sensible . . . that they enjoy the blessing of as mild and good a government as any people upon the globe." [4]

While Hutchinson was hoping, talking, and writing, John Mein had begun to take action. Mein was clever enough to realize that he would merely be wasting his effort if he based his counterattack on any appeal to something intangible like the spirit of liberty. He could not, he knew, simply argue or convince the people away from the radicals and nonimportation. He needed something visible and irrefutable that would raise "distrust and dissension." After "a few moments consideration" and a short examination of some customs papers, Mein found his tactic.[5]

On August 21, and continuing at intervals thereafter, Mein's Boston *Chronicle* began printing Custom House records showing the names of everyone who was importing English goods. The *Chronicle* ultimately ran fifty-five lists, showing that many of the so-called "well-disposed" merchants were breaking their own boycott. Every reader of the *Chronicle*'s 1,400-copy press run might well conclude that the merchant Sons of Liberty were utilizing the mob's muscle to destroy their competitors, "and that their Patriotism was founded on Self Interest and Malice." [6]

Publication of the manifests caused a sensation in Boston, but Mein did not rest. He printed 4,000 copies of the various lists and "circulated them, gratis, over all America, from Florida to Nova Scotia." He also put the entire series into a quarto pamphlet, likewise for free distribution in other colonies.[7] An effective nonimportation agreement depended upon intercolonial cooperation. The various seaports naturally envied and suspected one another. To have the merchants of, say, Philadelphia convinced by Mein's lists that the Boston-inspired agreement was merely a trading maneuver could well kill the idea forever. Adams might be able to soothe his irate townsmen. But as he had himself so adroitly proved with the fanciful "Journal of the Times," propaganda about local events, when shipped elsewhere, could never be entirely neutralized out-of-town.

Elimination of Mein and his influence was essential to the continued success of the nonimportation agreement and, indeed, of the entire radical program. His cleverness, courage, resourcefulness, and journalistic skill made the task of silencing him both necessary and difficult.

But Mein possessed several potential weak spots, and it was these which the radicals tried to exploit. Mein was an outsider; he had been in Boston only since 1764. Worse, he was a Scot. The attack on Gill had occurred a year and a half before Mein began printing the import manifests. But the final trial of Gill's civil action for damages did not take place until March 1769, and the last bit of legal maneuvering, Mein's futile motion for a new trial, was not finished until August, just about the time that the *Chronicle* exposé started. The memory and the odium thus remained fresh. Besides the deliberateness of the assault, people had been impressed with the physical disparity between the men; Gill was much smaller than Mein. Mein would be in a weak moral position to appeal for fair play when and if the Sons of Liberty should physically attack him.[8]

Mein's newspaper activities easily sufficed to earn him the radicals' hate. In addition, however, his successful bookselling and stationery business (he supplied the commissioners their writing paper) required him to depend heavily for inventory on London exporters. No business connection with the commissioners could increase a man's popularity. But it was Mein's relations with London which angered the radicals even more. From the start of the nonimportation movement, Mein had refused to cooperate. The radicals argued with him directly; they threatened him; they urged his customers to desert him; they wrote the selectmen of other towns, promoting a boycott; they ran advertisements in the newspapers calling him an enemy of America; they posted similar sentiments on trees and fences. All their tactics failed. Finally, at the uproarious town meeting of October 4, 1769, Mein's was one of the names handed to posterity as an enemy of his country.[9]

Mein having been in effect branded an outlaw, the radicals treated him like one. His person and perhaps even his life were now in open jeopardy, so he began to carry a pistol wherever he went. On a mid-October night, unidentified assailants with clubs attacked first one man who looked like him, then another. In each case the beating began so savagely that if the mistake had not been discovered, the victim (the Tories said) would have been killed.[10]

Swamped by anonymous threatening letters, warned by others and by personal word, on Tuesday, October 24, Mein finally went with his partner John Fleeming to Hutchinson's house. Troubled, perhaps by what the Ness-Molesworth affair that morning portended for him, Mein pressed the lieutenant-governor for assistance and advice. He was not presently fearful for his own safety, Mein said, but rather for whoever might attack him. His friends had told him they would assist him against any attack, and the resulting affray might lead to serious peace-breaking. Hutchinson replied that no "previous steps" could be taken to preserve the peace. Unless Mein could name his potential assailants, so they could be bound over to keep the peace, Hutchinson could not help him.

In that case, said Mein, perhaps he ought to present a memorial to Hutchinson and the council, outlining the situation, so that in the event of trouble, no one could blame it on him. This, Mein wrote later, Hutchinson "repeatedly advised me against & repeatedly objected to." Presumably, Hutchinson feared that any debate in the hostile council could not possibly help Mein, and would almost certainly further embarrass the government.

One final problem troubled Mein. Within two weeks, Boston would be celebrating November 5, "a riotous day in Boston." Could Hutchinson tell Mein the name of any particular justice of the peace on whom Mein might call for aid if need required? Hutchinson said he did not know any that would fail to do his duty. Well, asked Mein, was Hutchinson himself planning to be in town that night? He could not tell, Hutchinson replied, and repeatedly added that no previous steps could be taken.[11]

Whatever else might be said of Mein, he certainly had courage. Two days after Hutchinson had in effect told him he could expect no protection from the civil authority, the *Chronicle* carried a direct personal attack on the radical leaders. "Tommy Trifle, Esq." Mein called Cushing; "Muddlehead" did for Otis. "Johnny Dupe, Esq., alias the Milch-Cow" was the tag for Hancock, followed by this bitter and highly relevant description: "A good natured young man with long ears—a silly conceited grin on his countenance—a fool's cap on his head—a bandage tied over his eyes—richly dressed and surrounded with a crowd of people, some of whom are stroaking his ears, others tickling his nose with straws, while the rest are employed riffling his pockets." Following on the heels of the importation revelations, this kind of personal journalism roweled the radical leaders beyond endurance. Although as Hutchinson pointed out, they had for many years themselves "grossly abused and calumniated" Bernard, Hutchinson, Secretary Oliver and anyone else who opposed them, they were not at all inclined to concede a like license to the opposition. What Commissioner Hulton called Mein's "talent for humor" would no longer be tolerated.[12]

Some time after four o'clock on October 28, Mein and Fleeming left the bookstore, each carrying a pistol in his pocket. They crossed King Street and began walking along its south side, evidently heading for the Main Street (now Washington Street) and Mein's printshop. As they walked, Mein noticed that the shops on both sides of King Street appeared unusually crowded. Suddenly about twenty people surrounded the two printers. Mein recognized among others the radical

whip William Molineux, the merchant Edward Davis, the Whig trader and mariner Captain Samuel Dashwood, and the tailor Thomas Marshal, lieutenant-colonel of the Boston militia regiment. Angry and determined, the men began, as the *Evening-Post* account later put it, to catechize Mein. The talk grew hotter; Davis poked Mein's left abdomen with his cane, leaving a contusion which would still be visible and hard eight days later.

Davis's blow painfully assured Mein that the men around him would not be satisfied by a verbal exchange of views. He drew his pistol, cocked it, and leveled it at his inquisitors. Backing up King Street with Fleeming, Mein kept the growing crowd at a respectful distance; but he could not disperse it. With cries of "Knock him down! Kill him!" the mob advanced as fast as Mein retreated. Somebody tried to sneak behind Mein, desisting when he realized the editor meant to keep his threat to shoot the first man who touched him. As the crowd followed Mein up King Street, past the town whipping post near the corner of Pudding Lane (now Devonshire Street), a shower of brickbats flew through the air.

The flow of the crowd had naturally pushed Mein and Fleeming to the south side of the Town House, standing at the head of King Street. This accident proved a piece of luck for the two men, because it forced them toward the Main Guard on the south side of King Street across from the Town House. Here they could hope for some kind of protection; the Main Guard held the largest body of troops then under arms in the whole town. One of the crowd was later heard to say that the attack had begun too soon, too far down King Street. If only the ambush had been delayed until Mein and Fleeming had passed the Guardhouse, the mob would have "made sure" of him.[13]

Mistimed though the attack was, it almost succeeded. As he passed Joseph Waldo's shop, right near the whipping post, Marshal reached into the window and helped himself to an iron-edged shovel. When Mein and Fleeming reached the sentries outside the Guard, the officer of the guard, young Lieutenant James Basset of the Twenty-ninth, ordered the sentries to clear their posts. This permitted the printers to slip between the sentry boxes and reach safety. But while the sentries were pushing the mob from the front of the boxes, Marshal ran in from the side. As Mein, relieved at his escape, was "coolly stepping up the Guardroom steps," Marshal swung the shovel at his head. Whether from the unfamiliarity with the weapon, lack of balance after his run, or general miscoordination, Marshal missed his target. The heavy spade cut clear through Mein's coat, waistcoat, and shirt, opening a two-inch gash on his shoulder.[14]

Fleeming, a little way behind, came up. When Marshal spun away and sprinted off, Fleeming vainly struck at him with a stick he held in his left hand. Reeling, fighting to regain his balance, Fleeming reflexively contracted his right hand and discharged his pistol. Mein believed that the ball went into the ground; but a rumor arose immediately that the shot had torn the sleeve of one of the sentries, a grenadier from the Twenty-ninth. At any rate, no one was hurt.[15]

Inside the Guard, Mein could scarcely be called safe. From the guardroom, he hastily wrote to Hutchinson, asking "what protection the Law can afford to a person in my situation; and the names of the officers of the Law who will put that Law into execution." The mob outside was swelling. The crowd which drove Mein into the Guardhouse numbered about two hundred. Fleeming's shot attracted more. Eventually the throng in front of the sentries exceeded two thousand. The initial assailants had included not a single "low fellow." Someone saw Selectman Jonathan Mason (the one who had rescued Justice of the Peace James Murray), "one of the very gravest Personages in the Town." As the tumult grew, however, the mob took on more of a democratic character. The "Principal People" who had originated the attack remained, joined by others. A church bell began ringing.[16]

In the excitement and confusion, the people outside the Guard did not realize that it had been Fleeming's pistol which discharged. Everyone believed or assumed that Mein had deliberately fired into the crowd. If the rumor were true, then Mein had committed a criminal offense; seizing his person would accordingly become less of an act of personal vengeance and more of a civic duty. Thus inspired, the crowd surged against the Guardhouse. Only the bayonets of the sentries kept the mob from storming the citadel then and there. As it was, the press was so great that when the time came for the guard to change, the mob would not fall back far enough to permit the relief to form. Lieutenant Basset finally had to order the relief sentries off to their posts individually. Stymied at a direct assault, and aware that no one but a civil officer on authorized business could obtain admission to the Guardhouse, the radicals turned to the law.[17]

Pursuing the idea that Mein's alleged pistol-firing had been a criminal breach of the peace, Sam Adams and Molineux obtained from Justice of the Peace Dana a warrant to arrest him for firing a pistol upon the king's subjects, "lawfully and peaceably assembled together." It is of course possible that the radicals acted entirely from a desire to encourage respect for law enforcement. Mein did not think so. "Their plan," he wrote a few days later, "was to get me into the Custody of the Officer, & it being then dark, to knock [me] on the head; & then their usual saying might have been repeated that it was done by Boys & Negroes, or by Nobody." Someone else reported hearing two mem-

bers of the crowd say explicitly that it was intended the mob should
"rescue" Mein from the civil officers "and deal with him as they themselves should think proper." Adams and Molineux returned to the
Guardhouse, armed with Dana's warrant. Together with Deputy Sheriff Benjamin Cudworth and a constable, they began a careful search
for Mein. For over an hour they combed the guardroom without success, while Mein concealed himself in the garret. When they gave up,
he put on a soldier's uniform and made his way to Dalrymple's
house.[18]

The mob's push at the Guardhouse, coming so soon after the Ness-
Molesworth fracas, seemed to Dalrymple the start of that long-feared
direct combat between the soldiers and the townspeople. As soon as
the news reached him, he sent word to Hutchinson, and the lieutenant-governor hurried to Dalrymple's lodgings. Both men realized that
"things are got out of the reach of authority," and that there remained
to them only a few options. At Hutchinson's request, Dalrymple ordered the entire garrison under arms. Except for posted sentries, the
troops stayed out of sight in the various guardhouses and barracks.
Should the radicals choose to push the test further, the soldiers were
ready. Hutchinson, meanwhile, called together such of the council as
were in Boston, together with whatever local justices of the peace he
could reach.[19]

The onset of darkness had signaled the commencement of the New
England Sabbath. To George Gailer, the darkness meant the start of
an ordeal in some ways more terrifying than Mein's. Gailer had been a
crewman aboard the revenue cutter *Liberty*, the same vessel whose seizure had touched off the rioting in June 1768. She had been sold as
part of the vice-admiralty proceedings and turned into a customs en-
forcer. After a mob at Newport, Rhode Island, seized and burned her
in July 1769, Gailer signed aboard the Rhode Island sloop *Success*.
The sloop came up to Boston, and was shortly seized for landing uncustomed wine. Somehow the idea took root among the radicals that
Gailer had, in a colloquial as well as technical sense, "informed" on his
ship and had thus been responsible for the seizure. During the afternoon of October 28, a group of Liberty Boys located him and tried to
seize him. Managing to escape, he found shelter in a house which his
pursuers settled down to watch. At nightfall, when Gailer tried to slip
out, the radical sentries pounced.[20]

Dragging him to a cart waiting at the Town House, they stripped
him naked, replacing his clothes with a thick coat of tar, surmounted
by feathers. Thus attired, with a lantern in his hand to command attention, Gailer began a guided tour of Boston. To ensure that as many
onlookers as possible shared his triumph, the mob (estimated at be-

tween 1,000 and 1,500) insisted that the houses along the route display lighted windows. Only one person was reported to have refused this request; a barrage of stones soon shattered his darkened windows.[21]

The line of march led south along the Main Street toward Liberty Tree. When the yelling, cordstick-carrying mob reached Mein's house and the adjacent printshop, it paused. Several men tried to force the locked front door; others broke the windows. An apprentice inside loaded a musket with nothing but powder and fired it at the revelers to frighten them. Momentarily startled, they quickly regrouped, burst the door open in earnest and rushed inside. A thorough search of the rooms convinced them that Mein was out, so they contented themselves with doing "some mischief" to his books and confiscating two guns.[22]

Resuming Gailer's procession, the mob paused at Liberty Tree, where it listened to him swear never to be guilty of further informing. Then the crowd carted him up to the North End, over to the West End, and back to the Town House, occasionally swatting him with sticks or the back of a handsaw. From the Town House, the mob moved down to the Custom House, where Private Thomas Burgess of the Twenty-ninth stood sentry. Halting the cart before Burgess, the mob gave three cheers and moved in on him. Burgess told them to keep off his post. Some of the crowd then pushed into Royal Exchange Lane (now Exchange Street) and broke a few of the Custom House's windows. Again Burgess told them to clear off. Now the mob began to press him more ominously; thinking himself in danger, he loaded his musket, hoping to frighten his assailants. The maneuver failed. "[T]hey closed [me] up and struck at and abused [me] most grossly, threatening to Hoist [me] in the Cart and use [me] as they did the Man they had tarred and Feathered." But they did not execute the threat. Instead the rioters made Gailer renew his obligation to behave in the future; they made him ask pardon for his past offenses (whatever those might be); and they forced him to acknowledge their great lenity in not having put him to death. The formalities completed, they returned him his clothes. "[H]e was dismissed without further Damage." That winter, Gailer sued eight of his tormentors for £2,000. The case never came to trial; from the record, it appears to have been settled. Gailer's injuries did not prevent him from enlisting aboard *Rose* as an able seaman within a month of his mobbing.[23]

While Gailer was enduring his agony, Hutchinson was meeting with councilors and justices, trying desperately to find some way to reassert civil authority. This was the first real mob since the troops had arrived, and everyone realized that nothing would suffice to suppress it but calling on the troops to aid the civil magistrates. In addition to every

other argument which could be made against throwing troops at civilians, Hutchinson knew that the objects of this riot excited particular
odium. Mein was widely hated, as were informers. "I doubt not,"
Hutchinson wrote a few days later, "many persons were concerned in
this affair for the sake of punishing an Informer who would scruple
joining in acts of violence against any other persons." That kind of
mob would be impossible to control by ordinary means. Fortunately
for Hutchinson and the establishment, 9 p.m., the hour when their despair reached its nadir, coincided with the final festivities on King
Street. If, in the agonies of indecision, Hutchinson had happened to
look out the window, he would have seen the mob dispersing. The riot
was over.[24]

There remained the question of what to do with Mein, and the related problem of preventing future riots, or containing them if they
could not be prevented. The law's helplessness in Mein's case only emphasized its impotence generally. After issuing a proclamation which,
he confessed, would have no "other effect than to preserve the appearance of government," Hutchinson arranged for publication of an account of the evening's events. This peculiar item described the Gailer
mobbing in some detail, although omitting mention of the entry at
Mein's. And it barely mentioned Mein's own difficulty, not even giving
his name. Hutchinson's expressed reason was the impropriety of discussing the matter while a warrant was outstanding. It is more likely
that Hutchinson, recognizing Mein's overpowering unpopularity,
wished to play down the whole affair as much as possible, fearful that
a thorough report might again stir up the town.[25]

Earlier that same day, Hutchinson, meeting once more with the Boston justices of the peace, had laid out for them their legal obligations
in all cases of riot. Reminding them of their oaths, he emphasized the
destructive consequences of their neglect of duty. The justices uni-
formly disapproved the cruel treatment of Gailer and told Hutchinson
they were ready to exert themselves to execute the law against any
similiar future offenders. But Mein's case was different. One justice said
that although Mein would not be criminally prosecuted, there was
danger that the people would tear him to pieces, " 'for opposing the
whole continent in the only measure which could save them from
ruin.' " [26]

Hutchinson had never answered the letter Mein wrote from the
Guardhouse. Annoyed but undaunted, Mein began preparing his own
defense. He arranged to have some witnesses come to the house where
he was hiding to give affidavits under oath. But when he wrote to
Judge Foster Hutchinson (the lieutenant-governor's brother) asking
him to administer the deponents' oaths, Hutchinson refused. With

Fleeming and Dr. Richard Hirons standing by as witnesses, Mein wrote again to the lieutenant-governor. Reminding Hutchinson of their earlier talk, Mein observed that it was no longer a question of "previous steps"; the peace had in fact been broken, and Mein now had "some Title to claim a protection from further Insults." He offered to surrender, "provided I have a proper force to prevent any injury to my Person from a Licentious Mob." Believing he could clear himself of any criminal charge, he planned civil actions against those who assaulted him. But he wanted a military guard to assure his safety "to and from the Justices." [27]

Mein cavalierly closed this message, "in full Confidence of a speedy answer." Hutchinson, however, chose not to answer it at all. Mein could appear safely, he told the messenger, although the printer must remember "the Weakness of Government." This was nonsense. Hutchinson realized as well as Mein that Mein could appear publicly in Boston only if he wished to commit suicide. But if Hutchinson conceded this openly, he would somehow have to explain why he was refusing to call in the army. Mein fully appreciated this. Persuasion having failed, he tried desperately to goad Hutchinson into using troops. After pointedly reviewing his situation, Mein pressed his argument: "It therefore now rests with your Honour to Call in that assistance which the Wisdom of Administration has afforded you to support the Weakness of Government here," in the face of "a tumultuous Populace, with law in their mouths, but Rapine in their Hands, . . . where even the Civil Officers of the Crown are too timid, for it cannot be called Prudence, even to Speak, far less act." "If I go," he concluded menacingly, "I shall carry with me proper Authenticated Representations of the Power and Support being withheld while the most evident necessity demanded its being exerted. Every Person must then stand to the Consequences of his own behaviour." [28]

Hutchinson would not be stampeded. He knew that activating the soldiers would of itself probably lead to trouble; calling them out expressly to defend Mein, who the people, rightly or wrongly, regarded as a public enemy, would only make the bloodshed certain. Remaining idle caused him anguish, but his only hope, he felt, lay in the Home Government's taking some new definite step. The administration must either abolish the duties that seemed to be causing the discontent, or else enforce them with sufficient muscle to stifle the mobs, and especially to outlaw such extralegal combinations as the nonimportation agreement. Meanwhile, Hutchinson would "make it my chief view to avoid every thing which may unnecessarily irritate the minds of the people." [29]

So the helpless Mein remained a hideaway. Early in November, he abandoned his shoreside refuge and went to H.M. Schooner *Hope*,

where Lieutenant George Dawson sheltered him until Captain Caldwell of H.M.S. *Rose* offered him more commodious quarters in the captain's own stateroom and cabin. At Boston that very day, Mein's effigy
starred in the Pope's Day celebration. "Mean is the Man; M—n is his
name" ran one of the lines on the accompanying placard. Finally, in
mid-November 1769, all chances gone of returning to Boston, he transferred back to *Hope* and departed for England. He had threatened to
complain to the government about Hutchinson, and complain he did.
Too lengthy to set out here, the exhaustive memorial, written in Mein's
trenchant style, is larded with references to "the Refusal of the Civil
Magistrate to act while the most evident necessity demanded his interposition," "the timidity of the Magistrate," and "the weakness of Government and the officers of Government" in Massachusetts. Hutchinson
had fortunately taken Mein at his word. He sent Hillsborough a dis-
passionate account of the whole affair (contained in a letter which
Mein was kind enough to carry with him). Considering the rough verbal treatment which Mein was to give Hutchinson, it is an interesting
commentary on Hutchinson's fairness and integrity that he capped his
report thus: "I am fully convinced that Mr. Mein is a very great sufferer and that his sufferings took their rise from his opposition to the
doings of the Merchants and I could not deny him a just representation of his case to your Lordship." [30]

Mein's trouble, by any view, epitomized the political ills of Boston.
At a sabbath service held November 12 by the Sandemanian sect to
which Mein nominally belonged, elder Colburn Barrell preached a sermon analyzing the times. "A person would be in danger of having his
property demolished, & his person tore to pieces for speaking respect-
fully of the King," he said. "The Country [is] in open Rebellion, Diso-
bedience, & Disloyalty." Moreover, the "Clergy led in it." Barrell had
touched a radical nerve. The grand jury promptly indicted him for
breach of the peace.[31]

The Mein affair, Hutchinson wrote years later, "was the first trial of
a mob since the troops had been in town, and, having triumphed in defiance of them, a mob became more formidable than ever." Dalrymple,
writing the day after the riot, showed equal prescience. "Authority
here is at a very low ebb, indeed it is rather a shadow than a Substance." Of the abortive attack on the Guardhouse, he said: "The next
essay will be possibly more serious, at least if one may judge from appearances." Ailing and disheartened, the commander of the Boston
garrison saw no hope: "The Crisis I have long expected comes on very
fast, and the temper of the times is such that if something does not
happen of the most disagreeable Kind, I shall with pleasure give up
my foresight." [32]

CHAPTER 15

SEIDER THE MARTYR

With the arrival of the January 1, 1770, cutoff date, cracks began to appear in Sam Adams's nonimportation phalanx. Many of the merchants whose goods the committtee had either confiscated or locked up believed that as of New Year's Day they were properly entitled to resume selling. The radicals disagreed, arguing that such goods ought to remain in custody until other merchants had had a reasonable time in which to order and receive English goods. William Molineux roared as fiercely as ever, swearing that were it not for the law, he would with his own hands put to death every violater of the agreement. But instead of frightening his hearers, he disgusted them. Some hardy merchants began deserting the cause, and more were tempted to do so. Early in the month, two Scottish captains arrived to order four 230-ton vessels for their Glasgow principals. To finance the construction, they proposed to bring in and sell British merchandise. Aware of the impact of nonimportation, they refused to conclude the necessary shipbuilding contracts unless the merchants would vote that Boston retailers importing the goods would not be considered to have violated the nonimportation agreement. The shipbuilding trades circulated a petition to that effect. Within a few hours it drew seventy signatures.[1]

Delighted with their success, the sponsors met on the evening of January 12 to consider how best to present the petition. As they were debating, Justice of the Peace (and Selectman) John Ruddock walked in. After pointing out the subversive and ruinous nature of the subscription, Ruddock demanded to see the petition. When it was handed over, he promptly destroyed it. His influence was such that nobody protested. The shipbuilding scheme, so far as it concerned Boston, had died. The Scots took their plans to Newbury and let the contract there.[2]

Notwithstanding this temporary triumph, the radicals continued to feel their grip weakening. Hutchinson's sons Thomas and Elisha, having earlier permitted the Committee of Inspection to padlock their warehouse, ripped off the lock and removed the goods, principally tea, "to some other place unknown to the committee." Five other merchants who had previously agreed to keep English goods in storage now broke them out and began selling them. Despite a visit from the Committee of Inspection, they refused to quit. To counter this threat, Adams called a mass meeting in Faneuil Hall, chaired by Deacon William Phillips. Upon the committee's report of its failure, the meeting elected another committee to hale the defiant merchants down to the hall. But the committee soon reported that some of the recalcitrants could not be found and that the others absolutely declined to attend.[3]

The meeting thereupon unanimously voted to descend *en masse* upon each, and, with Molineux as spokesman, peremptorily to demand his goods. While this enterprise was organizing, startling good news came in from the North End: the Hutchinsons had now declared themselves ready to deliver up their unsold stock of tea as well as the proceeds from what had been sold. Delighted, the meeting deputed still another committee to visit the converts and take down their change of heart in writing. Meanwhile, Phillips, Molineux, Jonathan Mason, and Henderson Inches (the latter two both selectmen) led one thousand of what a Tory observer called "the very refuse of the town" up the slight rise from Faneuil Hall to the northeast corner of King and Main (now Washington) Streets. Here, doors firmly barred, stood the Sign of the Brazen Head, the shop of William Jackson, one of the hard-core holdouts.[4]

When Jackson looked out of an upper window, Molineux demanded admission and surrender of the goods. Both of these, he said with a characteristic mixture of nonsense and threat, his group "had an undoubted right to." Jackson denied the requests. "Sir," said Molineux. "Do you know that I am at the head of 2,000 men, and that it is beneath the dignity of this Committee to be parlied with in the street?" Without waiting for a reply, he marched the gathering back to the hall for another session of abusive, rancorous speeches by himself, Dr. Thomas Young, Adams, and others, directed at government generally and the Hutchinsons in particular. Although the lieutenant-governor's sons had not yet formally committed themselves, when the meeting broke up, the Sons of Liberty spent the evening "in high spirits," certain that once the Hutchinsons capitulated, the rest would fall easily.[5]

The celebration, it turned out, was premature. As the radicals were congratulating themselves, Jackson and two of the hold-outs, proclaiming their own determination not to concede, were berating the Hutchinsons for caving in. The next morning, when the confident radicals sent wagons to the lieutenant-governor's house (where the sons also lived), the Hutchinsons refused to deliver their tea. Upon the committee's reporting this to the merchants' renewed meeting in Faneuil Hall, "the Body," as the group was called, determined to take active measures. Someone proposed a mass visit to the Hutchinsons. At that, young attorney Josiah Quincy, the moderator's new son-in-law, stood up and plainly told the group that any plan to go in a body to Hutchinson's house would be an act of high treason, probably because it would be considered an attempt to apply direct force to the lieutenant-governor himself, the king's representative. The Hutchinsons, Quincy added, had doubtless invited such an illegal gathering for the express purpose of entrapping the Whigs.

Molineux, a little quieter than usual, rejected Quincy's objection. With unconscious irony, he compared the signers of the nonimportation agreement to a flock of sheep, some of which had broken out of the fold. Unless those could be brought back, he said, all the rest were ready to follow their example, and indeed seemed to wish for an opportunity. But Quincy still persisted, offering to bring the relevant legal treatises into the meeting. Finally, he turned to Dana and Otis, certain that they would support him. The old justice of the peace, however, remained silent. Otis did give a speech, but he was so incoherent that nobody could understand whether he condemned the measure or approved it.

By that time, even Molineux was willing to concede Quincy's point of law. Nonetheless, he argued, because there was no other way of obtaining redress, the "Body" ought to go ahead with its plan. Dr. Young was even less reserved. Such people as opposed or counteracted the general measures, he shouted, should be "deprived of existence"; it was high time for the people, to whom the government properly belonged, to take it into their own hands. Despite this torrid oratory, Quincy's words lay heavy on the minds of the faithful. When the radicals tried to elect a committee to lead the delegation to Hutchinson's, they found great reluctance among the erstwhile leaders. John Hancock, Henderson Inches, Otis, and Phillips all refused. Shocked, or perhaps merely play-acting, Molineux stood on a bench and announced he was going home, possibly to commit suicide. Young, alertly responding to his cue, shouted loudly, "Stop, Mr. Molineux! Stop, Mr. Molineux! For the love of God! Stop, Mr. Molineux! Gentlemen, if Mr.

Molineux leaves us we are forever undone! This day is the last dawn of liberty we ever shall see!"

Molineux, as an eyewitness reported slyly, "was upon this prevailed upon to return." Otis and Phillips, reconsidering, joined him, Adams, and Samuel Austin on the committee. Shortly after 2 P.M., with one thousand people behind them, they set out for the North End. At Hutchinson's house, the crowd paused in the street before the door. The lieutenant-governor opened one of the windows and asked what they wanted. "It is not you, but your sons we desire to see," said Molineux. One of the sons joined Hutchinson at the window. "I am the representative of the King of Great Britain, the greatest monarch on earth, and in his name require you to disperse," the lieutenant-governor told the crowd. The mob stayed where it was. Molineux read out the meeting's condemnation of the sons and the demand for the tea. Young Hutchinson replied that he had nothing to say to the committee, and the lieutenant-governor asked for a copy of the vote. This, Molineux refused, saying that he held only the original and was not at liberty to give a copy.[6]

Noticing Otis at the front of the throng, Hutchinson said he was greatly surprised to see him there. Surely Otis "could not be ignorant of the illegality of such proceedings." Moreover, Hutchinson added, he saw before him six or seven people who had been accessories to the pulling down of his house in 1765. "Gentlemen," he concluded, "when I was attacked before, I was a private person; I am now the representative of the greatest Monarch upon earth, whose Majesty you affront in thus treating my person." Somewhat embarrassed, the crowd left Hutchinson's to visit in a similar fashion Jackson, Theophilus Lillie, and two other recalcitrants. Although the crowd behaved quietly, it "received no satisfactory answer from any one of them." Lillie, indeed, said "they had already ruined him in his Business, and if they now wanted his life, they might take it when they pleased." Momentarily checked, the Body adjourned until 10 A.M., the next morning.[7]

Hutchinson's firmness convinced the Tories "they had gain'd a compleat victory." Many substantial merchants in the British trade whom fear had hitherto silenced stated publicly that should the Hutchinsons, Jackson, and others hold out for a few days, many others would join them, and their "bondage" would be ended. This wishful optimism did not raise an echo in the heart of the man most responsible, Hutchinson himself. After the mob had departed his home, the lieutenant-governor called a council meeting. He asked point-blank for help, urging "the necessity of some immediate steps being taken in order to discountenance and put a stop to so unlawful a proceeding" as the continuing meeting of the Body. The reply was numbing. "The Council debated upon this Proposal from his Honor but came to no determination."

At the same meeting, Hutchinson showed the council a letter he had just received from Jackson. Fearing the mob, Jackson, like Mein, was asking protection for his life and property. On the council's advice, Hutchinson called Sheriff Greenleaf and all the Boston justices of the peace to the council chamber. Jackson attended and told the group of several threats he had received. But he also admitted that he believed himself safe for the night, thus unintentionally undermining Hutchinson's already shaky position. The lieutenant-governor could now do nothing more than recommend to the sheriff and the justices "to be vigilant and faithful in the discharge of their duty as circumstances may arise." Even this mild injunction drew a rebuke. The justices told Hutchinson they were "of opinion that there was no danger of mischief tonight." Spurned by the council and the law-enforcement apparatus, Hutchinson encountered additional pressure from an unexpected source. That evening, as the temperature plummeted and the harbor froze over, several of the Tory merchants conferred with him. Their argument was simple: "in order to prevent violence to the persons of his sons, as well as to their property," he should advise to their delivering the goods.[8]

On the bitter morning of January 19, the Body met once again in Faneuil Hall, spirits low. People generally believed that the meeting would do nothing more than pass a few self-justifying resolves for newspaper publication and transmission to the other colonies. But before the Body had fully assembled, Hutchinson sent for Phillips and Captain Samuel Partridge of the Committee of Inspection. He told them that after further consideration, he was now ready to have his sons deliver up to the committee not only the tea remaining in their store but the cash for what they had already sold. Astounded, Phillips and Partridge hurried to the meeting to disclose the "extraordinary proposal." Hearing of Hutchinson's switch, another of the recalcitrants, Nathaniel Cary, wrote the Body that he, too, was willing to have his goods stored. The Body listened in amazed delight to a series of "scurrilous and abusive" speeches from Molineux, Adams, and William Cooper, and then adjourned until January 23. Well might the radicals exult. From a contemptuous spurning of the mob, Hutchinson in a few hours had deigned not merely to negotiate with it, but to accede to all its demands. That evening, two more merchants sent "proposals" to the committee.[9]

Why had Hutchinson changed so suddenly? He told Hillsborough his family's apparent interest in the dispute embarrassed his dealing with the whole situation. So long as his sons had a personal stake in the abolition of the agreement, he believed, he would have much more difficulty with the council and the radicals. He did not tell Hillsborough that the Tories, even those who had recommended it, resented his retreat. To himself, he admitted he had not sufficiently considered the circumstances; his "error in his publick trust" caused him more internal anguish than the destruction of his house. But to Hillsborough, he somewhat disingenuously reported that the other recalcitrant merchants "saw the reason" of his switch, though their own resistance to the Body "persevered to the end." [10]

To hearten the hold-outs, Hutchinson had "assured them of all the protection in my power." Small comfort, that. A little later, Hutchinson advised victims of the Body to sue their oppressors. The response was strongly negative. They would have "no chance with a Jury," the merchants told him. Even if they did, once an action was commenced "neither their Persons nor Property were safe while it was depending." Finally, even if they should "escape the injuries they faced and recover damages, their business would [fail] and nobody would dare to have any trade or dealing with them." Control of the jurors was firmly in partisan hands. Molineux is supposed to have boasted that the radicals "would always be sure of Eleven jury men in Twelve." [11]

During the Body's recess, Hutchinson kept meeting the council almost daily, trying vainly to promote support for a condemnatory proclamation. The councilors agreed to advise Hutchinson as to the measures he ought to take; but whenever he proposed anything concrete, they counseled against it. Not even an abortive attempt to burn down Jackson's house on the night of January 20 could stir them. Their point seemed to be simply that because the meetings were quiet and orderly, the government need take no active steps. Hutchinson himself conceded that the massive visitations were "without any degree of Tumult." But he reasoned, quite rightly, the mere presence in Boston of such large, Whig-led gatherings was "unwarrantable" and dangerous.[12]

"Illiberal, puerile, and very dishonorary," Hutchinson called the Body's deliberations. Yet he could not shake the council. The councilors, including those few who disapproved of what was going on, would not support even his urging the justices of the peace to exert their crowd-dispersing powers. Tolerantly conceding that although the councilors differed from him "in sentiment, I have no doubt of their doing what appears to them to be right," Hutchinson next turned directly to the justices. Because several of them had attended the Body's meetings and voted for its measures, Hutchinson could expect little support there; nonetheless he tried. They told him that unwarrantable though the meetings might be, "yet there were times when irregularities could not be restrained; that this was a time when the minds of the people were greatly agitated and disturbed, from a sense of danger to their just rights and liberties, which they hoped, in this way to preserve." The justices therefore did not feel themselves required to take any measures for interrupting the proceedings "unless there should be something more disorderly than yet had been." [13]

When the Body resumed deliberation on January 23, the meeting did not seem to fit the justices' prerequisites. Although it was the best-attended of the series, it was not at all disorderly. It did not need to be; the convolutions of the preceding week had accomplished most of the radicals' goals for them. Hutchinson spoke privately to Phillips and some others, warning them (if so powerless a magistrate as Hutchinson then was could be said to warn leaders of the force which controlled the town) that they were trying to "reform the law" by forcing repeal of the Townshend Acts; and that any mob violence would, in His Honor's opinion, "involve them all in the Guilt of High Treason." He might as well have shouted to the sea. Whatever the Body chose to do, it would do.[14]

First, the meeting considered the conduct of Lieutenant-Colonel Dalrymple in quartering his troops within the town, instead of Castle Island. This issue had been decided peremptorily in the fall of 1768, but the Body now felt sufficiently powerful to raise it again and actually to debate whether or not Dalrymple should be cashiered for his actions. Some of the radicals believed he had similarly exceeded his authority when he stationed a guard at the home of Nathaniel Rogers, one of the recalcitrant merchants. Despite lengthy discussion of both questions, neither came to a vote.[15]

When he learned what was happening, Hutchinson's temper snapped. He summoned Sheriff Greenleaf and had him carry to Phillips a "declaration," together with peremptory instructions to Phillips to have it read. This paper was nothing more than a summary of the arguments Hutchinson had been vainly urging on the council, the justices of the peace, and the Body leaders: the meeting was unlawful; the massive visitations were "of very dangerous tendency"; and the "persons of character, reputation, and property" present subjected themselves to the consequences of mob action however unwanted. Hutchinson concluded by requiring the assembly "without delay, to separate & disperse."

The reply, directed to Greenleaf, was a perfect example of the unctuous insolence Sam Adams sometimes affected when dealing from a position of strength. Hutchinson's declaration, the Body said, was "attended to with all that deference and solemnity which the message and the times demand; and it is the unanimous opinion of this body after serious consideration and debate that this meeting is warranted by law. And . . . they are determined to keep consciences void of offence towards God and towards man." [16]

Returning then to their interrupted business, the radicals pressed on to the final ostracism of the remaining recalcitrants. Jackson, Lillie, Rogers, and John Taylor were voted "obstinate and inveterate Enemies to their Country, and Subverters of the Rights and Liberties of this Continent." The Body resolved, as its "indispensible Duty to Ourselves and Posterity, for ever hereafter, to treat them as such, by withholding not only all commercial Dealings, but every Act and Office of common Civility." The men were voted to have "severed themselves from the Commonwealth." In an age which knew thoroughly the social-compact doctrines of Locke and Hobbes, this last in effect placed the four beyond the pale, as public enemies to be denied even the protection of the law.

Another vote branded six others (including John Mein) as deserving "to be driven to that Obscurity, from which they originated, and to the Hole of the Pit from whence they were digged." A final vote pledged and recommended total abstention from the use of tea "upon any Pretence whatever." Concluding its proceedings with a recommendation that the votes be pasted up "over the Chimney Piece of every public House, and on every other proper Place, in every Town" in all the colonies, the meeting adjourned quietly. This anxiety to "restrain all disorder at their breaking up" Hutchinson attributed to his declaration. His self-congratulation infected the Tories. One of them reported that Hutchinson had "greatly retreiv'd his Character and it is the universal opinion that the non Importation scheme is now at an end." [17]

Like so many of the loyalists' hopes this one, too, failed in the fulfillment. For about two weeks, the Sons of Liberty appeared "much dejected," and the Committee of Inspection stopped inspecting. Appearances, however, meant little. Hutchinson himself had correctly analyzed the situation in a summary so apt that it is worth fully setting out:

> If the Council had been in sentiment with me I think this Assembly might have been prevented or soon dispersed. Left alone, I had to consider the danger from such Meeting from day to day which I knew to be against Law and yet it consisted of several Justices of the peace who ought to execute Law, several professed Lawyers and a great number of Inhabitants of property together with three of the Representatives of the Town and a mixed multitude warmed with a persuasion that what they were doing was right and that they were struggling for the Liberties of America. I considered also the uncertain consequence of any thing Tragical from the Troops in suppressing acts of violence, if the Temper of the people should rise to it, occa-

sioned by a dispute upon a point in which so many Colonies warmly interest themselves.[18]

The basic helplessness of the government, which all the visible dejection of the radicals could not change, soon made itself evident. On February 8, the Boston *News-Letter* republished one of the newest "Junius" letters, just arrived from England, a bitter personal attack on the king. That day, like all Thursdays, was both a market day and a school holiday. At about 10 A.M., someone posted on the town pump a board bearing a large painted hand, beneath it the word "IMPORTER." The board was so fixed that the hand pointed directly at Jackson's shop, just across the street. A crowd of idle schoolboys and country people, in town for market, gathered around. Whenever anyone went in or out of the shop, the boys hissed and pelted him with dirt. Jackson tried several times to tear the board down; but whenever he did, the idlers, some of them armed with sticks, beat him back. Meanwhile, a group of "considerable Merchants" looked on, visibly pleased. Molineux, too, was there, and "took Care to distinguish himself in a particular manner." At 1 P.M., as mysteriously as it had appeared, the sign was removed. Dispersing, the boys and the yokels carefully spattered all of Jackson's windows with mud and dirt. The season of the "Exhibitions" had begun.[19]

During the following week, most of the recalcitrants, called simply "Importers," suffered broken windows, defaced signs, and similar marks of popular resentment. The Tories claimed that the radicals were setting these boys on. Peter Oliver reported that a radical minister, coming home from services, had watched a crowd smashing an importer's windows. "See how these boys fight for us," the clergyman is supposed to have said. On Thursday, February 15, the hand was again posted at Jackson's, this time decorated with the effigies of some of the Importers. A second sign promised that the following week the effigies of four of the commissioners (presumably all except Temple), five of their "understrappers," and some of the principal English hate-figures would adorn Liberty Tree. Four soldiers of the Fourteenth tried to tear the sign down, but the crowd defended it vigorously, seriously injuring one soldier and driving the rest away.[20]

Encouraged, perhaps, the radicals spent much of the next week promoting a no-tea-drinking subscription among Boston's female population. A local herb called labradore was recommended as a substitute for "the pernicious Practice of tea-drinking." Chocolate or coffee likewise won Whig approval; invalids were permitted to drink the genuine article. The Tories maliciously noted that although subscribers were properly enough using coffee and chocolate pots, the liquid dispensed therefrom always seemed to be tea. They also observed that sickness appeared to afflict by rotation, so that the ailing ladies could take turns entertaining their callers.[21]

This pleasant early form of antiprohibitionism did not particularly interest the radicals. They sought a more permanent confrontation, and on February 22, they finally got it. The night before, persons unknown smeared the importers' windows with tar and feathers. That day, as on the two preceding Thursdays, a hand went up at Jackson's. In addition, another one was erected on a post in the gutter outside the North End shop of Theophilus Lillie, "a very inoffensive man, except in the offense of importation." Besides his refusal to sign the agreement, Lillie had attracted the radicals' attention for his wit. Although less caustic than Mein, Lillie had the ability to touch Whig nerves:

> It always seemed strange to me [he had written in the Boston *News-Letter*] that people who contend so much for civil and religious Liberty should be so ready to deprive others of their natural liberty—that Men who are guarding against being subject to Laws [to] which they never gave their consent in person or by their representative, should at the same time make Laws, and in the most effectual manner execute them upon me and others, to which Laws I am sure I never gave my consent either in person or by my representative. . . . I own I had rather be a slave under one master; for I know who he is, I may, perhaps, be able to please him, than a slave to a hundred or more who I don't know where to find, nor what they will expect from me.[22]

Some of Lillie's numerous masters stood near his shop, surrounded by their "many hundreds" of juvenile auxiliaries. "The whole Street filled with People who would suffer no person to go to his Shop." Shortly after 10 A.M., Ebenezer Richardson, who lived about fifty paces away, appeared in the street. This was the same Richardson who had enraged the radicals in 1766 because of his activities as an informer for the customs service. The intervening years had improved neither Richardson's reputation nor his disposition. Many, particularly the radicals, considering him "the most abandoned wretch in America . . . His life would exhibit an atrocious volume." The day before, someone had heard him say he hoped there would be "a dust beat up" if any more effigies were posted, and that he wished the Fourteenth were there (thinking perhaps of the episode the preceding week), for "they would cut up the damned Yankees." Another time, speaking apparently of the radicals, he was heard to say he would "give the Devil a supper of them," adding that he would not hurt anybody unless they hurt him. On still another occasion, he was supposed to have said, "Let 'em come on me. I'm ready, for I've guns loaded." [23]

The radicals later tried to connect what followed to the commissioners. They suggested that Richardson was acting under orders when he went over to Lillie's. This may well have been an instinctive reaction to a propaganda opportunity; the Whigs certainly "took care to improve this affair to the utmost advantage" and succeeded so well that despite frantic published denials by Secretary Reeve, "it was almost universally believed that the Commissioners were abettors in this affair." The only discovered document of Richardson's own authorship bearing on the matter does not discuss this point.[24]

However unclear his initial motivation, Richardson's subsequent actions were unambiguous. He does not appear to have spent much effort on verbal persuasion. Instead, seeing in the street a horse and wagon belonging to one of the country people in town for market day, he tried to persuade the driver to run against the sign. When the man refused, Richardson made the same appeal to a nearby charcoal carter; again he was turned down. In rage and desperation, he seized the reins of a third wagon, and tried himself to topple the post.[25]

This finally diverted the schoolboys from their assault on Lillie's. They began pelting Richardson with dirt, sticks, and stones. As Richardson retreated toward his house, he met some of the Sons of Liberty. "Perjury! Perjury!" he shouted at Edward Procter, apparently referring to the blacklisting of Lillie. "What do you mean?" Procter asked. "By the eternal God," said Richardson, "I'll make it too hot for you before night." Thomas Knox also asked him what he meant; and Richardson likewise promised him a hot night.

Knox, Procter, and John Matchet followed Richardson to his door. "Come out, you damn son of a bitch," Knox shouted. "I'll have your heart out, your liver out." Richardson, who had gone into his house, came out "in a great rage, doubling his fists." He challenged the men and again said that it would be "hot enough" before night. To the boys, he said "Go off." They would not, they replied; they were as free as he to stand in the king's highway. More boys came over from Lillie's, showering the house with fruit peelings and other light missiles. The door opened and Richardson shook a stick at the crowd; some people thought it was a gun. He swore that if they did not disperse he would "make a lane" through them. As he took a step inside, a brickbat was tossed out. One of the adult members of the crowd picked it up and heaved it through a window. As if that were a signal, the boys surrounded the house completely. Sticks, stones, and eggs began to fly. More windows broke. A rock struck Richardson's wife; others whizzed past his two daughters.[26]

At his door, Richardson saw George Wilmot, a mariner who had commanded a company of Ranger bateauxmen in the French and Indian War. More recently he had belonged to *Liberty*'s crew. Like

George Gailer, he had lost his job when the Rhode Island radicals burned the cutter. He had petitioned the commissioners for reparation of his losses, but was at the moment apparently on the beach, out of work. The Sons of Liberty later tried to link Wilmot's presence with the commissioners, insisting that he had been on hand much earlier, and that in fact he had carried from the commissioners the instructions which sent Richardson to Lillie's. The commissioners and Wilmot denied it all. Five years later, Wilmot added that he had come to the North End after watching a similar demonstration at Jackson's, arriving at Richardson's just before the siege began in earnest.[27]

Whatever brought him, Wilmot told Richardson he would stand by him as long as he had breath, and asked if he had a gun. While Richardson was getting weapons for himself and Wilmot, the rock barrage increased. The window panes had long gone. Now the leading and frames followed. In the street, Matchet was saying Richardson deserved to be hanged years ago. Other men were there, laughing or acting unconcerned. When John Codman reproved the boys, one of the men told him, "You don't know what provocation the boys have had." Elias Dupee also tried to discourage them; another adult bystander told him, "The town will pay for it. 'Tis none of my business." [28]

Up in the house, Richardson brought his musket to the window. Unloaded though it was, he aimed it at the crowd and "snapped" the lock. At that, the mob broke open the front door; but nobody dared enter. The stone shower continued. Rocks cracked the ceiling. Through the bare openings that had once been windows, people could see Richardson and Wilmot holding muskets. Richardson came to the sill, knelt down, rested the barrel on the edge. In the street, eleven-year-old Christopher Seider (or Snider) stood idly, just stooping to take up a stone. A sailor, Robert Paterson, watched Richardson closely; so did others. No one believed that he would fire. Richardson fired.[29]

He had loaded with swanshot, pea-sized pellets. As the charge spread out, one slug went through sailor Paterson's trousers; two others hit the nineteen-year-old son of John Gore, wounding two fingers of his right hand and lodging in his thigh. Eleven slugs ended up in the chest and abdomen of young Seider.

A boy threw another stone. Richardson aimed his musket again. "Damn ye," he roared, "come here. I'm ready for you." Wilmot, shouting that he was helping Richardson, presented his weapon also. "Stand off or I'll fire," he said. Thus prevented from using the already-opened front door, the mob turned its attention to the rear. Meanwhile, Seider was carried into a nearby house. All the local doctors hurried to treat him but little could be done. Although still alive, he was clearly dying.[30]

Summoned by the bell of the New Brick Church on Hanover Street, which someone had begun tolling immediately after Richardson fired, reinforcements poured into the back yard from all over Boston. The crowd soon battered down enough of a wall to force an entrance and corner the men. Wilmot offered no resistance when Philip Ridgway snatched the musket from him. Unloading it, Ridgway found a charge which, he later testified, contained 179 shot, including 17 of the big swanshot. The pan looked as though it had flashed—which would mean that Wilmot had tried to fire—but Wilmot pointed to the lock. The screw pin was missing; he could not have fired. "It was not I but Richardson," he said.

Richardson did not give in so easily. With a cutlass, he fended off his captors, offering as he did to surrender himself to a proper officer. They told him he had killed a boy; as Seider was still alive, and would remain so for eight more hours, this was a slight exaggeration. "Damn their blood," said Richardson, still fighting. "I don't care what I've done." Finally, by weight of numbers they subdued him and brought him out.[31]

Richardson's reputation, his unrepentant intransigence, and the temper of the times almost combined to end his life on the spot. Mein, after all, had barely escaped death from a mob much less aroused. And he had offended only by publishing harmful facts and loyalists' propaganda. Could Richardson expect any mercy at all? For answer, someone brought a noose; others picked out a convenient sign post. Richardson would swing for the shooting and Wilmot would swing with him, just for being in the house. But as the battered pair were being hustled under the sign, providence, in the unlikely person of William Molineux, spared their lives. Perhaps the Whigs' strategy demanded it. That was Peter Oliver's view: "As they were pretty sure that they could procure a Jury for Conviction, so some of the Leaders of the Faction chose that he should be hanged by the Forms of Law, rather than suffer the Disgrace of Hangmen themselves." Perhaps Molineux feared that a court might some way hold him responsible for the hanging, he having, it was said, stirred up all the "tumultuous proceedings." Whatever his reasons, Molineux undertook to calm the crowd. He succeeded at least in stopping the lynching.[32]

Instead of killing the men outright, the mob now dragged them through the streets, cruelly abusing and battering them, until they came before Justice of the Peace Ruddock. Apparently unwilling to conduct the examination himself, Ruddock had the hearing transferred to Faneuil Hall, where Justices Richard Dana, Edmund Quincy, and Samuel Pemberton joined him. There, before one thousand spectators, they heard the witnesses and committed both Richardson and Wilmot to jail to await the next sitting of the superior court, scheduled for March 13. Such key witnesses as Ridgway and Paterson were put under £50 bond to appear then. Justice Dana's memorandum of the bonds set out the crime of which Richardson and Wilmot had been accused: "firing off & discharging a gun loaded with gun powder & swan shot at one Christopher Snyder thereby giving him a very dangerous wound." [33]

The crime was "giving him a very dangerous wound." Not murder, for Seider did not die until 9 P.M. Yet the men had almost been summarily strung up once, and would a second time be nearly lynched. As the constables hustled them off to jail, the crowd tried again to take them. Again, only the intervention of "some leading men of the popular side" removed the halters. Once more, the radicals had demonstrated violently that Boston's law and order rested solely in their hands. No one in authority had tried to disperse the original mob. When Hutchinson gave Sheriff Greenleaf "express directions . . . to go and suppress" that "unlawful assembly" before the shooting, Greenleaf said "he did not think it safe to attempt." As for the justices of the peace, not one, Hutchinson reported ruefully, "will appear on such an occasion." However optimistic about the peace-keeping apparatus he may have felt when talking to John Mein four months earlier, Hutchinson now had lost all faith in the justices. Nor could he obtain more willing or courageous replacements. In Massachusetts, the governor could not remove any magistrate, even for neglect of duty, without the council's consent.[34]

That evening, Seider finally died. The radical doctor, Joseph Warren, performed an autopsy and removed the shot. Almost immediately, a coroner's jury viewed the body and returned a verdict of death from being "wilfully and feloniously shott by Ebenezer Richardson." Now it was official. When they finally faced the court in three weeks, Richardson would stand trial for murder, Wilmot for being an accessory. If the mob let them live long enough to be convicted, they both could hang.[35]

Ailing and disheartened, Hutchinson tried desperately "to convince the Council of the necessity of their concurring with me in some measures to put a stop to these tumultuous assemblies, but to no purpose." The council, firmly in radical hands, refused to stop the disorders, lest importation somehow be encouraged. "The major part" of the councilors, he found, "as of every other order of men, wish success to the non-importers, and can dispense with a little illegality in the prosecution of them." So the attacks on the importers' houses in "the dead of night" continued. Lillie gave up his home, eventually moving to the country. Rogers, Hutchinson's nephew, was able to remain, guarded by soldiers. "Several of the others sleep with loaded guns by their bedsides." [36]

Presented with the great windfall of the Richardson affair, Sam Adams quickly began to extract maximum propaganda value. On Monday, February 26, aided by loud newspaper publicity, he staged Seider's funeral, "the largest perhaps ever known in America." A tremendous snowstorm, accompanied by thunder and lightning, had struck Boston two days before. Considering the primitive snow-removal equipment of the time, most of it must still have clogged the town's streets. Yet not even the elements could stop Adams's spectacular. The procession began at 5 P.M., at Liberty Tree. A board had been erected there with Biblical quotations which, as the Boston *Gazette* said, "Perhaps cannot easily be misapply'd." To anyone who might later sit on Richardson's jury, two of the sacred quotations were particularly applicable: "Thou shalt take no satisfaction for the life of a MURDERER —he shall surely be put to death." And "Though Hand join in Hand, the Wicked shall not pass unpunish'd." Between four hundred and five hundred schoolboys in couples preceded the bier, which bore Latin inscriptions appropriate to murdered innocence. Six youths carried the coffin, followed by the family and friends of the deceased and two thousand mourners. Thirty chariots and chaises closed the procession, which in its fullest length reached from Liberty Tree to the Town House, a distance exceeding five-eighths of a mile. Interment was in the Old Granary burial ground. "My eyes never beheld such a funeral," said John Adams, who stood in the street with John Rowe. In his diary, Adams made additional comments which show how successful Cousin Sam's production had been: "This Shewes, there are many more Lives to spend if wanted in the Service of their Country. It Shewes, too that the Faction is not yet expiring—that the Ardor of the People is not to be quelled by the Slaughter of one Child and the Wounding of another." [37]

Hutchinson, sourly noting the procession and the "inconceivable impression" it made, cynically remarked that if the Boston Sons of Liberty had had the power to resurrect Seider they "would not have done it, but would have chosen the grand funeral." He considered the ceremony merely another of those mass meetings which tended only to promote disorder. Once again, he tried to wring some assistance from the council. But after two days of the same futile deliberations which had so frequently tied his hands before, Hutchinson could win only a recommendation that he talk yet again with the sheriff and the justices of the peace, to "exhort them to do their duty." This he did, one suspects with little enthusiasm, because he had so fruitlessly pursued the same exercise many times before. This occasion was even more frustrating; "some of the Justices openly justified the proceedings." [38]

Seider's funeral, unique in America, had had a disturbing British precedent. Only two years before, at the riot over John Wilkes in St. George's Fields, London, panicky magistrates had ordered troops to fire on civilians. One of the soldiers pursued a young boy named William Allen and killed him in particularly outrageous circumstances. Wilkes's supporters immediately called the affair a "massacre." The Wilkesites gave Allen a massive public funeral whose aim, like Seider's, had been "to raise the passions of the people and to strengthen the . . . cause . . . in which their leaders had engaged them." The Allen case was a particularly troubling parallel, stressing as it did the combined themes of magistrates needlessly using troops, soldiers ruthlessly killing civilians, and martyrs enlisting large public sympathy. The radicals quickly drew the cases together in the Boston *Gazette* appearing on the day of the funeral, throwing in a cry for vengeance as well: "The Blood of *young Allen* may be cover'd in *Britain:* But a thorough Inquisition will be made in *America* for that of *young Snider,* which crieth for Vengeance, like the Blood of the righteous Abel." The Otis-Robinson affair and Hancock's *Liberty* case, the *Gazette* insisted, were all part of the same plot that killed Seider. "Young as he was, he died in his Country's Cause, by the Hand of an execrable Villain, directed by others, who could not bear to see the Enemies of America made the *Ridicule of Boys*." Those *"Oppressors!"* who killed Seider used other tools besides customs informers. Accordingly, the radicals hoped, Seider's death "will be a means for the future of preventing any, but more especially the Soldiery, from being too free in the Use of their Instruments of Death." On March 5 the *Gazette* carried another portentous notice: "The Particulars of several Rencountres between the Inhabitants and the Soldiery the Week past we are oblig'd to omit for Want of Room." [39]

CHAPTER 16

THE BOSTON MASSACRE

Boston was too small, the radical leadership too recklessly determined, to prevent the inevitable direct, fatal clash between civilians and soldiers. Like an arpeggio of conflict, the tensions had been rising: Panton's death; the Riley fracas; Robinson's battle with Otis; the Ness-Molesworth affair; John Mein's mobbing; and now Seider's death and commemorative funeral. Whatever the merits of British revenue policy, whatever the political practicalities of filling the customs service (and, for that matter, the governor's chair) with British place-seekers, the enterprise could succeed only if supported by American good will. But in Massachusetts, those who were prepared to acquiesce lacked the ability to make the acceptance general, while those who for their own reasons resisted imperial control possessed the genius to stir up the uncommitted, and the ruthlessness to use physical power as a necessary supplement to verbal persuasion. Because the violence attracted London's attention, and because the Tories on both sides of the Atlantic were willing to believe that force could control the violence, the troops had come to Boston.

But now, as February 1770 turned into March, the fallacy of sending the soldiers had become clear to the loyalists, the radicals, and, most important, even to the military. Gage summarized the situation precisely:

> The People were as Lawless and Licentious after the Troops arrived, as they were before. The Troops could not act by Military Authority, and no Person in Civil Authority would ask their aid. They were there

contrary to the wishes of the Council, Assembly, Magistrates and People, and seemed only offered to abuse and Ruin. And the Soldiers were either to suffer ill usage and even assaults upon their Persons till their Lives were in Danger, or by resisting and defending themselves, to run almost a Certainty of suffering by the Law.[1]

In New York City, soldiers and civilians had battled viciously around the Liberty Pole. The Boston *Gazette* had run what John Adams called "a pompous account" on February 19, trumpeting the citizens' victory. This detailed story "excited the resentment" of the Boston soldiers and raised "exultations among some sorts of the inhabitants." What had happened in New York could happen in Massachusetts.[2]

Looking back on the events of March 2, 3, 4, and 5, townsmen and soldiers alike would discern carefully laid plotting, always on the other side. Because the garrison at this time numbered six hundred, with no more than four hundred effectively able to mass at any point, it seems impossible that the military (or even the rank-and-file, acting in leaderless concert) could have been, as Sam Adams feverishly insisted, contemplating "a general massacre." Four hundred, or even six hundred, soldiers, simply could not withstand a population of sixteen thousand, its citizens adequately armed, supported by untold thousands of musket-bearing farmers ready to invest the town at the first flash of the tar barrel on Beacon Hill. Similarly, it is not reasonable to assume that Adams, however dedicated he was to the principle of removing the troops, would attempt to do so by a general engagement. Such a clash, besides producing an enormous bloodletting, would also constitute high treason and outright rebellion, neither of which Boston or the rest of America was yet prepared to accept. Roughing up individual soldiers in the streets and harassing them in the law courts was one thing; firing on the king's troops quite another.[3]

What the radicals needed, as they clearly must have realized, was some kind of incident in which the town rather than the army would appear as the injured party. The size and solemnity of the funeral staged for the Seider boy showed the ease and aptness with which Adams and the Sons could transform hitherto anonymous accident victims into martyrs for freedom. Given the intense feelings on both sides, an intensity which Adams had worked hard to increase, it could not be very long before the soldiers would stumble into a fatal error. As matters turned out, Seider's celebrated corpse had not been four days under ground when the incident the radicals sought occurred, and having occurred blossomed swiftly into just the happening to satisfy their most sanguine and sanguinary propaganda expectations. In trying to describe what happened, historians have been cursed by a plethora of eyewitness accounts. Like Joseph Warren's biographer Richard Frothingham, "I have constructed this narrative by a careful collation of the evidence that appears to be authentic; but it will be vain to attempt to reconcile all the statements in relation to this transaction." As Sir James Fitzjames Stephen said, in another connection, "The mere effort to see what is essential to a story, in what order the important events happened, and in what relation they stand to each other must of necessity point to a conclusion." [4]

Toward noon of March 2, a group of rope and cablemakers were laying rope in John Gray's extensive ropewalks, across from Commissioner Paxton's house, between what are now Pearl and Congress Streets south of Milk Street. Although the plant itself was massive—744 feet long—the business depended upon casual labor. A soldier looking for off-duty-hours work to supplement his meager pay might well come to the ropewalks, as indeed Patrick Walker of the Twenty-ninth did this very day. History concocts itself of insignificances. "Soldier, do you want work?" asked ropemaker William Green. "Yes, I do, faith," said Walker. "Well," said Green, in a triumph of ready wit, "then go and clean my shithouse." "Empty it yourself," said Walker. After more such exchanges, Walker, swearing "by the Holy Ghost" that he would have revenge, swung wildly at the ropemakers. Nicholas Ferriter, a one-day employee, "knocked up his heels"; a naked cutlass dropped from beneath his coat. Humiliated, drubbed, and disarmed, the soldier fled. In a few moments he was back, reinforced by eight or nine other soldiers, including Private William Warren. As the Redcoats squared off against the ropemen, the workers called for help. From other parts of the ropewalk, club-carrying assistance came, and the soldiers were repelled. Through the window of a nearby house, Justice of the Peace John Hill watched them retreat to the barracks. Within fifteen minutes, their number increased to near forty, they sallied again, armed with clubs and other weapons, and led by a tall black drummer. "You black rascal," Hill shouted, "what have you to do with white people's quarrels?" "I suppose I may look on," the man answered. Hill went out of the house and, in what was then a rare exercise for a Boston magistrate, commanded the crowd to keep the peace. Neither soldiers nor ropeworkers listened. The clubs on the one side and the ropemakers' wouldring sticks [i.e., wooden levers used in rope-twisting] on the other beat a loud tattoo as the parties battled around the ropeyard's tar kettle. A private named Mathew Kilroy fought notably, but so did Samuel Gray, a ropemaker. The civilians soon turned the battle and drove the soldiers out. Hill's good offices prevented a general pursuit; at the barracks, a corporal managed to control the soldiers and get them indoors. Both sides clearly regarded the interruption as temporary.[5]

On Saturday, Private John Carroll of the Twenty-ninth and two other soldiers tangled with a trio of ropeworkers. Reinforced by a sailor named James Bailey, the civilians battled the military to a draw. Then a journeyman tanner arrived with two "batts." He gave one to a bystander; together they cleared the soldiers from the walk. Private John Rodgers of the Twenty-ninth ended up with a fractured skull and arm. One of the ropemakers boarded with Benjamin Burdick. Believing that some of the soldiers were "dogging" him, the man asked Burdick for help. Through his window, Burdick could indeed see a soldier lurking near his house. The next day the soldier was back; Burdick went out and asked him what he was after. "I'm pumping shit," the soldier answered. "March off," said Burdick. "Damn you," the soldier said, and Burdick thrashed him until he ran.[6]

Alarmed at the pattern of direct, violent confrontation, Maurice Carr, lieutenant colonel commanding the Twenty-ninth, wrote Hutchinson, although exactly what he expected the helpless lieutenant-governor to do is unclear. That evening one of the Twenty-ninth's sergeants failed to answer a roll call. A rumor spread among the troops that he had been killed. Sunday morning, March 4, the sergeant still not having returned, Carr and some of his officers undertook without authority to search the ropewalks. Why they did so is a mystery, because as Carr later admitted, the sergeant had been seen alive on Saturday. Carr's embarrassment and the town's annoyance increased considerably when the sergeant shortly appeared, in full health. The reason for his absence has not survived; perhaps the general antimilitary bias did not extend to all of Boston's trades and professions.[7]

Certainly the soldiers' irritation had not prevented some of them from forming friendships with townspeople. Aware that the explosion must be near, they sought to warn their acquaintances. The radicals later pointed to these incidents as proof of a military plot. Such warnings seem rather the natural reaction of men aware that their fellows, full of "a pretty strong degree of resentment," would certainly "embrace any opportunity that chance might offer, consistently with their duty and the law, to take some revenge." Conscious though they were that the inevitable showdown had arrived, they tried to steer their friends away from injury. Civilians, too, were predicting trouble. The Reverend Andrew Eliot had known since Saturday that "many" townspeople looked forward to "fighting it out with the soldiers on the Monday." The "bells were to be rung to assemble the inhabitants together." A maid to Sarah Welsteed, Hutchinson's sister, spent Sunday evening with some of the ropewalk brawlers. Afterward, she informed her mistress that there would be a battle Monday evening between the inhabitants and the troops, and that the bells were to ring. Unfortunately, Mistress Welsteed appears not to have passed the intelligence on to Hutchinson until too late.[8]

At the council meeting on Monday, Hutchinson laid before the board Carr's complaining letter. Hoping for advice and assistance, he received what had come to be the council's normal response to any such request. The people, several councilors said, would never be satisfied with anything short of the troops' removal; "the Commissioners, too," Royall Tyler added. One man even said baldly that some of the town's leading citizens had several times met to consider the proper means for effecting this end. Unknown to everyone, Parliament was at that very moment beginning debate on a proposal to eliminate almost all the Townshend duties.[9]

The evening of March 5 turned out pleasant but chilly. About a foot of snow lay upon the streets, mostly frozen; it made cold walking. A white ice-cake covered King Street, with considerable broken ice littering the surface. Boston had no street lamps, and would not for four more years. Only a first-quarter moon, shining in the southern part of a cloudless sky, and reflected from the snow, lit the area between the Town House and the Custom House.[10]

To the south of the Town House, across a narrow fork of King Street, stood the Main Guard, Boston's military headquarters. A pair of small brass fieldpieces flanked the door, and a pair of soldiers occupied the sentry boxes. Down the street, at the corner of King Street and Royal Exchange Lane, Private Hugh White kept his solitary post near a small sentry box. White, the soldiers before the Main Guard, the squad at the Neck Guard, and other sentries posted at various places in Boston, all belonged to the Twenty-ninth Regiment, whose duty sections had assumed the guard at a forenoon ceremony. Thomas Preston, a forty-year-old Irishman whom even the radicals called "a sober honest man, and a good officer," was the captain of the day. Lieutenant James Basset, barely twenty, commanded at the Main Guard, as he had the day of Mein's troubles. Son of an army officer, Basset had so far enjoyed a vicarious military career. Although he had held a commission from the age of twelve, he had not served very much active duty; the preceding June, his father asked Carr to give the boy more leave. Because Basset had been absent four years from the regiment, Carr found the request "very unreasonable." So Basset stayed in Boston, and now he had the Guard. But typically, during the evening Basset remained in his quarters, one hundred yards away.[11]

The Custom House, on the south side of King Street, one block down from the Town House, was brick, with a three-step curbed front stoop before its centered door. Although the commissioners held their boards in the Concert Hall, on the southeast side of what the twentieth century called Scollay Square, the Custom House contained the heart of the Boston revenue-enforcement apparatus. Shipmasters went there to enter and clear their vessels and to pay any duties owed on their cargoes. The offices held all the Boston customs records and whatever revenue cash had been collected. It was for this reason that Private White had been posted in the little sentry box a few feet from the Royal Exchange Lane corner of the building. Besides the customs offices, the building housed the family of Bartholomew Green, a minor revenue official.[12]

The evening began quietly. White, pacing his post, saw Samuel Clark passing by on King Street. Knowing Clark, he asked him how things were at home. Clark went on, leaving the street empty. Captain-Lieutenant John Goldfinch of the Fourteenth came along. Edward Garrick, one of Piemont the wigmaker's young apprentices, arrived at the same time. "There goes the fellow that won't pay my master for dressing his hair," Garrick shouted. As Goldfinch had the receipt in his pocket, he passed haughtily on without acknowledging the insult. Garrick, looking across King Street to Quaker Lane (now Congress Street), could see a group of men carrying sticks. While Garrick stood by, Bartholomew Broaders, another of Piemont's apprentices, joined him. Broaders had just accompanied Bartholomew Green's daughter Ann and Mary "Molly" Rogers at their request to the apothecary's. Broaders, too, had noticed a group of club-carrying townsmen; he had encountered them at about 8 P.M., in King Street. They said some soldiers had attacked them. Broaders had followed the men south to the conduit in Dock Square, and then left them. Unknown to either boy, at the same time in other parts of Boston "clusters of the inhabitants were observed." ". . . Parties of soldiers were also driving about the streets, as if the one, and the other, had something more than ordinary upon their minds." [13]

As Broaders, Garrick, and the two girls stood on the Custom House steps, the big door opened. Ann's brother Hammond, a boatbuilder by trade, came out and ordered the girls in. The apprentices followed, stayed chatting a while, and then left for a tour of King Street and Quaker Lane. When they returned to King Street, Garrick decided to reopen the question of Captain Goldfinch's credit. Goldfinch, he said to three chance passers-by, was "mean" (i.e., penurious), and owed money. If Garrick's purpose was to taunt White, he succeeded. The sentry shouted that Goldfinch was a gentleman and would pay what he owed. There were no gentlemen in that regiment, Garrick answered. At that, White left his post, and came into the street. Garrick moved to meet him. "Let me see your face," White said. "I am not ashamed to show my face," Garrick replied. Without another word, White swung his musket, striking the side of Garrick's head. Reeling and staggering, the boy began crying in pain while White and Broaders exchanged insults.[14]

The ruckus attracted Hammond Green's attention. Together with his brother John and two more apprentice wigmakers who had been visiting, he went out the Custom House's back door and around by way of Royal Exchange Lane into King Street. From the direction of the Brattle Square Church, on the other side of Dock Square, came the sound of shouts. But in front of the Custom House, Green saw only eight or nine men and boys, including the weeping Garrick. Green went up the steps; the women let him in. Somewhere in the town a church bell began tolling, the alarm for fire. Men began shouting "Fire," and Hammond Green, safe inside, locked the door. Across town, Sarah Hutchinson Welsteed heard the bell. Ordinarily "terrified at the cry of fire, [she] gave herself little or no concern, very satisfied that it was the fray she expected." John Green, meanwhile, went up to the top of King Street near the Brazen Head. From there he could more clearly locate the shouting. It was coming, not from Dr. Charles Cooper's Brattle Square Church, but from Murray's sugar house on Brattle Street, where part of the Twenty-ninth had its barracks.[15]

As John Green reconnoitered the noise, White's difficulties were increasing. His set-to with the apprentices had left him "muttering and growling," apparently "very mad." This temper did not improve when the boys began daring him to come out and fight. "Lousy rascal," they called him. "Lobster son of a bitch! Damned rascally scoundrel lobster son of a bitch!" By the time John Green came back from the Brazen Head, the crowd had increased to fifty. Things had quieted down momentarily, but White was plainly frightened. He retreated to the Custom House steps—thus affording himself both elevation and a protected rear—and loaded his musket. Green went around to the back gate. In front, the verbal barrage resumed, augmented by snowballs. White fixed his bayonet; he lowered his musket, using it to keep himself clear. Like Private Burgess at the same post in the October riot, White feared himself in danger of being carried off his post. Henry Knox, a bookseller who had read widely about military matters, told White that if he fired he would "die for it." "Damn them," White answered. "If they molest me I will fire." Young Jonathan Williams Austin, in the middle of his first year as a law clerk to John Adams, heard the bells and came into King Street. When Austin told the people to "come away, and not molest the sentry," a few responded. But many remained. Fist-sized pieces of ice began to crash around White. He knocked at the Custom House door, but could not get in; he pounded the butt of his weapon on the steps, but the crowd kept on: "Kill him, kill him, knock him down. Fire, damn you, fire, you dare not fire." Town watchman Edward Gambett Langford tried to reassure him. These were only boys, he said, just young shavers; they would not hurt him. Unconvinced, White bellowed for help: "Turn out, Main Guard!" [16]

During the development of the Custom House crisis, a more violent and broader confrontation had been boiling a few blocks north. The "huzzaing" which the Greens had heard came not from Murray's Barracks themselves, but from the area directly in front. Many Boston streets in 1770, like some in the City of London today, were connected by covered passages tunneling through the separating buildings. One such passage, variously called Boylston's or Draper's Alley, led from the end of Cornhill (now Washington Street) to Brattle Street. Opposite the Brattle Street opening, that is, on the west side of the street, stood Murray's Barracks. Richard Hirons, the doctor who had befriended John Mein, lived on the east side of Brattle Street. Shortly after 8 p.m., Dr. Hirons noticed considerable activity in Brattle Street: soldiers variously armed with bayonets, clubs, and "one thing and another" were passing back and forth. From the direction of the Market and Dock Square, Hirons could hear noise and confusion; he could see people running to-and-fro. After ten minutes of this, a man rushed up Boylston's Alley toward Brattle Street, shouting loudly, "Town born, turn out! Town born, turn out!" In front of the barracks he repeated it twenty times, shouting first toward the south end of Brattle Street, then the north. Ensign Alexander Mall, at thirty, old for his rank, called to the barrack-gate sentry: "Who is that fellow? Lay hold of him." But the sentry did nothing and the civilians in turn ignored the sentry.[17]

Through the narrow passage now poured a crowd, whether civilian or military, Hirons could not tell. Armed with clubs and sticks, they thumped the sides of the passage so ferociously that Hirons locked his door, extinguished his front lights, and went upstairs to watch. Twenty or thirty townspeople clustered around the barracks gate opposite, facing four or five officers. A short man came up to the gate. "Why don't you keep your soldiers in their barracks?" he asked. The officers replied that they had done and would do everything possible to keep the men in. "Are the inhabitants," said the little man, "to be knocked down in the street? Are they to be murdered in this manner?" The officers tried vainly to reassure him. "You know the country has been used ill," he said. "You know the town has been used ill. We did not send for you. We will not have you here. We will—" In the uproar, Hirons could not distinguish the last words. They sounded like "—get rid of you," or "—drive you away." Once more the officers sought to pacify the man; they asked him to help disperse the crowd. Hirons could not tell the reply, but immediately the cry, "Home! Home!" went up. Nobody moved for a few minutes. Then the shout was repeated. About two-thirds of the people, huzzaing, "The Main Guard!" moved back through Boylston's Alley.

Shortly, however, more townspeople poured up from the Market. A little boy, seven or eight years old, ran toward the gate holding his head and screaming that he was killed. One of the exasperated officers grabbed him; "Damn you for a little rascal," he said. "What business do you have out of doors?" A soldier ran out of the barrack gate with his musket, kneeled down in the street, and pointed the weapon at Boylston's Alley, still packed with people. "God damn your bloods," he yelled. "I'll make a lane through you all." Mall and another officer knocked the soldier down, disarmed him, and shoved him back into the barrack. The noise increased. Another soldier came out with a musket, cursed the inhabitants, and, standing, brought the firelock to "present"; again Mall sent him sprawling and took the weapon.

Not all the soldiers had been confined. At the Cornhill end of Boylston's Alley, a knot of Redcoats armed with a single fireshovel were defending themselves against a snowball attack. Captain Goldfinch, passing by, saw the fight, and went over. Some of the civilians begged him to send the soldiers to the barracks, lest murder result. Working his way through the snowballs, Goldfinch succeeded first in pushing toward to the soldiers, and then in persuading them to follow him up to Murray's. The crowd followed so thick that soon the entire area between the barracks steps and the alley filled completely; more townsmen were pressing up the alley from Cornhill.

Fearing a real riot, Goldfinch, even though not a member of the Twenty-ninth, asserted his seniority and ordered the junior officers to confine the men. His fears were well founded. Even as Ensign Mall and Lieutenants Paul Minchin and Hugh Dickson were hustling the men into the barracks, the mob pelted them with snowballs and epithets: "Cowards," "Cowardly rascalls," "afraid to fight." Dr. John Jeffries, another neighborhood physician, had heard the shouting. Unable to force his way through the jammed alley, he managed to worm himself onto Hirons's front steps. As he arrived, a short man in a light brown surtout, or greatcoat, joined Goldfinch and the other officers. This was Boston merchant Richard Palmes, acting as a self-appointed mediator. The sight of the soldiers out of the barracks after 8 P.M. surprised him; he was blunt enough to tell the officers so. "Pray, do you mean to teach us our duty?" one asked. "I do not," Palmes answered hastily, "only to remind you of it." "You see," said the officer, "that the

soldiers are all in their barracks. Why do you not go to your homes?"
Any soldier who had injured a civilian, they promised, would be punished; the soldiers would not be allowed out that evening. "You mean
they dare not come out," someone shouted. "You dare not let them
out." The epithets continued, and so did the snowballs, which the
officers "stooped to avoid." "Gentlemen," said Palmes to the crowd,
"you hear what the officers say, and you had better go home." [18]

That was enough for most. "Let's go home," they shouted. But others
still looked for action. "Let's away to the Main Guard," was their cry.
Down the alley they swarmed, huzzaing and rapping the walls as they
went. Dr. Jeffries followed along behind. When he came into Cornhill,
the bell of the Old Brick Church, near the Town House, was ringing.
Jeffries walked along Cornhill to King Street. A gang stood outside the
Brazen Head. "Damn it," said someone, "here lives an importer." Others picked up chunks of ice and tossed them at the windows; four
panes broke. Andrew Cazneau the lawyer came over. "Do not meddle
with Mr. Jackson," he said. "Let him alone. Do not break his windows." They stopped throwing. Most of them went down King Street;
others pushed around between the Town House and the Main Guard.
Jeffries followed these latter. He saw them break into a run after they
rounded the Town House, and, without stopping at the Main Guard,
hurry down the street. From lower in King Street, Jeffries heard a
huzza.[19]

While one crowd had been jousting with White, and another with
the officers at Murray's Barracks, a third throng collected in Dock
Square. In his home at the corner of Royal Exchange Lane and Dock
Square, auctioneer William Hunter was entertaining a group of his fellow Scots. As they relaxed, David Mitchelson, a seal-engraver and
type-founder employed by John Mein, burst in. How could they sit
there so contentedly, Mitchelson wanted to know, when there was
such trouble between the soldiers and the inhabitants. The company
rushed upstairs to the vendue, or auction, room, with its balcony facing Dock Square. So many pushed on the balcony that Archibald Wilson, fearing it would fall down, withdrew and watched out a nearby
window. In Dock Square, a crowd of about two hundred swirled and
eddied. A throng carrying staves of wood came out of the North End.
They jammed into the narrow opening of Boylston's Alley, then ebbed
back into the square. As succeeding waves came in from the north,
they in turn made a push at the alley, followed by a retreat. Men who
lacked cudgels were breaking into the market stalls, ripping the legs
off the produce and butcher tables. The cry was "Fire," repeated frequently. "It is very odd to come to put out a fire with sticks and bludgeons," Wilson remarked to his companions.[20]

In the middle of Dock Square, a tall man wearing a white wig and a red cloak stood. Quieting down, the crowd gathered around him. The men at Hunter's could not hear his words, although he was obviously haranguing the mob. They did not know him. After a few minutes, having finished his speech, he went off. The people in Dock Square raised their hats, and gave a cheer for the Main Guard, with a promise to "do for the soldiers." Whistling through their fingers, shrieking, some of them striking their clubs on a store front as they passed, they headed for King Street. Some went over Cornhill, some by a narrow little alley; and the rest roared up Royal Exchange Lane to the Custom House.[21]

While the throngs from the barracks and Dock Square were pouring into King Street, augmenting the crowd already there, the bells were pulling still more townspeople toward the Custom House. Boston had no fire department; in the event of fire, the largely wooden-built town depended for survival on organized volunteers. Only ten years before, a terrible fire had erased almost every building from Milk Street to King Street, from what is now Devonshire Street to the water's edge (present Kilby Street). When a church bell rang the alarm, Bostonians hurried *en masse* to the site. Some manned the wheeled pumps called "engines" which were housed in convenient central locations throughout the town. Others brought bags (to help the stricken families save their belongings) and leather buckets (to help carry water). Bells might ring in the daytime for joy or for mourning. But in the night, an off-hour church bell meant only one thing. Thus when sometime after 9 P.M., first the Brattle Square Church bells, then those of the Old Brick, began to peal, the town reacted instinctively. At Windmill Point, half a mile south of the Town House, Robert Goddard heard the cry of "Fire" and hurried toward King Street. Men broke out the South End's engines and began hauling them up the Main Street. Out of the Town House came the engine kept there. Men with bags and buckets mingled with the eighteenth-century equivalent of fire buffs, and all rushed toward the sound of the bells. "Fire, fire, fire," they shouted.[22]

William Palfrey, the radical leader, at home recovering from an illness, sent a servant to see where the fire was. The servant came back with word that the soldiers were fighting the inhabitants in King Street. Sickness forgotten, Palfrey ran out into the snow. A little earlier, merchant Edward Payne, hearing a bell, came from across town toward his King Street home opposite the Custom House. On the way, someone told him the soldiers and townspeople had been fighting. Payne quickly went home to reassure Mrs. Payne that there was no fire. A conflagration, apparently, involved more personal risk than a pitched battle. Payne's across-the-street neighbor, Thomas Marshal, the tailor who served as lieutenant colonel of the Boston militia regiment, "had been warned not to go out that night." With the ringing of the bells and the collecting crowd, he "began to think it was fire." Temporizing, he stood in his doorway and watched.[23]

Magnetlike, the bells drew men and boys to King Street. Standing at his father's gate in Green's Lane (now Congress Street south of Milk Street), young Benjamin Davis saw Sam Gray. "There is no fire," Davis said. "It is the soldiers fighting." "Damn it, I am glad of it," said Gray, running off toward King Street. "I will knock some of them on the head." "Take care you don't get killed yourself," Davis called after him. "Never fear," shouted Gray. "Damn their bloods." A little further along, Gray met Nicholas Ferriter, who had been with him at the ropewalks during the recent battle. "Where are you going?" Ferriter asked. "To the fire," said Gray. He was carrying no stick; Ferriter thought he seemed calm as a clock. They went on to King Street together. What Ferriter saw did not disturb him; he decided to go home. Gray had said that if there were no fire he would leave. But for some reason he changed his mind.[24]

Samuel Maverick, seventeen years old, apprenticed to Isaac Greenwood the ivory turner, had worked at his master's till 8:30. Afterward he was eating supper at the home of Jonathan Cary, the kegmaker, with Cary's four young sons and another teen-ager. Maverick had some connection with the radicals. His half-sister, Elizabeth, was married to Ebenezer Mackintosh. When the bell rang, the boys told Cary they would eat a few more mouthfuls and go to the fire.[25]

At Thomas Symmonds's victualing-house (the equivalent of a present-day diner), much frequented by off-duty soldiers, a man who called himself Michael Johnson ate his supper. Variously described as a black and an Indian, Johnson said he came from New-Providence, in the Bahamas. He was in his late forties, standing a massive 6'2", a remarkable height in those days: in all the Twenty-ninth Regiment, only four men were as tall as 6'; only thirty-six (out of approximately three hundred) exceeded 5'10". Finishing his supper, Johnson went out into the tense town. With a cordwood stick about the thickness of a man's wrist, he led twenty or thirty sailors up Cornhill. Some carried clubs like his; others were whistling, huzzaing, and as one observer said, "making a noise." [26]

Other sailors found themselves in King Street. If we can believe Sam Adams, James Caldwell, a young mariner schooling himself "in the art of Navigation," came over to the Custom House from "the home of a reputable person in this town, to whose daughter he made his visits, with the honorable intention of Marriage." Robert Paterson, whose trousers, not two weeks before, had been cut by Richardson's swanshot, ran up from the North End to join the shouting, hooting mob.[27]

Many of the newcomers had left home fully aware that the ringing bells warned of something other than fire. Patrick Carr, an immigrant Irishman, lived in the household of his employer, a leather-breeches maker in Queen (now Court) Street. Well-experienced in the ways of Auld Sod mobs and of the soldiers called upon to quell them, he hid a hanger (a small cutlass) under his coat. Mr. Field, coming in as Carr was leaving, felt the sword. A brisk argument ensued, Field asking for the hanger, Carr holding to it. Finally, one of the neighbors who happened to be in the house persuaded Carr to leave the weapon. Another Celt, Benjamin Burdick, had at first gone from home unarmed. But his wife called after him, "It is not fire, it is an affray in King Street." Burdick came back. "If you are going," his wife said, "take this." She handed him his basket-handled highland broadsword. Others settled for less lethal weapons. Matthew Murray cut the handle off his mother's broom. Christopher "Kit" Monk, seventeen years old, came with a catstick, a slender bat used in tip-cat, the eighteenth-century equivalent of stickball.[28]

The noise in King Street increased. "Fire!" some shouted, even though there was none; up and down the street men cried loudly for an attack on the Main Guard, "Strike at the root; there is the nest!" To White's call for help from his outdoor prison on the Custom House steps, others added direct appeals. Edward Hill went up and told the people at the Guard that the mob might very well carry White off his post. William Jackson, Brazen Head himself, had been at his mother's, where Preston lodged. At the first bells, Jackson went out to reconnoiter. Basset was by now also at Preston's. When Jackson left, Basset and Preston went up on the roof to locate the fire. Before they could descend, Jackson had returned, and a corporal had come with a half-dozen soldiers to tell Preston the sentry was endangered. Preston was known for his coolness. "Had I wanted an Officer to guard against a precipitate action," Hutchinson said later, "I should have pitched upon him as soon as any in the Regiment." He belted on his sword, settled his hat over his wig, and went to the Main Guard.[29]

Men were still streaming into King Street. The radical doctor, Thomas Young, stood in Royal Exchange Lane, telling people the soldiers had "made a rumpus, and were now gone to their barracks, and now it was best for every one to go home." But he held a sword in his hand, and everybody seemed to take that as his true estimate of the situation; the surge toward King Street continued. The head of Royal Exchange Lane was "stopped up" with the crowd. Inside the Custom House, fear increased. Hammond Green checked the door. Thomas Greenwood took Ann Green, Molly Rogers, and Elizabeth Avery up to a little drawing room on the second floor in the corner of the house, directly over the sentry box. Standing in the dark, they watched what was happening. Terrified, as he said, lest the house be pulled down, Greenwood left by the back door. As he climbed the backyard wood-pile, in order to get over the fence, John Green returned and asked him to open the gate. "Not for anybody," Greenwood answered. Just before he jumped down to join Green, a passer-by shouted to him: "Heave over some shelales [shillelaghs]." Inside the house, Hammond Green went up to join the terrified women.[30]

In front of the Main Guard, Preston "walked up and down facing the Guard house for near half an hour," trying to decide what to do. He could see and hear the mob at the Custom House; in addition, various volunteers kept conveying predictions that the sentry's life was threatened. Yet while Preston appreciated that something must be done, the situation did not offer many viable options. *First,* he could try to reinforce White, hoping that the show of strength would cool the mob's temper long enough to permit a reasoned decision to disperse. Unfortunately, the crowd was so large, so angry, and so well armed that no one could fairly expect the sight of the handful of Redcoats at Preston's immediate disposal to frighten it into order. Further, as Preston knew, and the mob knew even better, troops could not be used to quiet civil disturbances unless some civilian authority specifically requested military action. "He had no Business to defend the Custom House unless legally called upon," Gage wrote later. *Second,* Preston could try to rescue White. This would involve assembling a force strong enough to break through any resistance, going down to the Custom House, and, more important, pushing back up to the Main Guard. Such a maneuver might well succeed in saving White's life. But it would also leave the Custom House fully open to the mob; and, perhaps equally significant to a military man, it would require Preston's violation of the order that had posted a sentry there in the first place. *Third,* Preston might do nothing; send word to Dalrymple, Carr, and Hutchinson; and leave the whole mess to his superiors. That, of course, would expose Preston to charges of dereliction, and just might cost White his life. In short, no course which Preston could conceivably take avoided, or even minimized, appalling risks.[31]

We have no record of Preston's reasoning. His explanation immediately after the event was that White's safety lay foremost in his mind. In a written statement composed after a short, tense interval, he said that the safety of the customs money motivated him also.[32] His initial response was probably more candid. Boston's activities since the Hutchinson riot indicated that the mob usually acted only upon individuals, and that the unguarded Custom House was safer than the besieged

White. Further, an assault on the king's money would have been such blatant treason that Preston could well have dismissed it from his mind as not worth worrying about. However, later on, after the rescue effort had produced wholesale death, it may have occurred to Preston and his friends that the Home Government would be much more likely to protect an officer whose woes stemmed from defending royal property against traitors than one who risked some lives, cost others, and provoked a major incident, all in a silly attempt to save a single easily replaceable private. In contemporary England, and even in Boston, soldiers, like slaves, were only with difficulty remembered as human beings.

These philosophical considerations could not command much of Preston's immediate attention. As ranking officer in the first battle of the American Revolution, he faced the necessity for immediate tactical decision. His inexperienced subordinate Basset, so visibly shaken that a bystander "pitied his situation," was nervously asking for orders. As a first step Preston had the guard, its heavy watchcoats off, form in front. The men were slow in responding. Preston, his own nerves obviously taut, swore impatiently "in a great flutter of spirit." "Damn your bloods, why don't you turn out?" When the troops finally formed, Basset again sought Preston. "What shall I do in this case?" he asked. "Take out six or seven of the men, and let them go down to the assistance of the sentry," Preston said.[33]

The relief party fell out, Corporal William Wemms and six privates, Carroll, Kilroy, Warren, Hugh Montgomery, James Hartigan, and William McCauley. All but the corporal were grenadiers, the biggest men in the regiment, made even taller by their high bearskin caps, the king's crest on the front (*"Nec aspera terrent"*) and a grenade with the number 29 on the back. Ordinarily, a party this small would require no more senior a commander than Corporal Wemms—indeed, the expression "a corporal's guard" fits it precisely. But the evident delicacy and danger demanded the presence of a commissioned officer. Basset prepared to lead. Preston, however, knew that he could not trust this assignment to the inexperienced boy. When the party stepped off, Preston placed himself beside it; Basset remained before the Main Guard.[34] In a column of twos, with Corporal Wemms at the head, as if for an ordinary relief, the party began moving down and across King Street, muskets shouldered, empty but with fixed bayonets. Their brisk pace slowed when they reached the thickening crowd. The soldiers' faces grew "very threatening"; their muskets came to the port, or diagonal position, so that the bayonets pricked any of the crowd who pressed too close. Nathaniel Hurd, the engraver, standing near the corner of Royal Exchange Lane, had a bayonet brush his hat. In the mid-

dle of King Street Nathaniel Fosdick, watching the Custom House, felt
a push at his back. He turned and found himself in the path of the
party. "Why are you pushing at me?" he said. "Damn your blood," said
the soldier, "stand out of our way." "I will not," Fosdick replied. "I am
doing no harm to any man, and I will not stand aside for anyone." The
column obligingly opened right and left, passing around him.[35]

Young bookseller Henry Knox was desperately trying, as even the
Tories later admitted, to do "everything in his power to prevent mischief on this occasion." Having fruitlessly sought to keep the boys from
bothering White, he came over and clutched Preston's coat. The officer
stopped, the party continued toward the Custom House. "For God's
sake, take care of your men," Knox said. "If they fire, you die." "I am
sensible [i.e., aware] of it," Preston answered in haste and agitation, as
he hurried to rejoin his men. While Preston and Knox talked, the soldiers reached the now-empty sentry box. Still in their files, they halted,
put butts of their muskets on the ground, and began to load. John Gridley, Otis's teammate in the September scrimmage, had been up the
street at Benjamin Kent's door, chatting with the Whig lawyer's daughter. When he saw the party go down, he followed, because he had
promised some companions at the Bunch of Grapes tavern a full report. During his walk along the Custom House side of King Street, he
heard no orders to load. Gridley reached the soldiers as they were
loading, and passed directly between the two lines, the Redcoats politely pulling their pieces back out of his path. In light of future events,
it is likely the muskets were double-loaded, the way the Neck Guard's
pieces were.[36]

When Preston arrived, his first thought was for White. He ordered
the sentry to fall in, which White did without serious interference.
Then Preston tried to march the party back to the Main Guard. The
crowd pressed around. Whether Preston could have pushed his squad
through is a question by its nature unanswerable. The need to use some
force simply to make a passage might well have touched off violence;
hemmed in by the crush, the troops would be able to employ neither
musket nor bayonet. There was little chance the crowd would permit a
quiet withdrawal. "Damn you, you sons of bitches, fire," some one
shouted at the now motionless Redcoats. "You can't kill us all." [37]

The party formed a single line, roughly semicircular, its right wing a
hitching post next to the corner of the Custom House, its left to the
street side of the sentry box. This was probably as good a deployment
as possible under the circumstances, protecting both flanks and the
rear, too. But men could still slip between the sentry box and the Custom House; during the next few minutes, several people did just
that.[38]

The soldiers stood about a body's width apart. No one knows the exact position of each one. Montgomery was on the party's right; Corporal Wemms was at the left. McCauley stood somewhere near the center. Carroll was third from the right, and Warren, a tall man, was third from the left. People recognized one or another of them. Jane Whitehouse lived in Royal Exchange Lane, near White's home. As she pushed near the soldiers, White put his arm out and thrust her toward the corner. "Go home," he said, "or you'll be killed." [39]

Preston stood slightly in front of the soldiers, shouting at the crowd, trying to convince it to disperse. For answer he got hoots, curses, and snowballs. People were daring the troops to fire; the bells kept on ringing; the civil authorities stayed hidden. Even the most courageous of the nonradical Boston justices of the peace did not dare to act. Apparently one did come to the scene, for a shout went up: "Here comes Murray with the Riot Act." And the crowd forgot the troops for an instant, long enough to pelt a scurrying figure with snowballs until it disappeared down Pudding Lane (now Devonshire Street). [40]

The Riot Act was not going to save Preston's men; nor, it seemed, was anything else. A large mob was pressing in upon them, the nearest people so close "you could not get your hat betwixt them and the bayonets." Those not in the front line were jumping up on the backs of those ahead, trying to see what was happening. Estimates of the crowd size vary. Captain Jeremiah French of the Twenty-ninth had been in the British Coffee House on King Street with James Forrest ("the Irish Infant") when the first cry of "Fire" began. The men went up to the roof, from where they could see the whole crowd. French later said that the mob could not contain "less than 300 or 400 people." Even allowing for French's obvious bias, and for his sometimes weak observative sense (he did not see Preston's party come down), his elevated vantage point makes his report more worthy of credit than the necessarily cramped and restricted view imposed upon any individual in the middle of the crowd. [41]

Physically as well as audibly, the crowd pressure increased. The soldiers were trembling, whether in fear or in rage, one could not say. Up and down the line, men dared the Redcoats to fire, called them cowardly rascals, challenged them to put down their weapons and fight. The shouts were so loud they might, as Gridley put it, "be heard to Long Wharf": "Why do you not fire? Damn you, you dare not fire. Fire and be damned." Musket barrels rang to the rapping of sticks and clubs. As the soldiers "payed," or thrust, with their bayonets, trying for breathing room, brief individual duels developed. [42]

Sam Gray clapped Joseph Hinkley's back. "Do not run, my lad," he

Richard Dana (1700–1772), by John Singleton Copley; courtesy, Richard H. Dana.

An enthusiastic member of the second-level radical leadership, Dana was the most outspoken anti-administration Boston justice of the peace. He seemed at his vituperous best (or worst) in cases involving soldiers. Not even his relationship to Tory Judge Edmund Trowbridge—Lydia Dana was Trowbridge's sister—modified Dana's open partisanship. His son became America's minister to Russia; his great-grandson wrote *Two Years Before the Mast.*

Boston Massacre Monument, Boston Common; photograph by Thomas F. Maffei, courtesy, the photographer.

Erected in 1889 after bitter controversy, this implausible mass of masonry suggests that the King Street killings burst assunder the chains of slavery. Whether this is what the monument properly ought to commemorate is at present difficult to settle.

Peter Oliver (1713–1791), by John Singleton Copley; courtesy, Andrew Oliver and the Frick Art Reference Library.

No lawyer, Oliver was an intelligent business entrepreneur whose polish drew praise even from John Adams. As a judicial craftsman, he appears to have been above average. It is, however, as an acidulous commentator upon his troubled times that he is best remembered. But *The Origin and Progress of the American Rebellion,* is, like red pepper, best used in small quantities carefully applied.

James Murray (1713–1781), by John Singleton Copley; courtesy, Frank Lyman and the Metropolitan Museum of Art.

A volatile Scottish merchant, Murray settled first in North Carolina, moving to Boston, for climatic reasons, in 1760. The irascible Murray was not the man to allay Boston's intense anti-Scottish, anti-Jacobite feelings. His open and continued adherence to the Crown position merely increased his unpopularity, which became irreversible when he leased his sugar warehouse to the army as a barrack for the Twenty-ninth Regiment.

Samuel Quincy (1734–1789), by John Singleton Copley; courtesy, Miss Grace Treadwell and the Museum of Fine Arts, Boston.

Brother of Josiah Quincy, Harvard classmate (1754) of John Hancock, and friend of John Adams (both were admitted to the bar the same day), Quincy was never quite certain which side of the political road he preferred to walk. His mental industry did not quite match his wit, so that his professional standing never exceeded the mediocre. His conduct as co-prosecutor of Ebenezer Richardson, Captain Preston, the soldiers, and the customs officials exemplifies his political ambivalence, his modest intellectual achievements, and his imperturbability (or indifference).

Blockade of Boston Harbor, by Christian Remick; courtesy, the Massachusetts Historical Society.

This is how Bostonians saw the Armada which landed the troops on October 1, 1768. After coming ashore on Long Wharf (at the middle bottom of the picture), the soldiers formed in what Paul Revere called "insolent parade" and marched up the wharf, on to King Street, into the heart of Boston.

Map of Boston (1769), by John Bonner; courtesy, Prints Division, The New York Public Library, Astor, Lenox and Tilden Foundations.
Key: 1. Neck Guard; 2. Gray's Ropewalk; 3. Old South Meeting House; 4. Old Granary Burying Ground; 5. Town House; 6. Main Guard; 7. Custom House and

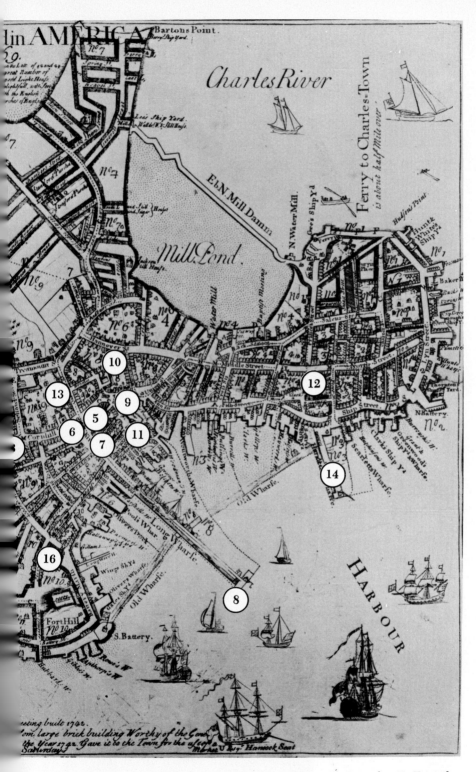

Massacre Site; 8. Long Wharf; 9. Dock Square; 10. Murray's Barracks; 11. Faneuil Hall; 12. Hutchinson's House; 13. Court House and Jail; 14. Hancock's Wharf; 15. Province House (Governor's residence); 16. Andrew Oliver's House; 17. Liberty Tree.

Plates from William Windham, *A Plan of Discipline* (1759); courtesy, Rare Book Division, the New York Public Library, Astor, Lenox and Tilden Foundations.

These figures are not wearing grenadier caps. Otherwise, they show how the soldiers stood in King Street on March 5, 1770: first, "with charged bayonet," trying to hold the crowd back; then, in firing position.

Gilbert deBlois (1725–1792), by John Singleton Copley; courtesy, Dr. Elizabeth deBlois and The Museum of Fine Arts, Boston.

A successful merchant, deBlois remained a steadfast loyalist, ultimately suffering exile and proscription. During the preliminaries to Captain Preston's trial, he furnished Preston with useful background information on prospective jurors, and even managed to have himself and four equally trustworthy Tories sworn on the jury.

Josiah Quincy (1744–1775), by Gilbert Stuart; courtesy, Edmund Quincy and the Museum of Fine Arts, Boston.

Eloquent in court or town meeting, fiery in his radical zeal, yet unstinting in his defense of Richardson, Wilmot, Captain Preston, and the soldiers, the cross-eyed "Wilkes" Quincy flashed through the pre-Revolutionary turmoil like a meteor through a New England summer's night. He died of tuberculosis in April 1775, coming home from a mission to London on behalf of the Boston radical leadership.

Plan of the Town House Area, attributed to Paul Revere; courtesy, the Boston Public Library.

Mellen Chamberlain, the nineteenth-century antiquarian who donated this plan to the Library, said it was drawn by Revere for use at the soldiers' trial. No other indication that it saw actual courtroom service has been found, either in counsel's trial minutes or in the printed transcript. The folds and a now-illegible notation on the reverse suggest that at one time it was at least part of a file of court documents. The significance of the numbers and the letters is not clear; neither is the reason for the omission of one of the victims and one of the soldiers.

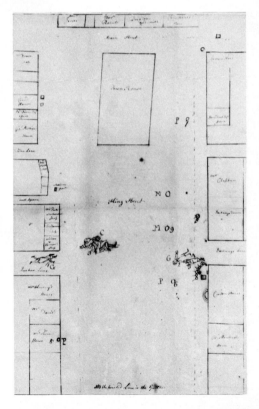

Charles Townshend (1725–1767); courtesy, The Duke of Buccleuch and the Scottish National Galleries.

Glib, charming, the spoiled darling of the House of Commons, "Champagne Charlie" Townshend proposed a mindless scheme of colonial taxation and revenue enforcement which, when enacted, stimulated the resistance that eventually led to revolt.

Engraving of View of Boston Common (ca. 1770), after Christian Remick; courtesy, Prints Division, The New York Public Library, Astor, Lenox and Tilden Foundations.

When the troops arrived on October 1, 1768, civilian resistance took the form of refusal to furnish appropriate quarters. Undaunted, the Twenty-ninth Regiment bivouacked on Boston Common, virtually in the front yard of John Hancock, whose Beacon Hill mansion may be seen in the background.

yelled. "They dare not fire." And he ran off, pounding the backs of others. Hinkley thought Gray was "a little in drink." However true that may have been, danger lay not in Gray's alcoholic exuberance, nor even in the currently popular grim flippancy that a man had but one life to lose and he ought willingly to lose it for his country. The real inciter of bloodshed was a fundamental legal misconception which the radicals had encouraged among Bostonians. It was based on an undoubted truth, that soldiers could not use force against civilians unless some civil authority so requested. Thus the rout of Murray doubtless enhanced the already strong belief that soldiers without a magistrate were legally helpless, and that this particular group of soldiers could not lawfully defend itself. Unfortunately and tragically, the purveyors of this supposed principle forgot its necessary corollary. No one, soldier or civilian, need without retaliation suffer a mortal attack. Whether with or without civilian approval, a soldier, like anyone else, retained the ordinary right of self-defense. If a man tried to kill a soldier, the soldier, without asking approval even of his own officer, could —if nothing else would save his life—kill his assailant. Of course in every case, civilian's or soldier's, the instantaneous issue would be whether, in fact, killing was necessary to preserve life. By definition, the circumstances were such as to preclude deep contemplation. So another fact entered the delicate balance on King Street. The Twenty-ninth had a reputation for quick temper. Hutchinson himself remarked that "they are in general such bad fellows in that regiment, that it seems impossible to restrain them from firing upon an insult or provocation given them." [43]

A heedless mob, playing with legal fire; a rash band of frightened soldiers, confused by the noise, distracted and provoked by the swearing and taunting in front of them. To this was now added an incitement from the rear, where a well-dressed, loud-mouthed gentleman was urging the soldiers to retaliate. "Fire," he said. "By God, I'll stand by you whilst I have a drop of blood. Fire!" [44]

Hope of avoiding tragedy sank fast. Theodore Bliss, whose mob experience dated back to Stamp Act days, worked his way to the scant neutral ground between the mob and the bayonets. "Are your men loaded?" he asked Preston. "Yes," the officer answered. "Are they loaded with ball?" Preston did not reply. "Are they going to fire?" "They cannot fire without my orders." Richard Palmes, the peacemaker at Murray's barracks, came over to Preston, carrying a large stick. Stepping between Bliss and the captain, he casually put his left hand on Preston's right shoulder. "Are your soldiers' guns loaded?" he, too, asked. "With powder and ball," Preston said. "Sir," said Palmes, "I hope you don't intend the soldiers shall fire on the inhabitants." "By no means," Preston answered, "by no means." He was, Preston pointed out, standing in front of the musket muzzles, and "must fall a sacrifice" if they fired. Besides, the pieces were on half-cock, held low, "My giving the word fire, under those circumstances, would prove me no officer." [45]

This was not a night for military precision. The crowd let out a mocking three cheers. Samuel Gray slapped the watchman Langford on the back. "Langford, what's here to pay?" "I don't know what's to pay, but I believe something will come of it by and by [i.e., very soon]," said Langford. A club arched through the moonlight, squarely catching Montgomery. Down on his backside he went, his musket dropping to the ice. Rising to his feet, in agony, rage, frustration, and fear, "Damn you, fire!" he roared, and pulled his trigger. From the party's first leaving the Main Guard, less than fifteen minutes had elapsed. No one seemed to be hit; perhaps the guns carried only powder, after all. Palmes swung wildly at Montgomery, striking his left arm; whirling, he brought the club down on Preston. Had the blow landed solidly, the captain's head might have split. Fortunately, Palmes slipped slightly on the ice at the height of his swing. The wood crunched on Preston's arm. Montgomery now thrust his bayonet at Palmes. Dodging, Palmes flipped his stick at the grenadier and ran safely into Royal Exchange Lane. Similar skirmishing took place elsewhere along the line. Fosdick, who had made the marching column part, ran in on the soldiers with a large stick. As the bayonets flicked, now at his chest, now his arm, he parried them off; but not before one long knife stabbed his biceps and another scraped the side of his chest.[46]

After that first shot, the crowd began to push toward Royal Exchange Lane, and down King Street, leaving the immediate center of the Redcoat line fairly clear. Some people departed more quickly than others. Andrew, a black servant of Oliver Wendell's, ran all the way to Dehone's at the head of King Street; Samuel Maverick started running toward the Town House. Between that first shot and the others which followed, there was a definite pause, long enough, people were to say later, to allow Preston time to order "Recover," which would have stopped the shooting. The estimates of that interval, however, varied from six seconds to two minutes. Like most of the events during the confusion in King Street, the rate of firing is clouded with uncertainty.[47]

The famous Pelham-Revere depiction of the Massacre scene shows the troops (only seven, instead of eight) standing in a straight line, firing simultaneously, while Preston, behind them, raises his sword in a gesture of defiance and command. In fact, the witnesses who described the firing unanimously recollected that the muskets banged almost at will. Preston indeed did not command a halt; but neither did he order a volley. In front of the troops at Montgomery's shot, he somehow got between or behind them as the firing continued. The crack of the discharge carried above the roar of the mob. At Murray's barracks, Captain Goldfinch, talking quietly with the officers, heard the shot. "I thought it would come to this," he said. "It is time for me to go." And he went off to join his regiment.[48]

The pause after the first shot quickly ended. Langford and Gray standing together watched Kilroy raise his weapon. "God damn you, don't fire," said Langford. Without aiming, Kilroy fired. Gray, his hands in his jacket pockets, spun around and fell on Langford's left foot. John Hickling ran to help him; feeling through the gushing blood, Hickling found a hole in Gray's head "as big as my hand." Another shot. Two bullets struck Michael Johnson's chest. He dropped his stick and fell, gasping and struggling, his head in the little gutter running just before the line of Redcoats. Someone suggested going in on the soldiers, to prevent their firing again. The mob advanced. More guns fired. The sailor Caldwell was standing in the crowd somewhere toward the middle of King Street. A bullet passed through his body; another lodged in his shoulder. He dropped on the spot. Paterson, the veteran of Richardson's siege, caught a bullet in the wrist of his raised right hand. The Irish mob expert, Patrick Carr, was just crossing King Street with shipmaster Charles Conner, heading toward the barber shop on the corner of Quaker Lane. A shot "went through his right hip & tore away part of the backbone & greatly injured the hip bone." As young Maverick fled at top speed toward the Town House, a bullet bounced crazily off some object and somehow struck his chest. He fell, dying.[49]

Edward Payne, standing inquisitively in his own doorway, took a bullet in the right arm. Kit Monk standing with his friend Brewer, about ten or fifteen feet from the soldiers, seemed to falter. "Are you wounded?" Brewer asked. "Yes," said Monk. But Brewer could not believe the guns contained bullets. "You are only frighted," he said. Hickling, until he felt Gray's shattered skull, had likewise been convinced that the soldiers had only fired powder. Even after the bodies lay in the street, people did not realize men had been killed. "I thought," Joseph Hilyer said later, "they had been scared and run away, and left their greatcoats behind them." [50]

What the soldiers thought, we do not know. Whether automatically, or from fear of a renewed assault, they reloaded and cocked their pieces, the click running ominously around the semicircle. Enraged, Preston asked his men why they had fired. They said they had heard the word "fire," and thought he was ordering them to shoot. The mob, which had dispersed somewhat, began to approach again. Its object this time was the bodies of the dead, dying, and wounded, but the overwrought soldiers mistook the crowd's intent. Up went the muskets into firing position. Preston hurriedly passed along the line, pushing the barrels with his arm, "Stop firing!" he shouted. "Do not fire!" Benjamin Burdick paused over the huge corpse of Johnson, stepped closer to the soldiers, and looked at them. "I want to see some faces," he said, "that I may swear to another day." Preston turned. For a moment Burdick stared into the captain's shocked face, pockmarked with smallpox. Preston said somberly: "Perhaps, sir, you may." [51]

The people inside the Custom House had watched the firing. Immediately Hammond Green let Elizabeth Avery out the front door and returned upstairs. His father Bartholomew came along then, so Hammond went again to the door and let him in. The men climbed the stairs together. Bartholomew opened the window, which Hammond hastily shut; then they opened it a second time and cautiously looked out. Hammond Green was frightened. Such activity could not help but attract attention. One of his acquaintances came to the door and asked Hammond by name to let him in. "If my father was out, or any of the Commissioners, I would not let them in," said Green. The friend thought he added, "because I have orders for so doing." [52]

In front of the Custom House, the scene rapidly cleared. As Boston had neither a hospital nor a mortuary, the dead and wounded were taken to various impromptu dressing stations. Captain Conner took Carr into a house in Fitch's Alley (now Change Avenue) and went for a doctor; later Carr was moved to his master's house in Queen Street. Johnson's corpse was carried to the Royal Exchange Tavern, across Royal Exchange Lane from the Custom House. A group of friends brought Gray's body to Dr. Loring's in Cornhill; but the door was locked, so, somewhat callously, they left him there. One of the other victims was taken to the prison house. Maverick went to his widowed mother's boarding house on Union Street in the North End, where, a few hours later, he died. [53]

The soldiers, too, left the area promptly. Preston formed the party and marched it without incident to the Main Guard. There, he turned out the entire guard and placed the soldiers in "street firings" on the narrow branch of King Street between the Guard building and the Town House. "Street firings" was a formation especially designed to permit small groups of soldiers to control large urban mobs. The basic unit was a file, with the front man kneeling. In theory, after firing, he would pass to the rear, while the second man knelt, fired, and, in turn, passed back. A small group of soldiers could thus command a narrow street; two such files, facing opposite ways, precluded encirclement. This formation, while properly employed at the upper, narrow portion of King Street, would of course have been useless before the Custom House, where the street was many yards wide.[54]

Preston had reason for fear. A rumor had reached him that four or five thousand people were in the next street preparing an assault. In fact, the crowd in King Street had swelled, soon after the shooting, to one thousand. Cries of "To arms," filled the night, together with the beat of the town drums, calling out the militia; all the church bells in Boston began to ring. Preston ordered his own drummer to beat "To Arms," thus sounding the general alert for the entire Boston garrison. He also sent Sergeant Hugh Broughton with an armed party to notify Dalrymple of the developments.[55]

The possibility of a real massacre now gripped Boston. Far out at the fortification, Ensign Gilbert Carter, who commanded the Neck Guard, found himself facing a mob throwing snowballs and stones. Carter turned out his guard, but the crowd quieted down. Meanwhile, at the Town House, the entire Twenty-ninth faced an ever-growing throng. Someone suggested taking the town's muskets from the storage place at Faneuil Hall. Dark stories circulated of armed reinforcements, waiting "on Tip Toe" and ready to pour in from the surrounding countryside.[56]

It was not a comfortable time for loyalists. Thomas Greenwood, the customs employee, broke the news to his superiors at Commissioner Burch's house, where the Burches were entertaining Commissioner Paxton and the board's secretary, Richard Reeve. When Greenwood told them the troops had killed some of the inhabitants, Reeve said "God bless my soul," and then felt it necessary to retire to another room. Greenwood spent the night in the comparative safety of the barracks at Wheelwright's Wharf.[57]

Officers trying to rejoin their regiments encountered particular difficulty. The uniforms invited insult and, in several cases, actual physical assault. Lieutenant Ross of the Fourteenth received a solid blow from a thrown stick; Ensigns Henry Hallwood and Andrew Lawrie of the Fourteenth were actually set upon and knocked down. Captain Goldfinch was punched in the face and robbed of his sword. Other officers had to clear their paths with swords. Captain French was still at the Coffee House, with Lieutenant Colonel Carr and Captain William Monsell of the Twenty-ninth. The crowd in King Street seemed so menacing that they "durst not attempt to joyn the regiment" until an armed escort came for them.[58]

The officers had strong ideas about the source of their woes. As the contingent at Murray's Barracks was paraded, Joseph Allen strode up, carrying, by his own later admission, "a stout cudgel." Three of the soldiers seized him and disarmed him. Lieutenant Minchin, restoring order, asked Allen why the inhabitants wrangled with the soldiers on the most trifling occasions. "Can a man be inactive," was Allen's indignant reply, "when his countrymen are butchered in the street?" "Mr. Molineux was the author of all this," said Minchin, politely returning Allen his stick.[59]

The massive confrontation developing at the head of King Street demanded the presence of the only man who could conceivably avoid catastrophic carnage. A succession of townspeople of all political persuasions ran to the North End to tell Hutchinson that "unless [he] went out immediately, the whole town would be in arms and the most bloody scene would follow that had ever been known in America." Hutchinson started for the Town House. Meanwhile, responsible citizens were also converging on King Street. Thomas Handasyd Peck, the province's leading fur exporter, went up to Preston, whom Peck highly esteemed as a gentleman as well as a soldier. "What have you done?" Peck asked. "Sir," said Preston, "it was none of my doings. The soldiers fired of their own accord. I was in the street and might have been shot." [60]

Joseph Belknap had been spending the evening with his neighbor, Councilor Royall Tyler. Hearing the hubbub, he flattered Tyler into accompanying him outside. "One word of yours, Mr. Tyler, will go further than ten of some other people's." In Dock Square, they heard the firing; Tyler went home, but Belknap continued to the Custom House. Although the bodies had gone, the blood remained, "near half a pail full in one place." Belknap started back to Dock Square. There, he met two radical chiefs, Selectman Jonathan Mason and Samuel Whitwell; all agreed that Hutchinson should be notified. As they walked toward the North End, they met Hutchinson, and reversed their steps to accompany him. At the conduit, or reservoir, just west of Dock Square, the party encountered a "great body of men, many of them armed with clubs and some few with cutlasses, and all calling for their firearms." Hutchinson identified himself and tried to convince them to listen to him. "Damn him," someone shouted, aiming a club at the lieutenant-governor, "I'll do his business." Fleeing for his own safety, Hutchinson followed Belknap back to Tyler's house, through the back yard, across a deserted part of the market place and up Pierce's Alley to King Street just east of the Custom House. As they walked up to the Town House, a throng pressing behind them, Belknap called Hutchinson's attention to the still-bloody snow.[61]

To the frightened Belknap, the troops arrayed at the head of King Street seemed ready to fire. "Here is his Honour, the Lieutenant Governor, come to talk with you," he called. "Where is your officer?" "Stand off, stand off," the equally nervous soldiers replied. Isaac Pierce went over to the right flank, where Preston stood. "There is His Honor, the Commander in Chief," he told the officer. "Where?" "There, and you are presenting your firelocks at him." Passing along the Redcoat front, "almost to the points of their bayonets," Belknap and Hutchinson reached Preston. "How came you to fire without orders from a civil magistrate?" Hutchinson asked angrily. "I was obliged to, to save my sentry." "Then you have murdered three or four men to save your sentry," Pierce growled. "These soldiers ought not to be here," Hutchinson said. "It is not in my power to order them away," Preston said, as if offended at being questioned; "Pray, sir, do you go up to the Guard House," he urged. "If you go," Belknap told Hutchinson, "I will attend you." Hutchinson was tempted, because he distinctly felt Preston's answer to have been "imperfect," as though he had more to say. But by going to the Guardhouse for a private talk with Preston, he would be taking a public stand, apparently approving what the officer had done. Such a move, Hutchinson must have realized, would have eliminated whatever popular support he still retained and would have put him finally into Samuel Adams's pocket. "I don't think it prudent for me to go to the Guard House," he told Preston.[62]

The push of the crowd was increasing. Belknap actively feared that the longer Hutchinson remained outdoors, the greater his physical jeopardy. "Pray, sir, go into the Council Chamber, and speak to the people." The crowd took up the cry: "The Town House, the Town House." Whether he intended to or not, Hutchinson found himself forced into the Town House and up to the second-floor council room, scene of so much frustration for him during the past half-year. More awaited. As soon as he arrived, Molineux and Whitwell asked him to order the troops back to their barracks. It was a trap. If he agreed, Dalrymple and Carr would either obey his order or they would not. If they obeyed, Hutchinson would be conceding that he did in fact have power to direct the troops, and hence that he could (if he wanted to) compel their removal from Boston. If the officers did not obey, the radicals would have a fine propaganda bonanza: they could trumpet to the world that in Boston the military refused to acknowledge civilian control. As before, Hutchinson moved with political shrewdness. He refused the request.[63]

Instead, he addressed the people from the balcony facing King Street, expressing his deep concern, assuring them that he would do everything possible to ensure a full inquiry, so that the law might take its course. Go home peaceably, he advised them. "The law shall have its course; I will live and die by the law." Many responded. But some damned him for a liar and an enemy to his country. Many remained. When Hutchinson went to the south window of the council chamber to talk to the officers, someone took over the east balcony, overlooking King Street, and told the inhabitants not to leave unless the soldiers left first. Molineux put the demand squarely to Hutchinson. The lieutenant-governor spoke to Lieutenant Colonel Carr again, relaying Molineux' ultimatum and suggesting as his own opinion that if the soldiers returned to their barracks, the civilians would likewise go home. This mode of communication left entirely in Carr's hands (at least formally) final deposition of the soldiers. Carr promptly marched the troops off, and the crowd dispersed.[64]

Among those who left quietly that night was John Adams. Still wracked by the death of his little daughter Susannah a month before, he had been meeting with friends in the South End when the commotion erupted. By the time he reached King Street, all was, as he later said, "quiet." Hurrying home to his pregnant wife, he cut through Boylston's Alley and Brattle Square. There Minchin had drawn up his soldiers under arms, bayonets fixed. They filled the square, leaving only a narrow space in front for foot traffic. As Adams passed before them, he ignored them and they him, as if "they had been marble statues." [65]

Sending the inhabitants and soldiers peaceably to bed was only half the evening's business. True to his promise, Hutchinson now set the machinery going to ascertain Preston's guilt and that of his men. Justices of the Peace Richard Dana and John Tudor came to the council chamber (as did Dalrymple, at Hutchinson's express request) to examine the evidence. Witnesses were called, in some cases from home, while the justices sought to decide whether there was, as we would say today, probable cause to hold Preston and any of his men for the next grand jury. Tension mounted in the chamber and on the streets. Preston could not be found; a feeling grew that he would try to avoid trial, perhaps by fleeing, as Mein had done. Outside, some of the soldiers apparently still wanted to work off excess belligerence. Corporal John Eustice of the Twenty-ninth and a party from the Neck Guard, the men's pieces double-loaded, bayonets fixed, surrounded Edward Crafts and John Halden. After assorted unpleasantries, Eustice swung his musket butt at Crafts' head. The civilian parried the blow with his arm, and the weapon "broke to pieces." A grand jury subsequently indicted Eustice for criminal assault.[66]

As the night wore on, the streets quieted. Inside, tensions did not ease until about 2 A.M., when, a warrant having been issued, Sheriff Greenleaf brought in first Basset, then Preston. The captain insisted he would have surrendered earlier, had he known of the warrant. It did not really matter. At the hearing, a witness who swore he had been within two feet of Preston when the muskets went off testified that

Preston did give the order to fire. Another said the captain not only ordered the shooting, but cursed the men for not firing at once. Others swore he had said "fire," but whether as part of "do not fire," they could not say. Still others testified they heard "fire," but could not tell if it came from Preston. Apparently impressed by the first witnesses, the justices sent Preston to jail about 3 A.M. Basset they released. The next morning, the eight soldiers surrendered and were in turn imprisoned.[67]

Later Hutchinson learned how close Boston had come to the bloodbath. The night of March 5, "expresses had gone out to the neighbouring towns and the inhabitants were called out of their beds, many of whom armed themselves but were stopped from coming into town by advice that there was no further danger that night. A barrill of tar which was carrying to the beacon to set on fire was also sent back." [68]

CHAPTER 17

PREPARATION
AND PROCRASTINATION

When he awoke on Tuesday morning after a few brief hours' sleep, Hutchinson found the town still ready to explode. Quickly he called a council meeting and hurried to the Town House to conduct it. Somewhere, probably in the Royal Exchange Tavern, where the body had been taken, Doctor Benjamin Church was beginning the autopsy of Michael Johnson. County Coroners Robert Pierpoint and Thomas Crafts were arranging for inquests on Johnson and the other victims. Doctors were treating mortally wounded Patrick Carr and the other living victims.[1]

At Faneuil Hall, a throng of townspeople—3,500, one wild estimate ran; 4,000, the radicals said—met to consider, or more accurately to receive orders for, the next step. Sam Adams, the "Matchiavel of Chaos," had taken firm command. The fatal result he had long predicted would follow placing a military garrison on Boston's back had at last fulminated. While the dead men's blood still lay on the King Street snow, Adams was arranging to press his palpable tactical advantage and drive the troops from Boston.[2]

When Hutchinson walked into the Town House, he found the Boston selectmen waiting. Pushing past them, he faced a frightened, angry, divided council. First, Royall Tyler delivered "an harangue." When Tyler finished, several councilors urged Hutchinson to order Dalrymple to remove the troops from Boston. Disclaiming such power,

Hutchinson refused. The selectmen, now being admitted to the chamber, likewise pressed Hutchinson to oust the soldiers; terrible consequences would ensue if he did not, they said. Boston's justices of the peace, together with some justices from neighboring towns, also arrived, bearing the same grim prediction. To both, Hutchinson repeated his earlier reply: he had no authority over the soldiers.[3]

At this point, a message came from Faneuil Hall, requesting the attendance of the selectmen. Samuel Adams was organizing a committee to visit the lieutenant-governor with what would now be the third renewal of the original request. The committee included the heart of the radical organization: Adams, Hancock, Molineux, and Deacon Philips. The message they delivered to the councilors and Dalrymple and Carr, present by Hutchinson's express request, was simple: "Nothing can rationally be expected to restore the peace of the town and prevent blood and carnage, but the immediate removal of the troops." Having put his enemy in the wrong, Sam Adams now led the committee into an adjoining room to await a reply.

Again many councilors begged Hutchinson to agree; only Harrison Gray and Samuel Danforth supported him; again he flatly refused to give the orders. Dalrymple now suddenly inserted himself into the discussion. Because the Twenty-ninth had originally been slated for billeting in Castle William, he said, and because that regiment seemed to be "peculiarly obnoxious to the town," he was willing to transfer it there, pending further word from General Gage. However deft an arbitrator Dalrymple fancied himself, he had now merely smoothed the road for Sam Adams and correspondingly pinned Hutchinson beyond hope. As soon as Adams heard the offer, he sprang: If Dalrymple could remove one regiment, he said, clearly he could remove both; it would, indeed, be at his peril that he did not. The room was silent.

Hastening to repair Dalrymple's blunder, Hutchinson turned on the committee members. They, he said bluntly, were the ones with the power to quiet the inhabitants. No, said Deacon Philips, if they should every one beg it upon his knees, it would have no effect. "If violence is the consequence of the illegal assembly of the people," Hutchinson replied, relying on the town meeting's having been called without legal notice, "and an attempt should be made to drive out the King's troops, everyone abetting and advising would be guilty of high treason." Not even this plain talk budged the committee; both regiments must go. Desperate, still intending to take no further notice of the request, Hutchinson rose to adjourn the meeting.

Once again Dalrymple thwarted him. Would not Hutchinson meet the council again in the afternoon, he asked. "I can do nothing further," Hutchinson said, moving toward the door. Dalrymple persisted.

Some of the councilors joined him; more followed. Almost before Hutchinson knew what was happening, he found himself calling for an afternoon meeting.

During the recess, Dalrymple collared Tyler and Harrison Gray and pressed on them his lastest peace proposal. If, he said, they would persuade Hutchinson to "desire" him to remove the troops, instead of "ordering" him to do so, he would certainly comply. The two councilors quickly passed the offer to their fellows. Meanwhile, at Faneuil Hall, the committee had reported the one-regiment offer. By 4,000 to 1, the crowd voted it unsatisfactory.[4] This time, the meeting had been lawfully called and convened. So many citizens and hangers-on had responded that Faneuil Hall could not accommodate them. Once again, the crowd had to move to the Old South Church, thronging as it did past the very doors of the Town House.

When Hutchinson called the afternoon meeting to order, he found "the Council to a man prepared." Captain Caldwell of the *Rose* also attended; he listened fascinated as the town committee reported the meeting's vote and again demanded that both regiments leave. Sam Adams later reported that Hutchinson's knees trembled. Well they might; when the committee retired, Tyler began the most violent speech of the day. It was "not such people as had formerly pulled down the lieutenant-governor's house which conducted the present measures," but "the people of the best characters among us—men of estates and men of religion." They had, Tyler continued, "formed their plan," which was "to remove the troops out of the town, and after that the commissioners." If the troops did not leave, Tyler warned, ten thousand men would come in from the country and wipe them out, "should it be called rebellion—should it incur the loss of our charter, or be the consequence what it would." James Russell and Samuel Dexter, having come in from Charlestown and Dedham respectively, confirmed what Tyler had said about the countryside; everyone else specifically adopted his words. They all said the troops must leave, and urged Hutchinson to ask Dalrymple to order them out. John Erving was even blunt enough to point out that if Hutchinson made the request and Dalrymple refused, the consequence would be the officer's responsibility, whereas if Hutchinson "should refuse to desire," the burden would all be his, since Dalrymple would certainly comply if Hutchinson asked.

Again and again the harried Hutchinson begged the councilors "to consider the consequence of their advice and not to persist in it." The unanimity continued. Desperately, he huddled with Carr, Dalrymple, Caldwell, and Secretary Andrew Oliver. All "advised to a compliance." The stoutly loyal Oliver admitted that he had changed his mind since the morning session; Hutchinson, he now felt, must now clear out the troops "or quit the Government." Wearily, Hutchinson accepted the inevitable. "What else could you do?" Dalrymple asked. "Retire to the Castle and remain there until the people come to their senses," said Hutchinson. "And take the troops with you," Dalrymple added.

A mere oral request would not satisfy Dalrymple, eagerly anxious to protect himself from any subsequent charge of violating the original orders posting the troops to Boston. He insisted upon receiving the request in writing, and then quibbled over the wording. To the Town, the distinction mattered nothing. When the committee returned to the Old South, the news "gave Great Joy to the Inhabitants" and, in John Rowe's belief, "a General Satisfaction, so that they went from the Meeting very Peaceably to their Habitations." As for Dalrymple and Hutchinson, each tried thereafter to blame the other for the military retreat.[5]

The next morning, military reaction set in. Dalrymple's officers appeared "greatly dissatisfied with being compelled by the people to leave the town so disgracefully." Expresses were sent to Gage for orders. When they finally reached him, on March 12, Gage directed Dalrymple to inquire "into the Conduct of the Soldiers," previous to the shooting, and to confine any who might be "found to have acted in any manner deserving Punishment." If it should appear "that the soldiers have fired Wantonly without a legal order for so doing," he wrote Hutchinson, "the Laws must no doubt have their due course." "[I]n any part where the Soldiers may have been in fault, they may be punished as they deserve." Of course, Gage added, if it developed "that they were dangerously attacked, and obliged to defend themselves and fired only in self-Defense to preserve their own Lives I trust you will do everything in your power, to prevent their falling a Sacrifice to the Resentment of Faction, against all principles of Justice, and by the perversion of the Laws of their Country." Believing that the evacuation was a *fait accompli*, Gage unqualifiedly approved. After receiving additional information indicating that the troops were still in Boston, he decided to use "every Argument" to keep the Fourteenth, at least, in town. Alarmed lest the evacuation not proceed, the radicals increased the pressure. Roxbury, Dr. Warren's home town, sent a special delegation to pray that Hutchinson would immediately order the troops out; he refused. On March 10, Boston itself held another town meeting; the resultant committee, with Adams at its head, visited Hutchinson. Adams pressed "the matter with great vehemence . . . intimating, that, in case of refusal, the rage of the people would vent itself against the lieutenant-governor in particular." Hutchinson, furious, peremptorily dismissed them. Unabashed, the committeemen now called upon Dalrymple, from whom they took greater comfort. Later that same day, with Molineux walking beside the troops "to protect them from the indignation of the people," the Twenty-ninth marched to the wharfs for ferrying down harbor to the Castle. The Fourteenth followed the next day. Gage's countervailing orders did not arrive until March 27, thirteen days after he sent them.[6]

The turmoil following the shootings had virtually paralyzed the town's normal life. At its March 7 gathering, the Suffolk Bar found a "thin meeting, and therefore agreed to proceed to no business" except a circular letter asking for the "concurrence and assistance" of other lawyers in the Province. Well might the meeting have been thin. Many of the members, like other citizens to a total of three hundred, had volunteered for the nightly armed watches that were maintaining order and ensuring no further bloodshed. Even John Adams, encumbered by musket, bayonet, broadsword, and cartridge box, reported in his turn for sentry duty at the Town House. The selectmen had urged Hutchinson to activate the militia. Unwilling to incur London's disapproval for calling "the Militia to keep the King's troops in order," he refused. Besides, lack of military expertise was dangerous. The Boston *News-Letter* had to print "A friendly Caution" urging the novices to put their guns where the children could not get at them. To ensure the militia's inactivity, Hutchinson specifically ordered Joseph Jackson, colonel of the regiment, not to authorize participation in the recruiting watch. Jackson ordered the militia out anyway.[7]

Whether or not the killings were, as each party insisted, the result of a preconcerted plot concocted by the other, radicals and Tories alike immediately realized the incident's tremendous propaganda value. From New York, Gage urged Dalrymple to prepare the military version of the shootings and the precedent provocations. At the first town meeting on March 6, witnesses told of overhearing remarks by soldiers indicating that the troops themselves had planned the whole affair. John Singleton Copley, the rising young portraitist, said he had heard a soldier say after the firing: "the Devil might give [the inhabitants] quarters [i.e., mercy]; he should give them none." So much other business confronted the meeting that the radicals could not take affidavits of all who had evidence to give. Within two days, a committee had been appointed to organize the rendition of such accounts. One by one, witnesses were brought before justices of the peace, sworn, questioned, and asked to sign written versions of their testimony. The resultant "depositions," Hutchinson said later, "were not generally in a form of words prepared by the deponents, but, when they had declared their knowledge of the facts, the form and words of the depositions were settled by the Committee or Justices—There was no cross examination and no body present to ask any questions to elucidate any parts of the depositions—no scrutiny was made into the credit, and characters of the deponents." The radicals, in their turn, insisted that the loyalists—including Dalrymple himself—had received ample notice; and that it was their own fault for neglecting to attend. Shortly after the shootings, Paul Revere carefully prepared a detailed, accurate plan of King Street. Whether it was designed for use at the trials, or to assist the various inquests, or for some other purpose, we do not know. The document, which is now in the Boston Public Library, appears to have been folded at one time so as to fit a court file. None of the trial papers even suggest that it was used in court. Because it only depicts four victims, it may well have been executed prior to Carr's death. At the appropriate place on the back one can barely make out some writing. Unfortunately, Mellen Chamberlain, who donated the plan to the Library, caused it to be pasted to a display board in such a way that the writing cannot be deciphered. Whatever the purpose of the diagram, no one could doubt the aim of Revere's other artistic effort. Within a few days of the shootings, young Henry Pelham, John Copley's talented half-brother, had produced an emotional drawing depicting with gross inaccuracy the events in King Street. Revere somehow obtained the Pelham cartoon and immediately engraved, printed, and sold it— all without permission or attribution. Although Pelham castigated Revere bitterly, the damage had been done. Thanks to Revere's swift piracy, the print, vividly colored, with heavy emphasis on reds, received wide circulation, presumably to Revere's profit, and undoubtedly to the prejudice of Preston and his soldiers.[8]

While the depositions were being prepared, a town committee, headed by Sam Adams, Hancock, Molineux, and Warren, wrote specially to former Governor Thomas Pownall. Carefully designed to "prevent any ill impressions from being made upon the minds of his majesty's ministers, and others, against the town," by unfriendly accounts, the letter stretched the truth wildly. Calling the soldiers "instruments in executing a settled plot to massacre the inhabitants," the committee seriously insisted that "our magistrates and courts of justices have appeared to be overawed by them."[9]

The radicals planned, in due course, to bring the law against the nine Redcoats languishing in the Boston jail. Meanwhile, they set to proving that what Sam Adams had already dubbed the Horrid Massacre was really the handiwork of the despised customs establishment. No conceivable evidence linked the commissioners themselves with the shooting. But lesser officials might be more vulnerable. First, Adams's "committee of enquery" had Benjamin Andrews, a carpenter, "take ranges" of the bullet holes in the buildings opposite the Custom House, to establish that guns had been fired from inside the house, as well as from the street outside. To spread the story even more widely and directly, the creators of the Pelham-Revere engraving drew a smoking musket barrel pointing out of the Custom House. Although this has been cited, somewhat naively, to prove that bullets really did come from the windows, in fact the engraving was prepared and distributed as pure propaganda; its accuracy should be judged accordingly. The Boston *Gazette* insisted that the Massacre, the Richardson affair, and the Otis-Robinson battle were united parts of "a Scene of Villainy acted by a dirty Banditti." [10]

The radicals' real attempt to taint the customs officers with the King Street blood took a quasi-judicial form. Samuel Drowne swore he saw two guns fired from the Custom House, the person who held one of them a tall man wearing a handkerchief over his face. Since Commissioner John Robinson was noted for his height, this was, as one of the councilors later suggested to Hutchinson, an indication that the commissioners had directly concerned themselves in the affair. The other witness, Charles Bourgatte, a fourteen-year-old French boy, servant to Edward Manwaring, a customs officer normally stationed in Gaspee, Canada, swore positively that he had actually been in the Custom House, and that he and his master had both fired muskets out the window.[11]

Armed with this dramatic evidence, the radicals tried to argue Justice of the Peace Richard Dana into committing Manwaring. But Drowne was "an idiot, or of . . . weak understanding." Bourgatte became entangled in contradictions; and Manwaring proved an alibi by the testimony of a friend, John Munro. Even Dana, "one of the chief Incendiaries in the Province," refused to apprehend Manwaring. Abashed, Bourgatte retracted his story, whereupon Dana sent him to jail instead. After a night there, the boy was ready to return to his original story, slightly embellished. Now, he insisted, not only Manwaring, but one John Munro, had been at the Custom House. Everyone went before Dana again. This time, Munro, having become an interested party, could not give evidence in his own behalf. Fortunately for the accused men, a person who had spent the evening of March 5 with them was able to supply the gap. Once more they were released; once more Bourgatte went to jail.[12]

While the radicals were busily gathering antimilitary, anticustoms depositions, the Tories, for once, beat them to the propaganda punch. Even before Gage's instructions arrived, John Robinson, having been sneaked aboard from a man of war's boat, sailed for London on March 16, carrying with him a parcel of military depositions generally tending to blame the town for the rowdiness and the shootings. He also carried an affidavit from Secretary Oliver, describing in full detail the council meeting of March 6, including Tyler's strong threats, and the meeting of March 7, in which the council had expunged the wild talk from the official minutes. On arrival in England, all these were delivered to the ministry; eventually they found their way into a pamphlet, *A Fair Account of the Late Disturbances at Boston.* Months later, reading the *Fair Account,* the radical leader, James Bowdoin, moaned: "Why this Deposition of the Secretary has defeated every thing we aimed at by the Narrative and Depositions sent home." This was high praise. The *Narrative,* hastily concocted by Bowdoin himself, shortly after Robinson left, had assumed in the most convincing, violent fashion that the Horrid Massacre resulted from sinister plots by the soldiers and the commissioners; it even stated flatly that "a number of guns were fired from the Custom House." Ninety-four of the ninety-six depositions appended to the *Narrative* (some of them taken even after Bowdoin had written it) bore out one or another aspect of these themes. The ninety-fifth was Hammond Green's largely neutral testimony; the ninety-sixth Thomas Greenwood's. Greenwood blamed the inhabitants for the trouble; but a footnote added by the town committee urged that "no credit ought to be given to his deposition." [13]

To increase the credibility of the other depositions, the committee obtained from Hutchinson a document bearing the province seal, certifying the status of the various justices of the peace before whom the assorted deponents had been sworn. At first the radicals tried without success to have him certify the facts as well; he agreed only to issue a perfectly routine document, calling for "full Faith and Credit" to be given to the "Acts and Attestations" of the justices. The radicals, and especially their English friends, however, insinuated falsely that Hutchinson's certificate established the truth of the depositions themselves.[14]

Printed, the pamphlets containing the *Narrative* and the depositions were sped to England as an antidote to the poison the radicals believed Robinson was preparing to spread. By vote of the Town, the copies not sent abroad were impounded, lest the publication in Boston "give an undue Byass to the minds of" prospective jurors. The radicals' good faith is open to serious question. They permitted (perhaps even directed) Edes and Gill to print the initial inflammatory letters; and they allowed copies of the pamphlet, either from their own stock or reprints of those sent to England, to circulate in Boston well before the trials. The English courts had long condemned such publications as prejudicial; but the Massachusetts court was in no position to restrain the radicals on this issue, or even to criticize them.[15]

Whether the *Narrative* substantially affected Boston opinion is hard to judge. Certainly enough antimilitary feeling existed in the immediate aftermath of the killings to render superfluous any attempt to stir up prejudice. As time passed and passions ebbed, the presence of the printed depositions and Bowdoin's intemperate introduction may well have reignited fading memories. The initial radical effort probably had more direct effect outside of Boston. The London newspapers gave the American version substantial play during April and May; Philadelphia papers faithfully reported the encounter as the "Bloody Massacre"; a South Carolina journal aped the Boston style by enclosing the report of the incident within heavy black rules. Oddly enough, New York, which had experienced the near-bloodshed of the Liberty Pole riot earlier in the year, handled the story coolly. The papers there published the news objectively, without referring to a "massacre." "Neither then nor later did the press present the patriot view of the incident or seek to use it to besmirch the local soldiery." [16]

In the weeks that followed the Massacre, the Sons of Liberty controlled Boston. It was true, as the radicals boasted, that officers could walk the streets unmolested. It was even true that a party from the *Rose* was permitted, astonishingly enough, to press a sailor thirteen days after the shootings. But these only emphasized the radical position. Like Mackintosh in the earlier time of trouble, Sam Adams, by his very inaction, unmistakably conveyed the threat of violence. Yet when necessary, he could flex the radical side's muscle. As Hutchinson confidentially reported to Gage, in any question involving British control of the colonies, "government is at an end and in the hands of the people." Hutchinson now stood "absolutely alone, no single person of my Council or any other person in authority affording me the least support." Dalrymple smugly endorsed Hutchinson's gloomy appraisal. "[H]e has no earthly weight or power here; a proposal coming from him would be for that reason sure to miscarry." "[I]f the people are disposed to any measure nothing more is necessary than for the multitude to assemble, for nobody dares oppose them or call them to account." [17]

Late in the afternoon of March 8, Adams took the occasion of the Massacre victims' funeral to stage a demonstration that left the pompous burial of young Seider just two weeks earlier a pale memory. By this time, the town had learned that the burly mulatto who had died under the name of Michael Johnson was really Crispus Attucks. Regarded today as America's first black hero, Attucks may in reality have been partly or even entirely Indian, a member of the Natick tribe living near Framingham. The radicals did not care. Black, red, or white, a martyr was a martyr. Whatever the deceased might have been in life, however insignificant or vicious, in death Attucks, Maverick, Caldwell, and Gray become murdered monuments to British oppression. One by one their coffins followed each other through town, around

Liberty Tree, and back up to the burying ground, as mourners genuine or contrived, ten to twelve thousand, marched behind. Reverend Mather Byles, looking on, turned to a companion. "They call me a brainless Tory," he said to a companion. "But tell me, my young friend, which is better—to be ruled by one tyrant three thousand miles away, or by three thousand tyrants not one mile away?" Another prospective sacrifice on the altar of freedom, the Irishman Patrick Carr, was unable to attend the ceremony, either as an object or as a participant. Although a team of doctors fought to save his life, he sank lower every day, finally succumbing on March 14. On March 17, appropriately enough, still another cortege wound its way over the now-familiar route, and Carr joined Seider and the four earlier Massacre victims in the Granary earth. It is not certain who read the burial service, since Carr died a Roman Catholic, and Boston had no priests.[18]

The show of force in Boston reminded everyone of the power at the radicals' disposal. News from Gloucester underlined the threat: the night of March 23, a mob, some of the men with blackened faces, others disguised as Indians, hauled the loyalist-leaning Jesse Savil out of his bed, walked him four miles barefoot, carted him through town, tarred him, and made him swear never to inform again. After making him thank the mob for its "gentle Discipline," they let him go. In Boston, the commissioners took nervous note of what was happening. They had held their last "board," or regular meeting, on March 9. Thereafter Burch and Hulton went to Hulton's house in Brookline; Paxton went to Cambridge; Robinson sailed for England. Only Temple, with his American wife and radical leanings, stayed on. By the end of March, Burch and Hulton, abandoning their families, had clattered up the post road to Portsmouth, New Hampshire. There, enjoying the hospitality of Governor John Wentworth, they fervently hoped that Paxton would not join them; his appearance, Wentworth had warned, would so provoke the local populace as to vitiate any guarantees of security. The commissioners (all except Temple) were perfectly content, so long as they and their families were not physically endangered, to remain incapable of conducting regular business; their enforced vacation merely lent credence to their frequent past complaints that efficient functioning of the customs service demanded the presence of royal troops to restrain New England rowdiness. Safe in Portsmouth, Burch and Hulton instructed Paxton to refer any customs officers with legal inquiries to the attorney-general, and settled down in safety.[19]

By the end of April, they were back in Brookline, unwilling to risk a trip to Boston. Around midnight on June 19, a mob came out and, drawing Hulton to the window by a trick, tried to assault him. He barely escaped back into the house; the mob worked off its frustration by smashing some of his panes. When the incident came to the council's attention, people like James Bowdoin and the Reverend Charles Chauncy grumbled that the whole affair had been staged by the commissioners themselves. With that, the commissioners and their families retired to the Castle.[20]

For Thomas Preston, the days immediately following March 5 were difficult indeed. Removed suddenly from the pleasant social life which even disaffected Boston shared with the army officers, thrust instead into the cold, dirt, and discomfort of the Boston jail—crowded, now, with Richardson, Wilmot, the eight soldiers, and Bourgatte—Preston must have considered his outlook grim. The Sunday after the shootings, the young Reverend John Lathrop preached a violent sermon in the Old North Church on Genesis 3:10: "The voice of thy brother's blood crieth unto me from the ground." He spoke of "sorrow for the dead, who fell victims to the merciless rage of wicked men; indignation against the worst of murderers." If a man "really intended to kill, unless in defence of his own life under absolute necessity, *he shall surely be put to death.*" Another zealous divine, the Reverend Charles Chauncy, tried to convince one of the wounded to sue Preston for damages. The man refused, since practically speaking, whatever the outcome of the criminal case, Preston would be effectively insulated from civil redress. Chauncy was unimpressed. "If I was to be one of the Jury upon his Trial," he said, "I would bring him in guilty, *evidence or no Evidence.*" John Rowe, visiting Preston during that first week, found the captain, to his surprise, "in much better spirits than I expected." But a rumor was running through the town that when the jury finally convicted Preston, Hutchinson would respite him; should that happen, the Sons of Liberty said, they would "Porteous" Preston —indeed they might even do it sooner. Captain John Porteous had commanded the guard at an Edinburgh execution in 1736. His soldiers had fired into the spectators, killing some. Porteous had been tried, convicted, sentenced, and reprieved, only to be lynched by a mob. Perhaps in an effort to calm the popular fever, Preston, without consulting Dalrymple, published in the Boston *Gazette* of March 12 a "card," or advertisement, to give "my Thanks in the most Publick Manner to the Inhabitants in general of this Town—who throwing aside *all Party* and Prejudice, have with the utmost Humanity and Freedom stept forth Advocates for Truth in Defense of my injured Innocence . . . And to assure them, that I shall ever have the highest Sense of the *Justice* they have done me . . ." When this reached Gage in New York, the general grimaced. "I wish he may not have been too premature in that Measure," he wrote Dalrymple. "And if illegal Proceedings are hereafter made use of against him, they will justify themselves by his own Words." For once, Gage correctly predicted an American response. Meanwhile the Sons of Liberty were already aiming their propaganda guns directly at Preston. They ran a false story that his servant had gone down to Scituate one night for a secret interview with Judge Cushing. The week after the "card" appeared, an anonymous correspondent remarked in the Boston *Gazette* that "no Person can be satisfied of his injured innocence, untill he is acquitted of the high Charge laid against him in a due Course of Law." Guilty until proven innocent, the radicals considered Preston. Desperate, he wrote to Gage, begging him "with all your interest & influence, to join my friends in petitioning for His Majestys pardon." [21]

On March 13, the statutory term of the superior court began. The first order of criminal business was the grand jury sitting. Then as now, an indictment was nothing more than a statement drawn up by the chief prosecutor (in those days, the attorney-general) outlining in precise legal terms the criminal charge which the government believed it could prove against a given defendant. In considering any indictment, the grand jury took whatever testimony it desired or needed, and then voted. If it felt the charges unfounded, the jury dismissed or "ignored" the indictment—the foreman wrote "Ignoramus" on the document. If the grand jurors believed that the case merited full trial, the foreman endorsed the indictment: "This is a true bill."

Attorney-General Jonathan Sewall drew up the indictments, using hackneyed legalisms redolent of the common law's medieval origins: "Not having the Fear of God before their eyes, but being moved and seduced by the Instigation of the devil and their own wicked Hearts," "did with force and arms feloniously, wilfully and of their malice aforethought assault one Crispus Attucks, then and there being in the peace of God and of the said Lord the King." Each indictment carefully described the instrument of death ("a certain hand gun of the value of twenty shillings") and the victim's wound ("in and upon the right Breast a little below the right pap of him the said Crispus, one mortal wound of the depth of six inches and of the width of one inch").[22]

We do not know exactly in what order the grand jury proceeded to its business. It probably had little trouble indicting Richardson and Wilmot. The indictment of the military people seems to have been delayed. The jury proceeded somewhat strangely. Apparently it had access to the signed statements which had been taken immediately after the killings. When Robert Goddard came to testify, the jury asked him to identify Preston. Accompanied by one of the jurors, Goddard went over to the jail. Several people were with Preston in his cell. The juror asked Goddard which was the man. Pointing to Preston, Goddard said he looked "very much like the man, and I verily believed he was the man that order'd the soldier to *Fire*." "Don't you say so," begged Preston. "Yes, sir," Goddard insisted, "you look very much like the man." "If you say so," said Preston, clapping his hands together, "I am ruined and undone." A minute of the identification was written across the foot of Goddard's original statement.[23]

However irregular the grand jury proceedings, the trials would not be held immediately after all. Judges Cushing and Trowbridge were ill, and Hutchinson resisted the radicals' suggestion that he appoint temporary judges to fill their places. Meanwhile, the Sons of Liberty pressed the case against Manwaring and Munro. Ann and Hammond Green, Molly Rogers, and Thomas Greenwood, all were called before the grand jury "once and sometimes twice a day for several days." They all stuck to one story: no one else was in the Custom House; no musket had been fired from the windows. "Every Method was made use of by threatening to make them fix it upon some person but to no effect." Notwithstanding proof of a perfect alibi for Munro and Manwaring, the grand jury on March 26 indicted them, as well as Green and Greenwood. "This excellent part of the English Constitution," Hutchinson wrote, "a Guard to the Lives of the Innocent, is improved to bring them into danger." The same indictment included the names of the military men. For good measure, the jury also indicted Ensign Alexander Mall of the Twenty-ninth for slashing a civilian "to the bone"; a warrant issued, but of course Mall, in the Castle, was safe from the sheriff.[24]

Thrown into jail the next day, the four civilians asked to be bailed. Despite the rumbling of the radicals and the surface irregularity of bailing anyone accused of a capital crime, the case against the civilians seemed so thin that the superior court was willing to consider the question fairly. The radicals vigorously opposed bail, suggesting that a flock of witnesses daily expected to arrive in town would indicate the strength of the prosecution's evidence. When the hearing began, however, only the discredited French boy and the idiot Drowne testified. Forty strong witnesses stood ready to testify for the civilians. Even so, external pressures restrained the court. Trowbridge was not sitting; the other three judges were not by any means unanimous. Judge Oliver felt there was "so little cause of Commitment" that bail ought to be granted forthwith, but Chief Justice Lynde inclined the other way. Old Judge John Cushing broke the tie: each civilian was bailed on a massive £400 recognizance with four different sureties on each separate bond. The soldiers and Preston, as well as Richardson and Wilmot, remained behind bars.[25]

Meanwhile counsel were preparing for the impending trials. Sewall, having drawn the indictments, left the grand jury and the court to their own devices, employing himself, as one displeased radical put it, "with the jurys of two Inferior Courts at Charlston [Charlestown] and Ipswich in ye petty Concerns cognizable before the General Sessions of the Peace." Sewall's behavior, while perhaps understandable in light of his loyalist tendencies, was thoroughly unprofessional. If he believed that the evidence would not fairly support indictment or conviction, he should either have refused to put the case to the grand jury (a futile gesture, because the jury could properly have indicted of its own volition) or he should have moved to nol-pros any indictment the jury might return. On the other hand, if he believed the evidence strong enough to require prosecution, he should have tried the case himself —his was a one-man office—or, if he felt convictions would entail miscarriages of justice, he should have resigned.[26]

Sewall merely disappeared. Left without a king's attorney, the court appointed Solicitor-General Samuel Quincy as special prosecutor. John Adams's "easy social and benevolent Companion" since their college days, Sam Quincy was a political trimmer. By now he stood far to the right of Adams and his own fiery brother Josiah. Apparently worried by Samuel's loyalist tendencies, the radicals moved to reinforce the prosecution team. They arranged to have first the Boston selectmen, then the town meeting itself, vote, ostensibly at the request of certain anonymous "Relatives of the Deceased," to pay the expenses of prosecuting Richardson, Preston, and the soldiers. To handle this important assignment, the leadership picked John Adams's perennial legal rival, Robert Treat Paine. A rough, sometimes overbearing opponent, Paine enjoyed a lucrative practice in southern Massachusetts and neighboring Rhode Island. Just ten days after the Massacre, he had ended lifelong bachelorhood (at the age of thirty-nine) by marrying Sally Cobb. William Molineux, notifying Paine of his appointment, sent him a copy of the *Short Narrative* to put him "into the Spirit of the thing," and exhorted him "to Espouse your Country's Cause, or that of Individuals, Who have Suffered by the hands of Execrable Villains and Professed Murderers."[27]

Even as Samuel Adams was trying to ensure strong representation for the crown, the loyalists had, in Molineux' slightly hysterical view, "Engag'd most or all of the Lawyers in Town." In fact, they had retained only three, with a fourth added shortly before the trials. Robert Auchmuty, the "dull, insipid" judge of the vice-admiralty court, had been early approached by Preston's friends; firm loyalist though he was, Auchmuty refused to commit himself. On Preston's behalf, someone asked Josiah Quincy. Normally "impetuous and vehement," and a wild enough radical to draw from brother Samuel the affectionate nickname "Wilkes" (after John Wilkes, who besides sharing Josiah's political incendiarism, owned, like him, a badly cocked eye), Josiah, too, hesitated.[28]

If John Adams's memories thirty-odd years after the event are accurate, both Auchmuty and Quincy were waiting for his lead. As Adams recalled it, the day after the killings the loyalist merchant James Forrest, "the Irish Infant," came to his office "with tears streaming from his eyes" bearing a message from Preston, "'who wishes for Council, and can get none.'" "'Council,'" Adams remembered saying pithily, "'ought to be the very last thing that an accused Person should want [i.e., lack] in a free Country.'" And with homilies on the bar's duty and his own disinclination to employ "Art or Address," "Sophistry or Prevarication," Adams accepted the case. "'As God almighty is my Judge,'" said Forrest, "'I believe him an innocent Man.'" Adams was unwilling to be drawn into that part of the controversy. "'That must be ascertained by his Tryal,'" was his lawyerlike answer. "'And if he thinks he cannot have a fair Tryal of that Issue without my Assistance, without hesitation he shall have it.'" [29]

The way Adams told it, the story bore such a glow of justice triumphant that one almost hesitates to point out its inaccuracies. Years later, as a loyalist trying to convince the London authorities that his special services for the king merited particular fiscal remuneration, Forrest submitted a thick file of laudatory material, some of it even written by others, including Gage. Yet nowhere in this collection is there the briefest mention of Forrest's part in achieving this representational coup.[30]

More importantly, John Adams's long-afterward account omits any suggestion that Samuel Adams and the radical high command played any role in his taking Preston's case. That Sam Adams and his cadre did indeed influence the retainer we know from an exchange of letters between Josiah Quincy, Senior, and his youngest son. The father, "shocked and bewildered" at hearing bitter reproaches uttered against his namesake, wrote on March 22 to learn first hand if the rumors were true that young Josiah had "become an advocate for those criminals who are charged with the murder of their fellow citizens." Somewhat testily, the son reminded his father "that these criminals, charged with murder, are not yet legally proved guilty, and therefore, however criminal, are entitled, by the laws of God and man, to all legal counsel and aid; that my duty as a man obliged me to undertake; that my duty as a lawyer strengthened the obligation." More important, "Wilkes" wrote, he had ended his initial refusal only after being "advised and urged to undertake it, by an Adams, a Hancock, a Molineux, a Cushing, a Henshaw, a Pemberton, a Warren, a Cooper, and a Phillips." In other words, young Josiah had not committed himself to his "duty" until virtually all the principal Sons of Liberty had approved.[31]

It is hardly conceivable that some kind of similar consultation did not precede John Adams's retainer. Thus the radicals had, in effect, chosen the prisoners' counsel almost as effectively as they had selected half the prosecution. Under the circumstances, why would the Sons be willing to throw such "men of parts," as Hutchinson correctly appraised them, against the very side which Sam Adams clearly wished to prevail? Did he intend that counsel should betray their clients? No evidence suggests it; what we know of John Adams's character flatly refutes it. Even Hutchinson, who was highly critical of John Adams's court performance, admitted that he "closed extremely well & with great fidelity to his Clients." I believe that in the flush of triumph at having finally seen the self-fulfilling prophecies of town-troop bloodshed enacted, the radicals failed to consider the possibility of an acquittal. Supremely confident that neither public opinion nor local jurors would return any verdict but condemnation, they were expansively willing to let the military have the best lawyers available; that way, no one could later taint the proceedings with unfairness. Further, if sound Whigs occupied defense counsel's table, no one need fear that the hearings would be turned into a trial of Boston's behavior. John Adams and Josiah Quincy, after all, had been two-thirds of a committee elected by the Town the week after the shootings to "write immediately" to the radicals' English friends "acquainting them with the Circumstances and Facts relative to the late horred Massacre, and asking the continuance of their good services in behalf of this Town and Province." [32]

In the passionate state of Boston's public opinion, neither Sam Adams nor his opponents saw any reason to believe a jury would acquit either Preston or his soldiers. Adams therefore pressed hard for immediate trials, while Hutchinson tried every conceivable maneuver to postpone them. He hoped to be able to utilize the illness of two of the judges as an excuse to put the trials over to June. Countering, Adams had the town meeting pass a resolution praying the appointment of special justices to fill out the court. Further delay, the Adams-written memorial insisted, might allow the escape of the prisoners. Besides, said Adams, many of the witnesses, being seamen, could not long afford to remain ashore waiting to testify; "possibly some of them may be under Temptation to absent themselves from the Tryal." Of course a ready means lay at hand for lessening the possible enticement: placing the restless sailors under bond to appear; or, if they could not post bond, imprisoning them as material witnesses. But Adams, naturally, did not mention that. Ultimate control of the trial "list" lay, of course, with the

judges. They inclined to delay, planning to adjourn the criminal business until the first week in June. Fearful lest passions cool unduly in
the interim, the radical leaders resorted to physical confrontation.
After dining at John Temple's, Sam Adams, Molineux, Warren, Hancock, and Cooper, followed by a "vast concourse of people," marched
right into the courtroom. While the judges quailed, Adams "ha-
rangued" them on the absolute "necessity of proceeding to the trial of
the Criminals this Term, particularly those concerned in the late
bloody Massacre." His message was clear: "Gentlemen, you must comply with our demand." The judges, Hutchinson reported, "had not firmness enough to abide by their determination." Proclaiming themselves
"under duress, and afraid to offend the town," they agreed to try the
Massacre cases in April. Hutchinson, meanwhile, tried vainly to resign.[33]

That left Richardson and Wilmot. Unlike the soldiers, who were
generally considered mere tools of the ministry, Richardson, by his earlier reputation and conduct, had achieved distinctly personal odium.
Neither the administration nor the court seemed willing to risk the popular fury a second time. "Had a trial been refused," Judge Oliver said
later, "it was rather more than an equal chance that the Prisoners
[meaning Preston and the soldiers, as well] would have been murdered by the Rabble; and the Judges exposed to Assassinations." Accordingly, on Monday, March 19, Richardson was arraigned; he
pleaded not guilty; trial was set for the Friday, March 23.[34]

When the clerk called the case that day, it became obvious that the
Boston bar's willingness to represent unpopular clients had a high degree of selectivity. Asked if he was ready for trial, Richardson told the
judges that he had applied to "almost every Lawyer in town," but
none would undertake his cause. The constables, he said, had refused to
summon his witnesses; the jailer prevented his conferring with his
friends; and every newspaper was "crouded with the most infamous
and false libels" against him, in order to prejudice the minds of his
prospective jurors. Now, Richardson concluded, without lawyer or witnesses, he was to be tried for his life.

Moved by this recital, the court put the trial over. In town, one radical grumbled that Richardson had won the postponement simply "because he had not an Evidence [i.e., witness] from Chelsea, but 2 miles
distant from ye Boston. O Tempora! O Mores!" Unruffled, the judges
tried to recruit counsel for Richardson. They asked each of the lawyers
present; each declined. The court thereupon ordered Samuel Fitch to
appear on Richardson's behalf. Fitch, the newly appointed advocate-
general of the vice-admiralty court, could by no stretch be considered
a radical; he was, indeed, a part of the loyalist establishment.[35] Yet

asked by the court to defend a one-time customs officer in a politically tainted and factually unjustified prosecution for murder, he "made use of a variety of arguments in order to excuse himself, which the Court did not judge sufficient." Finally, Fitch surrendered. Since the court had "peremptorily ordered" him, he said, he would undertake the defense, "but not otherways." To solve another of Richardson's difficulties, the court ordered Sheriff Greenleaf to give his deputies "particular instructions" with respect to summoning defense witnesses. The problem of newspaper-inspired prejudice remained beyond the judges' control.

While Fitch began to prepare for trial, Sewall remained out of Boston. The court, unable to dispatch any major criminal business in his absence, handled assorted civil matters and later, routine criminal cases, conducted, apparently, by court-nominated lawyers serving *ad hoc* as "King's Attorney." One of the civil cases bore political overtones. John Williams, the customs officer with Whiggish leanings, sued Thomas Ainslie, former collector at Quebec, for £3000 over Ainslie's conduct in seizing some of Williams's personal goods five years before. "Custom house officers," John Adams said during his argument for Williams, "[are] vested with very important power & if deviated from may become fire brands in the hands of Fools." The jury, receiving the case "late at night," brought in a verdict for £2700; the goods had been worth only £1041.[36]

On Friday, April 6, Richardson's case was called for trial. Fitch told the court he had learned "by an *anonimous* Letter handed into his House by an *unknown* person, that *somebody* could swear *something*" in Richardson's favor. Interpreting this as a request for additional preparation time, the judges put the case over. On April 7, still without having tried any of the prime defendants, the court adjourned for its regular week-long April sitting in Charlestown across the river. Meeting in Boston on April 17, the court called Richardson's case. Because Fitch again reported ill, still another postponement was necessary. The judges, exasperated, appointed Josiah Quincy, and on Friday, April 20, the trial finally began, before a wholly non-Bostonian jury. Meanwhile, the court of general sessions ordered Sheriff Greenleaf to "cause a New Gallows to be Erected on Boston Neck . . . the old one being gone to decay." The court also ordered that the "watch" at the jail be augmented to "six men constantly to watch there." [37]

"A vast Concourse of Rabble," was Judge Oliver's description of the crowd that packed the courthouse. Many of the spectators apparently stood, rather than sat; at least three of them had their pockets picked. Leaving Paine to sum up the case, Samuel Quincy opened for the crown and examined the prosecution's fairly straightforward witnesses.

Anticipating the defense argument that Richardson, besieged in his own home, his life endangered, had been justified in protecting himself by any means possible, even if death resulted, the prosecution tried to put in evidence that the besieging army was nothing but a gang of schoolboys. Sticks and stones, the prosecution argued, might break bones, but not being lethal weapons, they could not excuse Richardson's firing. Besides, whatever anyone else was doing at the fatal moment, young Seider had only been bending over to pick up a stone; his activity certainly did not threaten Richardson's life.[38]

The idea that reckless gunplay had killed an innocent boy underlay the town's feeling about the soldiers, as well as about Richardson. Compounded by the biblically inspired conviction that "blood requires blood," this concept posed a serious forensic difficulty for the defense. To counter it, Quincy and his associate, the dour Sampson Salter Blowers, put on witnesses, including Richardson's children, tending to show the extreme violence of the attack. If the jury could be convinced that Richardson fired in self-defense, then the law would protect him—or at least his attorneys so felt—because if the firing was justified the innocent Seider's death would nonetheless be excused.

After the defense rested, Josiah Quincy began his final argument. Today, a lawyer's closing speech concentrates exclusively on the facts, leaving the law to be summed up wholly in the judge's charge. In the eighteenth century, counsel were permitted, even expected, to argue law to the jury. Concocting a thick mixture of English judicial opinions and legal treatises, Quincy tried to soothe the anti-Richardson prejudice which infected Boston. Hopefully, such a reasoned approach might succeed, particularly with country jurymen like these. "A man's home is his castle," Quincy argued toward the end. "A man is not obliged to fly from his own House." It was a good job; under the circumstances, especially the short notice, it was outstanding. Even the Tories recognized Quincy's "bringing such pertinent authorities to support the facts, and making such just remarks on the same." They praised "his abilities as an Attorney," "his benevolence as a citizen," and "the faithfulness and impartiality he shewed for the Prisoner."

Paine's final argument for the crown has not survived. His courtroom notes suggest that he hammered at Richardson's burden of establishing justification. A man would be excused for killing someone who pursued him home, Paine urged, only if the assailant had actually entered the building. No one had broken into Richardson's house until after the shooting; Richardson therefore had had no right to shoot Seider.

When the lawyers finished, the judges took over. Generally, they agreed that Richardson, having acted in self-defense, could be held for nothing more than manslaughter. The crowd heard the charges restlessly. As Judge Oliver was commenting on the testimony of the Richardson children, "a general hiss," and cries of "Guilty!" filled the courtroom. Unshaken, Oliver went farther than the other judges; Richardson, he said, had committed no offense at all, not even manslaughter. The homicide was legally justifiable, he insisted. Seider's death should be charged to the promoters of the effigies and exhibitions, for it was they who had provoked the unlawful tumultuous assemblies. Warming to his theme, Oliver specifically included in his indictment the civil magistrates, who had failed to suppress the mobs. "Damn that Judge," shouted one of the crowd, "if I was nigh him, I would give it to him." Oliver ignored the interruption. As he remarked later, "This was not a Time to attempt to preserve Decorum; Preservation of Life was as much as a Judge dared to aim at." Oliver's charge aroused the already heated spectators. As the jury began filing out, the shouts increased. "Remember, jury," someone yelled, "you are upon oath." "Blood requires blood," somebody else shouted. "Damn him, don't bring it in manslaughter!" "Hang the dog! Hang him!" "Damn him, hang him! Murder, no manslaughter!"

The case went to the jury at about 11 P.M. Discussion commenced immediately, and went on, without interruptions for sleep, food, or drink, through the night. A large crowd remained in the courtroom until well past midnight, virtually imprisoning the judges. Richardson himself could not safely be taken to the nearby jail: it was whispered that the crowd had brought a rope into court, either to execute the expected sentence promptly, or perhaps to anticipate it. As the night wore on, the mob dispersed somewhat, enabling Richardson and the court to leave; but when the judges passed to their carriages, they were "hissed and abused in a most shameful manner." [39]

Into the dawn the jury deliberated, a circumstance which must have encouraged Richardson: it meant the jurors were at least considering the possibility of an acquittal. It might, of course, also mean merely that one or two jurors were holding out against the unanimity which the law required for a verdict either way. Not until shortly before court resumed the next morning did the jurors agree. The crowd again filled the courtroom. "How say you?" the clerk asked Jonathan Deming, the foreman. Wilmot, he replied, was not guilty, Richardson guilty of murder. "An universal clap ensued." "The Court Room resounded," in Judge Oliver's words, "with Expressions of Pleasure." Only when one of the radical leaders shouted, "For shame, for shame, Gentlemen," did the crowd quiet.

The verdict placed the judges in a difficult legal and political position. They could not tell whether the conviction had resulted from the jury's refusal to credit Richardson's witnesses, from its disinclination to

accept the legal postulates contained in the judges' charges, or from its
response to popular intimidation. "It was hard," as Hutchinson accurately observed later, "to be obliged to give judgment upon a verdict
which appeared to [the Court] to be directly against law; and it was
difficult, in the state of the town, to order the jury out a second time,
or to refuse or delay sentence after the verdict was received." The
judges' dilemma increased with their realization that they probably
could not lawfully ask the jurors the true basis for the verdict. Worse,
the then-state of English and Massachusetts law precluded the granting of a new trial. Playing desperately for time, the court formally received the verdict and ordered it to be recorded, simultaneously adjourning until May 29 without having passed sentence.[40]

Everyone expected that when court reconvened, "the trial of Preston
and the Soldiers must come on." Delay of the trials "is the only good
that can be done at present," Gage wrote Dalrymple. The colonel
agreed: "Procrastination is our only course." To the radicals' "party
zeal," pressing for immediate trials, was added now the discomfort of
the moderates. The somewhat later words of the Reverend Andrew
Eliot applied perfectly. "People complain of the delay of justice. Perhaps it was best to delay the trial at the first. The minds of men were
too much inflamed to have given him a common chance. But they are
as calm now as they are like to be at all, and if judges have power to
delay trials as long as they please, it certainly is in their power to say
whether there shall be any trial at all." [41]

Not even the news that Parliament had repealed all the Townshend
duties (except on tea) could lessen the pressure. The court attended to
its regular May sittings at Plymouth and Barnstable, in southern Massachusetts. On the way back to Boston, Judge Oliver fell from his horse
—purposely, Paine said. Judge Trowbridge was battling one of his pe-
riodic bouts of nervous illness, so when the court met at the May 29 adjournment, only Chief Justice Lynde and old Judge Cushing could attend. They immediately adjourned court again until May 31. By now a
new political diversion had arisen. The struggle for power between the
House and the lieutenant-governor turned attention somewhat away
from the Massacre trials. Acting under royal instructions, Hutchinson
had ordered the legislature to sit at Cambridge, safe from the Boston
mob. This, John Rowe correctly predicted, "will be the Cause of Quarrel between the Lieut. Governour & the House of Representatives."
From mid-March until the late April prorogation, the House yapped at
Hutchinson; he stood firm, refuting arguments and ignoring insults.
Boston, meanwhile, bubbled with renewed anti-importation activity.
The very day of Richardson's trial, Sam Adams staged an early-morn-
ing meeting of the merchants at Faneuil Hall. He told the mob that

another year of nonimportation would either see all "grievances redress'd or it would raise such a disturbance at home as would endanger the heads and necks of those great Men who were the promoters
of them." Voting itself "the Board of Trade," the meeting ordered committees of inspection to visit importers of goods and ascertain their
plans; masters and owners of vessels would be instructed to deliver no
goods to consignees without instructions from the "Board." The meeting adjourned promptly, to permit the leaders to attend Richardson's
trial.[42]

During the day, the inspectors went about their tasks. The provocative "hands" went up again outside Lillie's shop and others. Delega-
tions called on recalcitrant merchants. Well-to-do Gilbert Deblois de-
fied them openly; they "abused [him] in the grossest manner." Robert
Selkrig "absolutely refused." They threatened to "advertise" him and
"ruin his business." "I do not care a farthing for your advertising," he
replied. Radical merchant Henderson Inches had the last word: "Do
you know, sir, that both your life and property are in danger?" Well
might the more conservative John Rowe regard the "Board of Trade's"
votes with dislike. During April, Hutchinson tried vainly to promote
an "association" of loyal merchants. One of the first men he sounded
explained the problem: "Until Parliament makes provision for the punishment of the confederacies, all will be ineffectual, and the associates
will be exposed to popular rage." The anti-importation pressure would
continue throughout the summer, unaffected by the news of repeal.
While Hutchinson continued wishfully thinking that Parliament would
at last apply its "authority and power" against the unlawful combinations, the radicals solidified their hold on the province. By the lieutenant-governor's own estimate, "Representatives of seven-eighths of the
Towns appeared in the present [legislative] Session to be favourers of
non-importation." To show both their power and their displeasure at
the move to Cambridge, the representatives procrastinated ostenta-
tiously over the voting of Hutchinson's salary and those of the judges,
finally voting only a fraction of the customary sum, and that just before the April 26 dissolution.[43]

Hutchinson's foes did not at this time include Otis. Erratic in behavior throughout the winter, he had by spring become entirely uncontrollable. The day after Richardson's trial, he fired guns out of his window, attracting a large, frightened crowd. "His friends were obliged to
take him under their care, and he was removed into the country." When
the Town met on May 8 to select representatives for the new legislature, no one even mentioned him. Hutchinson's official career, by contrast, was thriving. Whatever his difficulties with the radicals, he had
clearly won the favor of Hillsborough and the king himself. One of the

ships which brought news of the tax repeal also carried the rumor—
which proved true a few months later—that Hutchinson was to replace
Bernard as governor in his own right; Secretary Oliver became lieutenant-governor and Thomas Flucker (the future father-in-law of Henry
Knox) the new secretary. Said Dalrymple, with some accuracy: "I do
not suppose they could have chosen three men more obnoxious to the
people." [44]

Actually, the trio did not stand alone in popular execration. With
completion of the deposition-taking, and printing of the product, accompanied by Bowdoin's inflammatory *Short Narrative*, the antimilitary feeling reached a peak. Relying on Massachusetts' strict vagrancy
laws, the authorities struck at the soldiers through their dependents.
On the theory that the families had no visible means of support, and
were therefore potential burdens on public bounty, the selectmen ordered the constables to "warn" Elisabeth "Hartick" and Isabella "Mon-
gomerry" (and her three children) "in his Majestys Name to Depart
this town of Boston in 14 Days." Soldiers and their wives were not the
only targets. A version of the Pelham-Revere cartoon published about
this time bore a doggerel slap at the court's refusal to sentence Richardson or to try the soldiers: "Should venal C——s the scandal of
the Land, Snatch the relentless Villain from her Hand, Keen Execra-
tions on this Plate inscrib'd Shall reach a *Judge* that never can be
brib'd." [45]

Out in the harbor, the two regiments uncomfortably jammed the old
Castle barracks beyond capacity. Gage, convinced that the additional
military strength did not justify leaving the soliders in such unsatisfactory
quarters, and aware of Boston's antagonism toward the Twenty-ninth,
ordered Dalrymple to send the regiment south. Delighted to see Carr's
men depart, the province nonetheless refused any assistance in the
way of carriages for baggage or quarters for en route bivouacks. Accordingly, on May 17, the troops were ferried to Dorchester Neck,
whence they commenced a march to Providence. The Rhode Island
metropolis afforded considerably more help; a fleet of "small vessels"
awaited, and carried the regiment to New Jersey, where it relieved the
Twenty-sixth in a string of small posts from the Hudson to the
Delaware.[46]

Boston's temper grew more violent. As usual, a committee had been
appointed to prepare the Town's annual "Instructions" to its newly
elected representatives. The product, written almost entirely by Josiah
Quincy, struck Hutchinson, recuperating at Milton from a brief illness,
as "the ravings of Men in a political frenzy." "Nothing can be more infamous." Quincy, Hutchinson sputtered, was a mere "Coxcomb." "He
bids fair for a successor to Otis and it is much if he does not run mad

also." [47]

The Instructions did indeed take an extreme position. The only purpose of the royal prerogative, Quincy wrote, "was the general emolument of the state; and, therefore, when any pretended prerogatives do not advance this grand purpose, they have no legal obligation; and when any strictly just prerogatives are exerted to promote any different design, they also cease to be binding." "*Obsta principiis* [resist the tyrant] is the maxim to be held in view." To protect provincial rights, the Instructions said, the representatives ought to make the militia's "despicable situation" "the object of your peculiar attention," thus to permit "more open, manly, bold and pertinacious exertions for our freedom." Such talk of military resistance struck Hutchinson as particularly relevant. Earlier in the year Lieutenant Colonel John Burgoyne had learned from a friend that someone in America had placed a large special order for military uniforms. The clothing was not apparently bound for any of the regular army regiments, nor for any of the colonial militia. Somewhere in America, somebody was preparing to outfit a military force. Ultimately, it seemed, the force would oppose royal authority: according to the report, the soldiers' caps would bear the legalistic motto: *vim vi repellere licet* [it is lawful to repel force with force]. Later in the year, however, the orders were canceled. [48]

Quincy's Instructions carried further astonishing suggestions. The Home Government's sending directions to the governor was, in Quincy's view, an "unwarrantable practice"; the legislature should deny appropriations to any local "instruments of government" if they seemed, through adherence to such instructions, to be subverting "the grand ends" of government. "We, also, recommend to you carefully to inquire into the state of criminal prosecutions, in our executive courts." This could only be interpreted as an invitation to the legislators to apply upon the judges whatever pressure seemed appropriate to hasten the soldiers' trials. Such an invitation on its face appears to be an improper attempt to influence the administration of justice; at the very least, it is a violation of the principle of separation of powers. Worse, it represents an appeal by counsel for prisoners awaiting trial that the trial be commenced forthwith. This was the radical party position, and understandably so, because the Sons wanted to take full advantage of whatever popular prejudices they could find or stir up. It was to counter this tide of prejudice that Hutchinson so desperately sought to have the trials postponed. Now here was Quincy, the men's own lawyer, joining in Sam Adams's hunt for their immediate blood.

Behind everything lurked still the threat of the mob. The afternoon of May 18, a couple of customs tidesmen, on duty aboard the schooner *Success*, at the Town Dock, observed peculiar activity around the nearby schooner *Martin*, of New London, Connecticut. Boarding the vessel, they "found the fore hold full of Hogsheads, Tierces & Barrels of Brown Sugar," all undeclared. The master begged mercy and offered first a bowl of punch, then money, "to make all things easy." For answer, the senior tidesman, Owen Richards, the man who had provoked the *Lydia* embroglio in April 1768, took a piece of chalk and put the admiralty's broad arrow on as many of the casks as he could reach. Having formally seized the offending cargo, he went topside and seized the vessel herself, chalking the mainmast with the same mark.[49]

When he learned of Richards' action, Deputy Collector William Sheaffe ordered the vessel shifted to a more convenient wharf; he also doubled the number of tidesmen on board. Toward 8 P.M., when the evening began to chill, Richards left *Martin* to go home for his watch coat. Lingering there, he did not return to the ship until after nine. As he passed through Dock Square, he found himself facing what he described shortly afterwards as "a great Number of disorderly men and Boys and Negroes also, with Clubs and Sticks crying out 'an Informer, an Informer!'" Laying on with his walking stick, Richards defended himself as best he could. The odds were too great. The crowd beat him nearly unconscious, dragged him to a cart, tossed him in, and pulled him to King Street. There, in front of the Custom House, on the very site of the Massacre, they stripped him of hat, wig, coat, waistcoat, shirt, and loose change. As he stood shivering in the cold, naked to his breeches, they poured tar over him, dumped feathers on the tar, and lit them. To Richards' besmeared chest they fixed a crude sign: "The True Informer."

By now the crowd numbered upwards of one thousand, its "very great Hallooing" audible all over town. Still shouting, the mob began moving the cart through the Boston streets. In a reversal of usual practice, the crowd began crying "Take your Lights from your Windows or you'll have 'em broke." Pitifully insisting that he had seized *Martin* in line of duty, not as an informer, Richards endured for almost four hours the taunts and threats of the boisterous throng. Hutchinson was at his Milton home; no one told him of the disturbance until the next day, long after it had ended. When he inquired why none of the justices of the peace had attempted to intervene, Justice Dana answered without embarrassment that he felt himself "under no obligations to make inquiry, as no Complaint had been made in form." So the fun was allowed to continue. Two smaller groups split off from the crowd. One went to *Martin*, barricaded the two tidesmen then on duty, and removed most of the contraband. The second group undertook to hunt down John Woart, the tidesman who had accompanied Richards in the original seizure. Cowering below deck aboard *Success*, Woart managed to elude them, largely because Captain Blake of that vessel told the crowd he was not there. The crowd, suspicious of Blake's good faith, swarmed aboard, found Woart, and dragged him across town to "New Boston," i.e., the Beacon Hill area, where Richards' escort had taken him. Events now trembled on the brink of chaos. Fortunately for both officers, "many who call themselves friends to Liberty" disapproved the entire rowdy proceedings. They intervened just enough to permit both men to escape.

The near-riot and the legislative turmoil enabled Hutchinson to parlay the statutory court schedule and some fortuitous judicial ailments into yet another postponement. When the court met again (ironically enough on May 29, a quasi-holiday honoring the restoration of the monarchy in 1660), only Cushing and Lynde were present. They promptly adjourned again to May 31. Meanwhile, the radicals were outsmarting themselves. They staged a massive two-day display celebrating their battle with Hutchinson. On the 29th, an ox was carried through the streets in triumph; the 30th, a "Fair, high day," while the legislature met at Cambridge, the ox was roasted whole on Boston Common, the Reverend Doctor Chauncy "preached an excellent sermon," 450 people consumed the ox at a Faneuil Hall dinner, and "ye day concluded with great Joy." [50]

Thus distracted, the radicals were unprepared for the court's next move. At 10 A.M., on May 31, once again only two judges attended. Trowbridge was still sick; Judge Oliver's horse had fallen as he was riding to Boston from his Middleborough home. At noon, Chief Justice Lynde adjourned the court *sine die*. Though the radicals grumbled that Oliver's mishap had been intentional, they could do nothing. Hutchinson had steadily refused to appoint a special judge; now the Ipswich sitting was coming up, to be followed closely by the grueling Eastern Circuit to Maine in late June and early July. Despite his weakness, Hutchinson had won: the soldiers could not possibly be tried before August 28, when, by statute, the court would next sit at Boston. [51]

The legislature, in selecting nominees for the council, had chosen, among others, James Bowdoin, one of the four Boston representatives. When Hutchinson assented to the choice, Bowdoin had to relinquish his House seat. At a special meeting held June 6, the Town replaced him with John Adams. Because Boston politics were solidly in the radicals' control, Adams's election indicates that the Sons of Liberty considered his representation of the soldiers to be entirely compatible with their own political aims. Indeed, immediately upon taking his seat, Adams assumed a prominent role in the battle with Hutchinson. Simultaneously, he was trying to maintain his private practice. There, he noticed a universal "Scarcity of Business," caused, he believed, by "the Non Importation agreement, and the Declension of Trade." Thus the lawyers, he insisted, were losing "as much by this Patriotic Measure as the Merchants, and Tradesmen." But Adams found business enough to warrant making the long horseback journey with the court to the Maine circuit towns. And during his spare moments, he seems to have been thinking of the great trials ahead. In his diary for June 28, he minuted a relevant passage from the great Italian penologist, Beccaria: "If, by supporting the Rights of Mankind, and of invincible Truth, I shall contribute to save from the Agonies of Death one unfortunate Victim of Tyranny, or of Ignorance, equally fatal; his Blessing and Tears of Transport, will be a sufficient Consolation to me, for the Contempt of all Mankind." [52]

While Adams wrestled in court, library, and legislative hall, the mob continued to rule Boston. John Mein's lists of the importing radicals were having good effect in New York and Philadelphia. The merchants there began to doubt the sincerity of the Boston Sons. When samples of Mein's pamphlet returned to Boston the radicals began comparing the type face with those of the various local printers. John Fleeming, Mein's partner and successor, took the hint. Before the mob could visit him, he fled to the Castle. [53]

In town, meanwhile, the incipient failure of the nonimportation movement seemed to be inspiring the radicals to more and more violence. The intransigent Theophilus Lillie had imported a stock of goods which had lain in the ship for a fortnight because the nonimportation committee would not suffer them to be landed. Anxious to capitalize on the increasing demand for British merchandise, Lillie and a Worcester County trader named Ebenezer Cutler worked out an arrangement for breaking the embargo. They planned simply to run the goods into the country the night of June 28–29. But as Cutler's two wagons, each pulled by "four good horses," thundered through the fortification and over the Neck at 2 A.M., an impromptu posse of committee vigilantes leaped to the saddle, followed, and finally caught them before they reached Little Cambridge, near the present site of Brighton. Angry and threatening, the mob turned the wagons around, tied Cutler to one of them, and brought everything back to town. In King Street, Cutler, threatened with tarring and feathering, surrendered his property to the committee for storage until the end of the nonimportation. Mrs. Henry Barnes remarked: "I look upon all goods seized and committed to that store as much forfeited to the owner as if they were in the bottom of the sea. For they begin to talk of selling them at vendue, and distributing the money to the poor. This will make the poor, as they call them, very assiduous in seizing everything that comes in their way. . . ." [54]

Another time, a mob attacked a wagon-load of goods belonging to Mrs. Barnes' husband, Henry. After abusing the driver, they opened a bag of pepper and carried off the contents in their handkerchiefs and hats. The rest of the load they put into the committee's storage. When Barnes asked Hutchinson for help, the lieutenant-governor could only advise a petition to the legislature; the courts, Hutchinson apparently now felt, could offer no redress. Even so, the treatment Cutler and Barnes received was light compared to that meted out to the three McMasters brothers, traders accused of antisocial importing. In early June, Dr. Thomas Young, "attended by Hundreds of Men and Boys," visited their store and "in a Magisterial tone" ordered them to shut up shop and depart within seventy-two hours. By "overtures repugnant to their inclinations," and the interposition of "a Gentleman of Influence and Character," the McMasters won a brief reprieve. Within two weeks, a rumor reached Boston that Parliament would shortly repeal the tea tax and recall the commissioners. Emboldened, the radicals returned in force at noon on June 19, pulled Patrick McMasters out of the house and heaved him, fainting from terror, into a cart where a pile of feathers and a barrel of tar awaited. No law enforcers opposed this bold daylight sally; only the mob's late-blooming reluctance to continue assaulting the cowering, gibbering wretch saved him from Richards' fate. Instead, they pulled him along to the Roxbury line, "where they made a lane through which they obliged him to pass, while they spit in his face." He broke away into the woods, pursued by about fifty Roxbury people. Hiding in the underbrush, he was able to make his way after dark to Castle Island. His two brothers, fortunately not at home when the mob arrived, also escaped; one of them had to run for his life successively in Marblehead and Salem. The Roxbury crowd worked off its energy that night by going out to Brookline and breaking Commissioner Hulton's windows. The McMasters brothers and Hulton's family all ended up in the Castle, while the council sardonically advised Hutchinson to order Attorney-General Sewall to prosecute the perpetrators.[55]

Captain Hall, who had brought back the rumors of repeal and recall, also carried something more substantially affecting Boston. This was a confidential letter from Hillsborough, conveying the king's direct orders, issued immediately upon receiving the first intelligence of the shootings, that, should Preston and his men be convicted, Hutchinson respite execution of the sentence until further express royal command. Such a scheme would have denied Boston judicial vengeance for the deaths in King Street; the bare rumor of Hutchinson's instructions gave prospects of "great uneasiness." Yet within a month English friends of the radicals were urging that in the event of any convictions, "the inhabitants do in a public town meeting agree on an address to the Governor to suspend their execution, & to convey to his Majesty their humble request that he will be pleased to extend his royal mercy & pardon them." Alderman Barlow Trecothick of London, member of Parliament and intimate correspondent of the radical leaders, explained this astounding proposal in terms not merely of "moral & religious virtue," but of practical politics. Such a gesture, he said, would give the government an opportunity gracefully and fully to respond and thus to encourage the permanent resolution of Anglo-American differences. Trecothick's suggestion at first drew open discussion among the radicals. Later, Hutchinson noticed "there seemed to be a desire to have nothing said of it"; Preston insisted the letter had been "secreted." The reason was clear: at a Boston meeting held about this time, "the spirit rose very high. Independence was a word much used." [56]

The ship which brought Trecothick's letter also carried definite word that Parliament had prorogued in mid-May without after all repealing the tea duties and without taking those firm measures which Hutchinson had long hoped for. Convinced that the ministry meant to maintain the irritant, without taking any effective steps to contain the unrest, Samuel Adams and others who were even then aiming at independence may well have concluded that wise policy demanded abandonment, rather than pursuit, of any measure calculated to effect or even encourage reconciliation. Oddly enough, at Harvard commencement, Thomas Bernard, son of Sir Francis, argued the affirmative of: "Is a Government tyrannical in which the Rulers consult their own interest more than that of their Subjects?" But a couple of days after the Parliamentary news arrived, a band of rowdies led by Thomas Young followed three flags through the streets, to the accompaniment of beating drums and a french horn. Shortly thereafter, the Reverend Dr. Charles Chauncy preached a sermon indicating the true radical attitude toward reprieve. Surely, said Chauncy, the governor "would not make himself a partaker in the guilt of murder, by putting a stop to the shedding of their blood, who have murderously spilt the blood of others! All such suspicions should be repressed." As the Sons of Liberty appreciated more than most, the best way to fan a rumor is to blow on it. Public opinion mirrored the radicals' pseudo-impartiality: "People seem universally to wish [Preston] a fair Trial—Tho a Tendency prevails that from Court Favor the Law will be eluded." [57]

Preston understandably took a grim view of the reprieve rumor; now the jurors, he wrote Gage, could with quiet consciences "the sooner find me guilty as they are told nothing bad will happen." Gage, perceiving a more dangerous possibility, ordered Dalrymple to assure

Preston and the soldiers of the certainty of a respite, "that they may not thro' Fear, and Hopes of Protection be cajoled by the People to perjure themselves, or make Declarations contrary to Truth and Fact." Doubts arose about the quality of Preston's defense. In March, Auchmuty had told Hutchinson he thought the evidence "very strong" that the captain had ordered the firing. As late as mid-August, Auchmuty's wavering persisted. Dalrymple feared he would "disappoint" Preston; if that were true of the ultra-loyalist Auchmuty, Dalrymple said, "the opinion of the others may be easily collected." Gage suggested calling in lawyers from other colonies. Apparently Preston was willing to trust his original counsel; no others were retained. In England, meanwhile, the king agreed to pay Preston's expenses himself, thus assuring that the figures would not "appear upon a Public Account." [58]

Other troubles now beset Preston. Back in March, even while the *Gazette* apprentices were setting his "card" into type, Preston had been preparing—or at least signing—a document much less complimentary to the town. This was the celebrated "Case of Captain Preston," ostensibly an account in the captain's own words of the King Street tragedy. Carried to England by Robinson, it had been promptly published in newspapers which returned to Boston in mid-Summer. Already primed to regard Preston as guilty until proven innocent, Boston read his printed "Case" with surprise and resentment, comparing the fulsome praise contained in the "card" with what people now assumed were Preston's true feelings:

> So bitter and inveterate are many of the Malcontents here [he had written] that they are industriously using every Method to fish out Evidence to prove it was a concerted Scheme to murder the Inhabitants. Others are infusing the utmost Malice and Revenge into the Minds of the People who are to be my Jurors by false Publications, Votes of Towns, and all other Artifices, that so from a settled Rancour against the Officers and Troops in general, the Suddenness of my Trial after the Affair, while the People's Minds are all greatly inflamed, I am though perfectly innocent, under most unhappy circumstances, having nothing in Reason to expect but the Loss of Life in a very ignominious Manner, without the Interposition of his Majesty's Royal Goodness.[59]

Sam Adams seized this tidbit as a falcon pins a sparrow. The Town organized committees, one to visit Preston, one to correspond with English friends. Full accounts filled the Boston *Gazette*, cleverly attacking Preston while proclaiming a desire to protect him. It must be conceded that Preston did not handle himself with honor. Asked to explain some of the more egregious accusations in his "Case," he told the committee that what was published in Boston differed materially from the original which he had sent to England. This was a flat lie, as a comparison of the original (now in the Public Record Office) with the *Gazette*'s version will show.[60]

The times did not foster candor. In early July, copies of the English reprint of the *Short Narrative* began to circulate in Boston. Edes and Gill, printers to the radicals, sought permission to sell their large stock of the pamphlet, impounded since March. The town meeting again voted to restrict distribution. So Edes and Gill ran off a printed-in-London title page, placed it on their own copies and sold them through a cooperating firm. It is impossible to believe this could have happened without at least the tacit approval of the radical chiefs.[61]

The radicals did not scruple greatly at outright lies. They assiduously spread the false story that Preston had exerted undue commercial pressure on Henry Quincy, ne'er-do-well son of Justice of the Peace Edmund Quincy and brother-in-law to Sewall. Although Henry Quincy subsequently acknowledged Preston's "great civility," the damage was done. The radicals naturally did not publicize an incident more typical of that benevolence and humanity which even the Sons of Liberty realized Preston possessed. Private William Clarke, one of Preston's men (not among the eight prisoners), had been tried and convicted of simple assault during the April sitting of the superior court and fined forty shillings. Thrown into jail for his inability to pay, he somehow attracted Preston's attention. Beset though he was with his own problems and fears, Preston sat down and wrote out a petition to Hutchinson praying a remission of the fine. As a result, the fine was remitted on July 23, and Clarke was released.[62]

Preston, of course, stayed in prison, terrified that the example of Captain Porteous would commend itself to the radicals and that they would come for him some night and lynch him. During the June unrest, "it was everybody's opinion poor Preston would be hanged." Justice of the Peace James Murray intercepted a rumor that a lynching was imminent and sent word to Hutchinson at Milton. Thoroughly alarmed, Hutchinson wrote Sheriff Greenleaf to take the jailkeeper's keys that night, so "that the Keeper himself if they should be demanded may not have it in his power to deliver them." Having sent out "scouts" to different parts of Boston, Hutchinson, still "extremely uneasy," came to Boston himself, and sat up until midnight, waiting. But although the people were "enraged" at Preston's newly published "Case," everything remained quiet. Later, Hutchinson learned that the official radical reaction to the lynching scare was an assurance that "whatever danger there may be after Trial it would be the heighth of madness to think of any such thing before." [63]

The rumor persisted throughout the summer, nonetheless. Gage suggested housing the prisoners on board one of the navy ships in the harbor, or else shifting them to the Castle. Hutchinson toyed with the idea of declaring the fort a prison, in order to justify such a transfer. Murray offered to lead two hundred regulars in a vigil at the former Boston barracks during the trial, a proposal which the military commanders sensibly rejected: The hated Murray, at the head of two hundred Redcoats, would almost certainly have provoked a real massacre. Gage assured Preston that "if there is any sufficient Reason to suspect any Designs of Violence on the Part of the People, . . . the Lieut. Governor will certainly order the 14th Regiment into the town." That same day, however, Dalrymple was writing Gage: "I do not then suppose that the Lieut. Governor will call the aid of the military." To increase the available armed force, Commodore Hood, after noting that "the outrage of the people daily increases," had on his own authority ordered H.M.S. *Martin* and *Bonetta* to reinforce H.M.S. *Hussar* and *Mermaid* on station in Boston Harbor. When Hillsborough learned what was happening, he asked the Admiralty to make Boston the naval "rendezvous" for the entire North American station, to "check further violences, prevent illicit trade, and to defend & support . . . the Magistrates in the enforcement of the Law." Although the presence of the ships doubtless gave some comfort to the frightened loyalists, it is not clear whether, on balance, the Navy was soothing the situation or exacerbating it. In late August, H.M.S. *Viper* stopped a coasting vessel and impressed one of her hands. When he learned of this, Hood exploded. Oblivious to the officer's insistence that he had merely recovered "a man who owned himself a deserter," Hood wrote specifically to James Bowdoin to assure the radicals that he disapproved of the conduct "exceedingly." [64]

The great English revivalist, George Whitefield, came to Boston on August 14, just as the Sons of Liberty were holding their annual celebration in Dorchester. Evangelistic whirlwind of the pulpit, Whitefield had by his fiery preaching in the 1740's infused with ascetic zeal a whole generation. Samuel Adams, it has been said, "hoped to do by means of a political revolution what George Whitefield had done through a religious awakening." Now, after a lifetime of preaching sixty hours a week, wheezing with asthma, Whitefield was making his seventh American tour. "I had rather wear out than rust out," he said.

Day after day he preached in stuffy, crowded churches, unaided, of course, by any voice-magnifying device. "Turn Ye to the Strong Hold Ye Prisoners, of Hope," was the appropriate text of an early Boston sermon. He visited most Boston pulpits, and many of the outlying towns, always in motion. On August 2, after speaking in Boston, he went to Milton for dinner with Hutchinson, returning afterward to town. For two weeks and a half, he tirelessly exhorted Boston to virtue; then he set out to the eastward. On September 29, he reached Newburyport, where he was to preach the next day. At 6 A.M. on September 30, taken suddenly with an asthmatic seizure, he died. "A good man may wish to be thus translated," Hutchinson wrote in his diary.[65]

Mob activity had seemed quieter in Boston during his visit. Some people attributed the change to Whitefield's emphasis of "Subordination to Government, and Obedience to Laws." With typical cynicism, Gage "rather inclined to attribute it to other causes." He may well have been right. The evening of September 8, Hutchinson had received orders to turn the fortifications on Castle Island over to Dalrymple. The regulars had, of course, been barracked on the island since mid-March; but the fort itself continued in the control of a provincial garrison. Aging pensioners and patronage placemen, the Massachusetts soldiers hardly qualified as militiamen, much less as expert artillerists. Nonetheless, their mere presence meant that the province, rather than the king, retained theoretical control over Boston Harbor.[66]

As the inevitable day of the Massacre trials approached, Gage, Hutchinson, and Hillsborough became convinced that the loyalists absolutely required army control of the Castle, to render it "a place of strength and security in any exigency." Gage even asked Hutchinson to concert with Dalrymple so that the troops could seize the fort if the situation demanded. The crown officials clearly foresaw the possibility of a general loyalist retreat to the island, followed by a full siege. Before Hutchinson and Dalrymple could concert their plan, however, the orders arrived, issued by the king himself. The next day, a Sunday, Dalrymple came out to Milton to plan the shift. It was a delicate business. The fort had been built at province expense; most of the military supplies there, and all the ammunition, had been purchased with province money. By giving it up, Hutchinson would in many minds be improperly relinquishing power entrusted to him by the province charter. Because the charter also gave the governor authority to control and garrison the fort, it occurred to Hutchinson that he might solve the dilemma by writing Dalrymple a Massachusetts militia commission, followed by an appointment to command Castle William. Dalrymple perceived a slight impropriety in simultaneously holding the king's commission and the province's, so Hutchinson resolved to write first to Gage for advice. The timing of the royal order was indeed unfortunate. Two recent actions by the superior court had irritated radical sensibilities; loss of the Castle might well provoke outright resistance.[67]

All summer, the judges had been struggling, trying to decide what to do with Richardson. They had also been contemplating the question of their own likely fates should he escape the noose. Twice Chief Justice Lynde came to Hutchinson "with his resignation in his pocket";

twice Hutchinson persuaded him to stay. Hutchinson thought Judge Trowbridge even more timid and unreliable in the face of pressure. Neither threats nor newspaper attacks daunted Judge Oliver; Hutchinson hoped Judge Cushing would follow his lead. In any event, the judicial quartet struck Hutchinson as sounder than any new judges he could have appointed who would have accepted the appointments or been acceptable to the radicals.[68]

Still nervous, Lynde joined some of the lawyers at John Adams's for the midday meal on September 6; then all proceeded to court for the examination of Richardson's jurors. The testimony quickly made clear that the exhortations of the courtroom crowd had indeed reached the jurors' ears. The jurors also revealed that from the beginning of their deliberations, most of them had wanted to convict. The only real hold-out, Thomas Lothrop, had finally come around about half an hour before the jury returned to the courtroom the next morning, when his fellows convinced him that the judges' unanimously expressed belief that Richardson was innocent meant that the court would take proper steps to save his life.[69]

Sampson for Blowers, arguing Richardson, put a mass of English case law before the judges. Unfortunately for him, and them, and Richardson, the law as it then stood afforded no real remedy in such cases. The inviolability of a jury verdict had become so sacred a principle that the court felt itself helpless. And yet the judges wanted desperately not to have to sentence Richardson, since the only possible punishment was death. Baffled and uneasy, they once again put the matter over for consideration. The public, unaware of the delicate legal problem, tended to regard the court's inaction as merely another example of judicial and loyalist chicanery.

The second provocative action of the court had followed hard upon the first. On September 7, Preston, the soldiers, and the four civilians were formally arraigned. Each man in turn pleaded not guilty. "How wilt thou be tried?" the clerk asked. "By God and my country [i.e., jury]," each said; no murder case could be judge-tried. "God send thee a good deliverance," the clerk answered. But the very next day, with ten days left before the next scheduled out-county sitting, the court abruptly adjourned the Suffolk sitting to the end of October. This upset both parties. The radicals saw it as yet another delay, a possible suggestion that the trials would never be held at all. Hutchinson and the military men wanted an immediate trial, for reasons of simple geography. Boston's present temper seemed reasonably conducive to as impartial a trial as might be expected. Moreover, should the case be tried in early September and the anticipated conviction result, Hutchinson would still have time to request a pardon from London and to receive it before the travel-stopping winter storms. So attractive had this strategy seemed to the defendants that Preston had even petitioned the court in early September for a prompt trial. Now, however, with the case put off until late October, even if the judges delayed sentencing until the next Suffolk term (March 1771), the pardon would not have time to arrive before that term opened. Once the defendants came up for sentencing then, the court would not dare to procrastinate further. Any additional delay in sentencing (or, for that matter, in execution) would almost certainly touch off a Porteous-type lynching or a severe civil disturbance.[70]

All this pressed on Hutchinson's attention as he tried to concoct some way of carrying out his orders without setting Boston, as he himself put it, "in a flame." His first inclination was to correspond further with Gage. But before the dispatch was ready, he realized that delay would only increase his problems. Word of the plan would almost certainly leak out, "and the execution of it be rendered," in Hutchinson's understatement, "more difficult, if not impracticable; and all the consequences of the delay would be charged upon [me]." He resolved, therefore, to act. After writing the necessary orders to the provincial commandant, he assembled the council, stated without calling for discussion the king's instructions, and immediately went out to the Castle to oversee the transfer ceremonies. Rather than commission Dalrymple, Hutchinson had chosen to regard him as merely the officer designated by the governor to command the Castle. To forestall other objections, he formally directed the provincial storekeeper to remain in custody of the supplies and ammunition; and he assigned another provincial officer to perform watchkeeping duties with respect to passing ships. He also tried to find employment for some of the provincial garrison displaced by the change.[71]

Although these precautions softened the reaction, they could not entirely mute it. Frightened, Hutchinson stayed at the Castle for a few nights until things quieted down. The legislature chivvied him about the transfer, and declared a day of fast and prayer for the House and council. But no serious trouble resulted. The crown officials now possessed a secure fortress of refuge should one be needed. Further, at least six warships rode to anchors in the harbor or rested at wharfs in the town.[72]

Perhaps one reason for the radicals' tameness on the castle issue was their growing realization that the nonimportation movement, so productive of passion and violence, was—temporarily at least—gently dying. The New York merchants had abandoned the cause in midsummer; Philadelphia was about to follow. By October 12, the Boston merchants had also decided to quit. If anything, the possibility of a fair trial had improved.[73]

CHAPTER 18

REX v. *PRESTON*

During the long interval which followed the joint arraignment on September 7, Adams, Auchmuty, and Quincy found themselves facing a difficult problem of tactics and what we today would call professional ethics. It was a problem which concerned Adams more than the others, since only he would be appearing and arguing in both trials. The difficulty arose from a simple fact: Captain Preston had not directly killed or wounded anyone. He stood accused simply of ordering his men to fire without sufficient provocation. All the killing had been done by the men. Captain Preston's best defense, therefore, would consist simply of a denial that he had ordered the shooting. Conversely, the men would want to show that in pulling the triggers, they had merely followed their officer's orders, as indeed on pain of death they were bound to do.

Gage, who generally tended to fulfill the stereotype of the supremely confident absentee client, did not regard this problem as serious. He recommended relying, in Captain Preston's as well as the soldiers' cases, entirely on a theory of self-defense. The prisoners, he argued, ought simply to prove "that the People were in search of them, which indicates premeditated Mischief, that they were grossly assaulted and attacked with Provocation, and to support the Degree of Violence in the attack to have been such, as to endanger their Lives." Whether Preston gave the order or not, Gage thought, "seems a Circumstance something stronger in his particular favour, and nothing more." [1]

Gage had grossly over-simplified. Underlying both cases was the legal principle that, once the fact of killing had been proved, the killer bore the burden of convincing the jury that the homicide was legally justified. But of course, before this burden could be thrust upon any defendant, the crown had to prove that that particular defendant had killed one of the victims. Proving that any given soldier had killed any given person was going to be difficult; proving that the firing as a whole had killed men would be simple. Lurking in the background was the argument that some of the deceased had died from civilian musketry; but it could be expected that the radicals would soft-pedal that argument during the trial of the military men. In any event, Auchmuty, the ultraloyal crown servant, would never participate in any attempt to vindicate the soldiers and Captain Preston at the expense of the civilians.

Thus, even though the crown might very well fail to prove that any particular soldier killed any particular victim, it might easily convince the jury that the killings, generally, were the captain's fault. Conversely, Captain Preston would be entirely content to see the prosecution establish beyond reasonable doubt that Kilroy, for example, had shot Gray, so long as the crown was unable to prove that Preston had given the fatal command. In short, trying Preston and his men simultaneously would almost certainly lead to the kind of mutual finger-pointing which would tempt the jurors, already hostile, and convinced by biblical instinct and radical propaganda that blood required blood, to convict all the defendants.

Severing the trials, however, would not solve John Adams's professional problem. His duty to Preston might, and probably would, require him to contend during the captain's trial for that which his duty to the soldiers would eventually require him to oppose. Today, one of the American Bar Association's Canons of Professional Ethics explicitly prohibits a lawyer from entertaining such a conflict of interests. He must relinquish one client or the other. In 1770, no such formal strictures bound attorneys. Adams and Quincy remained counsel in both cases. However, the day Preston's trial commenced, some of the soldiers raised the matter themselves. They petitioned that the superior court "would be so good as to lett us have our Trial at the same time with our Captain, for we did our Captains orders and if we don't Obay is Command we should have been Confine'd and shott for not doing of it." And, the petition continued, hinting at the reason for the lawyers' apparent insensitivity to the conflict, "we only desire to Open the truth before our Captains face for it is very hard he being a Gentelman should have more chance for to save his life than we poor men that is Oblidged to Obay his command." [2]

None of the surviving notes, correspondence, or diaries indicate that anyone else gave the problem significant attention. As late as October 23, the date to which the court had been adjourned, William Palfrey was still referring to "the trial" (in the singular) "of Captain Preston and the soldiers." By 8 A.M. the next morning, however, when the court opened, the question had been resolved. Despite his men's request to be tried with him, Preston stood alone in the dock.[3]

A legal skirmish developed immediately. Preston's counsel had of course realized from the start the overriding importance of ensuring, as much as the circumstances would permit, an impartial jury. Besides a still-inflamed public opinion, Preston had also to contend with the effects of Sam Adams's propaganda and of the perhaps inadvertent appearance in Boston of Bowdoin's printed *Short Narrative*. Selection of what lawyers call an indifferent jury would require shrewd judgment, based on knowledge of the personalities of the prospective jurors.

A statute required the veniremen to be picked by a method ostensibly impartial and unobjectionable. Upon the receipt of the *venire facias*, the court's writ commanding the selection, each town in the county would, from a list previously prepared by the selectmen, draw as in a lottery the names of as many veniremen as the writ commanded. Thus Boston would send eighteen veniremen, Dorchester three, Braintree two, and so on. The governing statute permitted the town meeting to discard the name of any prospective venireman who was, in the sole judgment of the Town, unable to serve as a juror. This power, the conservatives feared, would allow the radicals to pack the venire wherever (as in Boston) they controlled the town meeting. Moreover, the statute had expired in July; although it would be revived on November 15, in time for the men's trial, when the venire to try Preston was being selected, the towns were free to follow any procedure they wished, so long as it produced the required number of veniremen. "The nomination of Jurors," Dalrymple lamented, "is now more in the hands of people than ever before."[4]

Whether the radical chiefs' close connection to John Adams and Quincy might have influenced the former to refrain from loading the panel with Sons of Liberty is of course impossible to determine. No surviving documents discuss the point. The venire list in the court files includes only two names identifiable as Sons of Liberty, Solomon Davis, a ship captain and owner, and Fortesque Vernon, a merchant. Thus one could just as well argue that the venire was chosen without any regard to the politics of prospective veniremen.[5]

Defense counsel doubtless knew the names of all the Boston jurors. They probably did not have the veniremen from the country towns. And they had certainly not been furnished with a list of the full panel,

although a British statute guaranteed defendants in England the right
to receive a copy at least two days before trial. Auchmuty and Adams
made this failure their first resistance point. They did not move, as a
modern-day lawyer might, to quash the entire panel. Instead, they
argued that Preston's not having been given a copy of the panel constituted a valid "cause" for challenging individual jurors. The point was
worth belaboring, because in settling a jury to try Preston, his attorneys would be entitled to an unlimited number of challenges "for
cause." No Massachusetts statute governed the permissible number of
"peremptory" challenges—challenges for which no cause need be assigned. The Massachusetts courts had adopted the English common-
law rule which allowed twenty peremptory challenges in a murder
trial. Then, as now, lawyers tended to hoard "peremptories." The
judges "divided on the question" Preston's counsel raised, but apparently ruled against them. To prevent a recurrence of the issue, however, the court ordered "a panel of the Jury to be given whenever
asked for" in the future.[6]

Three additional technical points briefly occupied bar and bench.
The existing documents are either silent or cryptic, so it is difficult
accurately to reconstruct what happened. Apparently, the defense
argued that the indictments were insufficient, because they did not
charge each soldier with having shot each of the deceased. The indictment against Warren, for example, alleged only that he had shot Attucks. If the evidence at the trial tended to prove that not Warren but
White shot Attucks, could Preston be convicted of aiding and abetting
Warren in the killing of Attucks? This issue the court seems to have
disposed of by recourse to the principle which was to govern both the
trials: if any of the soldiers gave the mortal wound, anyone who was
present, aiding, and abetting in the shooting (as Preston would be if it
were proved he ordered the firing), was guilty as a principal.

Another dispute concerned the crown's right to challenge prospective jurors. Again, no record of resolution has survived. The figures on
Preston's challenges, however, coupled with a clear indication (which
we will shortly examine) that the prosecution would have challenged
certain jurors if it could, suggest that only the defense was permitted
to challenge. Finally, the lawyers and the court discussed—the precise
procedural context is unclear—a basic evidentiary question: would either side be permitted to offer evidence of "previous threats." No surviving record indicates the outcome, but no such testimony appears to
have been introduced.[7]

The preliminaries over, the actual impaneling began. Preston's lawyers apparently established early that they had not received the names
of two veniremen (including one from Adams's past and future home

town, Braintree). The prosecutors agreed the pair should not be sworn and that neither would cost the defense a "peremptory." We do not know just how the jury was picked. Presumably the clerk drew twelve names and seated the men in the jury box. The defense then exercised its challenges, the clerk substituting a new man for every one challenged. Despite its lack of a venire list, the defense did not face the array ignorantly. Plump Gilbert Deblois, the well-to-do Boston merchant whose stock-in-trade, along with his loyalist principles, had somehow survived the various nonimportation crises, had given Preston political background information about as many jurors as he could, particularly the ones from Boston.[8]

The exact order in which the veniremen came and went is still unknown. But the court files show that of the first twenty-two called (not counting the two challenged by consent), Preston challenged fifteen, seven of them from Boston. Of the seven jurors who had been seated, only two were Bostonians, one of whom, William Frobisher, the foreman, was Boston's leading soapmaker, well known for his potash-refining schemes and for his futile battles to wring monetary recompense for them out of the legislature.[9]

The clerk had now reached the end of the eligible veniremen. In 1770, as today, this meant that the appropriate officer (in those days, the sheriff) would collar spectators, or if necessary, passers-by, and convey them to the jury box. Seven such onlookers, talesmen, as they were and are called, came before the bench. Four of them Preston challenged, three others gave various excuses which convinced the court to let them go: Henry Bromfield was a justice of the peace; William Boardman had sat on the coroner's jury which investigated Gray's death; a Mr. Procter candidly declared himself "under Biass"—this may have been the high Son of Liberty Edward Procter who earlier in the year led the assault on Richardson and testified against him at his trial.[10]

Five seats remained empty. At this point, with the sheriff and his deputies seeking talesmen, Gilbert Deblois eased his way into the trial. By means unknown, he not only "got himself put on the Pannel," but brought with him four other men, each laboring under a loyalist "Biass" as heavy as the Whig variety which afflicted Mr. Procter. Philip Dumaresq's name had originally been drawn from the box at the Boston Town Meeting. But he had previously been heard to say that he "believed Captain Preston to be as innocent as the Child unborn," and that if he happened to be on the jury he "would never convict him if he sat to all eternity." It is not clear whether Dumaresq, conscious of his predispositions, had requested the meeting to relieve him, or if the managers had performed the service for him, unasked. At any rate, now that jurors were in short supply, here was Dumaresq, following Deblois into the jury box. Behind Dumaresq came William Hill, the baker who made a living supplying bread to the Fourteenth Regiment, quondam surety for the soldiers in the Riley riot. The next talesman was William Wait Wallis, Deblois's brother-in-law; juror Number Twelve was an avowed loyalist, Joseph Barrick.[11]

The word "pack" is used with frequent looseness in legal contexts, so perhaps we should not join the ultraradical William Palfrey in his violent denunciation of the "evident management to pack the jury." Still, recalling that Massachusetts practice required a unanimous jury for conviction, we can probably be fairly sure that before a single witness had been sworn, the outcome of the trial was certain. Not even a Richardson-type mob would be likely to frighten Deblois and Dumaresq. Nor would even the strongest evidence operate to drive them to convict Preston. In civil cases, a statute required the court on motion to ask each prospective juror whether he had "directly or indirectly given his opinion, or is sensible of any prejudice" in the case. This statute did not, by its terms, apply to criminal matters. Apparently no one pressed the inquiry upon the five talesmen. Why the radicals permitted the packing is a mystery, explicable, perhaps, by Sam Adams's absence from the courtroom.[12]

Because of the jury's composition, the only doubt and excitement depended upon the slender possibility that the evidence would turn out so overwhelmingly unfavorable to Preston that not even a loyalist could avoid his oath: "You shall well and truly try and true deliverance make between our sovereign lord . . . the king . . . , and the prisoner at the bar, whom you shall have in charge according to the evidence. So help you God." Apart from that small chance, the trial, as lawyers and judges must have known, was nothing but a propaganda battle. Yet everyone acted as though a life were really at stake. That continuing charade was the most significant aspect of the entire proceedings.

The jury's apparent predisposition to acquit lent irony to the Bowdoin committee's effort to suppress American distribution of the *Short Narrative*. And it rendered irrelevant the public appearance of the depositions in Boston during the summer. Whether the spread of the materials had been inadvertent or deliberate, with this particular jury, the *Narrative* stood little chance of inciting the conviction the radicals hoped for and the loyalists feared. What effect the *Narrative* would have produced had the trial been "straight" no one can tell. Copies of the pamphlet were lying on one of the courtroom tables during Preston's trial, and the men's too. Even under the favorable tactical conditions which prevailed in the jury box, John Adams, for one, felt that the publication was "an accidental misfortune" to Preston. Paine responded archly that, on the contrary, the printing of the evidence was "a service to" Preston, "as he knew how to shape his defense." My own conclusion, after comparing the depositions with several deponents' trial testimony, is that the latter followed the former pretty closely. Some of the discrepancies are, as will shortly appear, serious. None of them, however, justifies the judges' comment, relayed privately to Hillsborough by Hutchinson, that the crown's witnesses "differed materially in their evidence, from the Depositions." [13]

Only fifteen of the ninety-six deponents testified in Preston's trial. The real vice of the *Narrative* and its pre-trial Boston publication lay in the other eighty-one depositions, filled with gross hearsay, inadmissible evidence, and vividly irrelevant, one-sided case histories of soldier-civilian frictions. It is impossible, even today, to read the *Narrative* and the depositions without feeling at the end that the soldiers were aggressive, trouble-making bully boys, and that while perhaps they did not plan the Massacre exactly as it eventuated, they certainly were looking to do physical harm to the civilians. Had the trial not been fixed, the *Narrative*, coming as it did to a population preheated by the wild antimilitary fictions of Sam Adams's "Journal of the Times," would have been a classic example of the extrajudicial statement that prejudices a fair trial.

Acting as though the outcome were fairly doubtful, Samuel Quincy opened for the crown. As the junior member of the prosecution team, it would be his job first to describe the crown's evidence, then to examine the prosecution witnesses, and finally to summarize the testimony before the defense opened. We do not know whether he went on to cross-examine the defense witnesses, or if instead he left that job to Paine. At any rate, Paine, as senior crown counsel, would deliver the closing jury argument.

No substantial eyewitness account of either Preston's trial or the men's has come down to us, so it is difficult to depict it accurately. It took place in the still-new courthouse on Queen (now Court) Street. The courtroom, on the second floor, was approximately thirty-five feet wide, of an unknown depth. Before a chimney and fireplace stood the bench, so-called, a table long enough to accommodate the five-judge court. A witness stand, about six feet from the judges, a jury box, clerk's desk, and counsel tables spread in front of the bench. Somewhere behind the barristers' chairs, a bar must have run across the room; near that, a box for the prisoner, perhaps even a modified cage of some sort. The remaining free area of the courtroom was filled with standing spectators. Just how many onlookers the room accomodated, we do not know. By putting together bits of testimony from both trials, we can be fairly sure that about sixty nonparticipants attended the soldiers' trial; it is doubtful that any fewer would have watched Preston's. Members of the army, the navy, and the customs service predominated among the bystanders, and behaved, one of the radicals admitted, with "the greatest order and decorum." Dalrymple, in turn, described the Whig spectators' behavior in an identical phrase.[14]

All the preliminary arguments and the extended impaneling had left little time on the first day for evidence. The crown could put on only eight witnesses before the adjournment. A modern lawyer might think that eight witnesses in less than one trial day of a major case represented exceptional efficiency. Colonial practitioners worked considerably faster. The courts ordinarily turned over civil litigation at a rate frequently reaching six verdicts daily. Criminal cases took somewhat longer to try. But even there, the pace was rapid. Up to Preston's trial, no criminal case had ever required more than one day to try (although, as in Richardson's trial, the jury might occasionally argue overnight before returning a verdict).[15]

Samuel Quincy's opening, his terse statement of the crown's contentions and the evidence he anticipated introducing to support them, has not survived. The testimony of the first day's witnesses, however, made the prosecution's strategy quite clear. Edward Garrick, the young apprentice wigmaker, led off for the crown. He described his scuffle with the sentry, White, and said he had seen sword-carrying soldiers in the streets before the Preston party turned out. The second witness, Thomas Marshal, the tailor-militiaman, picked up the last point. He told the jury he had seen at least two such groups, one on King Street, the other on Royal Exchange Lane, both yelling: "Fire," and "Let them come, by Jesus." At first certain that the soldiers' shouts of "Fire" had preceded the bells, Marshal, on cross-examination, conceded uncertainty. But in recounting the actual shooting, he was sure that between the first shot and the others "there was time enough for an officer to step forward and give the word 'Recover' if he was so minded." That was a telling point. Before the crown had even put on a shred of evidence that Preston had ordered the firing, it was arguing that whether or not he initially gave the order, he could and should have acted to minimize the bloodshed.

At this point in the narrative, it might be well to emphasize a *caveat*. No analysis or description of a long-past trial can be any more accurate than the record upon which it is based. A contemporaneous letter by William Palfrey says that Justice of the Peace James Murray attended the trial and "employ'd a Scotch underling of [Mein's] to take down in Short hand all the Witnesses said in favor of Capt. Preston, and the arguments of the Council in his behalf, without noticing anything that was offer'd on the other side." Forty-six years later, Adams himself said much the same thing. In a letter to Gage after the trial, Preston reported that the testimony in his trial was recorded stenographically, and that Auchmuty was "correct[ing]" it. Nothing in Murray's published correspondence supports the assertion that he arranged for a reporter, and no transcript, slanted though it might be, has survived. Someone, however, took down at least part of the trial. A subsequent newspaper article by Richard Palmes included a stenographic-type account of his own testimony; he did not disclose who the reporter was.[16]

Without a transcript, how can one describe the trial? A summary of each witness's testimony was prepared immediately after the trial, apparently at Hutchinson's request, for transmittal to Lord Hillsborough. Robert Treat Paine's courtroom minutes have likewise survived.[17] Together, these give us, if not a verbatim transcript, the next best thing; indeed, the only thing. The degree of accuracy is admittedly an open question. Because, however, the two tend to corroborate each other, and because no one has been able to show any serious mistakes, I have decided to rely on them fully.

Neither courtroom minutes, summarized testimony, nor—in the soldiers' trial—the allegedly verbatim transcript demarcate between direct and cross-examination. One cannot say with precision just which phase of the testimony produced any given item of evidence. Wherever I have ascribed certain testimony to cross-examination, I have done so purely from (a) the context and (b) an informed surmise, reinforced occasionally by an acquired feeling that the matter in question is something no sane trial lawyer would willingly bring out on direct examination. (How frequently a witness may have "surprised" the side calling him is, of course, unascertainable; the possibility does increase my chance for error.)

Although the witnesses who followed Marshal testified that the townspeople were insulting the soldiers and taunting them, they also began to tie Preston to the firing. Peter Cunningham did not hear any order given to fire. On direct examination, as in his earlier deposition, he said he heard Preston give the command to prime and load; on cross-examination he admitted that the man who gave the order did so while his back was toward Cunningham. But he insisted vehemently that the man who gave that command was dressed in red, with a sash and no musket—in other words, dressed like an officer.

The last two witnesses of the day hurt Preston badly, or rather, would have hurt him had the outcome been truly doubtful. The first, William Wyat, said he had heard Preston say "Damn your bloods, fire, be the consequence what it will." He had also heard Preston warned

to be careful as he marched the men down. Wyat admitted the crowd
was shouting "Fire, damn you, fire." But he had no doubt that Preston,
wearing a "cloth-coloured surtout" (i.e., a neutral-colored overcoat),
had ordered the priming, loading, and firing.[18] Under cross-examination, he conceded that the overcoat-wearer was the man who first
spoke to Preston; and he also admitted that after the shooting, Preston
had struck up the gun barrels and damned the men for firing. Still,
that was what a quick-thinking officer, suddenly aware of a blunder,
might say in trying to gloss over his mistake. The next witness, John
Cox, pushed the point farther. He positively identified Preston, wearing a red coat and epaulet, and insisted that even after the firing Preston said "Damn your bloods, fire again, let the consequence be what it
will."

When it became obvious to the court that the trial would not be
completed in one day or even two days, steps had to be taken to protect the jury. Obviously, the judges could not follow the common-law
rule which deprived the jurors of food, drink, light, and fire until they
produced a verdict. But common-law practice would not allow the jurymen to return to their homes nightly. Even if this could lawfully be
done, common sense dictated that the jurors be sequestered from the
volatile Boston populace. Further, in those times of foot and horse
travel, jurors like Josiah Sprague, from Hingham, and Joseph Guild,
from Dedham, would have spent much of the recess just commuting.
Moreover, Judge Trowbridge, still in poor health, "ever had a tedious
way of doing business and was afraid of sitting after night lest the
people should offer insults." To solve all the problems, the prosecution,
the defense, and the court agreed that each side would name a keeper,
the two then to be locked up with the jurors in the nearby house of the
jail keeper. Bedding, food, and liquor would be supplied, the latter not
such a surprising item in those days when men "sought to refresh their
spirits and re-create their flagging energies by drinking enormous
quantities of cider, beer, wine, and rum." The county provided the
men with hearty breakfasts; at noon they got punch, biscuit, and
cheese; in the evening, punch, wine, flip, and toddy with their supper.
Pipes and tobacco were sometimes brought, and on Sunday, a large
dinner.[19]

When the trial resumed on Thursday morning, October 25, the
crown's case temporarily faltered. Theodore Bliss testified that Preston
admitted the soldiers' muskets were loaded. But although Bliss was
standing very close to Preston, he could not remember whether the
captain was wearing a surtout. Preston, he recalled, stood in front of
the guns. Somebody was shouting "Fire," but Bliss did not think it was
Preston. He did recall seeing snowballs and a three-foot-long stick hit

the grenadier who then fired the first musket; and he admitted that he himself tried to strike Preston after that shot.

Henry Knox told of Preston's stopping on the way down to hear Knox warn him that his life would answer for his men's firing. Knox was allowed to testify that he believed the sentry "scared, but in no danger." Cross-examination brought out that Knox had heard the crowd shouting "Fire, damn your blood, fire." On the tantalizing question of the surtout, Knox contributed his recollection that it had been Corporal Wemms who was thus attired. "I had none," he hastily added, lest someone conclude from Wyat's testimony that Knox had been the man who ordered the firing.

What Bliss and Knox had to say merely increased the confusion. If anything, their testimony strengthened the loyalist argument that the crowd's violence and taunting had provoked the tragedy. Benjamin Burdick, who came next, did nothing to help. He said he heard the word "Fire" come from behind the soldiers, but he could not testify that he had seen Preston give the command; the only order, indeed, which he attributed to Preston was the post-firing striking up of the muskets. He heard Preston say nothing else except "Perhaps you may," in "melancholy" response to Burdick's staring at the men for the announced purpose of later swearing to their identities. Weak as Burdick's testimony had been, the cross-examination demolished it entirely. Under pressure, Burdick admitted what he had until this time not publicly disclosed, not even in his published deposition, that he was carrying his highland broadsword. Carrying it, and preparing, should any soldier step out of rank to push a bayonet at him, to "cut his head off." Burdick also conceded that he "thought" he saw "something thrown over the heads." [20]

When the next witness, Robert Fullerton, could only repeat the familiar account of the shouts of "Fire" and "They durst not fire," the crown's case appeared to be crumbling completely. Fullerton could not even remember hearing an order to load. At this low point, Samuel Quincy put on the crown's best witness. Daniel Calef "heard the officer who stood on the right in a line with the soldiers give the word fire twice." Unlike some of the earlier witnesses, Calef had no doubts at all: "I looked the officer in the face when he gave the word and saw his mouth. He had on a red coat, yellow jacket, and silver laced hat, no trimming on his [waist]coat." It was a perfect description of Preston's uniform.[21]

Calef had not finished. "The prisoner is the officer I mean. I saw his face plain, the moon shone in it. I am sure of the man though I have not seen him since before yesterday when he came into Court with others. I knew him instantly." Then, for a final fillip: "The officer had no surtout on." If the jurors believed Calef and regarded their oath, the only possible verdict was "Guilty."

Quickly pushing his advantage, Quincy put on Robert Goddard. Although outwardly Goddard seemed "not capable of making Observations," and lacking "ordinary Understanding," he told a damning story. After the party came down, he said, about fifty boys gathered around, throwing snowballs. "Go home," Preston told them, "lest there be murder done." The boys threw more snowballs. Preston went behind the soldiers and told them to fire. One musket went off. A sailor or a "Townsman" struck Preston. In his deposition, Goddard had described the assailant as "a man like a sailor"; now by mentioning the possibility that Preston had in fact been assaulted by a Bostonian, rather than some nautical outsider, Goddard was giving the defense a highly exploitable opportunity. For the moment, however, Goddard's story greatly aided the crown. After being hit, Goddard testified, Preston stood behind the men with his sword drawn and swore "Damn your bloods, fire! Think I'll be treated in this manner?" Whereupon the men fired. Preston ordered them to prime and load again.[22]

The cross-examination sought to shake Goddard's identification of Preston. It failed miserably. Goddard described how he had positively identified Preston for the grand jury; and he related Preston's equivocal "If you swear that, you will ruin me everlastingly." Goddard was positive that Preston alone had given the fatal order. "I was so near the officer when he gave the word fire that I could touch him. His face was towards me." Again: "I looked him in the face." And still again: "When he told 'em to fire he turnd about to me. I lookd him in the face."

Having scored such impressive hits, why did not the prosecution rest then and there? Why did not the crown end its case on an upbeat, as sound trial strategy usually dictates? Two reasons suggest themselves. First, despite their dramatic impact on the written record, Calef and Goddard, in the flesh, may well have been so unimpressive that Paine and Quincy felt obliged to bring in more substantial witnesses. A likelier explanation, particularly in view of the trial's predetermined outcome, is that the prosecutors, especially Paine, felt that the evidence adduced thus far had not sufficiently depicted either the lack of provocation or the consequently unjustified nature of Preston's response.

Whatever the crown's aim, it missed. Obadiah Whiston, the battling blacksmith of the Ness-Molesworth affair, added nothing. Dimond Morton, a radical sympathizer, even subtracted something: he insisted Preston was wearing a surtout. Nathaniel Fosdick improved matters slightly. Preston, he insisted, was holding his sword; he wore regimentals and a wig, but no surtout. Fosdick heard no order to load. He did hear the word "Fire," but Preston's back was to him, so he only thought, albeit strongly, that it was the captain who gave the order. He saw no snowballs thrown, no blows at all given, no stick hit Montgomery.

The next witness faced an unusual difficulty. He was Jonathan Williams Austin, Adams's law clerk. Today, if an attorney's employee testified voluntarily against his senior's client, disciplinary action against one or both would almost certainly follow.[23] But in 1770, as we have had reason to appreciate, the concept of undivided loyalty to one's client had not yet reached its present intensity; no one questioned the propriety of Austin's testifying. There could be no issue of revealing client's secrets, because Austin merely testified to what he saw in King Street. The result was hardly worth the crown's while or the court's time. Austin "heard no orders to prime and load nor the word given, fire."

The prosecution's case continued to fizzle. Langford, the town watchman, insisted he had heard absolutely no words of assault, no shouts, no jeering. This is a good example of the sort of witness trial lawyers frequently encounter: in his desire to exhibit a helpful memory, he recounts a story so favorable to the side calling him that his testimony, completely at variance with the other witnesses', falls of its own absurdity. As if trying to compensate, Langford did say he remembered hearing the word "Fire"; typically, he could not identify the speaker. Francis Archibald, Jr., continued the feeble parade. In his deposition, he had sworn in fierce detail to the rowdy conduct of the soldiers in the Cornhill area during the evening of March 5. At the trial, naturally, he could not mention any of this, because it was irrelevant even to the issue of provocation. Like Langford, Archibald saw neither snowballs nor thrown sticks.[24]

It is an axiom of litigation that a case should open with a strong witness, and also close with one. In *Rex* v. *Preston*, the crown lawyers put all their good witnesses in the middle. They had nothing left for a suitable finale but Isaac Pierce, Joseph Belknap (Hutchinson's guide), and Selectman Jonathan Mason. None of this trio had seen the firing or its antecedents. They could only relate—with reasonable unanimity —Hutchinson's angry interview with Preston afterward at the head of King Street, and Preston's justification, variously remembered as "to save my sentry," "to save my men" (a switch from Belknap's earlier recollection: "I did it for my own safety"), and "his men were insulted and abused." This evidence, introduced to show Preston's state of mind at the time of the firing, was of course hearsay. It was admissible, however, by an exception to the hearsay rule which permits the court to receive and consider a defendant's admissions. Why did not the crown put on Samuel Drowne, whose deposition had been in Hutchinson's view "the strongest" against Preston? Perhaps the radicals "did not think fit to produce" as a star witness a man well known in Boston for his feeblemindedness.[25]

With this concerted whimper, the crown's evidence closed. Following usual practice, Samuel Quincy ought then to have summed up the testimony. The court, however, had heard fifteen witnesses that day, so Quincy only quoted a few appropriate legal treatises to the jury. "Not such killing only as proceeds from premeditated hatred or revenge against the person killed," he read, "but also in many other cases, such as is accompanied with those circumstances that shew the heart to be perversly wicked, is adjudged to be of malice prepense [i.e., aforethought], and consequently murder." A quotation from Lord Coke advised the jurors that under appropriate circumstances, even if an act be done without thinking, "the law implieth malice." And to ensure the jury's appreciation that to establish malice aforethought the crown need not prove extended advance planning, Quincy read from an opinion of the great English chief justice, John Holt: "He that doth a cruel act voluntarily doth it of malice prepense." With that, the crown rested.

The eighteenth century knew no such practice as moving for a directed acquittal at the close of the prosecution's evidence, so the end of crown's case would have afforded a convenient stopping place. But the judges, although realizing that the trial could not possibly finish that afternoon, chose to push on. Adams, therefore, rose to make his opening, of which no note or minute remains. Immediately thereafter he began calling witnesses. Like the prosecution, the defense started with scene-setting witnesses: Brazen Head Jackson told of Preston's summons; Edward Hill described the threats to the Main Guard and the sentinel, as did Benjamin Davis, Sr. Davis also told of being clapped on the shoulder and asked to "go and help fight the soldiers." He refused; his anonymous inquisitor told him to "note the clock," and rushed off shouting "Fire." None of the witnesses had much to say about Preston's activity at the Custom House. Hill saw him after the firing, pushing up a musket and telling the soldier: "Fire no more. You have done mischief enough." After this, the court, having heard eighteen witnesses, an argument, and an opening, finally called an adjournment.

The third trial day marked the high point of the testimony. Twenty-two witnesses took the stand, not counting Theodore Bliss, whom the crown called back twice for brief rebuttal. Preston himself did not testify. This was not mere invocation of the right against self-incrimination. By eighteenth-century rules of evidence, the accused in a criminal case, like the parties in a civil one, could not legally take the stand, even on his own behalf. In both instances, the law reasoned that the certainty of perjury by the interested litigant overcame whatever truth-finding value his evidence might afford. Preston was therefore a legally incompetent witness.

None of the men testified, either. They would have been eligible, and their testimony at least as to the provocation might have helped Preston. But they probably could have refused to give under oath answers which might have incriminated them. And if the unsuccessful petition for a joint trial reflected the consensus of the soldiers' recollections, their insistence that they fired only in response to Preston's orders might well have compelled a conviction. The crown had not called them, although it could have tried to do so, because, as suggested earlier, the more the men did to hang Preston, the harder would be the prosecution's later task of convicting them.[26]

Though neither Preston himself nor his men testified for the captain, the witnesses who did take the stand that twenty-sixth of October sealed his acquittal. Their testimony generally was so strong that even an honest jury would probably have acquitted him. The very first witness, Joseph Edwards, dispelled the lingering belief that Preston's ordering the men to load their empty muskets could somehow be utilized to support a conviction. It was the corporal, with the chevrons on his arm looking in the moonlight like rips, said Edwards, who had given the order to prime and load (and loaded his own weapon, too).

Preston's uniform had attracted two of the witnesses. John Frost and Benjamin Leigh, both apprentices, remembered his gaudy regimentals, the crimson silk sash around his body, the crescent-shaped silver gorget glinting on his chest, the sword in his hand. Like a half-dozen other witnesses who testified after them, Frost and Leigh recalled the taunts, shouts, and threats that the crowd spattered over Preston and his men. But who had put the cry of "Fire" into a command? Jane Whitehouse, White's friend, was sure the order came from a man standing behind the soldiers, dressed in dark-colored clothes. By statute in Massachusetts, witnesses and jurors swore their respective oaths simply by raising the right hand and repeating the ritualistic promise. At the end of Jane Whitehouse's testimony somebody in the courtroom recalled that she "thought there was no obligation from oaths administered by holding up the hand." So a Bible was brought, and she took the oath on it, probably retrospectively. Strangely enough, the only other witness who was thus sworn, a sailor named James Waddel, corroborated her story. He, too, had seen a "person like a gentleman walking behind the soldiers dressed in blue or black velvet or plush," telling them "Fire!"

The defense evidence certainly was beginning to create a picture of confusion, noise, and verbal threats. Whitehouse and Waddel had, at the least, raised serious doubts that the order to fire came from Preston. Other testimony made it seem likely that some deeper force than a simple military command had ignited the volley. "The soldiers," said Joseph Hilyer, "seemed to act pure nature . . . I mean they acted and fired by themselves."

The cumulation of testimony makes it impossible to say just when Preston's acquittal became assured. In a case so full of factual uncertainty and evidentiary conflict, one can hardly pick out the turning point. But two witnesses, testifying around midday on October 26, seem to have ensured the "reasonable doubt" which would hold even a "straight" jury from a verdict of guilty.

Richard Palmes, merchant and quondam Son of Liberty, recounted in explicit detail his peace efforts at Murray's barracks, his subsequent walk to King Street, and his approach to Preston. Theodore Bliss, Palmes said, was there already, asking Preston "Why don't you fire?" and "God damn you, why don't you fire?" Palmes himself was wearing a cloth-colored surtout; at last that particular mystery was solved. Palmes's testimony dispelled another: Palmes heard the command "Fire" at the moment when Preston's face was toward him; while admitting the possibility that the captain had in fact given the order, Palmes insisted that even though he stood with his hand on Preston's shoulder he could not say who gave the word. Despite the slight equivocation, and Palmes's remark that between the first gun and the second, Preston had had time "to have spoke to his men," Palmes's testimony pointed to an acquittal. With good reason, Adams later called him "the most material witness in the case." Standing by Preston, immediately next to the musket barrels, so close to the muzzles that the first shot's flash scorched one elbow of his conspicuous surtout, Palmes did not see Preston give the order. The defense had in effect proved a negative.

In an apparent effort to discredit Palmes, the crown immediately recalled Theodore Bliss. Bliss, in turn, sought to bolster his own now-impeached testimony by swearing that he had previously related an account of the affair to John Coffin. This was evidently a foundation for the calling of Coffin, who would hopefully describe Bliss's account in such a way as simultaneously to rehabilitate Bliss's credibility and destroy Palmes's. This tactic, which would probably not be permitted today, had little effect. When after some delay Coffin was called, presumably as a crown witness, he remembered well enough that Bliss had spoken to him, but only to tell him that Preston had said the men would not fire and that Bliss did not think Preston gave the order to fire. While this may have discredited Palmes's account of Bliss's exhortations, it only reinforced the doubt that Preston had commanded the musketry.

More intriguing than the crown's exhumation of the Bliss-Coffin conversation is the defense's failure to introduce as a witness John Hickling. Hickling had been standing immediately next to Palmes and Preston. His deposition in the *Short Narrative* indicates that he would have corroborated Palmes in every material particular. Better still, he would have testified that he heard the word "Fire" given, "but by whom I know not; but concluded it did not come from the officer . . . as I was within a yard of him and must have heard him had he spoke it." [27] Why did not the defense call him? No one now knows. Perhaps he was a mariner, away on a voyage. Perhaps he was dead. Perhaps Preston's lawyers thought their case sufficiently sure without him.

Whatever its reason for not calling Hickling, the defense was not yet closing. Matthew Murray recounted seeing Preston conversing with an unknown man (probably Palmes) just as a stick or piece of ice struck Montgomery, who fired without orders. Then the second of the defense's key witnesses took the stand. Andrew had no last name. The records variously refer to him as "a Negro Servant," "Servant to Oliver Wendell," or "the Black." Whatever the euphemisms, Andrew was a slave, owned by the merchant Son of Liberty Oliver Wendell (Harvard 1753), grandfather of the Breakfast Table autocrat, great-grandfather of the Justice.[28]

Andrew delivered a long, coherent, detailed account of all the doings in King Street, starting before Preston brought the party down. He told of the shouts, the snowballs, the halloos that greeted Justice of the Peace Murray and his Riot Act, and the barrage that drove him off. He described the boy taunting Montgomery ("Damn you, you bloody back lobster! Are you going to stab me?") and the grenadier's frustrated reply ("By God, will I!") Andrew was sure that a knot of people came down King Street huzzaing, shouting "Damn 'em, they durst not fire. We ant afraid of them. Knock 'em over." One of them was a husky mulatto with a stick. He pushed to the front of the crowd and swung the stick first at Preston, standing talking with some people, then at Montgomery. A brief duel began, wood against bayonet; "Kill him. Knock him over!" cried the crowd. The soldier worked his weapon free; the crowd yelled more. Preston was standing out in front of his men, looking at the crowd, his back turned toward Andrew. A voice different from the rest cried "Fire" and the first gun went off. Although Andrew could not see Preston's face, he was, he told the court, "certain the voice came from beyond him."

Neither of the prosecutors had raised any formal exception to Andrew's credibility. Nonetheless, the defense took the unusual precaution of calling Oliver Wendell. "Andrew has lived with me ten years," Wendell said. "His character for truth, integrity, and understanding is good. He can read and write." Literate or not, Andrew's testimony heightened doubts that Preston gave the fatal command, and also re-emphasized the physical danger the soldiers had faced in King Street.

History has made much of Attucks as the first martyr to independence. Nobody talks of the three blacks whose testimony helped to prevent the wrong of Attucks's death from spawning the judicial murder of one or more of the nine Redcoats. Besides Andrew, Jack, the black "servant" [i.e., slave] of Dr. James Lloyd testified to the snow-balls and the shouts of "Fire." Newton Prince, a free black pastrycook from the West Indies, said he saw Preston's party go down and heard the crowd threaten the Main Guard. A little later he also heard curses and dares shouted at the soldiers, and the sticks clanging against the muskets. The people were crying "Fire" as they hit the guns. But Newton Prince, watching Captain Preston standing in front of his men, "heard no orders given to fire." [29]

To counter whatever effect the crown's testimony about Preston's post-shooting responses had had upon either the record or the jury, the defense called James Gifford, a captain in the Fourteenth, shortly to leave the army and begin a distinguished career as a writer of Unitarian tracts.[30] Gifford had talked with Preston about ten P.M.; "He told me he had sent a party to protect the sentinel." The men had fired, Preston said, adding somewhat disloyally that he "gave 'em no orders and they must take the consequences." This was hearsay, but no one objected. Gifford gave the court a bit of character evidence about Preston: "mild tempered, prudent, discreet," and, in response to a question asked either directly by the captain, or at his suggestion, a little expert opinion: Officers, Gifford said, never give the order to fire from charged bayonet [i.e., from muskets held hip high, bayonets extended]. Anyhow, said Gifford, had the men fired in response to a command, "they would all have fired together, or most of them."

Thomas Handasyd Peck, the fur exporter who had hurried to King Street at the sound of the guns, also added a good word for Preston. He too had seen Preston shortly after the shootings. "What have you done?" he recalled asking. "Sir," said Preston, again passing the blame to his men, "it was none of my doings, the soldiers fired of their own accord. I was in the street and might have been shot." Peck was also permitted to comment on Preston's character. It was, he thought, "good as a gentleman and a soldier. I think it exceeds any of the corps."

Throughout the trial, both prosecution and defense witnesses had testified only about the events in King Street itself. Neither side had introduced evidence of earlier menacing activity either by soldiers or by townsmen. Now, as the case was drawing to an end, John Gillespie took the stand and told of seeing a gang of townspeople, armed with clubs, sticks, and swords, coming up out of the South End about 7 P.M., at least two hours before the firing. No other witnesses testified to any similar event, because John Adams, vigorously overruling Josiah Quincy, refused to permit it. Auchmuty, the senior barrister, apparently left the examination of the witnesses entirely to Adams. Quincy had "devilled," or prepared, the evidence, feeding the witnesses one at a time to Adams for direct examination. If, with a seemingly routine witness, Adams put a general, tell-what-you-know type of question, the resultant testimony might very well surprise Adams and even dismay him. This is what seems to have happened with Gillespie. After hearing the testimony, Adams told Quincy not to put any more evidence tending "to show that the expulsion of the troops from the town of Boston was a plan concerted among the inhabitants." When Quincy began to argue, Adams told him flatly that if Quincy insisted upon any further evidence of that sort, Adams would decline being further concerned in the case. Besides, he told Quincy, the case as it stood already contained evidence sufficient to bring an acquittal out of any jury, and (he may have added) especially out of this one. Whether Quincy felt that proof of a radical plot was necessary for some political purpose, we do not know. He may have felt that revealing the scheme might somehow ameliorate the popular indignation at the expected acquittal, thereby rendering it less likely that Preston would be lynched as he stepped from the courtroom. Or he may have believed the radicals were pressing too hard, too fast, and, as he had suggested at the nonimportation meeting the winter before, too far beyond the law. A thorough airing of the effects of these excesses might well have seemed to him both therapeutic and prophylactic.

However strong and logical Quincy felt his position to be, he put a temporary stop to this line of inquiry. The last evidence before the long session closed was dryly technical. Captain Brabazon O'Hara testified that the commanding officer placed the Custom House sentry for its safety, and that therefore the officer of the day had no authority to remove him. Obviously the defense hoped to forestall the argument that Preston should have avoided all the difficulty by taking White off his post when the snowballing first started and the situation, although touchy, was still under control.

Remembering Adams's outburst, Preston and his friends nearly panicked. Was the case to blow up just when victory—and justification—seemed assured? After court adjourned, they talked of obtaining another lawyer, as if such a switch, so late in the trial, could possibly help.

Adams, however, was not abandoning Preston. His insistence on leaving the townspeople out of the case sprang from two logical assumptions. First, he felt, with some justification, that Preston's acquittal did not require such evidence. Second, in diametrical opposition to Quincy, he feared that publication of what he considered unnecessary references to the radicals' scheme might well set off a reaction which could cost Preston's life, either quasi-legally through the kind of jury terrorizing that had convicted Richardson, or by a jail-storming and lynching. Common sense, a return of confidence, desperation, or Adams's exposition convinced the loyalists. When court reconvened on Saturday morning, October 27, the defense rested.[31]

By custom, the two defense lawyers would now give their closing arguments, first the junior man, Adams, then Auchmuty, the senior. As Adams rose to begin, Preston must have wondered whether in his summation the little barrister would continue pulling his forensic punches. He need not have worried. Adams's argument, as taken down by his opponent and professional rival, Paine, brilliantly capped the case. Paine did not bother to record the array of legal authorities on which Adams relied. But Adams's notes have survived, showing the points which he read to the jurors from thick treatises. "*Tutius Semper est errare in acquietando,*" he quoted from Hale's *Pleas of the Crown,* "it is always safer to err in acquitting." And from the same venerable author: "It is better five guilty persons should escape unpunished, than one innocent person should die." Fortescue, Adams's next authority, went even farther: better "twenty guilty persons" should escape.

"The law," Adams told the jury, quoting the martyred English Whig, Algernon Sidney, "no passion can disturb . . . 'Tis deaf, inexorable, inflexible." The law was also clear and certain in its application to the consequences of mobbings such as the affair in King Street. Adams smoothly laid it out for the jury: provocations justifying responsive killing; the law governing assaults, that is, threats to do corporal harm; the vicarious liability of every man in King Street for the force and threats of the actual rioters. Adams covered them all. "Self-defence," he paraphrased Blackstone for the jurors, "is the primary canon of the law of nature." And he reminded them that if a man who is assaulted retreats to where he can retreat no farther, he may to save his life kill his assailant; and if he is "assaulted in such a manner, and such a place, that he cannot go back without manifestly indangering his life," he may kill without retreating at all. Moreover—and this bore particular relevance to popular feeling—even Blackstone clearly showed that if in killing his attacker a man should inadvertently kill an innocent bystander, the law would hold him blameless.

The legal framework thus set, Adams now proceeded to finish the edifice masterfully. Conceding the "great bitterness between soldiers and inhabitants," he insisted that none of the evidence on that point applied either to the party or to Preston. Preston's duty was to "take all the care he could of his men and protect them." Why, said Adams, "had the sentry been a private citizen and the Captain a citizen, it was his duty to go and assist."

Then Adams began picking the crown's evidence apart. Hastily passing over William Wyat's testimony that Preston had ordered the firing, Adams tore into the rest of the crown testimony. Robert Goddard, who had positively recalled Preston's order, Adams dismissed as palpably not worthy of belief. Goddard had said that Preston had threatened the boys with "murder." This, Adams argued, only proved Goddard's unreliability. "The prisoner," Adams told the jury, "knows the use of language too well to say 'murder 'em.'"

The positive and damning testimony of Daniel Calef gave Adams somewhat more difficulty, but he handled it flawlessly. By burying his treatment of Calef's evidence in the middle of his argument, he minimized its adverse effect. Putting it at the beginning or the end of his analysis would have brought it too much into the limelight. Having placed it advantageously, Adams then treated Calef's testimony with absolute fairness—another excellent neutralizing tactic. Calef, Adams had to admit, was "nearly right with regard to [the] Captain's situation." The lawyer was "sensible [i.e., aware]" that it was "hard to account for [this] mistake." Almost imperceptibly, Adams had brought his argument around so that his characterization of Calef's insistence that Preston had said "Fire" as a "mistake" seemed quite natural.

Just labeling Calef's testimony thus would not suffice. Adams had to explain the error, explain it plausibly and convincingly, and in a way that would not accuse the honest-appearing Calef of perjury. "It must be this," he said. "[The] Captain said 'Fire by no means' when the people spoke to him," but Calef heard only "Fire." As a cameo of successful jury technique, that portion of the argument was a masterpiece. Even when Adams erred, he scored for his client. Nathaniel Fosdick, admitting he heard no order to load, had nonetheless given damaging evidence of Preston's ordering the firing. Adams thought he had said he did not actually see the loading. If Fosdick did not observe such an obvious activity, Adams told the jury, he was "therefore not cool." The rest of his evidence, Adams was suggesting, need not receive much credit.

At this point in the trial, if we can believe Paine's notes, Adams interrupted his argument to reopen the defense's case—a circumstance impossible without the assent of the bench and, almost certainly, the prosecution. Over to the witness stand walked the sheriff of Suffolk

County, Stephen Greenleaf. Why he could not or did not testify in season, we do not know. To intensify the puzzle, the summary of the trial which Hutchinson later sent to Hillsborough does not contain any account of Greenleaf's testimony. The sheriff's evidence was bland enough, hardly worth breaking up the order of the trial. It was mainly an account of his confronting Preston at the Main Guard. The captain told Greenleaf that he did not command the party, that it was a corporal's command, and that he did not order the firing.

Unruffled by this fairly useless interruption, Adams carried on. He calmly brushed off the positive testimony of Peter Cunningham that the man who ordered the loading was attired like an officer. "He is [of] warm temper and brisk spirits," Adams reminded the jury, turning Cunningham's certainty against him. "Natural for such a witness to suppose Captain gave orders."

Turning momentarily from his point-by-point refutation of the crown's witnesses, Adams cleverly edged into an explanation of the conflicts in the testimony. "Man is a social creature," he began. "His passion and Imagination [are] contagious. The circumstances had a tendency to move all the passions. [They] have had a tendency to produce gloom and melancholy in all our minds. [This] may account for the variation in the testimony of honest men." Another workmanlike, thoroughly professional job. Without calling anyone a liar, without overpainting the scene, Adams brought the jurors into Preston's situation and subtly reminded them that the unleashed "passions" in King Street might well have forced the soldiers' response and, incidentally, so confused the witnesses as to render their incriminating testimony, however honestly intended, entirely unreliable. Hearing Adams's virtuoso performance, a sour Paine could only note: "This is applicable to [the] aggravated account of assaults," that is, the assaults on the party.

His dissection of the prosecution's evidence finished, Adams now turned to treat Preston's side of the case. It is an apt commentary on Adams's forensic skill that his argument relied heavily on testimony that the crown's own witnesses had given. Before Adams could fairly start, however, another after-closing witness interrupted.

Thomas Hutchinson himself, the acting governor, took the stand in the very court whose chief justiceship he technically still held. Despite the incongruity of his present role, Hutchinson was, in one sense, a legitimate witness: like Gifford and Peck earlier, his recollections of Preston's behavior after the shooting bore directly upon the crown's suggestion that what Preston said and did comported more with guilt than with innocence. On that score, Hutchinson said he thought that Preston had wished to say more (to Hutchinson) than he had been able to. Moreover, "I heard him deny giving orders. I am very sure it did not occur to me that he had said anything in answer to my question in the street which would not consist with this denial." Hutchinson also served as a character witness, although, as he carefully noted, "I have no particular intimacy with Captain Preston." Most important, Hutchinson's presence in the witness box, testifying for the defendant, reminded everybody that the king's own representative, and by clear implication His Majesty too, was lining up at Preston's side.

Adams resumed his argument. Shrewdly, he noted that Knox's having stopped Preston as the party came down meant that the order to load must have been given before the captain rejoined his men. The subsequent wild antics of Benjamin Burdick, the highland-broadsword carrier, surely gave the soldiers reason to think the crowd was bent on killing, Adams said. Preston's answer ("Perhaps you may") to Burdick's threat of a future confrontation Adams cleverly turned to his own use. Such a response, he said, was "too cool for a man who had ordered to fire." Paine silently commented: "It was his trade."

At last it was time for Adams to utilize the defense's strongest evidence. Palmes, he began, was "an inhabitant of [the] Town, therefore not prejudiced in favor of soldiers." He was, Adams told the jury, "the most material witness in the case." His evidence showed that Preston knew the guns were loaded with ball. Yet he kept his place in front of the muskets. Surely, Adams urged, "self-preservation would have made [the] Captain alter his place at firing." What about the argument that after the single first shot, Preston had had time to order "Recover" and thus prevent further firing? Adams handled that in one artful word: "Surprise." Besides, said Adams, neatly shifting his ground, Preston, seeing no one fall at the first firing, might very well have concluded that the weapons were loaded only with powder, after all.

At this point, Adams may have felt he could afford a calculated gamble. William Wyat had testified that Preston first ordered the firing and then afterwards reprimanded his men for having fired. Adams risked emphasizing the damaging testimony in order to refute it. If Wyat's evidence were accurate, he said, it "must show [Preston] to be diabolically malicious." Yet all the other evidence of Preston's disposition proved him to be a man of good character. Thus, said Adams, Wyat, like others, must have been mistaken.

On he went, shoring up Preston's case with bits of remembered testimony. From Andrew's evidence: The people "thought they were in a riot"; that was why they were "crying Murray and Riot Act." From Hutchinson's testimony: "Had [the] prisoner been conscious of rashness, he would have gone off," that is, secreted himself. His open behavior, therefore, was "evidence of innocence."

In light of the eighteenth century's apparently insatiable hunger for dramatic oratory, Adams doubtless ended his argument with a per-fervid flourish. Unfortunately, no one bothered to record it. The after-noon was well advanced when Auchmuty rose to deliver the final de-fense argument. Preston later praised him for having particularly "ex-erted" himself "with great spirit and cleverness." If Paine's notes are accurate and complete, the admiralty judge—noted for his "voluble repetition" and "nauseous eloquence"—spoke briefly and ploddingly, generally covering the same legal ground as Adams, but leaving the facts pretty much alone, except for some fairly obvious remarks: "Palmes' evidence may be opposed to [i.e., set against] all the Crown evidence" and "Positive evidence always outweighs negative." Auch-muty finished talking at 4:30 P.M. Enough daylight remained before the Sabbath-beginning dusk to permit Paine at least to commence his final argument for the crown. The senior prosecutor, however, was feeling "unfit." Requiring him to proceed might well give the radicals a chance to berate the judges for placing an unfair burden on the prose-cution. To avoid the possibility, the court adjourned for the weekend. The decision was, as Judge Oliver wrote Hutchinson, "hard upon the jury," even though the jurors and their keepers were given the run of the locked courthouse.[32]

On Monday, October 29, Paine's postponed argument began. It was hardly worth the wait. Sick or well, he chose an approach so low-key it was virtually inaudible. Palmes's testimony, Paine insisted, was mis-taken; Andrew's was "unaccountable flights of fancy." Ignoring, per-haps for tactical reasons, the crown's burden of proof, Paine acknowl-edged that there was "some little confusion in the evidence," but in-sisted the defense was equally disadvantaged with the prosecution. Paine's one clever stroke came toward the end, when in arguing that the crowd's behavior was not unusually rowdy he noted that Palmes himself admitted standing in front of the muzzles. "Would he place himself before a party of soldiers, and risque his life at the muzzels of their guns, when he thought them under a necessity of firing to defend their life?"

The judges, following the usual practice, charged the jury one at a time, the junior judge, Trowbridge, commencing, the others following in reverse order of seniority. Trowbridge tried to put the case into a perspective of reason. There had been "no concerted plan on either side," he said. But the bickerings and insults had grown so heated that "any little spark would inkindle a great fire—and five lives [were] sac-rificed to a squabble between the sentry and Piemont's barber's boy." True, it had been "a saucy speech in the boy"; but "the sentry [had] no right to strike him."

Reminding the jurors that "the credit of the witnesses is entirely with you," Trowbridge then turned to a calm legal analysis of the case, setting a cool example for the jurors to follow. First, decide whether the party was a lawful assembly; then, whether the party was assaulted; next, whether the crowd was an unlawful assembly. Did Preston order the loading? "If it remains only doubtful in your minds whether he did order the loading or not, you can't charge him with doing it." If he did order the loading, did he do so because of the threats and assaults? Was he trying to "put himself in the best posture of defense?" Did he give the order to fire? Consider the conflicting testimony; consider whether Preston admitted it afterwards. And above all, remember, he urged, "'whoso sheddeth man's blood, by man shall his blood be shed' is a general rule [with] many exceptions to it."

"If you are satisfied that the sentinel was insulted and assaulted, and that Captain Preston and his party went to assist them, it was doubtless excusable homicide, if not justifiable. Self-defense [is] a law of nature, what every one of us have a right to, and may stand in need of."

Trowbridge, the only trained lawyer on the bench, had been so methodical and thorough that the other justices could add little. Peter Oliver stormed against the Pelham-Revere engraving, and the insult it had thrown at the court. He also reminded the jury of the contempt he had personally received during Richardson's trial. Judge Cushing and Chief Justice Lynde added little. "The principal question," they both agreed, "[is] whether the prisoner gave the order." "I fear the people came in too hostile a manner," Lynde concluded.

The four hours of charges had taken most of the afternoon. It was 5 P.M. before the jurors retired. Within three hours, someone reported later, they had reached a verdict. But the court did not then reconvene to receive it. At 8 A.M. the next day, October 30, when the court opened, the jury reported its verdict: Not Guilty. Considering the makeup of the jury and, to be fair about it, the nature of the evidence, the results surprised no one. The arch-radical William Palfrey had dismissed the entire proceedings as "nothing but a mere farce." Yet even he confessed that "in my own mind there still remains a doubt whether Captain Preston gave the orders to fire." [33]

Preston, though delighted with his acquittal, could not rest completely easy. Some of the disgruntled radicals were encouraging "one of the relations of the deceased" to reach into ancient legal history for a last try at Preston's neck. The procedure suggested was the "appeal of felony," a medieval relic having nothing to do with judicial review. In an appeal of felony, certain specified relatives of a decedent could bring a personal criminal action against the alleged killer. The accused was entitled to claim trial by battle. This gory feature may explain why the radicals were unable to bring the appeal past the talking stage.[34]

Balked in criminal vengeance, the Sons of Liberty sought to stimulate the prosecution of various civil actions by the people who had been wounded. They doubtless would have tried to stir up suits for wrongful death, too, but Massachusetts at that time did not permit such litigation. The threats of the personal injury actions were enough to drive Preston out of Boston. He retired to the Castle where, safe from would-be process servers, he wrote a fulsome thank-you letter to Auchmuty (but not Adams or Quincy) and turned his attention to helping prepare the soldiers' defense.[35]

CHAPTER 19

REX v. WEMMS et al.

Immediately upon Preston's acquittal, the court adjourned its Suffolk County sitting to November 20 and proceeded with its entourage of lawyers and clerks across the Charles River to Cambridge. After dinner, the party made its ceremonial way to the little courthouse just across the road from Harvard Yard and began the statutorily prescribed Middlesex County sitting. Plunging into the business at hand, Adams temporarily put the Massacre defendants out of his mind. With fortunate lack of success, he opposed his friend Jonathan Sewall's attempt to win freedom for Margaret, a mulatto woman claimed as a slave by the Muzzey family of Lexington. After that, he participated (apparently for the defense) in the lengthy trial of Jonathan Eaton and Martha Parker for adultery; both were acquitted.[1]

After the Cambridge sitting adjourned, bench and bar moved on to Salem, for the trial of "George a molatto man-slave," accused of the March tarring and feathering of customs officer Jesse Savil. George, the only member of the mob ever to be indicted, was promptly found guilty. Did the result presage a popular revulsion against radical strong-arm methods? The judges apparently hoped so. They sentenced George to stand at the gallows for an hour with rope around his neck, to be whipped thirty-nine lashes, and to suffer two years imprisonment, followed by seven years' bond to keep the peace (the eighteenth-century equivalent of probation).[2]

When the Salem sitting adjourned on November 10, the superior court faced no scheduled business until November 20, the date set for the soldiers' trial, and the lawyers were free to begin intensive preparation. On behalf of the Boston selectmen, Town Clerk William Cooper wrote Paine, urging an immediate trip to Boston for consultation with Samuel Quincy. The selectmen, Cooper wrote, "make no doubt of your exerting yourself to the utmost that a fair & impartial inquisition may be made for blood." To aid the search, the selectmen had employed a now-anonymous "person" to help Quincy and Paine gather evidence. On the defense side, Auchmuty, for some unknown reason, had not been retained to defend the soldiers. Adams now stepped into the senior counsel's role, while Josiah Quincy assumed the task of cross-examining the crown's witnesses and presenting the defense's case. To aid them in working up additional evidence, and especially to investigate thoroughly "the characters and principles," that is, the reputation and politics, of all members of the jury panel, Hutchinson had advised Preston to engage Sampson Salter Blowers, the Harvard classmate (1763) of Josiah Quincy's who had worked with Quincy in Richardson's defense.[3]

Blowers' performance, behind-the-scenes though it might be, could well determine the eventual outcome of the trial. The chances of obtaining a block of sympathetic jurors like the talesmen who clinched the Preston verdict was almost nil. Everything else aside, the question of guilt in the soldiers' case was much closer than in Preston's. The history of town-troop irritations, particularly the events of the weekend preceding March 5, had left many people willing to accept the argument that the soldiers had used the unrest in King Street as a mere excuse to extract mortal revenge.

Preston's acquittal only made the soldiers' defense more difficult. The captain had been saved, if one disregards the stacked jury, because the crown had failed to prove that he ordered his men to shoot. That being so, the soldiers must have fired without orders. If they fired without orders, so the thought ran, they must be murderers. Despite the education the people had received on the law of justifiable homicide from the Corbet, Richardson, and Preston cases, many Bostonians still agreed with the potential juror who reportedly said he believed "Captain Preston was innocent, but innocent blood had been shed and somebody ought to be hanged for it." Preston's escape could be accepted. He was, after all, in law and Boston society, a gentleman. The men, on the other hand, were brutes, ciphers. The town considered them virtually nonpersons, a feeling cruelly demonstrated by the eviction for "vagrancy" of Mrs. Hartigan and Mrs. Montgomery. Worst of all, so far as the Whig propagandists were concerned, many soldiers were Irish Roman Catholics. The radicals brought out the connection in a subtle yet unmistakable way on November 19, the day before the scheduled trial. An article in the Boston *Gazette* damned the crown's permitting Catholic missionaries to visit Nova Scotia—whence, it will be recalled, the Boston regiments had come. "Daring violations of law, and attacks upon the PROTESTANT RELIGION," the *Gazette* called the ministry's actions.[4]

The problem of jury prejudice, at least prejudice against the soldiers, could have been greatly avoided if, as Gage hoped, the Preston jury had also determined the second trial. Surprisingly, there may have been a real chance that the judges would follow this odd procedure. When the court met on November 20, it apparently had before it only the old jury panel, from which the Preston jury had been in part selected. The five talesmen, of course, having been brought in for Preston's trial only, were not members of that original panel. Whether from motives of propriety, fear, or an unwillingness to make any man sit through a second lengthy demanding trial, the judges determined to send for an entire new venire. They put the case over for one week and issued the writs necessary to summon the fresh panel. To fill the calendar, the court heard Samuel Fitch and Adams argue a complicated point of pleading in a case originally commenced in Essex County. Other matters followed for the rest of the week. By November 23, the new veniremen had reported. That day, John King, a Marine, stood trial for the killing of Seaman William Frazer during a quarrel in one of H.M.S. *Fowey*'s boats. Anyone who hoped to draw an omen from the result would probably be disappointed. The jury (including five men who later sat on the soldiers' trial) found King guilty, but only of manslaughter. He prayed benefit of clergy, took his branding, and went free.[5]

The pressure of anticipation must have weighed heavily on everyone who expected to be concerned in the trial, particularly the judges. The same four would sit who had heard *Preston*. Hutchinson, still nominally the chief justice, was again remaining off the bench; the aging Benjamin Lynde would once more preside. The judges must have known of Hutchinson's orders to respite any conviction; yet the need remained for correctness in law and deportment, for conducting a trial which was not only in fact fair, but (almost as important) which seemed to both political parties fair. Symbolically, the day before the trial opened, Lynde dined at Hutchinson's, and spent the evening with Hancock.[6]

The morning of November 27, a small difficulty appeared. Joseph Brown, a witness whose surrounding mystery is enhanced by the absence of his deposition among those collected in the *Short Narrative*, was found to be out of the province. Because Brown was said to have vital evidence to give against Kilroy and Hartigan, the crown did not

wish to proceed without him. To prevent still another general postponement, the court remanded Kilroy and Hartigan to jail. The remaining six soldiers would stand trial on the present evidence, those
two to be tried later.[7]

An audience of fifty or sixty people crowded the small courtroom.
Somewhere near the witness stand, John Hodgson, shorthand writer,
hunched over his notes. Unlike Preston's trial, this one would be tran-
scribed and published verbatim. Hodgson was not a trained court reporter. No one in Boston was: stenographic transcripts were virtually
unknown. The transcript's accuracy is therefore conjectural. John
Adams later thought Hodgson had not done justice to the closing arguments; but he made no criticism of "the testimonies of the witnesses." [8]

When the impaneling began, the court agreed that to prevent the
long wrangle with which Preston's trial had opened, the province law
with respect to challenges should control, the prisoners to have one
set of peremptory challenges among them. The judges also ruled that
the statutory inquiry about bias, which had not been put to the Preston
jury, should now be pursued. Perhaps because of this, selecting a jury
took a long time. Joseph Mayo of Roxbury occupied the foreman's
seat. A veteran of the great Louisbourg campaign of 1745, and a former neighbor of Governor Bernard, Mayo held a captain's commission
in the militia. Others soon joined him in the jury box: Edward Pierce, a
deacon from Dorchester; Isaiah Thayer, from Adams's home town of
Braintree; Samuel Davenport, one of the leaders in Milton, where
Hutchinson lived. But others were challenged: Samuel Bass, a Braintree innkeeper (perhaps Adams, an active temperance fanatic earlier
in his career, felt Bass, harboring a grudge, might not listen to Adams's argument with the kind of sympathetic ear the defense needed);
Harbottle Dorr, an avid Son of Liberty, who saved all the issues of the
Gazette and carefully annotated them, attributing all the anonymous
articles and cross-referencing the various propaganda strokes; all the
Boston veniremen. The court itself took a hand, rejecting, as illegally
chosen, the three veniremen from Hingham.[9]

Only nine jurors, not one of them from Boston, had been duly seated
when the pool of eligibles ran dry. Once again Sheriff Greenleaf began
corralling talesmen. Samuel Sheppard of Stoughton had been a venireman at Preston's trial, challenged peremptorily. Called as the first
talesman now, he was challenged again. One by one, four more talesmen were brought over and challenged for cause. Because the bystanders were mostly Bostonians, thus more likely than out-country-
men to have nurtured disqualifying antimilitary prejudices, filling the
last three jury seats seemed an impossible task. Then someone remembered the three men from Hingham. Although ineligible as veniremen,

they would make perfectly acceptable talesmen. Greenleaf put each in turn into the jury box. Neither side challenged them. The jury was now complete. Not one of the twelve men came from Boston. Sam Adams, mingling with the spectators, found this intolerable. Was not a jury of the "vicinage," in the ancient phrase, the best possible trier of facts? And was not its superiority based largely on its out-of-court, ante-trial personal knowledge of each witnesses's credibility? How unfair then, Adams insisted, to have out-of-towners deciding this case. Nobody took him seriously. Hutchinson's only comment on the jury was that it "was not so good" as the one that acquitted Preston.[10]

After Clerk Samuel Winthrop administered the jury's oath, the prosecution learned that the absence of its missing witness was likely to be permanent. Kilroy and Hartigan were again brought from jail. They agreed, doubtless after consulting their counsel, to accept the challenges made by the other prisoners and to consent to the jury as sworn. But just to make the matter certain, the court had Winthrop swear the jury once again.[11]

"Prisoners, hold up your hands," he then said. As the jurors looked at the defendants, Winthrop read the indictments and reminded the jury that each man had pleaded not guilty. "Your charge therefore is, to enquire whether they or either of them be guilty of the felony and murder whereof they stand indicted, or not guilty." "Good men and true," Winthrop concluded, "stand together and hearken to your evidence." Presumably they were allowed to sit during the long trial. Hearken they certainly did; both foreman Mayo and Deacon Pierce took notes of the ensuing testimony.[12]

Samuel Quincy opened for the crown, carefully, quietly: "The prisoners . . . were induced from some cause or other to fire on the inhabitants." He called the killings "the most melancholy event that has yet taken place on the continent of America," but cautioned the jury "that however interesting the question may be, the object of our enquiry is simply that of truth." Saying only that the anticipated evidence would come "from the testimony of credible witnesses," and "be sufficient to sustain the several indictments," he ended his brief opening and called his first witness, Adams's own law clerk, Jonathan Williams Austin.[13]

The prosecution's trial strategy was simple. Not even the defense denied that the five victims had died as result of gunshot wounds sustained in King Street. Quincy need really prove only that the defendants were present at the shooting and that each had fired his weapon. That done, he could wait for the defense to assume its burden of showing that the provocation the soldiers faced had sufficed to justify the killings. Indeed, it would ordinarily be considered improper for the crown to anticipate the defense evidence on this point. However,

Quincy and Paine proposed that the prosecution be permitted to introduce evidence of the threats and offensive behavior of the soldiers
preceding the King Street showdown. This idea may well have originated with Samuel Adams, who, after missing Preston's proceedings,
was a regular spectator of the men's trial. The court doubted the propriety, as well it might. Evidence of threats however violent, elsewhere
than in King Street, by soldiers not members of the party, could only
by a large effort be considered relevant to the mob's activity around
the Custom House. Auchmuty frankly did not like the proposal. But he
was no longer defense counsel; Quincy and Adams thought they saw
an advantage in the idea. They would agree to the crown's offer if the
defense, in turn, would be permitted the same liberty in proving provocative acts of the inhabitants. This suggestion made even less technical evidentiary sense than the prosecution's. Whatever evidence the
defense might adduce that Bostonians had been cruising the streets
shouting threats and waving clubs bore no legal relevance to the killings. The only evidence along those lines which properly counted
would be testimony that the shouting and the club-waving took place
in the sight and presence of the party (or possibly testimony that the
threats had been promptly communicated to the party). No violence
was legally relevant unless it threatened the soldiers, either actually, or
in their reasonable contemplation. Auchmuty suggested that the prosecution would find witnesses to outswear those the defense would introduce. As a mere onlooker, however, he could only grumble. Both sides
accepted the stipulation.[14]

The prosecution's case opened slowly. That first trial day, not enough
time remained after the preliminaries to call more than six witnesses,
three of whom had testified at Preston's trial; in all, twenty-four witnesses would be repeaters. Those first witnesses did little more than
generally set the scene and identify some of the prisoners as being
members of the party. Edward Langford, the town watchman, after
describing the "young shavers" pestering the sentry, made the only
major point of the day: he described how Kilroy's shot killed Gray.
With the final witness, Francis Archibald, Quincy began to utilize the
stipulation. Archibald told of a scuffle with some soldiers ("Damn you,
ye Yankie bougers, what's your business?") near the barracks that resulted in Archibald's breaking the wrist of a soldier who was trying to
pull himself off the ground.

On that note, at 5 P.M., the court adjourned. Sam Adams subsequently bemoaned this as a subtle attempt to "represent that it was
dangerous for the court to sit in the tumultuous town of Boston after
dark." But in fact the court throughout the trial sat full days, conven-
ing as early as 8 or 9 A.M., and not adjourning before 5 or 6 P.M. As in

the Preston trial, the jurors were kept together during the nights "by proper officers, appointed and sworn by the Court for that purpose." [15]

November 28 started badly for the prosecution. James Brewer, a water-front mechanic, intending to testify to Kilroy's freedom with the bayonet, stumbled into an admission that Christopher Monk, who later stopped a bullet, had been armed with a stick, and that "the people cryed Fire! Fire!—the word fire was in everybody's mouth." Although pressed on cross-examination, he denied that he noticed anyone else with a stick; he denied hearing cheers, name-calling, threats to kill the soldiers, or whistling; he denied seeing attempts to strike the soldiers or their guns. "No. I heard the people all around call Fire," he insisted stubbornly. "Did you take that to be the cry of fire, or bidding the soldiers to fire?" The question had been cleverly put; however Brewer answered, he would damage his own credibility. "I cannot tell now what I thought then," he answered weakly.

Fresh from this fiasco, the prosecution called Samuel Emmons. "I don't know any of the prisoners," he said, "nor anything. I was not in King Street. My brother was." The trial transcript contains no mention of this monument to mis-preparation, and counsel's notes omit indication of the laugh which must have sped Emmons from the stand.

A sailor, James Bailey, took Emmons's place. Unfortunately for the crown, he had indeed been present at the shooting. Identifying Montgomery as the man who fired the first shot, he testified on direct examination that earlier the boys had been bombarding the sentry with "pieces of ice . . . hard and large enough to hurt any man; as big as one's fist." And before he fired, Montgomery himself had been struck on the arm by a "stout man" and knocked down. Reminded of his oath, Bailey still called the blow "very violent." The crowd was fifty or sixty strong at the time, Bailey recalled. But when on cross-examination Josiah Quincy asked him if he remembered telling the justices of the peace in the Town House during the preliminary examination early on March 6 that the people "were throwing sticks and cakes of ice in the mob way," Bailey denied it. Yet before he left the stand, he testified to having seen Attucks in Cornhill a few minutes before the shooting, armed with "a large cord-wood stick" at the head of a "huzzaing, whistling" gang of sailormen, some of them "carrying their sticks over their heads."

Richard Palmes, whose testimony had saved Preston, followed Bailey, with just about the same story as before. Palmes admitted seeing Montgomery struck (but not knocked down) by a piece of ice. He was positive Montgomery had not fallen until after the firing, when, he admitted, he himself had walloped the grenadier. Here was a clear conflict between two of the crown's own witnesses. One of the judges tried to resolve the discrepancy by recalling Bailey to the stand. Whether from design or accident, whoever was questioning Bailey chose the "do-you-really-mean-what-you-said" technique of interrogation. This method has the advantage of not openly appearing to demolish the witness. But because it is based on the assumption that the questioner's implied disbelief will induce a change of testimony, it is not often effective. "Are you satisfied, notwithstanding what Mr. Palmes says, that Montgomery was knocked down by a blow given him, immediately before he fired?" "Yes, I am."

No surviving contemporary account has preserved the reactions of Samuel Quincy and Paine to this parade of witnesses "gone sour." Quincy, whose loyalism far overbalanced his vengefulness, may not have cared; Paine, expressly retained to make "a fair & impartial inquisition . . . for blood," probably felt the agony more strongly. And Sam Adams, back with the spectators, must have anguished with the peculiar despair vouchsafed a client whose "certain" victory has suddenly evaporated.

Doggedly, the prosecution continued. Perhaps John Danbrooke would put the case back on the march. Alas, he too turned out to be one of those witnesses who loses his sponsors much more than he gains them. True, he did not see anyone struck with any stick. And though he had watched "a little stick fly over their heads," it had not hit anybody. But Danbrooke did admit seeing Attucks leaning on a "long stick"; and he had indeed seen a party of twenty or thirty men dressed in sailor's clothes heading for the Town House, half of them carrying and waving cordwood sticks "as thick as one's wrist." Jedediah Bass, who followed Danbrooke, only corroborated him.

Another few witnesses like the group which had opened the day's evidence, and the crown's case might be irreversibly damaged. The picture they painted showed a crowd of armed sailors and missile-throwing boys attacking and (if one believed Bailey over Palmes) knocking down at least one soldier. Now if ever was the time to begin making use of the stipulation the crown lawyers had worked out with the defense at the beginning of the trial.

The witnesses who next came on gave vivid evidence of threats and assaults by soldiers other than the party. Nicholas Ferriter told of the ropewalk battle; Benjamin Burdick described how some soldiers had skulked around his house, stalking his roomer. Then the testimony moved closer to at least one defendant. Samuel Hemmingway, Sheriff Greenleaf's own coachman, described an evening one or two weeks before March 5 when he and Kilroy sat warming themselves in the snug kitchen of John Apthorp, Greenleaf's son-in-law. While the housekeeper and Apthorp's "Negroe" listened, Hemmingway heard Kilroy say that "he would never miss an opportunity, when he had one, to fire on the inhabitants, and that he had wanted to have an opportunity ever since he landed." Kilroy was sober when he said it, Hemmingway testified. "I said he was a fool for talking so. He said he did not care." [16]

This was more the sort of testimony the prosecutors had been hoping for. They kept up the evidentiary pressure. In all, ten witnesses told of pre-Massacre rough behavior by the military. Larded between them came additional provocative accounts. Nathaniel Fosdick not only told of receiving a bayonet thrust from one of the party, he opened his clothing and showed the scar. Joseph Hilyer reported that the sentry's waving his musket "had a tendency to exasperate the people." The only weak witness in the run was Josiah Simpson, a joiner, who "delivered his evidence as a schoolboy does his lesson." So detailed and stilted was Simpson's recital of the events that, Hutchinson later reported, "no credit was given to it." [17]

This brief flaw could not diminish the total force. Nor could the testimony of Robert Williams that "people [were] jumping on the backs of others trying to get in" cause the prosecution any worry. Not when, for example, twelve-year-old John Appleton told how a Redcoat had caught him in an alley. "Soldier spare my life," the boy said he cried. But, he told the jury, the soldier, raising his sheathed cutlass had growled, "No, damn you, we'll kill you all," and swung at Master John's head. "But I dodged and got the blow on my shoulder."

Small wonder the prosecutors regarded their case as just about finished. During the adjournment, Sam Quincy planned to work up his analysis of the evidence for delivery on the morrow, when the crown expected to rest its case. Unfortunately, his own fatigue and family problems prevented him from making more than a cursory summary. But the way the case was going, that seemed not a very serious lack. When court resumed, the prosecution threw what it must have hoped would be a pair of knockout blows. Joseph Crosswell saw Kilroy the morning of March 6, before he surrendered to the sheriff. The soldier's bayonet, Crosswell swore, was covered with dried blood for a distance of five or six inches from the point. Why the defense failed to object to this testimony is another of the case's many mysteries. Certainly a present-day court would exclude it on the commonsense ground that blood on a man's bayonet twelve hours or so after a killing does not tend to prove the soldier a killer, especially when the deceased died from a gunshot wound. Crosswell's testimony does not seem even to have drawn an objection. Indeed, all his story's gory details received prompt confirmation from schoolmaster James Carter, who also had seen Kilroy and the bloody bayonet. How close had Carter been to Kilroy? "As nigh as I am to you, sir," Carter replied, pointing to Paine, three feet away.

The crown might well have ended its case on that high note, but Quincy (or whoever was directing the flow of evidence) wanted to put on a few more minor witnesses. These added little. A crown pessimist might even have seen a bad sign for the prosecution in the fate of the final witness. Mary Gardiner was called to the stand. But before she could testify at all, she found herself, as Paine's cryptic, laconic minute says, "overruled."

Notwithstanding this check and the others which had preceded it, the last half-day's testimony, added to the morning's, must have given Samuel Quincy a most comfortable feeling on which to launch his argument. As behooved a front-runner, especially a tired one, Quincy kept his remarks simple. He named the soldiers, individually, carefully reminding the jury of the witnesses who had respectively identified each one. Then he began an intensive review of each witness's testimony. Such tactics today would, as the saying goes, lose the jury forever. In 1770, when entertainment was scarce, and men were accustomed to hearing double sermons on Sundays, Quincy's style found no objectors.

His summation, although tinged with an occasional and understandable slip, generally did substantial justice. He made full use of the testimony the stipulation had brought into the case:

> If you attend to the testimony of several of the witnesses, there were that evening in the streets at all parts of the town, a number of soldiers; they sallied out from Murray's barracks and every-where with clubs, cutlasses, and other weapons of death; this occasioned a general alarm; every man therefore had a right, and very prudent it was to endeavour to defend himself if attacked.

As Quincy was going over the various accounts of the actual shooting, a judge asked if there might not be such a thing in the law as voluntary manslaughter, that is, a deliberate killing not tantamount to murder. Someone else observed that to constitute murder, the homicide must be committed "with coolness and deliberation." Suavely, Quincy conceded both points. Indeed, he said, they applied particularly to Kilroy, of whom the evidence showed that he killed "in the manner which the law calls *sedato animo;* he was doing a deliberate action, with a cool and calm mind."

Nothing seemed to faze Quincy. Lieutenant Colonel Marshal had testified to astronomical impossibility. He had said he saw moonlight glittering on the drawn cutlasses of a party of soldiers on the south side of King Street; yet in fact the moon had been in the south part of the sky. "I cannot see it will make much one way or the other," Quincy

remarked equably, although the truth about the moon's position cast
the gravest doubt on the accuracy (if not the honesty) of Marshal's evidence. Marshal had also changed his earlier testimony. In Preston's
trial, he had said that the soldiers he saw were crying "Fire," and that
the bells rang on the cry; this time, he had been uncertain just when
the bells began. Added to the moonlight discrepancy, the tergiversa-
tion might be thought to have weakened Marshal's testimony. Not at
all, said Quincy. He would use it, he said, to emphasize the conduct of
the soldiers. "It is probable the word fire was a watch-word; it appears
to me, that if we can believe the evidence, they had a design of attacking and slaughtering the inhabitants that night, and they could have
devised no better method to draw out the inhabitants unarmed, than
to cry fire."

Quincy exploited the testimony of young John Appleton to its tear-
jerking limit: "the young master," "the little victim," "cruelty almost
equal to that of a *Pharaoh* or *Herod*." He neatly quoted, and turned back
on the defense John Adams's remark at Preston's trial that man is "a social creature," with contagious feelings, passions, and imaginations.
What happened to John Appleton, Quincy told the jury, "was food
enough for such passions, such imaginations to feed upon."

The conduct of the soldiers, in short, more than justified apprehension. Fear, together with the ringing of the bells as if for fire, drew the
townspeople to the center of town which "when there is a doubt where
fire is, becomes naturally the place of rendezvous." "I mention this,
only to take off the force of any evidence or pretence that may be
made, that there was an intention of the people to assault, or as it has
been expressed, swallow up the soldiers."

Openly admitting that most of the soldiers had not been proved to
have committed a specific killing, Quincy bore down hard on Kilroy,
"against whom I think you have certain [i.e., strong] evidence." All the
rest, however, would be liable as accessories. The prisoners' only hope,
Quincy said, lay in proving the justification of absolute necessity.

As Quincy began to analyze the evidence bearing on this defense,
Trowbridge interrupted him. It was improper, said His Honor, to anticipate the defense. All the other judges agreed. Quincy, unflappable
as ever, promptly closed, confident that "on the evidence as it now
stands, the facts, as far as we have gone, against the prisoners at the
bar, are fully proved, and until something turns up to remove from
your minds, the force of that evidence, you must pronounce them
Guilty." The prosecution rested.

Symbolic of the divisive political currents running through America,
yet symbolic in an oddly inverted way, Josiah Quincy now rose to follow his brother. Samuel, the easygoing loyalist, had shaped a work-

manlike argument to help hang the soldiers. Josiah, the fiery radical, began a desperate legal attempt to save their lives. In the face of the powerful evidence the crown had mustered, evidence which gained effect by contrast with the early-trial fiasco, Josiah Quincy's first task was to desensitize the emotions which the testimony and Samuel Quincy's adroit presentation had rekindled. Only after calming the jury could he hope to obtain any kind of fair hearing for the substance of the defense.

"The eyes of all are upon you," Quincy told the jurors. "Patience in hearing this cause is an essential requisite; candor and caution are no less essential." Not mere justice alone posited these requisites. "Nay, it is of high importance to your country, that nothing should appear on this trial to impeach our justice or stain our humanity." Although a skilled controversialist like Quincy certainly appreciated the propaganda values at stake in the trial, his comments did not refer simply to America's reputation. Without directly mentioning Richardson, Quincy was now telling the jury that another unreasoned verdict of guilty might provoke strong repressive action by the Home Government.

The town, Quincy remarked, had not considered the problem of the soldiers very clearly. This fuzziness had led to mischief. Many people, for example, thought "that the life of a soldier, was of very little value; of much less value, than others of the community." On the contrary, said Quincy, in "the equal eyes of the law" all men's lives stood alike. Another current "opinion equally foreign to truth and law" held "that no possible case could happen, in which a soldier could fire, without the aid of a civil magistrate." The law, Quincy thundered, "puts the citizen and soldier under *equal* restraint. What will justify and mitigate the action of the one, will do the same to the other."

Carefully sketching the background of the difficulties which brought the troops to Boston, Quincy told his listeners to forget the whole matter. "It poisons justice, when politics tinctures its current." The fear of some people that the soldiers would be "fastening, and riveting for ages, the shackles of their bondage," Quincy told the jurors to treat only as a simple fact. "With the justness of these apprehensions, you and I have nothing to do in this place . . . You are to think, judge, and act, as *Jurymen,* and not as *Statesmen.*"

The friction between civilians and soldiers was of course another fact to consider, and Quincy dealt on it at narrative length. Earlier he had complained that the entire case had "perhaps, too much engrossed our affections [i.e., emotions]—and, I speak for one, too much excited our passions." Now, he tossed another sharp barb at Samuel Adams and the radicals. "There are an order of men in every commonwealth who never reason, but always act from feelings. That their rights and liberties were filched away one after another, they had often been told. They had been taught, by those whom they believed, that the ax was now laid to the root of the tree, and one more stroke compleated its fall."

It was the end-product of the fears, rather than their validity or lack of it, which should concern the jury, Quincy insisted. And although the eyes of the world would scan Boston's way of doing justice, Boston itself was not on trial. Quincy hammered the point: "Boston and its inhabitants have no more to do with this cause [i.e., case] than you or any other members of the community. You are, therefore, by no means to blend two things, so essentially different, as the guilt or innocence of this town and the prisoners, together." Curiously, in light of the course the defense soon planned to take, Quincy minimized the threat the mob had posed. The inhabitants of Boston, he said, could not be "supposed answerable for the unjustifiable conduct of a few individuals hastily assembled in the streets."

Returning to his counsels of calm, Quincy read the jury lengthy excerpts from that still-respected paragon of moderation, John Dickinson, the "Pennsylvania Farmer." Dickinson's admired *Letters,* now three years old, abjured "hot, rash, disorderly proceedings." No political tract Quincy could have selected, indeed no legal treatise, would be so likely to bring the jurors to a contemplative state of mind.

Now Quincy was more safely able to resume sniping at the radicals' attempt to prejudge the soldiers. The prisoners, he said, must be tried solely upon "the evidence *here in Court* produced against them, and by nothing else." Without mentioning the *Short Narrative,* and explicitly avoiding accusations, he strongly denounced the depositions and the use the radicals had tried to make of them. "We were not present to cross-examine: and the danger which results from having this publication in the hands of those who are to pass upon our lives ought to be guarded against." Significantly, for the first time in his speech, Quincy had slipped into a familiar lawyer's locution: he used "we" instead of "my clients." "We say we are innocent, by our plea, and are not to be denounced guilty upon a new species of evidence, unknown in the *English* system of law."

Quincy had not finished pounding the Whigs. Figuratively standing again with his countrymen, he catalogued the radicals' attempts to prejudice the trial. "The prints exhibited in our houses," he said, meaning the Pelham-Revere cartoon, "have added wings to fancy; and in the fervour of our zeal, reason is in hazard of being lost." The pompous funerals, Quincy added, served likewise to "inspire a glow incompatible with sound, deliberative judgment." Be careful, he was warning the jury, "lest borne away by a torrent of passion, we make shipwreck of

conscience." "I have aimed," he added a little later, "at securing you
against the catching flame."

Only now did Quincy begin a legal analysis of the case. He had but
two major points; in making them he once more joined himself with
the soldiers. First, he argued, "we say that give the evidence for the
king its full scope and force, and our offence is reduced at least to
Manslaughter." This was a touchy argument. Lawyers generally do not
like to tell a jury, in effect, "my client is bad," even though they hastily add, "but he is not so bad as the other side says he is." The thin
line between a frank public admission of weakness and a damaging
concession of liability is one no advocate treads comfortably. Moreover, by emphasizing the potentiality of convictions for manslaughter,
Quincy risked raising in the jurors' minds the prevalent notion that
such a conviction entailed hardly any punishment. Shouts of "Hang
him! Murder, no manslaughter!" had followed the Richardson jury.
Quincy had no reason to believe the twelve countrymen he was presently addressing would not hear the same entreaties. They might even
now be thinking the same thoughts. Quincy tried to check them by
cataloguing the civil disqualifications attending a convicted man-
slaughterer and emphasizing that a man could claim the benefit of
clergy only once in his life.

Thus far, Quincy had not dealt in any detail with the evidence
which the crown had produced, nor had he disclosed the defense's expected testimony. Now, having calmed the jury's prejudices and faced
the manslaughter issue, he could dare to counter the mass of military-
misconduct testimony which the prosecution had thrown into the case.
Summarizing briefly what the witnesses had said about the soldiers in
other parts of town, Quincy handled the problem calmly. "We are
ready to admit, that their behaviour was altogether unjustifiable—for
we don't look upon ourselves as any way concerned in their conduct."
Should the jury accept this argument, the crown's (and the radicals')
damaging evidence would fall harmlessly. "If some of the witnesses
are not mistaken," Quincy slyly told the jury, those other soldiers that
night acted more like "madmen and barbarians, than like reasonable
creatures." But suppose the jurors believed the witnesses? Quincy took
the last step. "If *they* acted like savages or ruffians," he shouted, "what
is that to us?" Boldly, he was asking the jury to disregard the heart of
the crown's case.

Quincy went on to a lengthy and "minute detail" of all the crown
evidence, and then to a full statement of the anticipated evidence for
the defense. What he said has not been preserved. From some of John
Adams's notes it appears that he urged two important and still extant
rules of evidence. First, that a party "producing a witness is never to

discredit him," an apparent attempt to remind the jurors of the strong assistance the defense had received from some of the prosecution's own testimony. Second, that "A Person swearing a Positive is to be believed, *ceteris paribus*, rather than one swearing a negative." Quincy here was urging the jury to credit those witnesses who testified affirmatively about the snowballs, the whistling, the taunting, and the blows, and to ignore any evidence to the contrary. With that, the defense began calling its witnesses.

It was obvious from the start that Quincy intended to take full advantage of the pre-trial stipulation. Between the end of his opening and the court's adjournment at 5 P.M., he called fifteen witnesses, only two of whom actually saw the shootings. The rest all testified to unusual, club-swinging activity among the townspeople in various parts of Boston. The Scottish auctioneer William Hunter and the men who had been with him that evening described in detail the crowd in Dock Square. From their evidence (one might even say from their evidence only) came one of the future staples of Massacre mythology, the tall man in the white wig and red cloak, addressing the people in the square. Who he was, none of them said. No one else has ever supplied his name.[18]

When court adjourned, the tide may not have turned definitely in favor of the prisoners. But, as Quincy had said in another connection during his opening, it stood at "high-water slack." More witnesses like these last, and the jury would have no trouble deciding that the town's activities had posed, at the very least, a serious physical threat to all the garrison, not merely to the sentry and the relief party. Worse, from the radical viewpoint, the same thought would occur to everybody who read the trial transcript, whether in England or America. Abrupt measures would be needed to save not merely the convictions, but Boston's reputation. Samuel Adams directed his attention to the first, John Adams to the second.

Samuel Adams had been in court all along, taking notes. Either while there, or shortly after leaving, he wrote a disjointed memorandum to Paine. No trial lawyer likes to have his on-the-spot client calling the signals; we can reasonably assume that Paine, never noted for tact or tolerance of others' thoughts, either bristled at the suggestions or ignored them completely. Surely Paine did not need Adams to tell him the evidence of club-swinging Bostonians was "designed to prejudice the Characters of the Inhabitants as being the Aggressors." Nor was it necessary to remind him that testimony about the mob's breaking the legs off the market stalls could be countered by asking "Would not any person *at such a time* who was without a Weapon of Defense have done the same?"[19]

Adams offered some help in dealing with "the Scotch witnesses'" account of the red-cloaked man. This "lusty gentleman," Adams wrote, "might as probably have advised the people to have called the main Guard to quell the Soldiers." Doubtless Paine resented Adams's emphasis of the obvious: "Here is an artful Insinuation that at least one person of figure was a principal aggressor," and thus that the mob was not composed solely of out-of-town rowdies.

The memorandum covered the entire case, from Josiah Quincy's "flourish about the Narrative" as ex parte evidence ("Col. Dalrymple was notified," Adams insisted) to the underlying substantive law ("If eight men agree to do an unlawful Act, & one of them kills, are not all of them principals?"). Paine's notorious vanity must have flamed dangerously as he read Adams's postscript: "If the Prisoners Council bring on new matter, I mean Evidence to prove the Inhabitants were the aggressors & consequently that the Soldiers were not, should not the Council for the Crown have the Liberty to produce Evidence to invalidate theirs, by making it appear that the Conduct of the Inhabitants was the Effect of a just apprehension founded upon the *prior* Conduct of the Soldiers?"

Sam Adams's effort had been wasted. Not because Paine rejected the advice, but because even while Paine was considering it, his opposite number was making certain that the defense would not "bring on new matter." John Adams and Quincy had come to another serious falling out over the same issue that had nearly split them during Preston's trial. The younger man, having started the line of witnesses to the town's aggressions, wished to continue. He urged "giving very large Evidence against the Inhabitants to prove a premeditated design to drive out the Soldiers & frequent abuse as well as threats." Adams rejected the proposition summarily. While Blowers, the young attorney who had worked up the evidence, looked on horrified, Adams once again enforced his argument with a threat to quit. If Quincy and Blowers "would go on with such Witnesses who only served to set the Town in a bad light," Adams told Quincy, he would "leave the cause and not say a word more." Badly shaken, they acceded to his ultimatum and began revising plans for the next day's witnesses. Adams's behavior, dismaying to Quincy and Blowers, convinced the loyalist leaders that they had been betrayed. Commodore Hood "and others" flatly told Hutchinson "they expected the cause was lost." Hood even sent for Auchmuty and urged him to insert himself in the case instead of Adams. This fear-inspired reflex overlooked Auchmuty's lack of status. It also overlooked the practicalities. Auchmuty had not attended during the prosecution's evidence nor part of the defense. Obvious irregularities aside, he could not possibly "be sufficiently prepared to close the Cause." With Hutchinson's vigorous approval, Auchmuty declined. Like Preston, the soldiers would have to continue trusting John Adams.[20]

The first few witnesses that Quincy introduced on the morning of November 30, the fourth trial day, did not fully meet John Adams's prescription. Nothing has survived, however, to show that he made any further objection. Dr. Richard Hirons, who had the year before befriended the fugitive John Mein, related in impartial detail the misbehavior of both soldiers and civilians outside Murray's barracks. He also described the autopsy of his patient, Maverick, and identified the fatal musket ball, which Coroner Thomas Crafts produced in court.

Captain Goldfinch told of the insults he had received from the barber's boy earlier in the evening. Young Ben Davis, Jr.—only a "child," Sam Adams noted—testified to meeting Gray en route to King Street, and described the ropemaker's belligerent enthusiasm. Although a Son of Liberty, James Thompson swore to seeing some stick-carriers, perhaps fifteen in number, near King Street earlier. But compared to what had gone before, the evidence seemed tepid. Quincy abandoned the effort. Hardly another witness testified merely to the offstage violence. Almost everyone who took the stand after Thompson had actually been in King Street, either during the firing itself or during the provocations immediately before.

The testimony now began to unfold a picture of direct threats to the party. Through the short November day, Quincy methodically detailed a mass of evidence calculated to establish the real peril which the men had faced. No particular witness stood out, although occasionally the testimony raised a vivid image. Patrick Keeton described how Attucks had reached into a woodpile for two four-foot clubs, " 'Here, take one of them,' " Keeton recalled him saying as they passed together into King Street; later he heard Attucks "cursing and swearing at the soldiers."

Henry Knox told the same story he had at Preston's trial; this time he was on the defense's side. At the end of his testimony, whoever was handling the crown's cross-examination asked him if he had seen the corporal and if the corporal was wearing a surtout. Knox answered "yes." The stratagem was obvious. Because Preston's acquittal had partly been based on proof that the man who ordered the firing had been wearing a surtout (while Preston wore none), proof that Corporal Wemms had been wearing a surtout would tend to incriminate Wemms now.

On and on the evidence went. John Bulkely, Josiah Quincy's law clerk, testified for his master's side, thus perhaps offsetting the earlier performance for the prosecution of Adams's Jonathan Williams Austin.

Asked if he had expected the sentry to be carried off, Bulkely answered pungently: "I thought if he came off with his life he would do very well."

Newton Prince, the free black pastrycook, again testified for the defense. So, too, as the twilight began to fall, did Andrew. As at Preston's trial, he gave a thorough account, emphasizing Attucks's hand-to-hand scuffle with the grenadiers. "Did you yourself pick up everything you could find, and throw at them?" "Yes, I did," Andrew said. Once again the defense called Andrew's master, Oliver Wendell, to affirm "his general character for truth"; once again, Wendell vouched Andrew's credibility. Andrew's evidence must have had a strong favorable effect. A few months later, the first issue of the radical *Massachusetts Spy* ("Open to all Parties, but influenced by None") carried the following acronym:

> As Negroes and L--rs in judgment agree!
> No wonder that vice with her airs is so free!
> Device and low cunning do commonly stand!
> Related in friendship and join hand in hand!
> Experience doth teach us that poor black and white!
> When blended together, as one, will unite!! [21]

"Andrew's evidence, if not his judgment, was greatly rely'd upon," Sam Adams admitted after the trial, "the more, because his master, who is in truth an honest man, came into court and swore to his character." But, Adams added, "no man knows so little of the real character of his servant as the master does." The radicals' true position on racial matters appeared in Adams's next sentence, which also serves as an excellent example of his disingenuous style, affirming-by-denial: "It is well known that the Negroes of this town have been familiar with the soldiers; and that some of them have been tamper'd with to cut their master's throats: I hope Andrew is not one of these." [22]

From the opening of court on Saturday morning, the defense continued to follow John Adams's prescription. One after another, the witnesses held strictly to accounts of what happened in King Street. Blowers and Quincy had prepared the case well. The testimony was cumulating into a picture of riot and threat. Occasionally the preparation overreached itself and the pattern faltered. Charles Willis, an apprentice, began his testimony with the candid admission, "I know nothing worth the telling; I was not in King Street. . . . I came up Royal Exchange Lane and saw the firing, but was not near enough to see anything the people did." Thomas Symmonds, the victualer, told about an earlier hubbub; but his main contribution—overlooked by the harried stenographer—was a brief account of Crispus Attucks's last meal.

A man named John Williams (presumably not the inspector general of the customs) testified to a lengthy conversation with ropewalker Richard Kibbey about the ropemen's battles with the soldiers during the weekend before the Massacre and on March 5 itself. Such obvious hearsay drew a prompt objection from the prosecution, which the court overruled. Williams went on to relay Kibbey's account of the events in King Street. He said Kibbey had told him this during a sea voyage several months later. At that, "one of the prisoners' council" interrupted him and "declared in open court that it was not legal, and that it ought not to have the least weight in the minds of the jurors; upon which it was ruled that the witness should proceed no further, and he was dismiss'd." [23]

The stream of admissible exculpatory evidence continued. Deliberately or accidentally, Quincy was leading up to a midday climax. He put on Catherine Field (Patrick Carr's landlady) and John Mansfield to tell about Carr's trying to go out on the fatal evening carrying a concealed sword. Then he called Dr. John Jeffries. Harvard classmate of Quincy and Blowers and son of Boston Town Treasurer David Jeffries, Jeffries had been a student of Dr. James Lloyd (owner of the slave Jack, who testified for Preston). In May 1768, he sailed to Britain for further education, taking with him a letter to Province Agent Dennys DeBerdt from Sam Adams. Although the elder Jeffries had been forced, in his official capacity, to bring suit against Adams for his tax-collection deficit, Adams considered himself a friend of the family; both the Jeffries, in turn, retained radical leanings. When John returned, full of London learning and a "quickie" M.D. degree purchased from the University of Aberdeen, he and the treasurer joined the celebrating Sons of Liberty at the famous August 14, 1769, banquet.[24]

Jeffries' own recollections of the scuffling outside Murray's Barracks formed part of the testimony he was expected to give. But Quincy revealed the main reason for calling him with his very first question: "Was you Patrick Carr's surgeon?" Jeffries had been sent for at about 11 P.M. on the evening of the shooting; engaged in dressing Edward Payne's shattered arm, he had not gone to see Carr until the next morning. Dr. Lloyd, who was also treating Carr, encouraged Jeffries to question the patient on the circumstances of his shooting. Repeated virtually every day until Carr died, the conversation made for dramatic testimony. A voice from beyond the grave was coming to exculpate the soldiers.

> I asked him whether he thought the soldiers would fire. He told me he thought the soldiers would have fired long before. I asked him whether he thought the soldiers were abused a great deal, after they went down there. He said, he thought they were. I asked him whether

he thought the soldiers would have been hurt, if they had not fired. He said he really thought they would, for he heard many voices cry out, kill them. I asked him then, meaning to close all, whether he thought they fired in self-defense, or on purpose to destroy the people. He said he really thought they did fire to defend themselves; that he did not blame the man whoever he was, that shot him.

Jeffries' telling the jury what Carr told him was of course pure hearsay. It became admissible evidence as a result of Quincy's next question: "Was he apprehensive of his danger?" An exception to the hearsay rule permitted the introduction into evidence of a hearsay statement if the statement were made by someone with "a settled hopeless expectation" of impending death. In most courts today, Quincy would have been required to reverse the order of his questioning, that is, first to establish Carr's consciousness of death, and only then to bring out the substance of his statement. Whether Quincy's failure to lay the foundation sprang from the opposition's inattention or indifference, or whether, on the other hand, it represented settled Massachusetts practice, one cannot now say.

In any event, Jeffries' answer to Quincy's vital inquiry was somewhat less than explicit. But no objection appears to have been raised. "He was told of it," Jeffries said equivocally. "He told me also, he was a native of Ireland, that he had frequently seen mobs, and soldiers called upon to quell them." This is the sort of answer that lawyers call unresponsive; they mean overly responsive. Upon objection by the prosecution in a modern trial, Jeffries would have been stopped after his first sentence. But again, no one said anything. Jeffries continued: Carr also told him "that he had seen soldiers often fire on the people in Ireland, but had never seen them bear half so much before they fired in his life." The afternoon before Carr died, he had a last talk with Jeffries. "He then particularly said he forgave the man whoever he was that shot him, he was satisfied he had no malice, but fired to defend himself."

The Carr-Jeffries evidence had powerfully aided the defense. Later on, when Sam Adams was retrying the case in the newspapers, he deprecated Jeffries' evidence, and Carr's character. "[I]t is to be observed, he did not declare this under oath nor before a magistrate." Like many of Adams's propaganda blasts, this one dripped irrelevancy. Dying declarations are by definition unsworn; their admissibility depends not upon the sanction of the oath, but rather upon the premise, elegantly phrased by a later English judge, that no man "who is immediately going into the presence of his Maker, will do so with a lie on his lips." Adams, predictably, had a demagogic answer for that point. Carr, he said "in all probability died in the faith of a roman

catholick." Anyway, according to Adams, Carr had not really anticipated death: "His doctors had encouraged him that he would soon recover of his wounds, and he hoped to live to be a swift witness against
the soldiers." If that were true, one would have expected the prosecutors to bring it out on cross-examination of Jeffries, or by the independent witnesses which Adams claimed were "ready to be sworn." [25]

After the Jeffries bombshell, the remainder of the defense evidence
passed quickly and quietly. Two officers testified to the official placing
of the sentry; another witness told briefly of an out-of-King Street gang
with sticks; Theodore Bliss described again the provocation and the
shootings. That closed the prisoners' case. The crown had inserted an
out-of-order witness who, like Bliss, described the King Street activity.
Then, after the defense rested, Henry Bass, one of the Loyal Nine, and
the injured merchant, Edward Payne, testified as rebuttal witnesses.
Bass told only of rowdy activity by the soldiers earlier or elsewhere.
Payne, the sole victim of the musketry to give evidence, added little to
the prosecution's case. Indeed, he recalled commenting on "the foolishness of the people in calling the sentry to fire on them." He said the
mob, crowding "pretty nigh" the soldiers, numbered between fifty and
one hundred. It was a peculiarly quiet way for the crown to finish.
Paine offered additional evidence "to prove threats and behaviour of
Soldiers, but time would not admit." Inspired after all, perhaps by
Samuel Adams's mid-trial memorandum, Paine obtained, as his *quid
pro quo* for not extending the already record-length trial, an agreement that "there was reason for going armed and coming out that
night." The court thereupon adjourned, thus allowing the weekend for
counsel to prepare argument, and the judges to arrange their several
summations.

Josiah Quincy began for the defense on Monday morning. His argument lacked some of the verve and effect of his opening, but it carefully seized all the advantages the evidence had given to the defense.
"You are paying a debt you owe the community for your own protection and safety," he reminded the jurors. "And in your turn, a time may
come, when you will expect and claim a similar return from some
other jury of your fellow subjects."

The heavy evidence of military misbehavior he dealt with as he had
in his opening, urging the jurors to "distinguish between the transactions in Cornhill and those by the Custom House." Then he cleverly
used the evidence to argue that even "a very moderate person" might
hastily seek to extract vengeance from the Custom House party for
what other soldiers did elsewhere. "The law," however, "indulges no
man in being his own avenger." Self-defense? Of course; "upon the
right of self-defence and self-preservation we rely for our acquittal."

But the rest of the evidence showed that the people in King Street were not trying to preserve their own lives; they were frankly trying to obliterate the soldiers.

The "many commotions in various parts of town," Quincy said, disregarding his own earlier distinctions, showed that the inhabitants were "guilty of at least indiscreet conduct." But Quincy chose not to go deeply "into the tumult of the town, because I don't think it much to the point." And also, perhaps, because he did not want to risk John Adams's displeasure and its consequent bad effects on the defense.

The attack on the party allowed Quincy's analysis of the evidence to score heavily. "Where are we got if negative evidence shall outweigh positive?" he asked, as he emphasized Andrew's testimony, Carr's dying speech, and the conglomerate evidence that men had rushed in on the soldiers and struck them.

As to the firing itself, even that had not been satisfactorily proven. Some defendants had not been shown to have fired; the witnesses who testified that Montgomery fired also related extenuating facts. The evidence that Warren and Kilroy had been at the ropewalks "is nothing to do with this." The evidence bore hardest against Kilroy—the threats in the kitchen, the bloody bayonet. But even here, Quincy argued, quoting legal treatises, mere words were weak evidence on which to convict. Anyhow, if it were a matter of words, the jury should consider the mob's epithets ("lobster," "coward," "bloody-back," "dastard"). "Gentlemen of the jury," Quincy cried, "for heaven's sake, let us put ourselves in the same situation!" This was the weakest part of Quincy's argument; if the crowd, as he had earlier insisted, should not have taken vengeance for military assaults into its own hands, then even more should the soldiers have refrained from a violent response to mere words. Realizing his difficulty, Quincy deftly shifted ground. Under the circumstances prevailing in King Street, men should have tried to reassure the soldiers and calm them. Insults could only have the opposite effect. "You might as rationally expect," said Quincy, "that the flames of Etna would extinguish a conflagration."

Quincy left for Adams that pervasive problem, the absolute biblical injunction that "*whosoever* sheddeth man's blood" must die. He merely denied the applicability of the Mosaic law and quoted a mass of English precedent and authority to prove that the killings had been committed without fault. The wadded legal lore must have fallen heavily on, or more accurately around, the word-numbed jurors. Realizing this, Quincy tried to liven his peroration. He quoted from that old Whig favorite, John Locke, "to show the world that the greatest friends to their country, to universal liberty, and the immutable rights of man, have held tenets, and advanced maxims, favorable to the prisoners."

He threw another harpoon at the radicals and their *Short Narrative:* "They who are *under oath* to declare the *whole truth,* think and act very differently from by-standers, who, being under no ties of this kind, take a latitude, which is by no means admissible in a *court of law.*" Quincy then quoted from Shakespeare: Portia's "quality of mercy" speech. Finally, with a reminder that everyone would later "have an hour of cool reflection—when the feelings and agitations of the day shall have subsided," and a prediction that "then we shall all wish an absolving conscience," Quincy sat down.

The speech which John Adams now rose to give has never received its true measure of fame. Isolated paragraphs have occasionally been cited, invariably with vast approval, as part of the Massacre mythology. But never has it been praised for what it really was, a masterpiece of political tightroping and partisan invective, wrapped inextricably in a skillful, effective jury argument. From his opening mawkish quotation, inaccurately rendered, Adams successfully played both instruments. "I am for the prisoners at the bar, and shall apologize for it [as if an apology were either necessary or proper] only in the words of the Marquis Beccaria: 'If I can but be the instrument of preserving one life, his blessing and tears of transport, shall be sufficient consolation to me, for the contempt of all mankind.'" This produced an "electrical effect" on some of the spectators, although Adams had used it before, in Preston's trial. Adams's subsequent rhetoric must have produced a shock of alarm in the soldiers. Instead of an argument that the crown had not proved its case, he began citing to the jury that chestnut of the criminal law: "It's of more importance to [the] community, that innocence should be protected than it is, that guilt should be punished." "I shall take it for granted, as a first principle, that the eight prisoners at the bar, had better be all acquitted, though we should admit them all to be guilty, than, that any one of them should by your verdict be found guilty, being innocent." Adams was beginning his summation by virtually conceding the guilt of some of his clients.

Abandoning this risky strategy, Adams turned to the problem which had vexed Quincy, the popular belief that blood always requires blood. This, Adams flatly denied. "Had the prisoners been on the Plains of Abraham, and slain an hundred Frenchmen apiece, the English law would have considered it, as a commendable action." Adams had chosen his example well; Wolfe's dramatic victory at Quebec, only eleven years before, still raised grateful memories in the hearts of the people whose country, freedom, and religion the battle was widely considered to have saved. The thought was enough to carry the jury's attention through Adams's ensuing resumption of his law-book reading.

The law of self-defense, the "foundation" of liberty and property, as Adams called it, was the next topic of his discourse. Here he dropped the first of what Thomas Hutchinson later called "great indecencies . . . respecting the conduct of Administration in sending Troops here." [26] "You must place yourselves," Adams told the jury, properly enough, "in the situation of Wemms or Kilroy. Consider yourselves as knowing that . . . the people about you, thought you came to dragoon them into obedience to statutes, instructions, mandates, and edicts, which they thoroughly detested."

Then, just as abruptly as he had detonated the blast against the Home Government, Adams began to flay his own countrymen for the benefit of the jurymen, all from out-of-town, who had probably never seen a mob or heard one. He described in horrifying detail the scene in King Street, "the people shouting, huzzaing, and making the mob whistle as they call it, which when a boy makes it in the street, is no formidable thing, but when made by a multitude, is a most hideous shriek, almost as terrible as an Indian yell." Cleverly, Adams asked the jury to consider what might have happened if Gray, Attucks, and the rest of the victims had been part of a military watch planted by Lieutenant Colonel Marshal to keep order against bands of marauding soldiers. Suppose, he asked, such a band had attacked such a guard, as the crowd had assaulted Preston's party. "I confess I believe," said Adams, the civilians "would not have borne the one half of what the witnesses have sworn the soldiers bore, till they had shot down as many as were necessary to intimidate and disperse the rest."

Another lump of quotations from English authorities followed, seasoned with Adams's pungent comments, all directed toward emphasizing the common law's tender regard for the right of self-defense. In a mob situation, "[t]here is no occasion for the Magistrate to read the Riot Act," he said, thus deflating still another popular misconception. Further, "in case of an unlawful assembly, all and everyone of the assembly is guilty of all and every unlawful act" committed by any member of the crowd in pursuit of the mob's unlawful purpose. Adams's purpose here, as he said much later, "was to lay before [the people of Boston] the law as it stood, that they might be fully apprized of the dangers of various kinds, which must rise from intemperate heats and irregular commotions." "Rules of law," he told the jury, "should be universally known, whatever effect they may have on politics." The guilt shared by all members of an unlawful assembly "is the policy of the law: to discourage and prevent riots, insurrections, turbulence and tumults." But here Adams could not resist another propaganda shot. "At certain critical seasons, even in the mildest government, the people are liable to run into riots and tumults." This aptitude "to mutinies, seditions, tumults, and insurrections is in direct proportion to the despotism of the government." And he listed the forms of government in descending order of turbulent disposition: aristocracies, mixed monarchies, and "compleat republicks." "And under the same form of government, as in a limited monarchy, for example, the virtue and wisdom of the administration, may generally be measured by the peace and order that are seen among the people." By this little sally, Adams drew all blame for the Boston rioting away from the radicals who had directed it, tossing it instead on His Majesty's Government and its local representatives.

Adams threw the jury another thick blob of citations and quotations. One of the cases mentioned the subduing of "rebels." "I do not mean to apply the word rebel on this occasion," Adams hastily reassured the jury. "I have no reason to suppose that ever there was one in Boston, at least among the natives of the country; but rioters are in the same situation, as far as my argument is concerned."

To illustrate that argument, as well as to carry out his polemical purposes, Adams gently massaged another nerve. "Suppose a press gang should come on shore in this town," and carry off a sailor or householder. "How far do you suppose the inhabitants would think themselves warranted by law, to interpose against that lawless press gang?" The soldiers had no less right to resist the King Street mob than the people would have to "help an honest man there, against the press master."

The crowd's threat to the sentry, even if the people "had nothing in their intention more than to take him off his post, . . . tar and feather him, or to ride him," justified his defending himself. And if they threatened his life, he could deprive them of theirs. "That is a point I would not give up for my right hand," Adams said, "nay, for my life." The shedding of innocent blood in such a case would not alter the result; again Adams reminded the jury of "the Frenchmen on the Plains of Abraham." And even if the killings might be supposed not entirely justifiable, still they would be no more than manslaughter, albeit intentional, while the accidental deaths of the innocent bystanders would entail no guilt at all. To buttress his argument, Adams quoted still more English legal authorities. Deeper and deeper into his books Adams burrowed; "I will just read as I go along." One after another the weighty pronouncements of the old judges filled the courtroom, until suddenly five o'clock struck, and the court adjourned.

From the law, Adams turned the next morning to the evidence. Serially he dealt with the witnesses, spicing his analysis with occasional sharp observations. Nothing escaped his attention: the Kilroy-Hemmingway incident ("this is to prove that Kilroy . . . had the spirit not only of a *Turk* or an *Arab*, but of the devil"); the ringing of the bells ("probably copied from New York, a wretched example in this, and in two other instances at least"—referring to the Mein and Richardson affairs); a witness's errors (he "confounds one time with another, a mistake which has been made by many witnesses, in this case, and considering the confusion and terror of the scene, is not to be wondered at" —thus neatly avoiding having to call the witness a liar); the alleged blood on Kilroy's bayonet ("It would be doing violence to every rule of law and evidence, as well as to common sense and the feelings of humanity, to infer from the blood on the bayonet, that it had been stabbed into the brains of Mr. Gray after he was dead, and that by Kilroy himself who had killed him").

As the morning wore on, Adams began to unlimber his rhetoric.

> We have been entertained with a great variety of phrases, to avoid calling this sort of people a mob. Some call them shavers, some call them genius's. The plain English is, gentlemen, most probably a motley rabble of saucy boys, negroes and molattoes, Irish teagues and outlandish jack tarrs. And why we should scruple to call such a set of people a mob, I can't conceive, unless the name is too respectable for them. The sun is not about to stand still or go out, nor the rivers to dry up because there was a mob in Boston on the 5th of March that attacked a party of soldiers. . . . [S]oldiers quartered in a populous town, will always occasion two mobs, where they prevent one. They are wretched conservators of the peace.

With that neat hit at the administration, Adams returned to his evidentiary combing. The sentry had said he feared mischief; "and well he might, with so many shavers and genius's round him, capable of throwing such dangerous things." The shouts and threats of the multitude, the ringing of the bells, "the mob whistle screaming and rending like an Indian yell," Adams described them all once more. Montgomery had been knocked down; struggling to his feet, he was struck yet again. "What could he do? Do you expect he should behave like a Stoick Philosopher lost in Apathy? . . . It is impossible you should find him guilty of murder."

The idea of what a modern apologist would call "outside agitators" formed Adams's theme a second time. He started with the battling "stout Molatto fellow." "This was the behaviour of Attucks; to whose mad behaviour, in all probability, the dreadful carnage of that night, is chiefly to be ascribed. And it is in this manner, this town has been often treated; a *Carr* from *Ireland,* and an *Attucks* from *Framingham,* happening to be here, shall sally out upon their thoughtless enterprizes, at the head of such rabble of Negroes, &c. as they can collect together, and then there are not wanting, persons to ascribe all their doings to the good people of the town." This was Adams's clearest suggestion yet of a way that the jurors could acquit and yet retain quiet consciences. Blame the (dead) outsiders themselves for inviting their own deaths; clear the Bostonians of having provoked the riots. The idea seems to have been essential to the radical propaganda strategy; that is why Sam Adams took such umbrage at the red-cloak story, which suggested that the mob was Boston-led, if not Boston-bred.

His duty next impelled Adams to "a minute consideration of every witness produced on the crown side," and "the testimonies of the witnesses for the prisoners." Happily for an enjoyable appreciation of Adams's effort, these remarks were not recorded. The sun was at the zenith as he soared into his closing. "Facts are stubborn things . . . [N]or is the law less stable than the fact; if an assault was made to endanger their lives, the law is clear, they had a right to kill in their own defence; if it was not so severe as to endanger their lives, yet if they were assaulted at all, struck and abused by blows of any sort, . . . this was a provocation, for which the law reduces the offence of killing down to manslaughter . . . To your candour and justice I submit the prisoners and their cause."

Adams had almost finished. " 'The law,' " he said, quoting the great Algernon Sidney once again, " 'no passion can disturb. . . . 'Tis deaf, inexorable, inflexible.' " "On the one hand," he concluded, "it is inexorable to the cries and lamentations of the prisoners; on the other it is deaf, deaf as an adder to the clamour of the populace."

Adams, Hutchinson said shortly afterward, "closed extremely well & with great fidelity to his Clients." [27] He had done more; whatever political uses Adams had made of his closing, he had ensured an acquittal.

Paine, still "much fatigued and unwell," could offer no match for Adams's solid cleverness. "I have got the severe side of the question to Conduct," he candidly admitted. He did not conduct it well. Mostly, his argument took the form of denying the defense's points, rather than establishing his own; the prosecution had obviously lost the initiative entirely. Paine had to concede that Wemms's musket had not fired and that Montgomery's crime "can amount no higher than Manslaughter." Interrupted by the evening adjournment, Paine came back to speak for two hours the next day, beginning early, at 8 A.M. Only once did he show even a flash of talent. Should the jury conclude that the soldiers were unlawfully assembled, he urged, they must all be guilty, "for it has been abundantly proved to you by the numerous authorities produced by the council for the prisoners, that every individual of an unlawful assembly is answerable for the doings of the rest."

Paine's feeble best was not enough. When he finished up at 10 A.M.

the jurors faced three and one-half hours of charges from the court. Trowbridge's exhaustive and, if one believes the Whigs, partisan, summation parroted a great deal of the legal authority Adams had already cited.[28] The two speeches differed largely in their nonlegal content: Trowbridge was evidently trying, as was Judge Oliver a little later, to counteract some of Adams's "very great indecencies." "If upon the whole," said Oliver, "ye are in any reasonable doubt of their guilt, ye must then, agreeable to the rule of law, declare them innocent." The other two judges added little to what Oliver and Trowbridge had said; at 1:30 P.M., the case was finally delivered to the jury.

By 4 P.M. the jury was back. "Gentlemen of the jury," inquired Clerk of Court Samuel Winthrop, "are you all agreed in your verdict?" "Yes," they said. "William Wemms," said Winthrop, "hold up your hand." Wemms did. "Gentlemen of the Jury," continued Winthrop, "look upon the prisoner. How say you, is William Wemms guilty of all or either of the felonies or murders whereof he stands indicted, or not guilty." "Not guilty," said foreman Joseph Mayo. "Hearken to your verdict as the Court hath recorded it. You upon your oaths do say, that William Wemms is not guilty, and so you say all."

One by one, Winthrop led the prisoners through the formula with Mayo. Hartigan, not guilty; McCauley, not guilty; White, not guilty. At Kilroy, the pattern broke: "Not guilty of murder, but guilty of manslaughter." Warren, Carroll, both not guilty. Montgomery, manslaughter. Later, it was disclosed that the jury thought the soldiers should have waited longer before they fired. "[I]f it had been proved that they all fired they would have brought in all Guilty of Manslaughter." Only Kilroy and Montgomery having been proved to have fired, "[r]ather therefore than convict one of the six not proved to have fired who must be innocent the jury acquitted five who were Guilty." While the jailers kept Kilroy and Montgomery, readying them for the walk back to the prison and the wait for sentencing, the other six passed out of the courtroom, down the stairs, and into the town, where as the Boston *Gazette* reported, "They went their way thro' the Streets, with little, if any, notice." Nine months to the day after the killings in King Street, they were once again free men—or free soldiers, which was almost the same thing.[29]

CHAPTER 20

THE FLAME SUBSIDES

With the series of acquittals, Boston seemed at last to have broken the political fever which had raged since the soldiers' first arrival. True, Kilroy and Montgomery still remained in prison, technically liable to the death penalty, and the four civilians still awaited trial. But as Hutchinson reported to Hillsborough, "Take the whole together, it is a favorable Event." The day following the verdicts, Preston, bearing Hutchinson's praise for "having been very assiduous in furnishing every necessary help for the Trial of the soldiers," left for home aboard H.M.S. *Glasgow*. With him as passengers went two other central figures of the times: Lieutenant Alexander Ross of the Fourteenth, and irascible Justice of the Peace James Murray.[1]

Paine, ill and disappointed, returned to Taunton. No one knew when the civilians' trial might come on. The exhausted judges did not resume sitting until late in the afternoon of December 11; even then, they only met in order to adjourn. That evening, Hutchinson summoned Chief Judge Lynde and Judge Trowbridge to his official residence at the Province House. "He urged continuing [i.e., postponing]," Lynde noted in his diary, which suggests that Hutchinson, strangely enough, did not seem willing to seize the moment of calm. He preferred to put the civilians' case over to the future.[2]

Despite the acting governor's wishes, the next morning, Manwaring and his three co-defendants were brought to the bar. Sewall and Paine remaining absent, and the Town's committee, Selectmen Inches and Mason, declaring themselves unauthorized to retain a special prosecutor, Samuel Quincy, "in Furtherance of the Business of the Court," offered to conduct the trial. It proved, as Quincy told Paine later, "another Windmill adventure," in which Quincy "came off . . . like poor Quixot in a like Instance." The name of defense counsel has not been recorded. It is possible, even likely, that Manwaring and his friends stood trial without a lawyer.[3]

Unwilling to summon an entire new venire for the trial, the court used the same panel which had furnished the soldiers' jury. The impaneling went forward quickly; none of the jurors came from Boston; ten of the twelve had been challenged in the earlier trial, seven peremptorily, three for cause. The crown called four witnesses, all of them pathetically weak. Samuel Drowne told of seeing musket flashes at an upper window and balcony of the Custom House. But Drowne was "an idiot," and the crown found it necessary to call Timothy White specially to bolster his credibility. Even White conceded that "some people thought [Drowne] foolish." Gillam Bass saw the soldiers fire. "Two or three flashes seemed four or five feet higher than the rest." But, Bass admitted, "I saw no firing from the Custom House." [4]

That left the crown's chances up to Charles (or Charlotte) Bourgatte, Manwaring's French servant boy. Born in Bordeaux, Bourgatte spoke enough English to deliver his testimony without an interpreter. The testimony, if believed, would surely hang Manwaring, and might well convict John Munro and Hammond Green. According to Bourgatte, Manwaring fired a double-loaded musket into King Street, while a mysterious "tall man" (perhaps an insinuating reference to John Robinson) forced Bourgatte, on pain of death, to fire two guns, one after the other, out the same window. Bourgatte said he had managed to fire each musket in a safe direction. Green and Munro had been present in the house, although not in the same room with Bourgatte. Immediately afterward, the tall man offered Bourgatte money not to tell what happened. Bourgatte said he went to Manwaring's lodgings, where he found only the landlord and landlady. At that, the crown rested. "The prisoners," says the printed report of the trial, "desired the following witnesses might be sworn and examined." This tends to suggest the defendants had no counsel. None really was necessary; the witnesses told straightforward stories. Messrs. Bethune, Davis, Harrison Gray, Jr., and Edward Payne (the latter still scarred by the bullet that had struck his arm) had all been standing across the street from the Custom House, in perfect position to observe any shooting from the second-story windows. Unanimously, they said they had seen none. Elizabeth Avery denied the firing and, more important, said that neither Manwaring nor Munro nor Bourgatte had been in the Custom House that night; Ann Green confirmed this.

Manwaring's landlady, Elizabeth Hudson, testified positively that her husband had been out of town on March 5, and that her boarder together with Munro and Bourgatte had been in the house continuously from the time the bells began ringing until after ten o'clock. When Mrs. Hudson finished, the judges asked the still-present Bourgatte if he had heard and understood her testimony. Yes, he had, he said, and her account was false; what he had just declared in court was "the truth and nothing but the truth." Still seeking to unravel the mystery, the court swore four interpreters, including schoolmaster John Lovell and the Preston trial juror, Philip Dumaresq. Through them, Bourgatte was again examined, this time in French. He stuck to his story.

James Penny, who as an imprisoned debtor had shared jail quarters with Bourgatte in late March, testified that Bourgatte had told him and another debtor that "what he testified to the Grand Jury and before the Justices on his examination with regard to" Manwaring's and Munro's firing out of the Custom House "was in every particular false, and that he did swear in that manner by persuasion of William Molineux, who told him he would take him from his master and provide for him, and that Mr. Molineux frightened him by telling him if he refused to swear against his master and Mr. Munro the mob in Boston would kill him." Further, Penny said, Bourgatte told him that a Mrs. Waldron from the North End "gave him the said Charles gingerbread and cheese, and desired him to swear against his master."

The court had shifted its attention; Bourgatte was the real defendant now, not the four prisoners. Desperate, the French boy hotly denied having said any such thing to Penny or anyone else, and "stood to his account with consummate impudence." [5] He insisted the judges call still another debtor, cabinet maker William Page. But Page did little for Bourgatte's riddled credibility. After admitting that Molineux had indeed taken the boy into the jailkeeper's house for a quiet talk, Page could only say that Bourgatte had later insisted "Mr. Molineux never urged or required him to say anything but the truth." Penny's testimony, at best, was excludable hearsay. No one seems to have objected, however, and the evidence closed shortly before noon. No record survives of any closing argument or indeed of any charge. Perhaps nobody thought such formalities necessary. Certainly the jurors did not; they "acquitted all the Prisoners, without going from their Seats."

The result was unimpeachable. Although the historian Edward Channing has argued that guns really were fired from the Custom House, he based his contention on slippery ground: the Pelham-Revere print (a demonstrably and designedly inaccurate propaganda piece) and Manwaring's later petition for reimbursement of his defense expenses.[6] Such a request by a customs official to be reimbursed for financial losses incurred in a real sense in the line of duty cannot by any means be considered tantamount to an admission of guilt. The trial evidence confirmed what many had suspected from the start: the indicting of Manwaring and the others had been induced by the radicals in order to implicate the customs service, particularly the commissioners, in the King Street bloodletting.

None of the Whig leaders, including Molineux, ever faced criminal charges in this connection. Whatever protected them did not extend to Bourgatte. Immediately after the trial, the judges, struck by the inherent impossibility of his story, ordered him committed pending grand jury action. At the next regular superior court sitting, the grand jury indicted him for perjury, the petty jury convicted him, and the court sentenced him to an hour in the pillory and twenty-five lashes at the whipping post. The radicals did not abandon him completely. When the sheriff's men set about the flogging, a crowd stopped them; they had to return two days later, "to execute in a hasty manner the sentence of the law." [7]

Meanwhile, Kilroy and Montgomery remained in jail. Some of the crown officials wanted to spare the soldiers the burning on the thumb which was the necessary judicial price for invoking the life-saving "benefit of clergy." Someone asked Hutchinson to remit the branding. Fearing that such lenity would "have a tendency to irritate the people," Hutchinson hesitated while "Dalrymple and other Officers" surprisingly urged him to deny the request. Assuring himself that the question "was of little consequence to the prisoners," Hutchinson finally declined. On December 14, Montgomery and Kilroy came, guarded, into court. Asked if either had any reason why sentence of death should not be passed, each promptly "prayed clergy." While at least one of their lawyers, John Adams, looked on with pity, Kilroy and Montgomery, protesting their innocence, held out their right thumbs for Sheriff Greenleaf to brand. The barbaric ceremony completed, the prisoners were discharged and the Boston Massacre, legally speaking, passed into history.[8]

The feelings the event and its aftermath had engendered, however, did not fade so easily. Even before the branding, Samuel Adams had taken to the Boston *Gazette* in a bitter attempt to retry the cases. Writing as "Vindex," Adams followed what Supreme Court Justice Felix Frankfurter once called the "practice familiar in the long history of Anglo-American litigation, whereby unsuccessful litigants and lawyers give vent to their disappointment in tavern or press." Critical of the way the court and counsel had conducted the trial, vicious in its assault on key defense evidence, particularly Carr's dying declaration, the "Vindex" series rode cavalierly over the truth. Adams, deprived of a juridically chosen scapegoat, seemed determined to win a propaganda victory anyway. In his burning passion to convince the world that the soldiers had indeed attacked the mob, Adams resolutely refused to allow simple fact or clear law to impede him. He misstated testimony and, ostensibly in the guise of leading the reader back to a consideration of "the temper the Soldiers in general discovered [i.e., revealed]," palmed off as genuine some of the *Short Narrative* depositions whose authors had not even appeared as witnesses at any of the trials. Worse, Adams rekindled the "blood requires blood" fallacy: "As the lives of five of his Majesty's subjects were *unfairly* lost on the evening of the 5th of March last, it follows that some persons must have been at fault." [9]

Jonathan Sewall, writing as "Philanthrop," tried to neutralize Vindex's venom. "I think," Hutchinson wrote Hillsborough, "[he] will lay open to view of the Public the Artifices which have been employed to deceive & abuse them." But the truant attorney-general was never a polemical match for Adams. His "Philanthrop" series, lawyerly and judicious, lacked the fire the occasion demanded. Curiously, while Adams publicly tried to prove that justice had miscarried, his ardent supporter, the Reverend Samuel Cooper, was telling Benjamin Franklin that the acquittals ought to "wipe off the imputation of our being so violent and blood thirsty a people, as not to permit law and justice to take place on the side of unpopular men; and I hope our friends will make this use of them." [10]

While the newspaper battle warmed up, the Sons of Liberty took more direct action. The night following the acquittal of the civilians (December 12), someone pinned on the door of the Town House a paper bearing a few lines from Thomas Otway's still-popular political play, *Venice Preserved; or A Plot Discover'd*. As altered to fit the occasion, the speech complained of the court's having cheated "the injured people with a shew of justice" and called on the Town "to rise up at the great call of nature and free the world from such domestic tyrants." Taken down and carried to the judges, the placard so infuriated them that they threatened to adjourn the court session instanter. After brief reflection, they sent the paper to Hutchinson, who laid it before the council; a proclamation offering a suitable reward for information was published, "which," Hutchinson remarked tartly, "there was no room to suppose would have any effect." [11]

But Boston was visibly quieting down. The commissioners of the customs, who had precipitously fled in March, now came back; in Hutchinson's opinion, they could safely have returned a month earlier.

Before the end of December they were, with the governor's explicit approval, again holding their board meetings in town, making "no complaints of Insults or any sort of Molestation." The verdicts, Hutchinson observed, "instead of incensing the People of the Country against the Jury have incensed them against the Town and their Committee of which Mr. Bowdoin was Chairman which drew up the Narrative." Hutchinson was delighted with the jury's demonstrated ability to sift the evidence; "[P]retty good distinctions for an American jury," he said. Pleased by the acquittals, the governor planned to reward foreman Joseph Mayo by promoting him to major of militia. Mayo had a radical reputation, Hutchinson wrote, "but proved an honest man & would not go against his conscience." [12]

The regulars, of course, had long since cleared the town. The Fourteenth was still at the Castle, the Twenty-ninth in the Jerseys. Dalrymple wanted the acquitted men to rejoin the latter regiment as soon as possible, but doubted whether he could march them south. "A bad disposition appearing in the Soldiers who were confined I shall send them round by Sea. We have but too much reason to suspect their ententions to desert they are not at all to be depended upon." Before the party embarked, Montgomery confided to his counsel "that he was the man who gave the word fire which was supposed by some of the witnesses to come from the Captain; that being knocked down and rising again, in the agony from the blow he said Damn you, fire and immediately he fired himself and rest followed him." [13]

In England, the Massacre and its aftermath had attracted wide attention. Even before word of the soldiers' acquittals had reached home, a demand had built up for information about Preston's trial. One bookseller said that if he had a report of the testimony, he "could soon sell a thousand copies of it." Preston himself, it was widely anticipated, would receive "some compensation for his confinement." The king paid expenses of £264:7:0 for Preston and the men. The captain also received a £200 annual pension and retired from the army. When John Adams heard of Preston's good fortune, he grumbled slightly. "If C. Preston is to be reimbursed his Expences, I wish his Expences, at least to his Council, had been greater." The lawyers had divided fees totaling £140:2:0. [14]

For political purposes, if not commercial ones, Hodgson's stenographic notes were being rushed into transcript and then print. The shorthand reporter, fatigued from the effort of keeping up with the week-long flow of oratory, had not been able to take down Paine's closing. Samuel Quincy, Blowers, and even Judge Oliver all urged Paine to reconstruct his argument, so that the finished report would be complete. But Paine, pleading another bout of indisposition, could only put together some rough jottings, which never found their way into the published trial. When Adams reviewed Hodgson's version of his own speeches, he found the product so offensive that he eliminated much of his evidentiary analysis. It was not until mid-January that Fleeming's press was able to turn out final copies. Hutchinson, having previously sent Hillsborough a set of rough minutes, hurried the sheets to London.[15]

Symbolically, the very next day, the Queen's Birthday, brought "fine weather." Guns fired interminably to celebrate the "jovial" occasion. That evening, a "very Grand Assembly" gathered at Concert Hall. Hutchinson was there, Dalrymple, all the high military officers, the commissioners, and, in John Rowe's enthusiastic words, "all the Best People in town." It was, he said, "A General Coalition so that Harmony Peace & Friendship will once more be Established in Boston— Very Good Dancing & Good Musick but very Bad Wine & Punch." Hutchinson, perhaps deluded by the sudden relaxing of tensions, was sure the tide had turned. "I am told," he wrote, "that I have succeeded beyond what the friends of Government expected and that it is now the sense of a great part, perhaps the majority of the people of the Province, Boston excepted, that the late measures are not to be justified." [16]

Anxious lest burgeoning "Harmony Peace & Friendship" dull the edge of antiministerial resentment, Samuel Adams moved promptly to keep the memory of the killings red in America's eye. Catering to the Boston appetite for anniversary celebration, he arranged to have March 5 set aside as an annual day of mourning, complete with bell tolling, lighted-picture displays, and oratory. Every March 5 from 1771 through 1784, when, belatedly, July 4 assumed its proper place in the holiday hierarchy, selected orators delivered what Bernard Bailyn has accurately called "some of the most lurid and naive rhetoric heard in eighteenth-century America." The speakers touched only briefly on the actual facts of the King Street killings. Instead, they used the occasion to lambaste constituted authority and (after independence) the general English evils. The topic of the speeches was so divorced from the legal and factual issues involved that John Adams could seriously consider accepting an invitation to give the 1773 version. "The Subject of the Oration," he agreed, "was quite compatible with the Verdict of the Jury," even, Adams added, "with the absolute Innocence of the Soldiers." He nonetheless declined the offer. "The World in general," he believed, "were not capable or not willing to make the Distinction" he had drawn. He was right. By Sam Adams's persistent efforts, "a great part of the people were induced to think the acquittals to be unjust and illegal. The action continued to be spoke of as a massacre, a bloody massacre, and the like." Men, Hutchinson noted, talked about the killings just "as if the jury had found those concerned in it guilty of murder." [17]

Popular feeling very clearly did not rejoice in that triumph of justice over prejudice which later Bostonians have seen in the acquittals. Adams himself always considered his participation in the defense "one of the most gallant, generous, manly and disinterested Actions of my whole life, and one of the best Pieces of Service I ever rendered my Country." The death sentence, he wrote in 1773, "would have been as foul a Stain upon this Country as the Executions of the Quakers or Witches, anciently. As the Evidence was, the Verdict of the Jury was exactly right." Some of his townsmen violently disagreed. They heaped "abuse" on Adams and Quincy. The lawyers heard their names "execrated in the most opprobrious terms whenever [they] appeared in the streets of Boston." "To this hour," Adams complained in 1815, "my conduct in it is remembered, and is alleged against me to prove I am an enemy to my country, and always have been." [18]

Adams did not perceive, as Hutchinson quite clearly did, that for all the dropping of "great indecencies" concerning the presence of the troops, his performance in the trials had seriously prejudiced the radical argument that Bostonians were essentially quiet folk, being prodded to violence by barbaric Redcoats. "The Counsel for the prisoners," Hutchinson wrote shortly after the trial, "have done more to hurt the general cause in which they had been warmly engaged than they ever intended & I think it not impossible if they could have forseen it they would have declined engaging or measures would have been taken to discourage them from it." [19]

An inkling of the lingering popular dissatisfaction with the outcome may be seen in the action of the Suffolk Court of General Sessions, composed of all the county's justices of the peace. The superior court, concerned at the length of the trials and the consequent effect on the livelihoods of the sequestered jurors, had recommended that the sessions grant the jurors a suitable "reasonable Allowance." The jurors promptly petitioned the sessions for the money, but after an all-day hearing, in which "[t]he two Quincys, Otis and Adams, argued," the sessions denied the petition. Lack of statutory authority was the stated reason; it is probable that behind the decision lay a strong unwillingness to grant the jury anything remotely resembling a reward, or even a vote of approval.[20]

Resentment of the acquittals did not diminish the attempts to apotheosize the Massacre itself. On the night of March 5, 1770, John Adams later boasted, "the foundation of American independence was laid." But he felt similarly about Otis's speech against the writs of assistance. Does it matter which is more deserving the palm? The men in Boston and London, radicals and Tories alike, had long struggled blindly to control, for whatever purpose, a growing historical wind whose power and direction they could only feel. The deaths on King Street were but an eddy in that growing tempest.[21]

For five years preceding the shootings, order had gradually disappeared from the streets, untrammeled law had slowly been barred from the courts. For five years, violence had become so common in Massachusetts and the attempts to restrict it so absurdly futile that killing must surely come, on one side or the other. Men believed it then, as we, looking backward, believe it even more firmly now. Courage and imagination on the loyalist part, restraint and moderation by the radicals might have delayed the bloodshed; but they could not have avoided it. True, less demagoguery by Sam Adams afterward might have kept the incident's fame proportional to its actual significance; but such accommodation would not have prevented the Revolution. Somehow it seems fitting that an event so historically inevitable and yet so basically insignificant should have taken place on a moonlit night, before scores of people, without leaving any two witnesses able to give the same account of what happened.

If the trials were attempts to establish the truth, they failed; no one yet knows what really happened. If they were only attempts to do justice, perhaps they were somewhat more successful. But were the trials really fair? No matter what went on at the court, the defendants would not have been executed. Preston's jury was safely packed; the soldiers if convicted would have received reprieves and pardons. Does not fairness, in the legal sense, presuppose doubt? Is a "bagged" acquittal of an innocent man a just result? The trials, in short, leave one with the uncomfortable feeling that although the outcome was indeed, in John Adams's words, "exactly right," it was right for reasons which if not wrong, were at least questionable. No wonder that years later, when Preston and Adams met on a London street, they passed without speaking.[22]

The fog surrounding the Massacre and its sequels has never been dispelled. In the mid-1800's, some people began to link the death of Crispus Attucks with the idea of emancipation and civil rights, a connection which Attucks's contemporaries would have found novel, if not repugnant.[23] Today, the Boston Equal Rights League annually conducts a commemorative ceremony at the corner of State Street where the Bostonian Society years ago erected a bronze plaque: "The Boston Massacre Took Place Here." In truth, the Massacre took place across the street: the complex myth that rose from the bloody snow of King Street needs no factual support. Yet even more relevant now than the spurious legends are the true lessons of the Massacre and the violent confrontations which preceded it.

BIBLIOGRAPHY

(Short Title List)

A.L.R.
  American Law Reports Annotated, Rochester, N.Y., 1919–.
ABA, *Canons*
  American Bar Association, *Canons of Professional Ethics*.
ABA, *Code*
  American Bar Association, *Code of Professional Responsibility*.
Acts, Privy Council (Col.)
  Acts of the Privy Council of England, Colonial Series, 1613–1783,
  ed. W. L. Grant, James Munro, Hereford, 1909–1912; 6 vols.
Adams, *Diary and Autobiography*
  Diary and Autobiography of John Adams, ed. L. H. Butterfield and
  others, Cambridge, Mass., 1961; 4 vols.
Adams Family Correspondence
  Adams Family Correspondence, ed. L. H. Butterfield and others,
  Cambridge, Mass., 1963–.
Adams, *Independence*
  Thomas R. Adams, *American Independence*, Providence, 1965.
Adams, *New Light*
  Randolph G. Adams, *New Light on the Boston Massacre*, Worcester,
  Mass., 1938 (also in Amer. Antiq. Soc., *Procs.* 47:259 (1938), with
  a pagination factor of plus-256).
Adams Papers
  Adams Papers, MHS.
Adams, *Works*
  *The Works of John Adams, Second President of the United States:
  with a Life of the Author*, ed. Charles Francis Adams, Boston, 1850–
  1856; 10 vols.

Adams, *Writings*
The Writings of Samuel Adams, ed. Harry Alonzo Cushing, New York, 1904–1908; 4 vols.
ADM
Admiralty documents, PRO.
Alden, *Gage*
John R. Alden, *General Gage in America,* Baton Rouge, La., 1948.
Alden, "Letter from Molineux"
John R. Alden, "A Letter from William Molineux," *NEQ* 17:107 (1944).
Alden, "Mein"
John E. Alden, "John Mein: Scourge of Patriots," Col. Soc. Mass., *Pubns.* 34:571 (1942).
Amer. Antiq. Soc., *Procs.*
American Antiquarian Society, *Proceedings.*
Anderson, "Mackintosh"
George P. Anderson, "Ebenezer Mackintosh: Stamp Act Rioter and Patriot," Col. Soc. Mass., *Pubns.* 26:15, 348 (1924–26).
Andrews, "Boston Merchants"
Charles M. Andrews, "The Boston Merchants and the Non-Importation Movement," Col. Soc. Mass., *Pubns.* 19:159 (1917).
Andrews, *Colonial Period*
Charles M. Andrews, *The Colonial Period in American History,* New Haven, 1938; 4 vols.
Andrews, "Letters"
"Letters of John Andrews," MHS, *Procs.* (1st Ser.) 8:316 (1865).
Annual Register
The Annual Register (London, 1766–1771).
AO
Audit Office documents, PRO.
Army List
A List of the General and Field-Officers . . . in the Army . . . for 1770, London, n.d.

B. Chron.
Boston *Chronicle*
B.E.P.
Boston *Evening Post*
B. Gaz.
Boston *Gazette*
B.N.-L.
Boston *News-Letter*
Bailyn, *Origins*
Bernard Bailyn, *The Ideological Origins of the American Revolution,* Cambridge, Mass., 1967.
Bailyn, *Pamphlets*
Bernard Bailyn, *Pamphlets of the American Revolution, 1750–1776,*

vol. 1, 1750–1765, Cambridge, Mass., 1965.

Barrington-Bernard
The *Barrington-Bernard Correspondence*, ed. Edward Channing, Archibald C. Coolidge, Cambridge, Mass., 1912.

Barrow, *Trade*
Thomas C. Barrow, *Trade and Empire*, Cambridge, Mass., 1967.

Belknap Papers
Belknap Papers, MHS.

Bernard Papers
The collected papers of Massachusetts Governor Francis Bernard, Sparks Manuscripts, Harvard University.

Boston Rec. Comm., *Reports*
City of Boston, Record Commissioners, *Reports*, Boston, 1876–1906; 39 vols.

Bowdoin-Temple
Bowdoin-Temple Papers, MHS, *Colls.* (6th Ser.), vol. 9 (1897).

Bowdoin-Temple MSS
Bowdoin-Temple Manuscripts, MHS.

Boyle, "Journal"
John Boyle, "Journal of Occurrences in Boston, 1759–1778," *NEHGR* 84:142, 248, 357; 85:5, 117 (1930, 1931).

Brennan, *Plural Office-Holding*
Ellen E. Brennan, *Plural Office-Holding in Massachusetts 1760–1780*, Chapel Hill, 1945.

Britannica (11th ed.)
The *Encyclopedia Britannica*, 11th ed., New York, 1910–1911; 30 vols.

Brown, *Hawley*
E. Francis Brown, *Joseph Hawley, Colonial Radical*, New York, 1931.

Brown, "Hawley"
E. Francis Brown, "Major Joseph Hawley," *NEQ* 4:482, 502–08 (1931).

Caldwell, Log
Benjamin Caldwell, Log, Caldwell Collection (CAL/101), National Maritime Museum, Greenwich, England.

Camb. Hist. Soc., *Pubns.*
Cambridge (Massachusetts) Historical Society, *Publications*.

Cary, *Warren*
John Cary, *Joseph Warren*, Urbana, Ill., 1961.

Chalmers Papers
Sparks Manuscripts, Harvard Library, volume 10; 4 sub-volumes.

Chamberlain Papers
Mellen Chamberlain Collection, Boston Public Library.

Channing, *History*
Edward Channing, *A History of the United States*, New York, 1912–1925; 6 vols.

Charnock, *Biographia Navalis*
John Charnock, *Biographia Navalis* (London, 1794–1798); 6 vols.

CHOP
  Calendar of Home Office Papers of the Reign of George III, 1760–1775,
  ed. Joseph Redington, Richard A. Roberts, London, 1878–1899; 4 vols.
CO
  Colonial Office documents, PRO.
Coke, *Littleton*
  Edward Coke, *First Part of the Institutes of the Lawes of England; or,*
  Commentarie upon Littleton, 2d ed., London, 1629.
Col. Soc. Mass., *Pubns.*
  Colonial Society of Massachusetts, *Publications.*
Colson, *Lord George Gordon*
  Percy Colson, *The Strange History of Lord George Gordon,* London,
  1937.
"Cooper-Pownall"
  Frederick Tuckerman, "Letters of Samuel Cooper to Thomas Pownall,
  1769–1777," *American Historical Review* 8:301 (1903).
Copley-Pelham
  Letters and Papers of John Singleton Copley and Henry Pelham, 1739–
  1776, MHS., *Colls.,* vol. 71 (1914).
Corner, Diary
  John Corner, Diary Kept by Captain Corner, House of Lords Record
  Office.
Cox C. C.
  Reports of Cases in Criminal Law . . . , ed. Edward W. Cox and others,
  London, 1846–1941; 31 vols.
Cushing, "Judiciary"
  John D. Cushing, "The Judiciary and Public Opinion in Revolutionary
  Massachusetts," in *Law and Authority in Colonial America,* ed. George
  A. Billias, Barre, Mass., 1965.

Dana, Pleas
  Pleas before Richard Dana Esqr. Beginning January 5th 1768 Ending
  March 8th 1772, MHS.
Dana, Writs
  Book of Writs &c. returnable befr R. Dana Esqr begin'g ye 27th of
  September AD. 1763 Ending ye 5th May 1772, MHS.
Davidson, *Propaganda*
  Philip G. Davidson, *Propaganda and the American Revolution 1763–*
  1783, Chapel Hill, 1941.
Dexter, "Suffolk Bar"
  George Dexter, "Record Book of the Suffolk Bar," MHS, *Procs.* (1st
  Ser.) 19:141 (1881–1882).
Dickerson, *Military Rule*
  Boston Under Military Rule, 1768–1769, As Revealed in a Journal of the
  Times, ed. Oliver M. Dickerson, Boston, 1936.
Dickerson, *Navigation Acts*
  Oliver M. Dickerson, *The Navigation Acts and the American Revolution,*

Philadelphia, 1951.
DNB
The Dictionary of National Biography, ed. Leslie Stephen, Sidney Lee, N.Y. and London, 1885–1900; 63 vols. and supplements.
Dorr Papers
Harbottle Dorr Papers, MHS.
Drake, *Boston Landmarks*
Samuel Adams Drake, *Old Landmarks and Historic Personages of Boston*, Boston, 1873.
Drake, "Henry Knox"
Francis S. Drake, "Henry Knox," *NEHGR* 34:347 (1880).
Drake, *History*
Samuel G. Drake, *The History and Antiquities of Boston*, Boston, 1856.
Dumbauld, *Declaration*
Edward Dumbauld, *The Declaration of Independence and What it Means Today*, Norman, Okla., 1950.

Edes, "Dr. Young"
H. H. Edes, "Memoir of Dr. Thomas Young, 1731–1777," Col. Soc. Mass., *Pubns.* 11:2 (1906).
Edes, "Sandemanians"
H. H. Edes, "The Places of Worship of the Sandemanians in Boston," Col. Soc. Mass., *Pubns.* 5:109 (1899).
"Eliot-Hollis"
"Letters from Andrew Eliot to Thomas Hollis," MHS, *Colls.* (4th Ser.) 4:449 (1858).
Eng. Rep.
The English Reports; 176 vols. A collection of all the early English law reports.
Evans, *American Usage*
Bergen Evans, Cornelia Evans, *A Dictionary of Contemporary American Usage*, New York, 1957.
Everard, *Twenty-Ninth*
H. Everard, *History of Thomas Farrington's Regiment subsequently designated the 29th (Worcestershire) Foot, 1694 to 1891*, Worcester, England, 1891.

F.R.D.
Federal Rules Decisions, St. Paul, 1933–.
F.2d
Federal Reporter, Second Series, St. Paul, 1925–.
Fair Account
A fair Account of the late Unhappy Disturbance At Boston in New England; . . . London, 1770. (All references are to the appendix unless otherwise indicated.)
Fiore, "Temple-Bernard"
Jordan D. Fiore, "The Temple-Bernard Affair," Essex Institute, *Histori-*

cal Collections 90:58 (1954).

Fisher, "Attucks"
J. B. Fisher, "Who Was Crispus Attucks?" *Am. Hist. Record* 1:531–533 (1872).

Forbes, *Revere*
Esther Forbes, *Paul Revere and the World He Lived in,* Boston, Sentry ed., 1962.

Ford, "Wilkes"
Worthington C. Ford, "John Wilkes and Boston," MHS, *Procs.* 47:190 (1914).

Forester, *Hornblower*
C. S. Forester, *Hornblower and the Atropos,* New York, Bantam ed., 1962.

Frothingham, *Warren*
Richard Frothingham, *Life and Times of Joseph Warren,* Boston, 1865.

Frothingham, "Sam Adams Regiments"
Richard Frothingham, "The Sam Adams Regiments in the Town of Boston," *The Atlantic* (June 1862), 701.

Gage, *Correspondence*
The Correspondence of General Thomas Gage with the Secretaries of State, 1763–1775, ed. Clarence E. Carter, New Haven, 1931–1933; 2 vols.

Gage Papers
Papers of General Thomas Gage, William L. Clements Library, University of Michigan.

Gay Transcripts
Frederick L. Gay, Transcripts Relating to the History of New England, 1630–1776, MHS.

Gipson, *Empire*
Lawrence Henry Gipson, *The British Empire Before the American Revolution,* 1936–; 13 vols.

Gordon, *History*
William Gordon, *The History of the Rise . . . of the Independence of the United States of America . . . ,* London, 1788; 4 vols.

Guttmacher, *King*
Manfred S. Guttmacher, *America's Last King,* New York, 1941.

Harvard Catalogue
Harvard University, *Quinquennial Catalogue of the Officers and Graduates 1636–1920,* Cambridge, 1920.

Hinkhouse, *Preliminaries*
Fred J. Hinkhouse, *The Preliminaries of the American Revolution as seen in the English Press, 1763–1775,* New York, 1926.

Hood, Log
A Journal of the Proceedings of His Majestys Ships and Vessels under the Command of Samuel Hood Esqr Commander in Chief . . . [in 4

vols., April 9, 1768 to November 7, 1770], ADM 51/798.
Howe, "Quincy"
Mark A. De W. Howe, "Journal of Josiah Quincy During His Voyage
and Residence in England from September 28th 1774 to March 3d
1775," MHS, *Procs.* 50:433 (1917–1918).
Hulton, Account
[Henry Hulton], Some Account of the proceedings of the People of
New England from the Establishment of a Board of Customs in Amer-
ica, to the breaking out of the Rebellion in 1775, MS, Princeton Uni-
versity Library, Andre deCoppet Collection of American Historical
Manuscripts.
Hulton, *Letters*
Anne Hulton, *Letters of a Loyalist Lady,* Cambridge, Mass., 1927.
Hutchinson, "Additions"
Catherine Mayo, "Additions to Thomas Hutchinson's *History of Massa-
chusetts Bay,*" Amer. Antiq. Soc., *Procs.* 59:11 (1949).
Hutchinson, Almanac
MS journal kept by Thomas Hutchinson in Nathaniel Low, *An Astro-
nomical Diary; or Almanack For the Year of Christian Æra, 1770,* Eger-
ton MSS, British Museum.
Hutchinson, *Diary*
The Diary and Letters of . . . Thomas Hutchinson, ed. Peter Orlando
Hutchinson, Boston, 1884–1886; 2 vols.
Hutchinson, *History*
Thomas Hutchinson, *The History of the Colony and Province of Massa-
chusetts-Bay,* ed. Lawrence Shaw Mayo, Cambridge, Mass., 1936; 3 vols.
Hutchinson, Opinion
Thomas Hutchinson, untitled opinion concerning the statutes of 28
Henry 8, 11 & 12 William 3, 4 George 1, and 8 George 1, Mass. Arch.
44:527–531.

IND
Digest of Admiralty In-Letters, PRO.

Knollenberg, *Origin*
Bernhard Knollenberg, *Origin of the American Revolution: 1759–1766,*
rev. ed., N.Y. 1965.

Lathrop, *Innocent Blood*
John Lathrop, *Innocent Blood Crying to God From the Streets of Boston,*
London, 1770, Boston, 1771.
Legal Papers
Legal Papers of John Adams, ed. L. Kinvin Wroth, Hiller B. Zobel,
Cambridge, Mass., 1965; 3 vols.
Levy, *Origins*
Leonard W. Levy, *Origins of the Fifth Amendment,* New York, 1968.

Lloyd, *Nation and Navy*
Christopher Lloyd, *The Nation and the Navy*, rev. ed., London, 1961.
Longley, "Mob Activities"
R. S. Longley, "Mob Activities in Revolutionary Massachusetts," *NEQ* 6:98 (1933).
Lynde, *Diary*
The Diaries of Benjamin Lynde and of Benjamin Lynde, Jr.; with an Appendix, Boston and Cambridge, Mass., 1880.

Marcus, *American Jewry*
Jacob Rader Marcus, *American Jewry—Documents—Eighteenth Century*, Cincinnati, 1959.
Mass.
Reports of Cases Decided in the Supreme Judicial Court of Massachusetts, Boston and Exeter, 1804–.
Mass. Acts
The Acts and Resolves . . . of the Province of the Massachusetts Bay, ed. Ellis Ames, Abner C. Goodell, and others, Boston, 1869–1922; 21 vols.
Mass. Arch.
Massachusetts Archives, State House, Boston.
Mass. House Journal
Journal of the Honorable House of Representatives of His Majesty's Province of the Massachusetts-Bay in New England.
Matthews, "Preston"
Albert Matthews, "Captain Thomas Preston and the Boston Massacre," *Col. Soc. Mass., Pubns.* 7:2 (1905).
May, *Naval Dress*
W. E. May, *The Dress of Naval Officers*, London, 1966.
MB
Minute Books, Superior Court of Judicature, Office of the Clerk, Supreme Judicial Court for Suffolk County, Boston.
Metzger, *Catholics*
Charles H. Metzger, *Catholics and the American Revolution*, Chicago, 1962.
MHS
Massachusetts Historical Society, Boston.
MHS, *Colls., Procs.*
Massachusetts Historical Society, *Collections, Proceedings*.
Miller, *Origins*
John C. Miller, *Origins of the American Revolution*, Boston, 1943.
Miller, *Sam Adams*
John C. Miller, *Sam Adams, Pioneer in Propaganda*, Boston, 1936.
Morgan, *Stamp Act*
Edmund S. Morgan, Helen M. Morgan, *The Stamp Act Crisis*, rev. ed., New York, 1963.

Morison, *Maritime History*
  Samuel Eliot Morison, *The Maritime History of Massachusetts,* Boston, 1921.
Morison, *Three Centuries*
  Samuel Eliot Morison, *Three Centuries of Harvard,* Cambridge, Mass., 1946.
Moscowitz, "Trial of a Criminal Case"
  Grover M. Moscowitz, "Some Aspects of the Trial of a Criminal Case in the Federal Court," 3 F.R.D. 380 (1944).
M. Spy
  Massachusetts Spy
Murray, *Letters*
  Letters of James Murray, Loyalist, ed. Nina Moore Tiffany, Susan I. Lesley, Boston, 1901.

Naval Documents
  Naval Documents of the American Revolution, ed. William Bell Clark, Washington, 1964–.
NEHGR
  New England Historical and Genealogical Register
NEQ
  New England Quarterly
New Jersey Archives
  Documents Relating to the Colonial History of the State of New Jersey (1st ser., vol. 27), ed. William Nelson, Paterson, N.J., 1905.

O'Donnell, *Fourteenth*
  Henry O'Donnell, *Historical Records of the Fourteenth Regiment,* Devonport, England, 1893.
OED
  The Oxford English Dictionary, Oxford, 1933; 12 vols. and supplement.
Oliver, *Origin*
  Peter Oliver's Origin and Progress of the American Rebellion, ed. Douglass Adair, John A. Schutz, San Marino, Calif., 1961.

Paine Papers
  Robert Treat Paine Papers (including diary and notes on the Boston Massacre trials), MHS.
Postgate, *Wilkes*
  Raymond W. Postgate, *That Devil Wilkes,* New York, 1929.
PRO
  Public Record Office, London.
Prown, *Copley*
  Jules David Prown, *John Singleton Copley,* Cambridge, Mass., 1966; 2 vols.

Quincy, *Quincy*
Josiah Quincy, *Memoirs of Josiah Quincy, Junior, of Massachusetts: 1744–1775,* ed. Eliza Susan Quincy, 2d ed., Boston, 1874.

Quincy, *Reports*
Josiah Quincy, Jr., *Reports of Cases Argued and Adjudged in the Superior Court of Judicature of the Province of Massachusetts Bay, between 1761 and 1772,* ed. Samuel M. Quincy, Boston, 1865.

Rec.
Records, Superior Court of Judicature, Office of the Clerk, Supreme Judicial Court for Suffolk County, Boston.

Rippon, Log
A Journal of the Proceedings of His Majesty's Ship *Rippon* Between the 21st of January 1768 and the 20th of January 1770, ADM 51/788.

Rippon, Muster Book
Muster Book of H.M.S. *Rippon,* between the 30th April and the 30th June, 1769, ADM 36/7483.

Robson, *American Revolution*
Eric Robson, *The American Revolution in its Political and Military Aspects, 1763–1783,* New York, 1955.

Romney, Log
A Journal of the Proceedings of His Majesty's Ship *Romney* Between the 24th of February 1768 and the 8th of May 1769, ADM 51/793.

Romney, Muster Book
Muster Book of H.M.S. *Romney,* between the 8th of May 1769 and the 30th of June 1769, ADM 36/7488.

Rose, Log
A Journal of the Proceedings of His Majesty's Ship *Rose,* Benjamin Caldwell, Esqr Commander: Commencing the 27th of April 1768 and Ending the 30th of April 1769 [and a journal identically titled except for the dates, which are "1st of May 1769" and "30th of April 1770"] ADM 51/804.

Rose, Muster Book
Muster Book of H.M.S. *Rose,* April 29, 1768 to June 30, 1770, ADM 36/7943.

Ross, *Cornwallis*
Charles Ross, *Correspondence of Charles, First Marquis Cornwallis,* London, 1859.

Rowe, *Diary*
Letters and Diary of John Rowe, Boston Merchant, 1759–1762, 1764–1779, ed. Anne Rowe Cunningham, Boston, 1903.

Rowe, "Diary"
Edward L. Pierce, "Diary of John Rowe," MHS, *Procs.* (2d Ser.) 10:11 (1896).

Rowe, MS Diary
John Rowe, Manuscript Diary, MHS

Sagittarius
[John Mein] *Sagittarius's Letters,* Boston, 1775.
Savage, Diary
MS journal kept by Samuel Phillips Savage in Nathaniel Low, *An Astronomical Diary; or Almanack For the Year of Christian Æra, 1770,* Samuel Phillips Savage Papers, MHS.
Schlesinger, *Prelude*
Arthur M. Schlesinger, *Prelude to Independence, The Newspaper War on Great Britain 1764–1776,* New York, 1958.
SCJ
Superior Court of Judicature.
Sessions, Minute Book
Minute Book, Suffolk County Court of General Sessions of the Peace, Office of the Clerk of the Supreme Judicial Court for Suffolk County, Boston.
SF
Early Court Files and Papers, Office of the Clerk of the Supreme Judicial Court for Suffolk County, Boston.
Shaw, *Topographical Description*
Charles Shaw, *A Topographical and Historical Description of Boston,* Boston, 1817.
Short Narrative
A Short Narrative of the Horrid Massacre in Boston . . . To which is added, An Appendix . . . , Boston, 1770. (All references are to the appendix unless otherwise indicated.)
Shy, *Toward Lexington*
John Shy, *Toward Lexington,* Princeton, 1965.
Sibley-Shipton
John Langdon Sibley, Clifford K. Shipton, *Biographical Sketches of Graduates of Harvard University, in Cambridge, Massachusetts,* Cambridge, Mass., and Boston, 1873–.
Smith-Carter Papers
Smith-Carter Papers, MHS.
"Sons of Liberty—1769"
List of Sons of Liberty in 1769, MHS, *Procs.* (1st Ser.) 11:140 (1869–1870).
Sparks, *Franklin*
The Works of Benjamin Franklin, ed. Jared Sparks, Boston, 1836–1840; 10 vols.
Sparks Papers
Manuscripts collected by Jared Sparks, Harvard Library.
Stacey, *Quebec*
C. P. Stacey, *Quebec, 1759,* New York, 1959.
Stark, *Loyalists*
James H. Stark, *The Loyalists of Massachusetts,* Boston, 1910.
Steckler, "Management of the Jury"
William E. Steckler, "Management of the Jury," 28 F.R.D. 190 (1962).

Stephen, *Criminal Law*
  James Fitzjames Stephen, *A History of the Criminal Law of England*, London, 1883; 2 vols.
Str.
  John Strange, *Reports of Cases in the courts of Chancery, King's Bench, Common Pleas and Exchequer*, London, 1755; 2 vols.
Sumner, *East Boston*
  William H. Sumner, *A History of East Boston*, Boston, 1858.
Sumner, *Memorandum Book*
  Increase Sumner, *Memorandum Book*, MHS.

T
  Treasury documents, PRO.
Thwing, *Crooked and Narrow Streets*
  Annie Haven Thwing, *The Crooked and Narrow Streets of the Town of Boston, 1630–1822*, Boston, 1920.
Tourtellot, *William Diamond's Drum*
  Arthur Bernon Tourtellot, *William Diamond's Drum*, New York, 1959.
Tudor, *Diary*
  Deacon Tudor's Diary, ed. William Tudor, Boston, 1896.

Ubbelohde, *Vice-Admiralty*
  Carl Ubbelohde, *The Vice-Admiralty Courts and the American Revolution*, Chapel Hill, 1960.
U.S.
  United States Reports, Supreme Court, Boston, New York, and Washington, 1875–.

Va. Gaz.
  Virginia *Gazette*
Van Doren, *Franklin*
  Carl Van Doren, *Benjamin Franklin*, New York, 1938.

Watkins, "Tarring and Feathering"
  Walter Kendall Watkins, "Tarring and Feathering in Boston in 1770," *Old-Time New England*, 20:30 (1929).
Wells, *Adams*
  William V. Wells, *The Life and Public Services of Samuel Adams*, Boston, 1865; 3 vols.
Wemms Trial
  The Trial of William Wemms [and others] . . . , *for the Murder of Crispus Attucks* [and others] . . . , Boston, 1770.
"Wilkes-Palfrey"
  George M. Elsey, "John Wilkes and William Palfrey," Col. Soc. Mass., *Pubns.* 34:411 (1943).
Williams Papers
  Israel Williams Manuscripts, MHS.

Winsor, *Boston*
  The Memorial History of Boston, Including Suffolk County, 1630–1880, ed. Justin Winsor, Boston, 1880–1881; 4 vols.
Wolkins, "Boston Customs"
  George G. Wolkins, "The Boston Customs District," MHS, *Procs.* 58:418 (1924–1925).
Wolkins, "Liberty"
  George G. Wolkins, "The Seizure of John Hancock's Sloop 'Liberty'," MHS, *Procs.* 55:239 (1921–1922).
Wolkins, "Malcom"
  George G. Wolkins, "Daniel Malcom and Writs of Assistance," MHS, *Procs.* 58:14 (1924–1925).
Wolkins, "Paxton"
  George G. Wolkins, "Letters of Charles Paxton," MHS, *Procs.* 56:343 (1922–1923).
Wroth & Zobel, "Trials"
  L. Kinvin Wroth and Hiller B. Zobel, "The Boston Massacre Trials," American Bar Association, *Journal* 55:329 (1969).

Zobel, "Law Under Pressure"
  Hiller B. Zobel, "Law Under Pressure: Boston 1769–1771," in *Law and Authority in Colonial America*, ed. George A. Billias, Barre, Mass., 1965.
Zobel, "Newer Light"
  Hiller B. Zobel, "Newer Light on the Boston Massacre," Amer. Antiq. Soc., *Procs.* 78:119 (1968).
Zobel, "Sewall"
  Hiller B. Zobel, "Jonathan Sewall: A Lawyer in Conflict," Camb. Hist. Soc., *Pubns.* 40:123 (1966).

NOTES

1. His Majesty's Province of Massachusetts Bay

1. Boston population: Shaw, *Topographical Description*, 294. Other figures: *Britannica* (11th ed.) 17:547, 8:941; 16:965 (all by extrapolation). Colonies: see, e.g., Daniel Dulaney, "Considerations on the Propriety of Imposing Taxes in the British Colonies" (Annapolis, 1765), in Bailyn, *Pamphlets*, 607, 638.

2. Mayhew sermons: *Sibley-Shipton*, 11:453.

3. Adams, *Diary and Autobiography*, 1:184–186.

4. Bernard's entry: Bernard to Barrington, Aug. 7, 1760, *Barrington-Bernard*, 15. Family connections: *ibid.*, xvi; Hutchinson, *Diary*, 1:320–321. Finances: Bernard to Barrington, Feb. 18, 1760, *Barrington-Bernard*, 9–10.

5. Third-rate abilities: Channing, *History*, 3:4. Bernard and Gage: Alden, *Gage*, 12.

6. Bernard as anecdotist: Hutchinson, *Diary*, 2:319. Optimism: Bernard to Barrington, April 19, 1760, *Barrington-Bernard*, 11, 12. Fair prospect: same to same, Aug. 7, 1760, *ibid.*, 15. Comments on speech: Adams, *Diary and Autobiograpy*, 1:186. Epilepsy: Hutchinson, *Diary*, 2:76.

7. New dormitory and Harvard fire: Morison, *Three Centuries*, 94, 95. Bernard as architect: Hutchinson, *History*, 3:76n.

8. Mount Desert: Bernard to Barrington, Feb. 20, 1762, *Barrington-Bernard*, 50; on possible *quid pro quo*, see Brennan, *Plural Office-Holding*, 53–54 and sources there cited. Doggerel: *B. Gaz.*, Feb. 29, 1768.

9. Sewall: *Sibley-Shipton*, 6:561–567.

10. New attorneys: Adams, *Diary and Autobiography*, 1:316. Bar regulation: *Legal Papers*, 1:lxxviii–lxxx. Judicial qualifications: Adams, *Diary and Autobiography*, 1:168.

11. Trowbridge: *Legal Papers*, 1:cxi–cxii. Prat: *ibid.*, cvi; *Sibley-Shipton*, 10:229. Gridley: *Legal Papers*, 1:ci; Adams, *Diary and Autobiography*, 1:83. Otis, Sr.: *Legal Papers*, 1:civ–cv.

12. Hutchinson: *Sibley-Shipton,* 8:149–165. Otis's threat: Bernard to Lord Shelburne, Dec. 22, 1766, in Gipson, *Empire,* 10:121–122n.; Hutchinson, *B.N.-L.,* April 7, 1763, in *Sibley-Shipton,* 11:251; Brennan, *Plural Office-Holding,* 30–31.

13. Eyesore: Hutchinson, *Diary,* 1:66. Trowbridge incident: *Sibley-Shipton,* 8:515. Hutchinson as judge: Quincy, *Reports, passim.*

14. Hutchinson and Adams: Oliver, *Origin,* 83. Hutchinson as judge: Hutchinson to John Sullivan, March 29, 1771, Mass. Arch., 27:136.

15. Hutchinson's background: *Sibley-Shipton,* 8:149–162. Adams's tribute: John Adams to Joseph Ward, Oct. 24, 1809, quoted in *Sibley-Shipton,* 8:159. Hutchinson and hard money: Hutchinson, *Diary,* 1:54.

16. Land Bank and Adams's father: *Sibley-Shipton,* 10:421–422. Adams's *Quaestio:* Morison, *Three Centuries,* 91.

2. Imperial Prologue

1. Hutchinson: Quincy, *Reports,* 411. *Petition of Lechmere: ibid.,* 412–414; *Legal Papers,* 2:106–147.

2. Pitt: Gipson, *Empire,* 10:111. Trade and navigation acts: Knollenberg, *Origin,* 157–160; Miller, *Origins,* 4–7; Andrews, *Colonial Period,* 4:85–367.

3. *Legal Papers,* 2:133–134.

4. Writs: *Legal Papers,* 2:107–113. Merchants' petition: Quincy, *Reports,* 412–413. Otis: *Sibley-Shipton,* 11:252; *Legal Papers,* 2:140. Generally: Gipson, *Empire,* 10:120–121.

5. Argument: *Legal Papers,* 2:106–107, 134–144.

6. *Ibid.,* 2:115.

7. Molasses requirements: Channing, *History,* 3:3. Adams on taverns: Adams, *Diary and Autobiography,* 1: *passim.* Rum as currency: Knollenberg, *Origin,* 138–139.

8. Value: Knollenberg, *Origin,* 131, 251n.; Gipson, *Empire,* 10:218. Outward cargoes: Knollenberg, *Origin,* 139; Gipson, *Empire,* 10:214.

9. Compounding: Gipson, *Empire,* 10:219; Knollenberg, *Origin,* 131. Diminished entry: Timothy Orne to George Dodge, July 18, 1758, extracted in Knollenberg, *Origin,* 132, 252n.: "Vessells . . . have been admitted to Enter about One Eight or Tenth part of their Cargo paying 6d sterling per gallon Duty for what is entered." Circular letter: Gipson, *Empire,* 10:111n.

10. Informer bill: Gipson, *Empire,* 10:129. Advisory opinion: Bernard to Barrington, May 1, 1762, *Barrington-Bernard,* 52. Vacation: same to same, Feb. 20, 1762, *ibid.,* 49. Popularity: same to same, May 1, 1762, *ibid.,* 51. Hutchinson's research: Adams, *Diary and Autobiography,* 1:232–233. Otises: Hutchinson, *History,* 3:69–70; *Sibley-Shipton,* 11:256–257.

11. English situation: Gipson, *Empire,* 10:180–199. Insufficient indemnity: *ibid.,* 50–51. Canada: Bernard to Barrington, Feb. 18, 1760, *Barrington-Bernard,* 11. Indians: Channing, *History,* 3:19–24.

12. Grenville: *DNB.*

13. Knollenberg, *Origin,* 164–168; Gipson, *Empire,* 10:226–231; Channing, *History,* 3:41–44.

14. Hutchinson as special agent: Gipson, *Empire,* 10:211–212. "Summa Potestatis": Adams, *Works,* 10:286. Thatcher's opposition: Hutchinson, *History,* 3:77.

15. Boston Rec. Comm., *Reports,* 16:116.

16. Instructions: Bailyn, *Pamphlets,* 472–473; Boston Rec. Comm., *Reports,* 16:120–122. Adams: Miller, *Sam Adams,* 24.

17. High duty: Hutchinson, *History*, 3:78. Calculations: Bailyn, *Pamphlets*, 357. Official connivance: Hutchinson, *History*, 3:79. Customs figures: Gipson, *Empire*, 10:241.

18. For the over-all account: Fiore, "Temple-Bernard." The details of Cockle's behavior: Hutchinson, *History*, 3:117–118; see also Quincy, *Reports*, 423–424. Hutchinson on Bernard and Temple: Hutchinson, *Diary*, 1:67.

19. Hutchinson, *History*, 3:117.

20. Affidavit of Salem Custom House clerk Samuel Toovey, Sept. 27, 1764, in Fiore, "Temple-Bernard," 74–75.

21. Hutchinson, *History*, 3:117.

22. Fiore, "Temple-Bernard," 64–65, 69–70.

23. *Ibid.*, 66–67.

24. Distinction between *in rem* and *in personam*: Hutchinson, *History*, 3:117. Auchmuty-Bernard-Cockle: Fiore, "Temple-Bernard," 66–68.

25. Bribe attempt: Fiore, "Temple-Bernard," 71–72. Salem and Boston celebrations: Rowe, *Diary*, 64–65. Clamor against Cockle and Bernard: Hutchinson, *History*, 3:118.

26. Bernard's pecuniary obsession: *Barrington-Bernard, passim*. Bernard's explanation: Bernard to Richard Jackson, Oct. 5, 1764, Bernard Papers, 3:256, and same to same, Nov. 30, 1764, *ibid.*, 3:267, quoted in Quincy, *Reports*, 423–424. Hutchinson on Bernard: Hutchinson to Richard Jackson, May 5, 1765, Mass. Arch., 26:138.

27. Depression: Rowe, *Diary*, 74–75. Hutchinson's letter (to Richard Jackson, July 23, 1764): Morgan, *Stamp Act*, 269–273. Massachusetts protest: Knollenberg, *Origin*, 184–186; Gipson, *Empire*, 10:232–235; Morgan, *Stamp Act*, 53–54. Hutchinson's role: Knollenberg, *Origin*, 186; Gipson, *Empire*, 10:234. Vituperation: Adams, *Diary and Autobiography*, 2:80.

3. Violence Over Stamps

1. Stamp Act generally: Morgan, *Stamp Act*, 74–92; Gipson, *Empire*, 10:257–271; Knollenberg, *Origin*, 204–209; Miller, *Origins*, 110–112. No good faith: Morgan, *Stamp Act*, 91. "Sons of Liberty": Knollenberg, *Origin*, 206. Passage and royal assent: *ibid.*, 207–209; Guttmacher, *King*, 75–86.

2. News of debates: Hutchinson, *History*, 3:84. Act: *ibid.*, 3:85; Boyle, "Journal," 118. Catalogue: Morgan, *Stamp Act*, 96; see also the statute itself: 5 Geo. 3, c. 12 (1765).

3. English taxation compared: Gipson, *Empire*, 10:279. Additional provisions: Miller, *Origins*, 114.

4. Nonimportation and no lamb: Hutchinson, *History*, 3:84. Funeral: Boyle, "Journal," 166.

5. News arrives: Boyle, "Journal," 168. Circular letter: Hutchinson, *History*, 3:85. Stamp Act Congress: Knollenberg, *Origin*, 210; Morgan, *Stamp Act*, 139–152.

6. Patrick Henry: Morgan, *Stamp Act*, 122–123. Resolves: *B. Gaz.*, July 1, 1765. Otis on Resolves: Hutchinson, *History*, 3:86n. Commencement July 17: Rowe, *Diary*, 86. Gerry: Morison, *Three Centuries*, 91. Gerry, Sr.'s ship: Rowe, *Diary*, 87.

7. Loyal Nine: Morgan, *Stamp Act*, 160 and works there cited. Boston riots: Bailyn, *Pamphlets*, 582. Anti-Catholicism: Metzger, *Catholics*, 7–24; see also John Adams, "A Dissertation on the Canon and Feudal Law," Adams, *Works*, 3:449, 453, 456.

8. Mackintosh: Anderson, "Mackintosh," *passim.*

9. Pope's Day 1764: Rowe, *Diary,* 68. Mackintosh's hearing: *ibid.,* 76. Caucas Clubb: Adams, *Diary and Autobiography,* 1:238. Mackintosh's nomination: Anderson, "Mackintosh," 27.

10. Bailyn, *Pamphlets,* 585.

11. Parade: Oliver, *Origin,* 54. "Ardour of liberty," etc.: *B.E.P.,* Aug. 18, 1765. Oliver and Ingersoll: Hutchinson, *History,* 3:85–86; *B. Gaz.,* Aug. 12, 1765. Effigy prepared by Loyal Nine: Anderson, "Mackintosh," 31. Crowd at Elliot's: Rowe, *Diary,* 88. "Tree of Liberty": *B. Gaz.,* Sept. 16, 1765. Sam Adams: Adams, *Diary and Autobiography,* 1:295. Council and sheriff: Hutchinson, *History,* 3:87.

12. Crowd and cutting down image: Rowe, *Diary,* 89. Through Town House, assault on Oliver's house: Hutchinson, *History,* 3:87–88; for an excellent description of the outrage, see Morgan, *Stamp Act,* 161–165. Adams's report and reaction: Adams, *Diary and Autobiography,* 1:259–261.

13. Resignation and reaction: Hutchinson, *History,* 3:88; Rowe, *Diary,* 89. Anniversary celebration: Rowe, *Diary,* 139, 172, 191, 205, 248, 316; Adams, *Diary and Autobiography,* 1:341–342.

14. Adams, *Diary and Autobiography,* 1:260–261. Currency dispute: Hutchinson, *History,* 3:72. Sam Adams's technique: Miller, *Adams,* 24.

15. Depositions and Hallowell's report: Hutchinson, *Diary,* 1:67. Events of Aug. 15: Hutchinson, *History,* 3:88–89. Hutchinson's windows: Drake, *Boston Landmarks,* 167.

16. Reward: Hutchinson, *History,* 3:87; Boyle, "Journal," 169. Timidity: Hutchinson, *History,* 3:89. Mayhew's sermon (Galatians 5:12–13): *Sibley-Shipton,* 11:465; Hutchinson, *History,* 3:89. Rowe's involvement: Hutchinson, *Diary,* 1:67; Rowe, *Diary,* 89.

17. Hutchinson's home described in detail: Drake, *Boston Landmarks,* 167. Hutchinson's home as target: Diary of Ebenezer Parkman, cited in Morgan, *Stamp Act,* 166; *Sibley-Shipton,* 11:465. Hutchinson and the rumors: Hutchinson to Jackson, Aug. 30, 1765, Mass. Arch., 26:146, printed with only minor errors in Anderson, "Mackintosh," 32–34. The riot preliminaries: Hutchinson, *History,* 3:90. Locations: of Paxton's house, Drake, *Boston Landmarks,* 273; Hallowell's house, *ibid.,* 148; Story's house, Thwing, *Crooked and Narrow Streets,* 141. Activities: at Paxton's house, Longley, "Mob Activities," 108–109; at Story and Hallowell houses, Hutchinson, *History,* 3:90; Joshua Henshaw to ?, *NEHGR* 32:268–269 (1878). Hutchinson's worth: AO 13/46.647.

18. Hutchinson to Richard Jackson, Aug. 30, 1765, Mass. Arch., 26:146; Sally's "Resolution fixed to stay and share his Fate" is confirmed in an apparently contemporaneous account by Josiah Quincy, Quincy, *Reports,* 169; see also Hutchinson, *History,* 3:90.

19. Henshaw to ?, Aug. 28, 1765, *NEHGR* 32:268–269 (1878); Quincy, *Reports,* 169–170.

20. Hutchinson to Richard Jackson, Aug. 30, 1765, Mass. Arch., 26:146. Adams, *Diary and Autobiography,* 1:306; on the Philadelphia incident, see Hughes' letters, extracted in Morgan, *Stamp Act,* 314–315.

21. Merchants raising the mob: Hutchinson, *Diary,* 67. Adams on the mob: Adams to Dennys DeBerdt, Nov. 15, 1766; Adams, *Writings,* 1:100 and Adams to John Smith, [Dec.] 20, 1765, *ibid.,* 1:60. Adams on Hutchinson and the Stamp Act: *Sibley-Shipton,* 10:428. Whately drafter of Stamp Act: Morgan, *Stamp Act,* 78–80. Hutchinson's opposition: Hutchinson, *Diary,* 70; see also Morgan, *Stamp Act,* 269–274.

22. Richard King: *Legal Papers,* 1:106–140. Providence: Adams, *Diary and*

Autobiography, 1:300.

23. Maine land: *Legal Papers,* 2:255–258; (Miller, *Sam Adams,* 59, says without documentation that Samuel Adams took "a flyer in Maine lands.") Destruction to prevent title search: Gordon, *History,* 1:180. Hutchinson's allusion: Hutchinson, *History,* 3:90n.

24. Hutchinson on Mackintosh: Hutchinson, *History,* 3:91, 101; Hutchinson, *Diary,* 1:71. On Moore: Bernard to Hillsborough, Aug. 29, 1768, CO 5/767. On Atkins: recollection of Hannah Mather, quoted in Forbes, *Revere,* 172–173.

25. SF #100480, #100493, #100494; #100599 (jail return).

26. Chase and Speakman firm: Adams, *Diary and Autobiography,* 1:294. Avery and the Loyal Nine: Morgan, *Stamp Act,* 160. Avery at Harvard: *Harvard Catalogue,* 158.

27. Richardson and Bliss: MB 81, March Term, 1765. Warren's note: SF #100482. Warren at Harvard: *Harvard Catalogue,* 158. Warren and Samuel Adams: *Sibley-Shipton,* 10:425.

28. Mayhew to Hutchinson, Aug. 27, 1765, in *Sibley-Shipton,* 11:465–466.

29. Hutchinson's kindness to Quincy: Quincy, *Reports,* 151. Quincy's patriotism: *ibid.,* 168. Hutchinson in court: *ibid.,* 170.

30. Hutchinson's address: Hutchinson, *Diary,* 1:69–70; Quincy, *Reports,* 171–173. Quincy's thoughts: *ibid.,* 173.

31. Town meeting: Boston Rec. Comm., *Reports,* 16:152; Hutchinson, *Diary,* 1:70. Council meeting and sequel: *ibid.,* 71. The threat of new violence was not exaggerated. "In the Beginning of the Evening [of Aug. 27] there was a Number collected and opposed the Cadets, knock'd one of them down with a stone. Colo. Jarvis order'd them to advance and level their peices, which they did and soon scatter'd them, they broke a few Squares in the Town House Windows but were peacable the Remainder of the Night." Joshua Henshaw to ?, Aug. 27, 1765, *NEHGR* 32:269 (1878); see also generally Hutchinson, *History,* 3:91–92.

32. Mackintosh as potential informer: Hutchinson, *Diary,* 1:71. Apprehension and jail break: *ibid.,* 70; Hutchinson, *History,* 91. Moore: Bernard to Hillsborough, Aug. 29, 1768, CO 5/767.

33. SF #100599; MB 81.

34. Kent's argument: Quincy, *Reports,* 194–195.

35. Adams to office: Boyle, "Journal," 170; see also Hutchinson, *History,* 3:96–97. Otis in the Stamp Act Congress: Bailyn, *Pamphlets,* 551. Adams's description: Adams, *Diary and Autobiography,* 1:271.

36. Court harmony: Quincy, *Reports,* 197. Quiet Nov. 1: Morgan, *Stamp Act,* 173 (an excellent description); Hutchinson, *History,* 3:98. North–South peace Nov. 5: Hutchinson, *History,* 3:98; *Sibley-Shipton,* 9:581; Anderson, "Mackintosh," 42; Adams, *Works,* 2:177n. All assume that "Swift" was lawyer Samuel Swift, Harvard 1735, see *Legal Papers,* 1:cxi; I think it more likely that "Swift" was the "Henry Swift, Shipwright" indicted for the Pope's Day riot of 1764; among other reasons, Samuel Swift lived on Pleasant Street, which was in the South End, *Sibley-Shipton,* 9:580; John Bonner Map of Boston (1769) in *Legal Papers,* 3:opp. 69. Conflicting interpretations of the quiet: Hutchinson, *History,* 3:98.

37. Nonimportation: Boyle, "Journal," 171. Adams's description: Adams, *Diary and Autobiography,* 1:264–265.

38. Storm: Adams, *Diary and Autobiography,* 1:265. Loyal Nine: Henry Bass to Samuel Savage, Dec. 19, 1765, in MHS, *Procs.* 44:688–689 (1911).

39. Oliver's resignation: Hutchinson, *History,* 3:101 (where the oath is set out); Anderson, "Mackintosh," 43; Morgan, *Stamp Act,* 180–181. Dana: Quincy, *Re-*

ports, 312n.; and see Chapter 12, below.

40. Opening of Custom House: Morgan, *Stamp Act*, 181. Town activity: Boston Rec. Comm., *Reports*, 16:158–159. John Adams's notification, reaction, and actions: Adams, *Diary and Autobiography*, 1:265–274. Samuel Adams's thoughts: *ibid.*, 274.

41. Argument before the governor and council: Quincy, *Reports*, 200–209.

42. Molineux and the judges: Boston Rec. Comm., *Reports*, 16:161. Hutchinson and the probate court: Hutchinson, *History*, 3:102–103; *Sibley-Shipton*, 8:177–178. Adams's research: Adams, *Diary and Autobiography*, 1:273.

43. Opening of inferior court: Adams, *Diary and Autobiography*, 1:292. Adams and the Loyal Nine: *ibid.*, 1:294. Bernard's woes: Bernard to Barrington, May 9, 1768, *Barrington-Bernard*, 156–157. Bernard's warship: Colvill to Admiralty, n.d., *CHOP*, 2:2.

44. Prophecies of forces: Adams, *Diary and Autobiography*, 1:309. Gage's belligerence: Gage to Barrington, Jan. 10, 1766, Gage, *Correspondence*, 2:334. Bernard's ignorance: Bernard to Barrington, Sept. 1, 1766, *Barrington-Bernard*, 114. Bernard's choice: *ibid.*, 115.

45. English newspapers: Hinkhouse, *Preliminaries*, 58. Nonimportation: Gipson, *Empire*, 10:365; Knollenberg, *Origin*, 211; Morgan, *Stamp Act*, 369–370. King on Grenville: *DNB*, 23:116. Rockingham ministry and merchants: Miller, *Origins*, 153–155. Passage of Repeal and Declaratory Bills: Gipson, *Empire*, 10:lxxv; Miller, *Origins*, 158. (The acts were effective March 18, the day the king signed the bills, Gipson, *Empire*, 10: lxxv.) News reaches Boston: Hutchinson, *History*, 3:106; Rowe, *Diary*, 95.

46. Peter Oliver and lawyers' reluctance: Bernard to Lords of Trade, March 10, 1766, in Quincy, *Reports*, 216. "Political finesse": Quincy, *Reports*, 215; Adams, *Diary and Autobiography*, 1:305. The single civil case was apparently *Prince* v. *Salisbury*, MB 81, March 1766; the criminal trial was *Rex* v. *Ward*, but it may possibly not have been tried until April 29; the chronology does not readily emerge from the Record or Minute Book, MB 81, March 1766; Rec., 1766–1767, fol. 2.

47. Plymouth and Boston sittings: Adams, *Diary and Autobiography*, 1:308. April 29 sitting: *ibid.*, 310. The court adjourned to May 9 and then to June 3, when, with a full bench, normal business resumed, MB 81, March 1766; Rec., 1766–1767, fol. 2.

48. Adams, *Diary and Autobiography*, 1:311.

4. Violence Over Customs Duties

1. News of repeal, Boston illumination: Rowe, *Diary*, 95. Festivities and crown officers: Hutchinson, *History*, 3:106. Adams: Adams, *Diary and Autobiography*, 1:312.

2. Boston Rec. Comm., *Reports*, 16:183; the meeting reaffirmed the point on March 16, 1767. Suing for freedom: *Legal Papers*, 2:48–67. Harvard: Morison, *Three Centuries*, 117–118.

3. Adams's re-election: Boston Rec. Comm., *Reports*, 16:177; Rowe, *Diary*, 93. Chosen clerk: Adams, *Diary and Autobiography*, 1:313; Rowe, *Diary*, 97. Clerk voting: Hutchinson, *History*, 3:107. Power during recesses: Miller, *Sam Adams*, 94–95.

4. Young: *Adams Family Correspondence*, 1:208n.; Edes, "Dr. Young," *passim*. Molineux: Rowe, *Diary*, 286; John Andrews to ?, MHS, *Procs.* (1st Ser.) 8:379 (1865) ("imprudent pitch"); John Eliot to Jeremy Belknap, Nov. 8, 1774, in Davidson, *Propaganda*, 28 ("noble principles"). Reputation of Molineux and

Young: see Miller, *Sam Adams,* 267. Mayhew: *Sibley-Shipton,* 11:468; Rowe, *Diary,* 103.

5. Paxton birth: Wolkins, "Paxton," 345; Stark, *Loyalists,* 319, indicates 1704 or 1707. Customs officer: Barrow, *Trade,* 218. Offices: Quincy, *Reports,* 421n. Paxton on Boston: Adams, *Diary and Autobiography,* 1:313. "Summoned home"; Channing, *History,* 3:86. "Remodelling": Quincy, *Reports,* 422n. "Essence": Adams, *Works,* 10:298. Bernard: Bernard to Barrington, July 25, 1766, *Barrington-Bernard,* 111. Departure: Rowe, *Diary,* 105. Stamps: *B. Gaz.,* July 28, 1766.

6. Falmouth riot: Quincy, *Reports,* 466n.; Gipson, *Empire,* 11:34–35; *Sibley-Shipton,* 12:215–216. Rescues: Bernard to Lords of Trade, Aug. 18, 1766, in Quincy, *Reports,* 446n.

7. The best treatment of the Malcom affair is in Wolkins, "Malcom," where the depositions of the principals and the witnesses are printed *in extenso;* see also Gipson, *Empire,* 11:36–38; Channing, *History,* 3:92–93; Quincy, *Reports,* 447–449n. Initial confrontation: Wolkins, "Malcom," 26–27; 39–40.

8. Bernard and council: Wolkins, "Malcom," 27–28; Quincy, *Reports,* 447n. Hallowell's writ of assistance: Quincy, *Reports,* 434. Search warrant: Wolkins, "Malcom," 28. Foster Hutchinson: *Sibley-Shipton,* 11:237–238; *Legal Papers,* 1:cii.

9. 'Change: Morison, *Maritime History,* 131. Hallowell/Sheaffe–Malcom meeting: Wolkins, "Malcom," 41. Otis Malcom's lawyer: Bernard to Shelburne, Dec. 22, 1766, in Quincy, *Reports,* 446n. Hallowell on soldiers: Wolkins, "Malcom," 44–45. Malcom's preparations: *ibid.,* 41.

10. Greenleaf's efforts: Wolkins, "Malcom," 35. Sheaffe and Greenleaf, Harvard Class of 1723, *Sibley-Shipton,* 7:143. Quiet onlookers: Wolkins, "Malcom," 46. Greenleaf's efforts to enlist the J.P.'s: *ibid.,* 36–37. Ruddock's weight: Andrews, "Letters," 322.

11. Tudor: Wolkins, "Malcom," 30–31. Riot Act: *Legal Papers* 3:70–71n. (and sources there cited). Riot: *ibid.,* 3:252 and note. "Paul Rivere": Wolkins, "Malcom," 52.

12. Wolkins, "Malcom," 38.

13. School and Greenleaf's request and fortitude: *ibid.,* 46–47. Tudor: *ibid.,* 31. Writ valid only in daytime as to houses: *Legal Papers,* 2:146. Good night toast: Wolkins, "Malcom," 45.

14. Richardson: Wolkins, "Malcom," 47, 30. Richardson's background: *Legal Papers,* 2:396 and sources there cited, giving his birth year as 1718; compare Richardson deposition, Feb. 27, 1761, T 1/408.155, giving his birth year as 1721. Jackson-Henshaw affair: *Legal Papers,* 2:397; *Sibley-Shipton,* 6:301, 323–324. Cotton-Molineux: Adams Papers; SF #101149; Rowe, *Diary,* 179.

15. Trowbridge's recommendation and Richardson's employment with Paxton: Richardson, petition, Jan. 14, 1775, T 1/517.258. Barrons' interview: Richardson, deposition, Feb. 27, 1761, sworn to before Judge Russell, T 1/408.155–156.

16. Barrons' background and desire to ingratiate: Barrow, *Trade,* 169–170. Barrons on merchants: Richardson, deposition, Feb. 27, 1761, T 1/408.156. John Adams: Adams, *Works,* 10:210. Samuel Adams: Adams, *Writings,* 1:95; Boston Rec. Comm., *Reports,* 16:194.

17. Rowe: Rowe, *Diary,* 111. Sheaffe, Hallowell, and other witnesses: Wolkins, "Malcom," 26–33.

18. Boston Rec. Comm., *Reports,* 16:187–188.

19. Weasel word: Evans, *American Usage,* 549.

20. Depositions: Boston Rec. Comm., *Reports,* 16:188–190; Wolkins, "Malcom," 39–58; Rowe, *Diary,* 112. Letter to DeBerdt: Boston Rec. Comm., *Reports,*

16:191–194; Adams, *Writings,* 1:89–95.

21. Transmission to Shelburne: See Wolkins, "Malcom," 50n. Russell's departure: Boyle, "Journal," 251. Adams on Russell: Adams, *Diary and Autobiography,* 2:90. Russell's death: *Sibley-Shipton,* 9:87; Russell died at Guilford, England, Nov. 24, 1766; Shelburne received Bernard's letter Dec. 12, 1766, which suggests that Russell did not carry the letter after all; see Wolkins, "Malcom," 50n. Auchmuty: *Legal Papers,* 1:xcvi. Trowbridge: *ibid.* cxii. Gridley: *ibid.,* ci; Rowe, *Diary,* 141. Sewall: *Legal Papers,* 1:cix; AO 13/48.495.

22. Harrison: Morgan, *Stamp Act,* 32; Rowe, *Diary,* 114; Wolkins, "Boston Customs," 429. Rockingham left office July 23, 1766: Gipson, *Empire,* 11:77. Money scarcity: Andrews, "Boston Merchants," esp. 180–183; James Bowdoin to Alexander McKay, Nov. 29, 1770, *Bowdoin-Temple,* 241–242; Gipson, *Empire,* 11:137, suggests that Massachusetts was "blessed with specie," but Bowdoin, *Bowdoin-Temple,* 241, talks of "a scarcity of such money," alleviated only by import of "Portugal & Spanish coin." Dollars from Salem: Adams, *Diary and Autobiography,* 1:322.

23. Adams, *Diary and Autobiography,* 1:323–324.

24. General Court activities: Hutchinson, *History,* 3:114; Rowe, *Diary,* 114; Gipson, *Empire,* 11:20–22. Petitions: Mass. Arch. 88:182 (Hallowell), 183 (Story), 199–201 (Hutchinson), 202–203 (Oliver).

25. Vote: Gipson, *Empire,* 11:22. English reaction: *Annual Register, 1766,* 174–182, setting out Secretary Conway to Bernard, March 31, 1766; Bernard's speech to the legislature, June 3, 1766; and the House's reply to the latter.

26. Hawley: Hutchinson, *History,* 3:212–213; the standard biography is Brown, *Joseph Hawley;* Brown, "Hawley," 502–508 is, from a lawyer's viewpoint, inadequate. Berkshire affair: Quincy, *Reports,* 248–250; Hutchinson, *History,* 3:114; Hutchinson, *Diary,* 1:72–73; Adams, *Diary and Autobiography,* 1:326; SF #157338, #157388; MB 83, SCJ Springfield, Sept. 1766; Rec., 1766–1767, fol. 133.

27. Wells, *Adams,* 1:127.

28. Delay for approval: Hutchinson, *History,* 3:114; see resolve of Boston Town Meeting, Dec. 1, 1766, instructing the Town's representatives "to use their Endeavors to the passing of said Bill into a Law," Boston Rec. Comm., *Reports,* 16:195. Effort against amnesty: Gipson, *Empire,* 11:24. Passage by House (Dec. 5, 1766): Rowe, *Diary,* 117. By council (Dec. 6, 1766): Boyle, "Journal," 251. Bernard's doubts: Hutchinson, *History,* 3:115. Amounts received: Mass. Arch., 88:207 (Hutchinson, £3194:17:6; Hallowell, £385:6:10; Oliver, £172:4:0; Story, £67:8:10). Aftermath: Hutchinson, *Diary,* 1:73. Disallowance (May 13, 1767): *Acts, Privy Council (Col.),* 5:86, 87; the best concise, documented account of the entire compensation question is Gipson, *Empire* 11:18–26. Samuel Adams: Adams, *Writings,* 1:394 (as "Alfred" in *B. Gaz.,* Oct. 2, 1769).

5. The Customs Commissioners

1. Shy, *Toward Lexington,* 40, suggests that the militia could "maintain law and order," giving as examples control of Indian hostility and of slave insurrections. He cites no instances of the militia's controlling the type of riot which was beginning to plague Massachusetts in the mid-1760's, and I believe him to be closer to the mark when he admits later in the same paragraph that the militia was "an instrument of either order or insurrection, depending on circumstances."

2. Transient troops: Hutchinson, *History,* 3:122. Bernard's attitude: Bernard to Barrington, Dec. 13, 1766, *Barrington-Bernard,* 119.

3. Arrival of Artillery: Rowe, *Diary*, 115. Quartering Act (5 Geo. 3, c. 33 [1766]); Shy, *Toward Lexington*, 163–190, especially 187n.; Channing, *History*, 3:45, 52–53. Provisioning: Hutchinson, *History*, 3:122; Miller, *Origins*, 238; Shy, *Toward Lexington*, 254. Crisis: Hutchinson, *History*, 3:122–123; Gipson, *Empire*, 11:30–32; Miller, *Origins*, 238–239 has some valuable details, but erroneously suggests that the supplies were not provided.

4. Shelburne: Shelburne to Gage, Dec. 11, 1766, *CHOP*, 2:97, 98. Johnson: Hutchinson, *Diary*, 1:10, quoting *Taxation No Tyranny*. Minority: *Annual Register, 1767*, 229.

5. House's attitude: Miller, *Origins*, 251. Townshend's character: *Britannica* (11th ed.), 27:112. Proposal: Gipson, *Empire*, 11:106. Acts: 7 Geo. 3, c. 41, 46; 8 Geo. 3, c. 22 (1767). £40,000: *Britannica* (11th ed.), 27:112; see also Barrow, *Trade*, 213–218, which takes a more charitable, and hence perhaps more accurate, view of Townshend than mine. Foolishness of policy: Robson, *American Revolution*, 31, 44, 45; see generally, Miller, *Origins*, 247–252; Gipson, *Empire*, 11:70–135; Channing, *History*, 3:81–85.

6. Boston as leader: Paxton to Lord Townshend, Feb. 24, 1768, in Wolkins, "Paxton," 348. Object: Gipson, *Empire*, 11:135.

7. Popular control: Paxton to Lord Townshend, Feb. 24, 1768, in Wolkins, "Paxton," 348 (written some months after the events in the text, but nonetheless applicable). Hawley-Hutchinson: Hutchinson, *History*, 3:126–127; see also *ibid.*, 213.

8. Hawley: Hutchinson to Cushing, July 30, 1767, MHS, *Procs.*, 44:524 (1911); SF #157477, #157559; MB 90, Hampshire, Oct. 1769; Rec. 1767–1768, fol. 46. Trowbridge: *Legal Papers*, 1:ln.; Adams, *Diary and Autobiography*, 1:230; Rowe, *Diary*, 127. Hutchinson's stroke: Lynde, *Diary*, 191.

9. Charge: Quincy, *Reports*, 247. On charges and politics: Cushing, "Judiciary," 169. Celebration: Rowe, *Diary*, 139.

10. Hutchinson: Hutchinson, *History*, 3:129. Bernard: Bernard to Barrington, Feb. 7, 1768, *Barrington-Bernard*, 144.

11. Gage to Shelburne, April 28, 1767, in Gipson, *Empire*, 11:130.

12. Paxton-Lord Townshend: Adams, *Diary and Autobiography*, 2:177; 1:344. Lord Townshend at Quebec: Stacey, *Quebec*, 153. Boston location: William Samuel Johnson to Jared Ingersoll, Nov. 12, 1767, in Gipson, *Empire*, 11:118n. Temple: *Sibley-Shipton*, 11:522; *Legal Papers*, 2:148. Temple's marriage: Boyle, "Journal," 251; whether or not Bowdoin's radicalism preceded his daughter's marriage, it most certainly flourished afterward, Hutchinson, *History*, 3:211; Hulton, *Letters*, 123–124; *Sibley-Shipton*, 11:522–523. Commission: Channing, *History*, 3:85n.; compare Gipson, *Empire*, 11:120n. (Sept. 14, 1767). Gazetting: *Annual Register, 1767*, 173. Hulton: Hulton, *Letters*, viii, 4; Andrews, *Colonial Period*, 4:220n. Burch: Stark, *Loyalists*, 319. Traveling companions: Boyle, "Journal," 253; see also Barrow, *Trade*, 222. Robert Temple: Adams, *Diary and Autobiography*, 2:92.

13. "Unwelcome cargo": Boyle, "Journal," 253. Rain: Rowe, *Diary*, 145. On the landing generally, see Quincy, *Reports*, 450; Hutchinson, *History*, 3:132; Paxton to Lord Townshend, Feb. 24, 1768, Wolkins, "Paxton," 348. Paxton's effigy: Channing, *History*, 3:86–87. Devils and laughter: Hulton, *Letters*, 8. Town meeting and Otis: Hutchinson, *History*, 3:131–132. Commission: Paxton to Lord Townshend, Feb. 24, 1768, Wolkins, "Paxton," 348; Hulton, Account, 28, says the date was Nov. 16. First meeting: *B. Gaz.*, Nov. 23, 1767. Concert Hall: *Legal Papers*, 3:315. Custom House: T 1/476.156b.

14. Blake: Rowe, *Diary*, 146. Silver: Boston Collections Account, Jan. 5, 1770–

Jan. 5, 1771, T 1/476. Temple: Wolkins, "Paxton," 350. Efficient service: Channing, *History,* 3:88–91; see also Wolkins, "Liberty," 241n., which shows from documents that in the year commencing Jan. 5, 1768, ports in the commissioners' jurisdiction netted revenues of £36,756:12:2¼, of which £8734:1:4½ came from Boston; compare Gipson, *Empire,* 11:241, which puts the American net for Sept. 8, 1767 to Jan. 5, 1769 at £12,474:10:7¾, and Channing, *History,* 3:90, which puts the average annual American net for Sept. 8, 1767 to Jan. 5, 1774 at £17,000. The gross at Boston and Salem-Marblehead, respectively, during the year commencing Jan. 5, 1770 was £5923:17:3½ and £2900, Boston Collections Account, Jan. 5, 1770–Jan. 5, 1771, T 1/476. The Townshend duties for the period Sept. 8, 1767 to Nov. 5, 1770, including about £1900 worth of seizures, totaled £18,276:16:9¾, according to Temple, Bowdoin to Thomas Pownall, Nov. 12, 1770, *Bowdoin-Temple,* 236. Adjournment at 2 P.M.: Bowdoin-Temple MSS 7:58. Hulton's house and chattels: Hulton, *Letters,* x–xi; AO 13/46.464bff.; Hulton was also "Principal Receiver in America for the [six-penny monthly payments from mariners for maintenance of the] Royal Hospital at Greenwich," England, a sinecure which produced him £208 annually, AO 13/46.467b, 478; see also Andrews, *Colonial Period,* 4:208, 220n. Bernard: AO 13/74.9; the naval officer's duties emphasized paperwork rather than enforcement, see Andrews, *Colonial Period,* 4:188–190; Barrow, *Trade,* 78. Steuart: T 1/476.151ff.

15. Quincy: "Hyperion," *B. Gaz.,* Oct. 5, 1767. Adams: Massachusetts House of Representatives to DeBerdt, Jan. 12, 1768, Adams, *Writings,* 1:146; similar language appeared eighteen years later in the Declaration of Independence: "He has . . . sent hither Swarms of Officers to harrass our People, and eat out their Substance"; see the discussion in Dumbauld, *Declaration,* 116–117.

16. Mein: *Legal Papers,* 1:152, and sources cited there. "Mean": *ibid.,* 1:201n.; Hulton, *Account,* 135 suggests "Mayne". Adams as patron: Adams, *Diary and Autobiography,* 1:338. Weekly gross: Mein, memorial, n.d., T 1/478. Constable: Boston Rec. Comm., *Reports,* 16:164. First issue and Otis's reply: *Legal Papers,* 1:152. Radicals setting press: Hutchinson to John Cushing, Aug. 5, 1768, MHS, *Procs.* (2d ser.), 20:536 (1906–1907).

17. *Legal Papers,* 1:151–157.

6. The *Liberty* Riot

1. *Britannica* (11th ed.), 8:460 (under "Downshire," the title he acquired in 1789).

2. Franklin: Van Doren, *Franklin,* 383, 384–387. Walpole: *Britannica* (11th ed.), 8:461. King: George III said he did "not know a man of less judgment than Lord Hillsborough," George III to John Robinson, Oct. 15, 1776, quoted in *DNB,* 9:879. Frigate: IND 4807, Sept. 5, 1765. Bernard: Barrington to Bernard, April 16, 1768, *Barrington-Bernard,* 151; Barrington to Bernard, Feb. 20, 1768, *ibid.,* 147.

3. News: The news reached Boston around Feb. 20, 1768; see Bernard's letter of that date cited in note 2, above. Circular letter: Bernard to Barrington, same letter, *ibid.,* 145–146; the best account of the whole episode is Miller, *Sam Adams,* 103–133.

4. Warren: *B. Gaz.,* Feb. 29, 1768. Bernard's efforts: Bernard to Shelburne, March 5, 1768, CO 5/766. Hutchinson charge: Quincy, *Reports,* 262–270. Grand jury: Bernard to Shelburne, March 12, 1768, CO 5/766; see *Legal Papers,* 1:206; Hutchinson, *History,* 3:135; when the text of Bernard's letter was published about a year later, the radical merchant Harbottle Dorr annotated his copy: "A Notorious

Falshood!", Dorr Papers.

5. Parade: Bernard to Shelburne, March 19, 1768, CO 5/766. Burch's home: Bernard to Shelburne, March 19, 1768, CO 5/766; Bernard to Barrington, March 4, 1768, *Barrington-Bernard*, 148. Madeira: Bernard to Shelburne, March 21, 1768, CO 5/766; Bernard to Barrington, March 4, 1768, *Barrington-Bernard*, 147–148; Hutchinson, *History*, 3:137; it is not clear to whom the cargo belonged; Hulton, Account, 126–127, says Hancock; Hillsborough to Bernard, July 11, 1768, CO 5/765, quoting the commissioners' report, says Malcom; see also Barrow, *Trade* 228. Woolton: Woolton, deposition, March 18, 1768, Gage Papers. Harvard: Hutchinson, *History*, 3:135–136; see also Morison, *Three Centuries*, 133.

6. Bernard to Barrington, March 4, 1768, *Barrington-Bernard*, 148–149.

7. Nonimportation: Rowe, *Diary*, 152–155; Bernard to Shelburne, March 21, 1768, CO 5/766; in his copy of the printed version, Harbottle Dorr wrote opposite Bernard's report of the pressure exerted on the merchants, "Falsehoods," Dorr Papers; "European" included English goods. Adams and nonimportation: Miller, *Sam Adams*, 193–201; Andrews, "Boston Merchants," *passim*. Adams's peculations: *Jeffries v. Adams*, MB 86, Suffolk, Aug. 1767; Rec., 1767–1768, fol. 122; Boston Rec. Comm., *Reports*, 16:92, 143, 201, 218, 241–243; Adams, *Writings*, 1:199; Rowe, *Diary*, 157; Miller, *Sam Adams*, 98–101.

8. Colors: Bernard to Shelburne, March 19, 1768, CO 5/766. Effigies: Rowe, *Diary*, 157; Hutchinson, *History*, 3:136. Cutting down: Rowe, *Diary*, 157. Loyal Nine: Morgan, *Stamp Act*, 160; Adams, *Diary and Autobiography*, 1:294. Dinners: Rowe, *Diary*, 156; at the Whig dinner, one toast honored the grand jury, *Legal Papers*, 1:206. Mob: Rowe, *Diary*, 157; Bernard to Shelburne, March 19, 1768, CO 5/766; see also Hutchinson, *History*, 3:136; Hulton, Account, 84.

9. Williams: Adams, *Diary and Autobiography*, 1:344. Boasts: Hulton, Account, 112. "Reception": Bernard to Shelburne, March 19, 1768, CO 5/766. Kindred spirit: Williams's connection with the radicals has never been explored; he was close enough to them so that his son Jonathan could later become John Adams's law clerk, *Legal Papers*, 1:cxiii, and he acted as political guide to Josiah Quincy during Quincy's London visit in 1774–1775, Howe, "Quincy," *passim;* he is supposed to have been a brother-in-law of Benjamin Franklin, *ibid.*, 437n. Adams: Miller, *Sam Adams*, 140–142. Dust-licking: *B. Gaz.*, March 14, 1768. No damage: Rowe, *Diary*, 157.

10. Trifling: The council, in a later, more radical phase, called the matter "trivial," Council to Gage, Oct. 27, 1768, CO 5/86; after investigating, Gage concluded that it was indeed trifling, Gage to Hillsborough, Oct. 31, 1768, CO 5/86. Troops: Paxton to Lord Townshend, May 18, 1768, Wolkins, "Paxton," 349. Naval: Hood to Admiralty, July 11, 1768, CO 5/767; Hillsborough to Admiralty, June 15, 1768, IND 4807. Dalrymple: Rowe, *Diary*, 160.

11. *Lydia:* Rowe, *Diary*, 159; Owen Richards and Robert Jackson, deposition, May 12, 1768, T 1/465; see also *Legal Papers*, 2:174; Barrow, *Trade*, 229–230; Ubbelohde, *Vice-Admiralty*, 120–121; Dickerson, *Navigation Acts*, 234–235. Sewall: Commissioners (including Temple) to Treasury, May 12, 1768, T 1/465; Fitch to Commissioners, April 15, 1768, T 1/465; *Legal Papers*, 2:178n.

12. *Liberty:* Generally, *Legal Papers*, 2:173–210. Freight and rumor of smuggling: Hutchinson, *History*, 3:137. Boasts and examination of tidesmen: Hallowell, testimony, July 21, 1768, T 1/468. Harrison: *Acts, Privy Council (Col.)*, 5:254. Marshall: Drake, *Boston Landmarks*, 170; Boyle, "Journal," 254.

13. *Romney:* Hood to Admiralty, July 11, 1768, CO 5/767; Boyle, "Journal," 254; *Romney*, Log. Impressment: Charnock, *Biographia Navalis*, 6:576; *Romney*, Log. Statute: 6 Anne, c. 37 §9 (1707); similar language in 19 Geo. 2, c. 30

(1746); see also *Legal Papers*, 2:278, 283, 323. Furlong: *Romney*, Log. Bostonian unrest over impressment was nothing new; in 1747 impressment activities had provoked three days of riot and tumult, Hutchinson, *History*, 2:330–333; even after independence, the problem remained, this time in the United States Navy; "A Furious Press this morning to Man the Fleet", Rowe, *Diary*, 329–330, July 12, 1779.

14. Hallowell, testimony, July 21, 1768, T 1/468; Kirk, deposition, June 10, 1768, T 1/465.

15. Harrison and Hallowell to Commissioners, June 11, 1768, T 1/465; Hallowell, testimony, July 21, 1768, T 1/468.

16. Warren and Hulton's suggestion: Hallowell, testimony, July 21, 1768, T 1/468; see also Wolkins, "Liberty," 252. Seizure: *Acts, Privy Council* (*Col.*), 5:255. *Romney*'s participation: *Romney*, Log; Hallowell, testimony, July 21, 1768, T 1/468.

17. Riot: Generally, Bernard to Shelburne, June 11, 1768, CO 5/766; see also Hutchinson to Richard Jackson, June 16, 1768, Mass. Arch., 26:310. Irving's rank: Schedule annexed to Bernard to Shelburne, June 17, 1768, CO 5/766.

18. Boats: Hood to Corner, May 2, 1768, Wolkins, "Liberty," 272: "no Boat to be suffered to be kept waiting on any Account." Dispersing: John Robinson, testimony, June 26, 1770, *Acts, Privy Council* (*Col.*), 5:253; Hulton, *Letters* 12. Radicals on March incidents: Bernard to Shelburne, March 19, 1768, CO 5/766. Rowe: Rowe, *Diary*, 165. Council: Council to Gage, Oct. 27, 1768, CO 5/86. Adams: Adams, *Writings*, 407; he added: "It was not a numerous Mob; nor was it of long Continuance, neither was there much Mischief done." Adams's exhortation: Richard Sylvester, deposition, Jan. 23, 1769, Chalmers Papers, 3:12.

19. Commissioners to *Romney*: *Romney*, Log. Bayonets: Hulton, *Letters*, 12. Temple: Hutchinson, *History*, 3:140; *Legal Papers*, 2:176n.

20. Hallowell, testimony, July 21, 1768, T 1/468.

21. Legal battle: *Legal Papers*, 2:177–210. Otis's bill for services, Chamberlain Papers, M.110.102. "Drudgery": Adams, *Diary and Autobiography*, 3:306. Sewall: Bernard to Commissioners, Jan. 6, 1769, Bowdoin-Temple MSS, 7:239. "Journal": *Legal Papers*, 2:184.

22. Malcom as grand juror: SF #101222; Bernard, testimony, June 27, 1770, *Acts Privy Council* (*Col.*), 259. No evidence: Bernard to Hillsborough, Sept. 9, 1768, CO 5/767. King's attitude: Hillsborough to Bernard, Oct. 12, 1768, CO 5/765.

7. "A Most Unequal War"

1. Entertainment: Hulton, *Letters*, 12; Corner later requested and received 150 guineas from the Navy Board for "the great expense he was at in receiving on board the Officers of the Customs," IND 4807, June 15, 1769. Placards: Bernard to Hillsborough, June 14, 1768, CO 5/766. Liberty Hall: Bernard to Hillsborough, June 16, 1768, CO 5/766. Weather: *Romney*, Log. Crowd and proceedings: Hutchinson, *History*, 3:138; Rowe, *Diary*, 165.

2. Meetings: Rowe, *Diary*, 165; Bernard to Hillsborough, June 16, 1768, CO 5/766; Hutchinson, *History*, 3:138–139. Petition: *ibid.*, 3:353–354.

3. Reception: Rowe, *Diary*, 165; Bernard to Hillsborough, June 16, 1768, CO 5/766. Response: Boston Rec. Comm., *Reports*, 16:256. Bernard's success: Bernard had previously negotiated with Corner and the selectmen; a few days after the petition, he boarded *Romney* with Councilors William Brattle, James Bowdoin, and Royall Tyler, and concluded a satisfactory agreement, Bernard to

Hillsborough, June 16, 1768, CO 5/766; Rowe, *Diary*, 165, 166; Report of Brattle, Bowdoin, and Tyler, June 16, 1768, Mass. Arch., 44:438–441; the committee "observed with Pleasure the friendly Disposition of Captain Corner to the Province in general, and to the Town in particular," *ibid.*, 441; see also Boston Rec. Comm., *Reports*, 16:254–257; Bernard to Barrington, June 18, 1768, *Barrington-Bernard*, 160; Charnock, *Biographia Navalis*, 6:576. *Romney's* shifts: *Romney*, Log. Corner's agreement: *B. Chron.*, June 20, 1768. Commissioners to Castle: Rowe, *Diary*, 167; the rest of *Romney's* guests disembarked June 27, *Romney*, Log. Hulton, Burch, Temple: Hulton, *Letters*, 15. Harrison: Harrison, testimony, June 27, 1770, *Acts, Privy Council (Col.)*, 5:255. Socializing: Hulton, *Letters*, 14–15. Hallowell: Bernard to Barrington, June 18, 1768, *Barrington-Bernard*, 160; Hallowell, testimony, July 21, 1768, T 1/468; Rowe, *Diary*, 167.

4. Otis: Bernard to Hillsborough, June 16, 1768, CO 5/766. Instructions: *Legal Papers*, 278n. Text: Boston Rec. Comm., *Reports*, 16:257–259.

5. Commissioners: Commissioners to Gage, June 15, 1768, CO 5/86. Consultation: Bernard to Barrington, March 4, 1768, *Barrington-Bernard*, 148. Circular: *Annual Register, 1766*, 174. Gage: Gage, *Correspondence*, 2:27, 29.

6. Need: Bernard to Barrington, July 20, 1768, *Barrington-Bernard*, 167. Gage's orders: War Office to Gage, Oct. 24, 1765, Gage, *Correspondence*, 2:27n. Gage's response: Gage to Commissioners, June 21, 1768, CO 5/766.

7. Bernard's fear: Bernard to Barrington, Nov. 23, 1765; March 4, 1768; May 9, 1768; July 20, 1768, *Barrington-Bernard*, 102, 147, 148, 149, 159, 167, 168. Permanent solution: Same to same, Nov. 23, 1765; Feb. 7, 1768, *ibid.*, 101, 141, 143, 145. Better job: Same to same, Feb. 7, 1768; June 29, 1768, *ibid.*, 142–144, 161–162; Barrington to Bernard, May 9, 1768, *ibid.*, 154. Bernard's war: Bernard to Barrington, July 30, 1768; Nov. 23, 1765, *ibid.*, 170, 102. Increased net worth: Same to same, Nov. 15, 1765, *ibid.*, 80. Climate: Same to same, Feb. 7, 1768, *ibid.*, 142; Bernard had been worrying about the problem for years, see Chapter 3, text at n. 44, above.

8. Son: Bernard to Barrington, April 20, 1768, *Barrington-Bernard*, 152. Trouble: Same to same, Dec. 12, 1764, *ibid.*, 85.

9. Orders received: Bernard to Hillsborough, June 17, 1768, CO 5/766. Fireship: Bernard to Barrington, June 18, 1768, *Barrington-Bernard*, 160. Recision: See generally Gipson, *Empire*, 11:151–152. Bernard's optimism: Bernard to Hillsborough, June 17, 1768, CO 5/766. Bernard's tactics: Hutchinson, *History*, 3:141. Tax relief: Bernard to Hillsborough, May 26, 1768, CO 5/766. Hutchinson recall: Hutchinson, *History*, 3:145; he was called June 24, when the court, having adjourned at Ipswich the day before, MB 85, was enroute to Falmouth; when the court sat at Falmouth June 28, Hutchinson was there, MB 87. Sample of oratory: *Sibley-Shipton*, 11:274–275. Vote: Hutchinson, *History*, 3:143; Bernard to Hillsborough, June 25, 1768, CO 5/766. Ninety-two: Fifteen Sons of Liberty commissioned Paul Revere to fashion a commemorative silver bowl (weighing a significant 45 ounces and holding 45 gills, the figure 45 being sacred to John Wilkes); suitably engraved, the bowl made its first public appearance Aug. 1, 1768, Rowe, *Diary*, 171; Forbes, *Revere*, 134. Purge: Miller, *Origins*, 264; see also Miller, *Sam Adams*, 130.

10. Commissioners' plea: Gage to Bernard, June 24, 1768, CO 5/86. Orders: Gage to Bernard, June 25, 1768, CO 5/86 (received by Bernard July 2, 1768, see Bernard to Hillsborough, July 30, 1768, CO 5/767); Gage to Dalrymple, June 25, 1768, CO 5/86. Nova Scotia activity: Hood to Admiralty, July 11, 1768, CO 5/767. Gage's unwillingness: Alden, *Gage*, 159. Prior orders: Hillsborough to Gage, June 8, 1768, CO 5/86. Gage's receipt: Gage, *Correspondence*, 2:78n.; ten

weeks was the normal passage, Bernard to Hillsborough, Sept. 10, 1768, CO 5/767.

11. Bernard to Hillsborough, July 9, 1768, CO 5/766.

12. Bernard to Hillsborough, July 9, 1768, and supplement of July 11, 1768, CO 5/766.

13. Bernard to Shelburne, June 16–18, 1768, CO 5/766.

14. Bernard to Hillsborough, July 18–19, 1768, CO 5/767; see also Rowe, *Diary*, 170; Hutchinson, *History*, 3:146.

15. Visitors: Rowe, *Diary*, 170. Radicals and absence of leaders: Bernard to Hillsborough, July 18–19, 1768, CO 5/767.

16. Odium: Hutchinson, *History*, 3:146; the king, however, approved Williams's "Spirited & proper conduct," Hillsborough to Bernard, Sept. 14, 1768, CO 5/765. Council: Rowe, *Diary*, 171; the council also met July 23 and 27, but the question of calling for troops was settled July 29; see Bernard to Hillsborough, July 30, 1768, CO 5/767. Council's advice: Bernard to Gage, July 30, 1768, CO 5/86; Bernard to Barrington, July 30, 1768, *Barrington-Bernard*, 169. Rumors: Rowe, *Diary*, 171. Secrecy: Hutchinson, *History*, 3:146–147.

17. Irish regiments: Hillsborough to Shelburne, July 27, 1768, CO 5/86. Admiralty and instructions to ships: Hillsborough to Admiralty, July 28, 1768, CO 5/86. Normal allowance: Barrington to Shelburne, Jan. 29, 1768, *CHOP*, 2:299. *Rippon:* Hillsborough to Gage, July 30, 1768, CO 5/86.

18. Letter: Hillsborough to Bernard, July 30, 1768, CO 5/765. Statute: 35 Hen. 8, c. 2 (1544). Impressment: Hillsborough enclosed vintage formal opinions of Attorney-General Sir Edward Northey (1715/16) and Attorney-General Sir Dudley Ryder and Solicitor-General Sir John Strange (1740); both opinions concluded that the American exemption from impressment under 6 Anne, c. 37 §9 (1707) no longer existed; see also *Legal Papers*, 2:324 and note.

8. Troops To Boston

1. Nonimportation: Rowe, *Diary*, 171, 172. "Mob-Law": Bernard to Hillsborough, August 9, 1768, CO 5/765.

2. Celebration: Rowe, *Diary*, 172; Hutchinson, *History*, 3:146; Boyle, "Journal," 255. Toast: *B. Gaz.*, Aug. 22, 1768; "Walkerizing" undoubtedly refers to an incident at Montreal in 1766, when soldiers of the Twenty-eighth Regiment cropped an ear of Justice of the Peace Thomas Walker, who had tried an officer of the Twenty-eighth for illegally occupying quarters; see Shy, *Toward Lexington*, 162. Moore: Bernard to Hillsborough, Aug. 29, 1768, CO 5/767.

3. Adams on printers: John Adams to Abigail Adams, July 4, 1774, *Adams Family Correspondence*, 1:23. *Gazette*, court adjournment, and Bernard: Hutchinson to John Cushing, Aug. 5, 1768, MHS, *Procs.* (2d Ser.), 20:536 (1906–1907). Robinson: *Annual Register, 1768*, 254–255. Return to the Castle: *B. Gaz.*, Sept. 5, 1768, which says he lodged the night of Sept. 4 at Dorchester.

4. Troops by New Year's: Bernard to Hillsborough, Aug. 9, 1768, CO 5/767 (this may have referred to the projected termination of the nonimportation agreement on that date). Bernard's coyness: Hutchinson to John Cushing, Aug. 5, 1768, MHS, *Procs.* (2d Ser.), 20:536 (1906–1907). Freemasons: Hancock: *Sibley-Shipton*, 13:426; Otis: *ibid.*, 9:248; Crafts and Warren: Cary, *Warren*, 56; Rowe, *Diary, passim*. Revere: Forbes, *Revere*, 60–61. Masonry and radicals: Forbes, *Revere*, 61 (unfortunately, here as elsewhere this gifted writer refuses to give her sources); later, army officers joined the lodge, see Chapter 12, at note 9 below. Arms: Bernard to Hillsborough, July 9, 1768, CO 5/766; Bernard to Gage, Sept.

16, 1768, CO 5/86.

5. Shirreff: Gage to Bernard, Aug. 31, 1768, in Frothingham, "Sam Adams Regiments," 713–714. Bernard to Gage, Sept. 5, 1768, CO 5/86; Gage to Hillsborough, Sept. 7, 1768, CO 5/86; Alden, *Gage,* 159–160. I have dated the meeting from: (a) the day that Shirreff is known to have reached Boston (Frothingham, "Sam Adams Regiments," 713), and (b) the date of the orders which Shirreff forwarded to Dalrymple (Dalrymple to Gage, Oct. 2, 1768, CO 5/86). Shirreff-Bernard arrangement: Bernard to Gage, Sept. 5, 1768, CO 5/86. Artillery: Dalrymple to Gage, Oct. 2, 1768, CO 5/86. Gage's orders: Gage to Bernard, Aug. 31, 1768, in Frothingham, "Sam Adams Regiments," 714; Gage to Hillsborough, Sept. 7, 1768, CO 5/86. Bernard's suggestions: Bernard to Gage, Sept. 5, 1768, CO 5/86.

6. *Gazette* piece and risk to crown officers: Bernard to Hillsborough, Sept. 16, 1768, CO 5/767; *B. Gaz.*, Sept. 12, 1768. Franklin: Van Doren, *Franklin,* 344.

7. Bernard's scheme: Bernard to Gage, Sept. 16, 1768, CO 5/86; Bernard to Hillsborough, Sept. 16, 1768, CO 5/767. Bernard's leaks: Bernard to Hillsborough, Sept. 16, 1768, CO 5/767; Rowe, *Diary,* 174. Circulation of news: Bernard to Hillsborough, Sept. 16, 1768, CO 5/767.

8. *Senegal* carrying orders: Hood to Admiralty, Oct. 12, 1768, CO 5/767. Discontent, fear, and alarm: Corner, Diary. Quiet on Saturday nights: Hutchinson, *Diary,* 1:334. Barrel, beacon, meetings, and removal: Hutchinson, *History,* 3:147; Bernard to Hillsborough, Sept. 16, 1768, CO 5/767; Corner, Diary. See also Rowe, *Diary,* 174. Barrel empty: Bernard to Gage, Sept. 16, 1768, CO 5/86; Corner, Diary; see also *Sibley-Shipton,* 7:186–187. Removal: Hutchinson, *History,* 3:147.

9. Rumors: Corner, Diary; Bernard to Hillsborough, Sept. 16, 1768, CO 5/767. Meeting at Warren's: Corner, Diary.

10. Speeches and *Magdalen:* Corner, Diary. Resolves: Boston Rec. Comm., *Reports,* 16:260.

11. Bernard's reaction: Boston Rec. Comm., *Reports,* 16:261. Bernard's lying: In addition to sources cited in note 5, above, see Gage to Hillsborough, Sept. 16, 1768, CO 5/86, which clearly indicates that Bernard, not Gage, set the size of the Boston-bound force and its placement. Reinforcements: Bernard to Gage, Sept. 16, 1768, CO 5/86.

12. Oratory: Bernard to Hillsborough, Sept. 16, 1768, CO 5/767. Resolves: Boston Rec. Comm., *Reports,* 16:261–264; see generally Hutchinson, *History,* 3:148–149, and Miller, *Sam Adams,* 149–151. Statute: Act of Nov. 29, 1693, *Mass. Acts,* 1:128.

13. Sylvester: Deposition of Richard Sylvester, Jan. 23 1769; Chalmers Papers, 3:12. Letter from DeBerdt: Corner, Diary. English reaction: *ibid.;* Bernard to Gage, Sept. 16, 1768, CO 5/86; DeGrey-Dunning opinion, Nov. 25, 1768, CO 5/767. Boston reaction: Corner, Diary. Transports and Gage's attitude: Gage to Hillsborough, Sept. 26, 1768, CO 5/86.

14. Events in Ireland: *CHOP,* 2:370–374. Transports: Gage to Hillsborough, Jan. 5, 1769, Gay Transcripts, 11:131; same to same, Mar. 4, 1769, *ibid.,* 11:135. *Hussar:* Same to same, Jan. 5, 1769, *ibid.,* 11:131.

15. Activities at Halifax: *B. Gaz.*, Oct. 10, 1768; Hood, Log; Wolkins, "Liberty," 247–248; Dalrymple to Gage, Oct. 2, 1768, CO 5/86; the eighty-four men from the Fifty-ninth were filling in temporarily for men in the Twenty-ninth whom Dalrymple had not had time "to withdraw, or relieve" from Nova Scotia outposts. Dalrymple: Shy, *Toward Lexington,* 353; O'Donnell, *Fourteenth,* 41n.; Gage to Hillsborough, Sept. 7, 1768, CO 5/86; Hulton, *Letters,* 63. Carr: Gage to Barrington, Jan. 16, 1766, and June 15, 1766; Gage, *Correspondence,* 2:333, 357. Descrip-

tions: *New Jersey Archives*, 27:237, 532, 557; Everard, *Twenty-Ninth*, 73.

16. American enlistments: Shy, *Toward Lexington*, 143. Officers: Adams, *Diary and Autobiography*, 1:188. Dislike of peace-time army: see "Instructions of the Town of Boston to its Representatives in the General Court, May 1764," Adams, *Writings*, 1:6. Standing army-police: Of particular help in shaping my thoughts have been: Bailyn, *Pamphlets*, 41–43, 71–72, 120; Shy, *Toward Lexington*, 190, 376–377.

17. English mobs: Adams, *Writings*, 1:237; Benjamin Franklin to John Ross, May 14, 1768, Van Doren, *Franklin*, 381; see also accounts in *CHOP*, 2:*passim*. Barre: Quincy, *Reports*, 463. English and Irish experience: Shy, *Toward Lexington*, 394–395. St. George's Fields: Postgate, *Wilkes*, 134–135; Shy, *Toward Lexington*, 396–397; Bailyn, *Pamphlets*, 72.

18. Gage: Gage to Hillsborough, Sept. 26, 1768, CO 5/86. English preoccupation: Hinkhouse, *Preliminaries*, 140–141; news of the *Liberty* riot, however, did lower London stock prices, *ibid.*, 144.

9. The Occupation Begins

1. Orders and Bernard's leave: Bernard to Gage, Sept. 16, 1768, CO 5/86. Quartering: Bernard to Hillsborough, Sept. 16, 1768, CO 5:767; Bernard understood that Otis had explained the legal strategy thus:

> There are no Barracks in the Town, and therefore by Act of Parliament [5 Geo. 3, c. 33 (1765)] they must be quartered in the public Houses: but no one will keep a public House on such Terms, and there will be no public Houses; then the Governor and Council must hire Barns, Outhouses, &c. for them, but no-body is obliged to let them, no-body will let them, no-body will dare to let them. The Troops are forbid to quarter themselves in any other manner than according to the Act of Parliament under severe Penalties; but they can't quarter themselves according to the Act, and therefore they must leave the Town, or seize on Quarters contrary to the Act. When they do this, when they invade Property contrary to an Act of Parliament, we may resist them with the Law on our Side.

Ibid.; well might Bernard reply, as he did: "Indeed the Act is impracticable enough without all this Contrivance," *ibid.* Gage: Bernard to Gage, Sept. 24, 1768, CO 5/86. See also: Bernard to Hillsborough, Sept. 26, 1768; Oct. 1, 1768; Oct. 5, 1768, CO 5/767; Hutchinson, *History*, 3:150–151.

2. Fast: Corner, Diary. Byles: *Sibley-Shipton*, 7:464–490; Stark, *Loyalists*, 275–279. Hymn: *Sagittarius*, 109. Boston militia: Corner, Diary. Number of delegates: Hutchinson, *History*, 3:151; Corner, Diary, says forty-four; by Sept. 27, the delegates numbered between eighty and ninety, "Eliot-Hollis," 428; the best account of the convention is Miller, *Sam Adams*, Chapter 6; see also Hutchinson, *History*, 3:151–153. Cushing and Adams: Bernard to Hillsborough, Sept. 27, 1768, CO 5/767. Otis's absence: Corner, Diary; Bernard to Hillsborough, Sept. 27, 1768, CO 5/767. Squabble with Bernard: *ibid.* Gales: Corner, Diary.

3. "Result": Hutchinson, *History*, 3:152–153; Bernard to Hillsborough, Oct. 3, 1768, CO 5/767. Otis-Adams: *ibid.* Eliot: "Eliot-Hollis," 428. Arrival of flotilla: Corner, Diary. "Scalded hogs": *Sagittarius*, 81n.

4. Heavy weather: Dalrymple to Gage, Oct. 2, 1768, CO 5/86. Bernard-Dalrymple: *ibid.;* Bernard to Hillsborough, Oct. 1, 1768, CO 5/767.

5. Flotilla complete: Rowe, *Diary*, 175. Council meeting: Bernard to Hillsborough, Oct. 1, 1768, CO 5/767.

6. Council meeting: Dalrymple to Gage, Oct. 2, 1768, CO 5/86; Bernard to

Hillsborough, Oct. 1, 1768, CO 5/767. Dalrymple's concern: Dalrymple to Gage, Oct. 2, 1768, CO 5/86.

7. Montresor: Dalrymple to Gage, Oct. 2, 1768, CO 5/86; Bernard to Hillsborough, Oct. 1, 1768, CO 5/767. Gage's reaction: *ibid.;* for a sample of the intelligence Gage was receiving, see "Paper of Intelligence" from "a Gentleman who left Boston [Sept. 14, 1768]," CO 5/86.

8. Dalrymple and quartering: Dalrymple to Gage, Oct. 2, 1768, CO 5/86. Ships moving: Bernard to Hillsborough, Oct. 1, 1768, CO 5/767. Description of spring: Forester, *Hornblower,* 222. Revere: see the inscription on the famous Revere-Remick view of the landing; a version is reproduced in Gipson, *Empire,* 11: facing 164. Potential trouble ashore: "Eliot-Hollis," 34: "At present, people do not seem disposed to resist the troops, but their tempers are in such a ferment that they may easily be pushed on to the most desperate measures; and if the troops attempt to quarter in the town, I greatly fear the consequence."

9. Landing and lack of opposition: Dalrymple to Gage, Oct. 2, 1768, CO 5/86; Bernard to Hillsborough, Oct. 1, 1768, CO 5/767; Revere-Remick view, Gipson, *Empire,* 11: facing 164. Colors and uniforms: O'Donnell, *Fourteenth,* 40, 270–275, 295; see also Everard, *Twenty-Ninth,* 58–60. Molesworth: Stark, *Loyalists,* 439–440; *Britannica* (11th ed.), 3:822, 22:62.

10. Manufactory: Drake, *Boston Landmarks,* 302–303; Hutchinson, *History,* 3:153, 155; Dalrymple to Gage, Oct. 2, 1768, CO 5/86.

11. Dalrymple and the selectmen: Dalrymple to Gage, Oct. 2, 1768, CO 5/767; Rowe, *Diary,* 175–176. Faneuil Hall, *ibid.;* Hutchinson, *History,* 3:153.

12. Town House: Hutchinson, *History,* 3:153–154.

13. Castle: Gage to Hillsborough, Oct. 31, 1768, CO 5/86. Salem and Newbury: Bernard to Gage, Oct. 1, 1768, CO 5/86. Quartering Act: 5 Geo 3, c. 33 (1765). Gage's view: Gage to Hillsborough, Oct. 31, 1768, CO 5/86.

14. Housing: Rowe, *Diary,* 177; *Short Narrative,* 9 (text). Guard house: Rowe, *Diary,* 177. Desertion: Hutchinson to Thomas Whately, Oct. 17, 1768, *Mass. Arch.,* 25:283; "Eliot-Hollis," 432. Encouragement of desertions: See *Rex* v. *Geary* (Garry) (information for "encouraging" a desertion on Oct. 6, 1768; found not guilty), MB 86; Rec., 1767–1768, fol. 370. Wilson: Rowe, *Diary,* 178 (which incorrectly states he was bound over to the sessions); SF #101301a (the indictment); *B. Gaz.,* Nov. 7, 1768; the superior court Minute Books and Record contain no mention of this matter, which suggests that the indictment was nolprossed; John Mein, too, commented on the paradox of Boston's containing slaves, *Sagittarius,* 38–39. Hill: AO 13/46.337.

15. Gage's impatience: Gage to Bernard, Oct. 2, 1768, CO 5/86. Gage's arrival and review: Rowe, *Diary,* 177. Gage and council meeting: Bernard to Hillsborough, Nov. 1, 1768, CO 5/767.

16. Greenleaf's adventure: Bernard to Hillsborough, Nov. 1, 1768, CO 5/767; Hutchinson, *History,* 3:155; Drake, *Boston Landmarks,* 303; Rowe, *Diary,* 177; *Sibley-Shipton,* 7:187. Boyle, "Journal," 256 suggests that this event occurred on Oct. 12; the other sources confirm the Oct. 20 dating. Gage's portrait: Prown, *Copley,* 1:80. Gage on Boston: Gage to Hillsborough, Oct. 31, 1768, CO 5/86. Commissioners: *ibid.;* "Eliot-Hollis," 427. Grenville Temple: Rowe, *Diary,* 178.

17. Bernard, council, and justices: Bernard to Hillsborough, Nov. 1, 1768, CO 5/767. Ames: Rowe, *Diary,* 178; Boyle, "Journal," 257. Officers' leasing: Bernard to Hillsborough, Nov. 1, 1768, CO 5/767. Quartering: Boyle, "Journal," 256–257; *Fair Account,* 4, 9, 11; Drake, *History,* 777; Drake, *Boston Landmarks,* 284. Otis: Bernard to Hillsborough, Sept. 23, 1768, CO 5/767. Molineux: Alden, "Letter from Molineux," 107–108; Drake, *Boston Landmarks,* 358 (which suggests that

Molineux was merely acting as agent for the Apthorp interests).

18. Straw: Bernard to Hillsborough, Nov. 1, 1768, CO 5/767. Councilors: Bernard to Hillsborough, Nov. 14, 1768, CO 5/767.

19. Quiet: Gage to Hillsborough, Nov. 3, 1768, CO 5/86. Soiree: Rowe, *Diary*, 178–179. Robinson: *ibid.*, 179.

20. Hancock case: *Legal Papers*, 2:180–181, 186–188. "Groundless": William Bollan to Samuel Danforth, March 19, 1770, *Bowdoin-Temple*, 188. Crown honor: Bernard to Hillsborough, Dec. 12, 1768, CO 5/767. Gage: Gage to Hillsborough, Nov. 3, 1768, CO 5/86. Hillsborough: Hillsborough to Gage, Dec. 24, 1768, CO 5/86.

21. Bernard to Hillsborough, Dec. 12, 1768, CO 5/767.

22. *Ibid.*

23. Bernard's overstatements: "Eliot-Hollis," 433: "[H]e hath been more minute in his representations home, than was any way necessary, and . . . many things have been noticed, which might very well have been passed over"; James Bowdoin to Thomas Pownall, *Bowdoin-Temple*, 143: "[H]e has a peculiar knack at making mountains of mole hills, & idle chitchat, treason." Commissioners and Sewall: Minutes of Commissioners, Aug. 8, 1768, T 1/471. Advocate General: Adams, *Diary and Autobiography*, 3:287–289. Adams to Boston: *ibid.*, 3:286. Adams's career: "Eliot-Hollis," 427, 434.

10. Trumpets of Sedition

1. Transports: Lieut. Meredith to Admiralty, Nov. 23, 1768; Nov. 25, 1768, CO 5/767. *Hussar and Raven:* Same to same, Nov. 23, 1768, CO 5/767; see also Hutchinson, *History*, 3:156n.; Boyle, "Journal," 258. Remainder: *B. Gaz.*, Dec. 19, 1768. Hartigan and Montgomery: *Legal Papers*, 3:9n.

2. Hood's arrival: Rowe, *Diary*, 179; Boyle, "Journal," 257. Fleet's wintering: *B. Gaz.*, Dec. 19, 1768. Hood: *Britannica* (11th ed.), 13:665; *Bowdoin-Temple*, *passim*. Commissioners' return: Rowe, *Diary*, 179. Rowe and commissioners: *ibid.*, 181, 184. Assemblies: Hulton, *Letters*, 19.

3. Calm: Hutchinson, *History*, 3:157. Gage: Rowe, *Diary*, 180. Dispatches: Hood to Admiralty, Dec. 12, 1768; Jan. 31, 1769; Feb. 27, 1769, CO 5/767; Bernard to Hillsborough, Feb. 25, 1769, CO 5/767. Liquor, behavior, and commanders: "Eliot-Hollis," 437–438. Bernard: Bernard to Hillsborough, Dec. 26, 1768; Feb. 25, 1769, CO 5/767. Hutchinson: Hutchinson, *History*, 3:161.

4. Adams: Adams, *Diary and Autobiography*, 3:289–290; Adams, *Works*, 10:200; in both places, Adams refers to a "Major Small" as the officer in charge; the *Army List* shows no such officer in any of the Boston regiments; but an Alexander Mall (pronounced Maul) was an ensign in the Twenty-ninth, part of whose troops were barracked on Brattle Street; see Adams, *Legal Papers*, 3:181n., 183n.; and a Captain John Small served on Gage's staff, *Copley-Pelham*, 77–78n. Pomeroy's orders and anecdote: Hutchinson, *History*, 3:161–162. Rich: Rowe, *Diary*, 181.

5. Debates: Gipson, *Empire*, 11:234–238. English letters: Hutchinson, *History*, 3:160.

6. Fire: Boyle, "Journal," 257, 258; "At the late Cry of Fire, a Military Gentleman was heard to give Orders to a Soldier or Servant, 'Go directly to the General and inform him that it is no RIOT, but only a Fire,'" *B. Gaz.*, Feb. 6, 1769. Military: Rowe, *Diary*, 183; *B. Gaz.*, Feb. 6, 1769; Donnelly and his companions, Abel Badger, "an Infant," and Michael Carmichael, "Mariner," were indicted for arson and for jailbreaking; they were acquitted of the first charge

and convicted of the second, MB 89; Rec., 1769, fol. 39.

7. Sustained effort: Davidson, *Propaganda*, 237. "Journal": Schlesinger, *Prelude*, 313; Dickerson, *Military Rule, passim*. Bernard's reaction: Bernard to Hillsborough, Jan. 23, 1769; Feb. 25, 1769, CO 5/767.

8. Adams's aims: Bernard to Hillsborough, Feb. 25, 1769, CO 5/767; Hutchinson, *History*, 3:162. Hutchinson's warning: Hutchinson to Israel Williams, Jan. 1, 1769, Williams Papers, 2:162. Edes & Gill: Bernard to Hillsborough, Jan. 25, 1769, CO 5/767. Effect: Hutchinson, *History*, 3:162.

9. Harrassment: Bernard to Hillsborough, Feb. 25, 1769, CO 5/767; court documents suggest that soldiers (called "labourers") were frequent defendants; the merits of the cases cannot of course be now determined. Adams's prophecy: Adams, *Writings*, 1:299.

10. An excellent "Note on Conspiracy" appears in Bailyn, *Origins*, 144–159. Adams's view: Adams, *Writings*, 1:389. John Adams: Adams, *Diary and Autobiography*, 1:90.

11. "Cabinet Council": Bernard to Hillsborough, Jan. 24, 1769, CO 5/767. Letters: Bernard to Barrington, April 12, 1769, *Barrington-Bernard*, 200; Rowe, *Diary*, 186.

12. Bowdoin to Hillsborough, April 15, 1769, CO 5/767.

13. Bernard on conspiracy: Bernard to John Pownall, Aug. 6, 1761, Quincy, *Reports*, 426. News of the baronetcy reached Bernard April 26, 1769: Bernard to Hillsborough, April 29, 1769, CO 5/767.

11. Death Before Impressment

1. Desertions: Hood to Admiralty, May 5, 1769, ADM 1/483. Recruiting problems: Philip Stephens to Robert Wood, April 26, 1769, *CHOP*, 2:466; for an indication of the low wages, see Lloyd, *Nation and Navy*, 138. Orders: Hood to Caldwell, April 3, 1769, ADM 1/483; see also Hood, Log, April 3, 1769.

2. Hood to Caldwell, April 3, 1769, ADM 1/483.

3. *Rose* guns: "List of the Navy, July 1st, 1770," T 1/14. *Rose* complement and marines: *Rose*, Muster Book. Caldwell: *DNB*; Caldwell to Admiralty, April 30, 1768, ADM 1/1609. Naval Academy: Lloyd, *Nation and Navy*, 143 (the admiral was Lord St. Vincent). Panton: *Rose*, Log. Forbes: *Rose*, Muster Book; Caldwell to Admiralty, June 4, 1768, ADM 1/1609. Midshipmen: Caldwell to Admiralty, Nov. 20, 1771, ADM 1/1609; *Rose*, Muster Book; *Legal Papers*, 2:298. (Another sprig of the nobility serving on a Boston-stationed ship at this time was Lord George Gordon, then a seventeen-year-old midshipman, Rowe, *Diary*, 188; Colson, *Lord George Gordon*, 23, 28.) Deserters: *Rose*, Muster Book.

4. Shirley's party and voyage: *Rose*, Log. Damage: Hood to Admiralty, Nov. 11, 1768, Dorr Papers, 913–914. Winter: *Rose*, Log.

5. *Rose*, Log; *Rose*, Muster Book.

6. *Ibid*.

7. *Rose*, Log.

8. The account which commences in this paragraph comes from these sources: (a) Caldwell, Log; (b) *Rose*, Log; and (c) my best reading of the testimony at the subsequent trial, *Legal Papers*, 2:293–322.

9. Uniform: IND, Jan. 23, 1768; May, *Naval Dress*, 18.

10. Drunkenness: *B. Chron.*, May 1, 1769.

11. Body remaining aboard: *ibid.*, April 27, 1769. Muster Book: *Rose*, Muster Book.

12. Sailing data in this and the next paragraph: *Rose* Log; Caldwell, Log.

13. *Rose* work: Caldwell, Log. Funeral: *B. Chron.*, May 1, 1769. Discharge: *Rose*, Muster Book.

14. Examination: Caldwell, Log; *B. Gaz.*, May 8, 1769. Account: *B. Chron.*, May 1, 1769.

15. Cabinet council: see Chapter 10, text at n. 11, above. Court: *Legal Papers*, 2:276, 279.

16. Statutes in this and the following paragraph: *Legal Papers*, 2:275–276; Hutchinson, Opinion.

17. Transfers: *Romney*, Muster Book; *Rippon*, Muster Book; *Rippon*, Log. Hooper: *Legal Papers*, 2:x. Adams's memory: Adams to William Tudor, Dec. 30, 1816, Adams, *Works*, 10:224. Otis's boast and Fitch's research: *Legal Papers*, 2:287.

18. Hood to Admiralty, May 5, 1769, ADM 1/483; Hood, Log.

19. Generally: Chapter 6, especially n. 13, and Chapter 7, especially n. 4, above; *Legal Papers*, 2:278, 283, 323; Zobel, "Law Under Pressure," 192.

20. See generally *Legal Papers*, 2:278–279; Zobel, "Law Under Pressure," 191. Benefit of clergy arose from the medieval rivalry between the English royal courts and the church courts. A cleric accused before a royal court could, upon proof of his status, refuse to be tried by any but an ecclesiastical court. Because the ability to read distinguished the clergy, eventually any literate defendant could obtain the "benefit," generally by reading aloud Psalm 51, verse 1, the "neck verse." By 1707 even this test was abolished. So long as the crime was "clergyable" (as murder, for example, was not), a first offender could escape with only a branding on the thumb, the latter to ensure that he would not receive the benefit again. In certain statutory crimes the law prescribed "death without benefit of clergy." This did not mean that the convict would be denied last rites, but merely that the death penalty was mandatory. See *Legal Papers*, 3:31n.

21. Mackay arrival (on April 30): Boyle, "Journal," 230. Request: Adams, *Writings*, 1:340, 341; Boston Rec. Comm., *Reports*, 16:278. Response: Mackay to Gage, May 4, 1769, Gage Papers.

22. Trial date and summons: Hood to Admiralty, May 5, 1769, ADM 1/483. Wentworth: *Sibley-Shipton*, 13:650.

23. Pleas: Adams to David Sewall, Jan. 29, 1811, Adams, *Works*, 9:629. See also Adams to William Tudor, Dec. 30, 1816, Adams, *Works*, 2:224–225. Text of plea: *Legal Papers*, 2:288–292, especially 291.

24. The chronology underlying this and the following few paragraphs follows and amplifies that set out in *Legal Papers*, 2:279. Sitting of May 23; *ibid.* Court House: Boyle, "Journal," 257. Sewall-Fitch: *Legal Papers*, 2:287. Bernard: Hutchinson, *Diary*, 1:74. Hutchinson: Adams to David Sewall, Jan. 29, 1811, Adams, *Works*, 9:629.

25. Opening of Court: *Legal Papers*, 2:287; Hutchinson, *History*, 3:167; Hutchinson, *Diary*, 1:75.

26. Argument: *Legal Papers*, 2:288. Sewall concession: Hutchinson, *History*, 3:167. Hutchinson on selection, Bernard on extradition, and Otis on venire: *Legal Papers*, 2:288.

27. Hutchinson's reasoning: Hutchinson, Opinion; see also *Legal Papers*, 2:288.

28. May 25: *Legal Papers*, 2:279; James Robertson to Gage, May 24, 1769, Gage Papers (this letter refers unmistakably to events of May 25; I am therefore convinced that although Robertson may have begun it on May 24, he did not complete it until the next day). Hood's health: John Pomeroy to Gage, May

29, 1769, Gage Papers; Mackay to Gage, June 12, 1769, *ibid.* Reference to England: Robertson to Gage, May 24, 1769, *ibid.*

29. Hutchinson, Opinion; Hutchinson, *History,* 3:167; Hutchinson, *Diary,* 1:75.

30. Interest: Adams to Jedidiah Morse, Jan. 20, 1816, Adams, *Works,* 10:209–210. Otis: Boston Rec. Comm., *Reports,* 16:294.

31. *Legal Papers,* 2:305; the entire account of the trial is taken from *Legal Papers,* 2:293–335; accordingly, I have omitted specific citations.

32. A suggestion of Silley's character appears in *Rose,* Log, Nov. 2, 1769: "punish'd . . . Jam[s] Silley with a Doz[n] Lashes . . . for Drunkeness," and Jan. 24, 1770: "Punish'd Jam[s] Silly a Marine with 2 Doz[n] lashes for Drunkeness & abusing his officers."

33. *Ryan* v. *Peacock:* SF #101703. Brig's people: *Legal Papers,* 2:313–320. Hill: *ibid.,* 317.

34. Wilks: *Rose,* Muster Book. On Nov. 13, 1769, Raynsford deserted while on "Leave ashore at Boston," *ibid.*

35. See *Legal Papers,* 2:280, which collects the sources. I have concluded, after reconsidering the chronology, that Adam's abortive argument did take place late on June 16, and that the court then commenced deliberation, adjourning for the night; see *ibid.,* note.

36. Time of return: *B. Chron.,* June 19, 1769. Bernard and Auchmuty: Adams to J. Morse, Jan. 20, 1816, Adams, *Works,* 10:207–208; see also Adams to William Tudor, Dec. 30, 1816, *ibid.,* 2:225–226.

37. Hutchinson, *History,* 3:167.

38. Adams to William Tudor, Dec. 30, 1816, Adams, *Works,* 2:226; Adams to J. Morse, Jan. 20, 1816, *ibid.,* 10:209.

39. Bernard correspondence: CO 5/758. Ryan: *Legal Papers,* 2:280–281. Writ: SF #101703. Hood's interest: Hood to Bowdoin, April 24, 1770, *Bowdoin-Temple,* 175; August 7, 1770, *ibid.,* 210. Marriage: Adams to J. Q. Adams, Jan. 8, 1808, MHS, *Procs.,* 44:424 (1910–1911). Council: Hutchinson to Hillsborough, Dec. 20, 1769, CO 5/759.

40. Adams to John Jay, June 26, 1785, Adams, *Works,* 8:275–276.

41. *Legal Papers,* 2:219.

12. Soldiers and the Law

1. Boyle, "Journal," 259; Hood to Admiralty, July 10, 1769, CO 5/758.

2. Mackay and Pomeroy: Shy, *Toward Lexington,* 311. Butler: Gage to Mackay, May 8, 1769; Butler to Gage, June 12, 1769; Gage to Butler, June 18, 1769; Mackay to Gage, June 19, 1769; Carr to Gage, June 25, 1769; Gage to Mackay, June 28, 1769; all in Gage Papers.

3. Authority: Hillsborough to Gage, March 24, 1769, Gage, *Correspondence,* 2:87. Reinforcements: Gage to Mackay, May 29, 1769, Gage Papers; thirty men went to the Twenty-ninth, fifty to the Fourteenth. Deployment: Gage to Mackay, June 4, 1769, Gage Papers; the House refused use of the Castle, so both regiments remained in town, Hutchinson, *History,* 3:180.

4. Opinion: Gage to Mackay, June 4, 1769, Gage Papers. Bernard's reaction: Bernard to Hillsborough, June 25, 1769, CO 5/767. Recall order: Bernard to Barrington, May 30, 1769, *Barrington-Bernard,* 203.

5. Embarkation plans, resolves, cancellation: Hood to Admiralty, July 10, 1769, CO 5/758; Bernard to Hillsborough, July 7, 1769, *ibid.;* Hutchinson, *History,* 3:173–174. "Uneasiness" and Adams: Hutchinson, *History,* 3:174; Bernard to

Hillsborough, July 7, 1769, CO 5/768.

6. Resumption of embarkation: Bernard to Hillsborough, July 7, 1769, CO 5/768. Conclusion of evacuation: Admiralty to Hillsborough, Sept. 9, 1769, CO 5/768; Boyle, "Journal," 259. Adams's amendment: Bernard to Hillsborough, July 11, 1769, CO 5/768.

7. Final battles: Bernard to Hillsborough, July 17, 1769, CO 5/768; Hutchinson, *History*, 3:176–179. Circumstances of departure: Samuel Thompson to Admiralty, Sept. 3, 1769, ADM 1/2590; Hutchinson, *Diary*, 1:22. Calm: Miller, *Sam Adams*, 173 (citing no authority). Bernard and troops: Hutchinson, *History*, 3:180. Celebration: Boyle, "Journal," 259; Hutchinson, *History*, 3:182; Rowe, *Diary*, 190.

8. Gage to Hillsborough, July 22, 1769, CO 5/233.

9. Expenses: Gage to Barrington, June 14, 1769, Gage, *Correspondence*, 2:514. Social life: Rowe, *Diary*, 184; Rowe, MS Diary, *passim*. Masons: Frothingham, *Warren*, 115.

10. Cato: Rowe, *Diary*, 58. Timmons: Private John Timmons, deposition, July 7, 1770, CO 5/88. Paymount: Hutchinson, *Diary*, 1:76, 77.

11. "Exercise": Private James Corbin, deposition, July 24, 1770, Gay Transcripts, 12:121. Promise of land: see *Fair Account*, 8–9, 12. Eliot: "Eliot-Hollis," 444; Samuel Cooper boasted that "Hundreds of the Troops" had deserted by February 18, 1769, "Cooper-Pownall," 305. Reward: Gage to Dalrymple, Sept. 25, 1769, Gage Papers. Rescue: Dalrymple to Gage, Oct. 28, 1769, Gage Papers; Pomeroy to Gage, Feb. 2, 1769, *ibid*. Return-wish and Mackay's lament: Mackay to Gage, May 4, 1769, *ibid*.

12. Dukesberry: Pomeroy to Gage, Feb. 2, 1769, *ibid*. Dana on soldiers' credibility: Ensign Alexander Mall, deposition, Aug. 12, 1770, Gay Transcripts, 12:101.

13. "Poyson'd": Mackay to Gage, June 12, 1769, Gage Papers. Attorney-General: Mackay to Gage, June 12 and June 25, 1769, *ibid*. No redress: Sergeants William Jones and Richard Pearsall, deposition, July 28, 1770, Gay Transcripts, 12:127. Otis: Dalrymple to Gage, Dec. 28, 1769, Gage Papers.

14. Boston jury: Gage to Pomeroy, Dec. 19, 1768, Gage Papers. Obedience to law: Gage to Mackay, May 15, 1769, *ibid*. Mackay's view: Mackay to Gage, May 25, 1769, *ibid*.

15. Statute: *Mass. Acts*, 1:52. Incident: Mackay to Gage, June 12, 1769; Gage to Mackay, June 18, 1769, Gage Papers.

16. Settlement: Mackay to Gage, June 19, 1769, *ibid*. Moyse's case: *Legal Papers*, 2:436–437; Mackay to Gage, June 19 and June 25, 1769; Gage to Mackay, June 28 and July 2, 1769, Gage Papers. See also Mackay to Gage, July 6, 1769, *ibid*., calling Moyse "a Rascall."

17. See generally: *Legal Papers*, 2:433–435, and sources cited there. Grenadiers: *Britannica* (11th ed.), 12:579. Fordyce died a hero's death during the Revolution. *Naval Documents*, 3:188.

18. Fellows: Hutchinson, *History*, 3:364; SF #131768; MB 85; Rec., 1769, fol. 71–72; Fellows withdrew a not guilty plea and was permitted to plead *nolo contendere*—thus admitting the crime for purposes of punishment but not in such a way as to constitute an admission which might be held against him in any subsequent civil action; he was fined £10 and required to post £50 to keep the peace for two years; see also Ford, "Wilkes," 205. House of Representatives: Mass. House Journal, 1769, 83 (session of Saturday, July 15, 1769). "Journal of the Times": Dickerson, *Military Rule*, 119–123. Wilkes: William Palfrey to Wilkes, July 26, 1769; Ford, "Wilkes," 205–206.

19. Preliminary hearing: Lieutenant Alexander Ross, deposition, Aug. 25, 1770,

Gay Transcripts, 12:43. Trial and aftermath: *Legal Papers*, 2:432–435. Ross's career: *DNB;* Ross, *Cornwallis*, 76n.

20. Ness incident: Ensign John Ness, deposition, Aug. 25, 1770; Sergeant James Hickman, deposition, Aug. 25, 1770, CO 5/88; Ensign John Ness, deposition, Nov. 3, 1769; Lance Corporal Archibald Browning, deposition, Nov. 3, 1769, Gage Papers; *B.E.P.*, Oct. 30, 1769. Guardhouse: Adams, *Writings*, 1:257. Pierpoint: SF #152686; the town had elected Pierpoint on March 13, 1769, to collect the taxes which Sam Adams had been unable to produce, Boston Rec. Comm., *Reports*, 16:272. Gridley: Ness's indictment, SF #101482. Molesworth: Captain Ponsonby Molesworth, deposition, Nov. 3, 1769; Lieutenant Hugh Dickson and Lieutenant Thomas Buckley, deposition, Nov. 12, 1769, Gage Papers. Ness's prudence: Dalrymple to Gage, Oct. 28, 1769, *ibid.* Molesworth's rashness: Dalrymple to Gage, Nov. 30, 1769, *ibid.*

21. Scene at Dana's: Ness, deposition, Aug. 25, 1770, CO 5/88; Dana, Pleas, No. 53.

22. Molesworth marriage: Rowe, *Diary*, 186; Boyle, "Journal," 258. Activities: SF #101398, #89659; *B.E.P.*, Sept. 25, 1769. Dana, Writs, also shows that at least three suits were brought against Molesworth in 1770; no details concerning the actions are indicated.

23. Molesworth, deposition, Nov. 3, 1769, Gage Papers.

24. Ness, deposition, Aug. 25, 1770, CO 5/88.

25. Statute: *Mass. Acts*, 3:305; 4:324. Hearing: Ness, deposition, Aug. 25, 1770, CO 5/88; Hickman, deposition, Aug. 25, 1770, CO 5/88; SF #101482.

26. Molesworth, deposition, Nov. 3, 1769; Lieutenant William Monsell and Ensign David St. Clair, deposition, Nov. 12, 1769, Gage Papers.

27. Ness's indictment and trial: SF #101482; MB 89; Rec., 1769, fol. 252; Ness, deposition, Aug. 25, 1770, CO 5/88. Molesworth's indictment: SF #89239, MB 89.

28. "Alfred," *B. Gaz.*, Oct. 2, 1769; Adams, *Writings*, 1:392.

29. Heat of expression: Dalrymple to Gage, Nov. 30, 1769, Gage Papers. Conviction and motions: MB 89.

30. Dalrymple to Gage, Oct. 28, 1769, Gage Papers.

31. Situation of troops: *ibid.* Galway juries: Dalrymple to Gage, Dec. 28, 1769, Gage Papers. Galway and lynch law: *Britannica* (11th ed.), 11:432. McKaan: Private James McKaan, deposition, July 24, 1770, Gay Transcripts, 12:116. "Tyranny": Dalrymple to Gage, Nov. 30, 1769, Gage Papers. Hutchinson's helplessness: Dalrymple to Gage, Oct. 28, 1769; Nov. 30, 1769, *ibid.* Grand jury: Dalrymple to Gage, Dec. 7, 1769, *ibid.*; James Bowdoin to Thomas Pownall, Dec. 5, 1769, *Bowdoin-Temple*, 159; Hutchinson, *History*, 3:189 (which says the bills were nol-prossed by the king's order); a copy of the indictment in Hutchinson's hand is in CO 5/88.

13. Coffee House Brawl

1. Celebration: Adams, *Diary and Autobiography*, 1:341–342; Rowe, *Diary*, 191; "Sons of Liberty—1769." The forty-five toasts represented yet another salute to John Wilkes and the celebrated Number 45 of his *North Briton*. Character of Balch: Drake, *Boston Landmarks*, 341.

2. See generally, Miller, *Sam Adams*, 202–203; Hutchinson, *History*, 3:185; Hutchinson, "Additions," 15.

3. Rowe: Rowe, *Diary*, 190. Rogers: Rogers to ?, Oct. 25, 1769, Chalmers Papers, 3:44. Limit of Jan. 1, 1770: "Eliot-Hollis," 446.

4. Letters: Hutchinson, "Additions," 14; Adams, *Diary and Autobiography*, 1:340. Otis's conviction: *B. Gaz.*, Sept. 4, 1769. Conferences: *B. Chron.*, Sept. 11, 1769; Adams, *Diary and Autobiography*, 1:342.

5. "Cooking up": Adams, *Diary and Autobiography*, 1:343. Article: *B. Gaz.*, Sept. 4, 1769.

6. Otis: Adams, *Diary and Autobiography*, 1:343. "Bedlamism": *ibid.*, 1:225.

7. Otis: Adams, *ibid.*, 1:271. Stick: *B. Chron.*, Sept. 18, 1769.

8. British Coffee House; Winsor, *Boston*, 4:582; Edes, "Dr. Young," 7. Bystanders: The capias in the case of Robinson, Brown, and Dundass lists as witnesses (among others) O'Hara, French, Forrest, and Mein; SF #89228; admittedly, it is possible that some or all of these were not present at the outset, but came in later; there is, on the other hand, no evidence that they were not present; on balance, given the circumstances of the event and the nature of the Coffee House, I believe it more probable than not that they all were there from the beginning. O'Hara: *Legal Papers*, 3:80. French: Everard, *Twenty-Ninth* 68, 72. Dundass: Rowe, *Diary*, 175, 176, which also gives a striking sample of Dundass's arrogance and rudeness; Robinson later insisted that Dundass was not present during the brawl, *B. Chron.*, Sept. 18, 1769; I believe Robinson was wrong (or lying), else why would Paxton have been so concerned over the possibility of an attempt to serve process aboard a man-of-war (see n.15, below)? Forrest: *Legal Papers*, 3:6n., and sources there cited. Mein: *ibid.*, 1:151–152. Browne: He is listed as William Burnet Brown in the court documents, and is described as being "late of Salem," SF #89228; Sessions, Minute Book, Nov. 1769; see also Rowe, *Diary*, 193; Hutchinson to Bernard, Sept. 6, 1769, Mass. Arch., 26:373, says he was formerly from Beverly, currently from Virginia; see also Hutchinson, "Additions," 15; Clifford K. Shipton identifies Browne as the loyalist rescinder William Browne, John Adams's Harvard classmate; *Sibley-Shipton*, 13:552–553; because Browne was a grandson of former Massachusetts Governor William Burnet, Stark, *Loyalists*, 449, I concur. But another Browne (William "Virginia Billy" Burnet) may have been the man. See *Sibley-Shipton* 8:124.

9. Statute: Act of Aug. 27, 1728, *Mass. Acts*, 2:516–517. Nose-tweaking as insult: *B. Chron.*, Sept. 11, 1769; see *Brattle* v. *Murray*, SF #100740, #100808; MB 81; Rec., 1766–1767, fol. 13–14. Encounter: *B. Chron.*, Sept. 11, 1769; *B. Gaz.*, Sept. 18, 1769 (from which the dialogue was taken).

10. Thomas Dupee, deposition, July 26, 1771, and James Lloyd, deposition, Sept. ?, 1769, SF #102135; *B. Gaz.*, Sept. 18, 1769; Thomas Young to John Wilkes, Sept. 6, 1769, Ford, "Wilkes," 209.

11. Dupee, deposition, July 26, 1771, SF #102135; *B. Gaz.*, Sept. 18, 1769.

12. Fever and recovery: Nathaniel Perkins, deposition, July ?, 1771, SF #102135; Thomas Young to ?, n.d., Edes, "Dr. Young," 6; Thomas Young to John Wilkes, Sept. 6, 1769, Ford, "Wilkes," 209. Adams: Adams, *Diary and Autobiography* 1:344. Town: Boston Rec. Comm., *Reports*, 16:297, 301. Rumor and Adams: ? to ?, Oct. 30, 1769, Chalmers Papers, 3:48. "Never the same man": Channing, *History*, 3:118; see also Drake, *Boston Landmarks*, 60; I do not mean to suggest that Otis was as good as new afterwards; in December 1769, he told Dr. Sylvester Gardiner that he was not physically able to accept a proffered retainer; within a short time he was "the sport of the young gentlemen at the Barr," Andrew Oliver to Francis Bernard, Dec. 3, 1769, Sparks Papers, 12:163–164; and on Jan. 16, 1770, John Adams reported: "Otis is in Confusion yet. He looses himself. He rambles and wanders like a Ship without an Helm." Adams, *Diary and Autobiography*, 1:348. My point is simply that the mental deterioration proceeded independently, and "is to be imputed, not to any effects of

the affray with Mr. Robinson, but rather to the high tone given to [Otis's] animal frame by the strength of his passions, and a failure in the point of temperance," Gordon, *History*, 1:308.

13. Marriage: Boyle, "Journal," 261. Boutineau: Stark, *Loyalists*, 448; Drake, *Boston Landmarks*, 253. Stoning: Robinson to Joseph Harrison, Oct. 5, 1769, Chalmers Papers, 3:38. "Liquorish boys": Boston Rec. Comm., *Reports*, 16:315. Adams: Adams, *Writings* 1:424. See also Chapter 7, text at n. 11, above.

14. Radical activity: *B. Chron.*, Sept. 11, 1769. Otis's description: *ibid.*, Sept. 18, 1769. Rowe: Rowe, *Diary*, 192. Dalrymple: Dalrymple to Gage, Sept. 6, 1769, Gage Papers.

15. Meeting: Adams, *Writings*, 1:384. Warning: Adams, *Diary and Autobiography*, 1:343. Army: Dalrymple to Gage, Sept. 6, 1769, Gage Papers.

16. Browne in hiding: Hutchinson to Bernard, Sept. 6, 1769, Mass. Arch., 26:373. Crowd: Rowe, *Diary*, 192. Murray and hearing: Murray, *Letters*, 159–161. Mason as Son of Liberty: Adams, *Legal Papers*, 1:civ; the recognizance, SF #89235, is dated *August* 6; I believe this to be an inadvertence by Justice Dana, who filled out the printed recognizance form; but it could conceivably pertain to some earlier incident; the coincidence of the day ("sixth"), the names (Murray, Browne, Gridley, and Dana) and the alleged offense (assault) argues strongly for the error theory, as does the modern common cognate experience of dating a check by the preceding month; it is a little harder to explain why Sessions, Minute Book, Nov. 1769, should perpetuate the misdate; probably either no one noticed the discrepancy, or the court, having noticed it, felt that the date on the recognizance must control and that the error was formal only. Mein: Young to ?, n.d., Edes, "Dr. Young," 6.

14. King Street Showdown: John Mein

1. Adams: Miller, *Sam Adams*, 202–203. Town meeting: Notice dated Sept. 28, 1769, Chalmers Papers, 3:37.

2. "The Proceedings of a Town Meeting. . . ," Chalmers Papers, 3:37; see also Boyle, "Journal," 260.

3. George Mason to ?, Oct. 20, 1769, Chalmers Papers, 3:40.

4. Mackintosh, common argument, and deacon: George Mason to ?, Oct. 20, 1769, Chalmers Papers, 3:40. Hutchinson: Hutchinson to John Pownall, Nov. 17, 1769, CO 5/758.

5. Mein, memorial, n.d., T 1/478.

6. Lists: Andrews, "Boston Merchants," 288n. Press run and "Self Interests": Mein, memorial, T 1/478.

7. Mein, memorial, T 1/478.

8. Mein's life: *Legal Papers*, 1:152n., for a collection of the sources; that account, like this one, owes much to Alden, "Mein." Scots and prejudice: Chapter 5, text at n. 16, above; see also Dumbauld, *Declaration*, 19.

9. London suppliers: *Legal Papers*, 1:199–200. Commissioners: Incidental expense warrants of Commissioners of Customs, Boston, Oct. 10, 1769–Oct. 10, 1770, T 1/476; Mein sold stationery valued at £97:16:10 3/4 from April 15, 1768, to April 27, 1770. Harrassment: Mein, memorial, T 1/478. Enemy: Boyle, "Journal," 260.

10. George Mason to ?, Oct. 20, 1769, Chalmers Papers, 3:40.

11. Mein to Hutchinson, [Oct. 29, 1769], Mass. Arch., 25:455–456b. Because Nov. 5 fell on a Sunday, the celebration would take place Monday; see Rowe, *Diary*, 194.

12. Personal attack: *B. Chron.*, Oct. 26, 1769; "A Key to a Certain Publication," Chalmers Papers, 3:45. Calumniation: Hutchinson, *History*, 3:186. "Talent": Hulton, Account, 135.

13. Descriptions of the assault: Mein to Joseph Harrison, Nov. 5, 1769, Chalmers Papers 3:51; George Mason to ?, Oct. 28, 1769, Chalmers Papers, 3:47; *B.E.P.*, Oct. 30, 1769; Hutchinson, *History*, 3:186 and "Additions," 15–16. Rowe, *Diary*, 194, and Boyle, "Journal," 260–261, also have descriptions, but I believe them inaccurate. Marshal: Mein pilloried Marshal's lack of learning some years later, *Sagittarius*, 112. Contusion and ambush: Mein to Harrison, Nov. 5, 1769, Chalmers Papers, 3:51. Whipping post: *Legal Papers*, 3: opp. 68.

14. Clearing posts: Mein to Harrison, Nov. 5, 1769, Chalmers Papers, 3:51. Basset: Private Thomas Burgess, deposition, July 24, 1770, CO 5/88; Everard, *Twenty-Ninth*, 72.

15. I have followed Mein's account, Mein to Harrison, Nov. 5, 1769, Chalmers Papers, 3:51; for a slightly different version, see Hutchinson to Hillsborough, Nov. 11, 1769, CO 5/758; and see sources cited in n. 17, below. Grenadier: Rowe, Diary, 194; *B.E.P.*, Oct. 30, 1769.

16. Inquiry and crowd of 200: Mein to Hutchinson, [Oct. 28, 1769], Mass. Arch., 25:459. Crowd of 2,000, Mason, and composition of mob: Mein to Harrison, Nov. 5, 1769, Chalmers Papers, 3:51.

17. Belief that Mein fired: Hutchinson to Hood, Oct. 31, 1769, ADM 1/483; Rowe, *Diary*, 194; Boyle, "Journal," 260–261; *B.E.P.* Oct. 30, 1769. Push on Guardhouse and Basset: Burgess, deposition, July 24, 1770, CO 5/88. No admission: Mason to ?, Oct. 28, 1769, Chalmers Papers, 3:47.

18. Adams, Molineux, and Dana: Mein to Harrison, Nov. 5, 1769, Chalmers Papers, 3:51; *B.E.P.*, Oct. 30, 1769; Hutchinson, *History*, 3:187. Plot, search, and escape: Mein to Harrison, Nov. 5, 1769, Chalmers Papers, 3:51; Mason to ?, Oct. 28, 1769, Chalmers Papers, 3:47.

19. Hutchinson-Dalrymple conference and "out of the reach": Dalrymple to Gage, Oct. 29, 1769, Gage Papers. Hutchinson's request and his meeting with council: Hutchinson to Hood, Oct. 31, 1769, ADM 1/483.

20. Sabbath: Dalrymple to Gage, Oct. 29, 1769, Gage Papers. *Liberty: Legal Papers*, 2:179–180. Gailer: *B.E.P.*, Oct. 30, 1769. Suspected as informer: Hutchinson, *History*, 3:187, "Additions," 16; *B.E.P.*, Oct. 30, 1769; Boyle, "Journal," 260; Rowe, *Diary*, 194. Pursuit and capture: *B.E.P.*, Oct. 30, 1769; the identity of his pursuers is not known, although in his subsequent law suit, Gailer named seven, including Eleazar Trevett, master of the brig *Triton*, *B.E.P.*, Oct. 30, 1769, and Pool Spear, a Boston tailor, *Legal Papers*, 1:41.

21. Tarring: Mason to ?, Oct. 28, 1769, Chalmers Papers, 3:47; Rowe, *Diary*, 194; Burgess, deposition, July 24, 1770, CO 5/88; *Legal Papers*, 1:41; *B.E.P.*, Oct. 30, 1769, says only Gailer's shirt and jacket were removed. Size of mob, lighted windows, and refusal: Mason to ?, Oct. 28, 1769, Chalmers Papers, 3:47.

22. Mason to ?, Oct. 28, 1769, Chalmers Papers, 3:47; Mein to Harrison, Nov. 5, 1769, Chalmers Papers, 3:51; *B.E.P.*, Oct. 30, 1769 (which says three guns were taken).

23. Route: Enclosure in Hutchinson to Hillsborough, Oct. 31, 1769, CO 5/758. Handsaw: *Legal Papers*, 1:41. Custom House: Burgess, deposition, July 24, 1770, CO 5/88. Terminal ceremony: *B.E.P.*, Oct. 30, 1769; Mason to ?, Oct. 28, 1769, Chalmers Papers, 3:47. Suit: *Legal Papers*, 1:41–42. Enlistment: *Rose, Muster Book* (it occurred Nov. 14, 1769).

24. Meeting: Hutchinson, *History*, 3:187; Hutchinson to Hillsborough, Oct. 31, 1769, and enclosure, CO 5/758. Mob's composition: Hutchinson to Hillsborough,

Oct. 31, 1769, CO 5/758. Nine P.M. conclusion: Dalrymple to Gage, Oct. 29, 1769, Gage Papers; enclosure in Hutchinson to Hillsborough, Oct. 31, 1769, CO 5/758; *B.E.P.*, Oct. 30, 1769.

25. Proclamation and news account: Hutchinson to Hillsborough, Oct. 31, 1769, and enclosure, CO 5/758; the account appeared in *B.E.P.*, Oct. 30, 1769; the enclosure to Hillsborough was a cutting from galley proof.

26. Hutchinson, *History*, 3:187.

27. Mein to Hutchinson, [Oct. 29, 1769], Mass. Arch., 25:455–456a.

28. Mein to Hutchinson, n.d., Mass. Arch., 25:457–458.

29. Hutchinson to Hood, Oct. 31, 1769, ADM 1/483; Hutchinson, *History*, 3:189–190; Hutchinson to Hillsborough, Nov. 11, 1769, CO 5/758.

30. Mein afloat: Mein to Harrison, Nov. 5, 1769, Chalmers Papers, 3:51. Pope's Day: *Legal Papers*, 1:201. Mein's return: *B.E.P.*, Nov. 20, 1769; Andrew Oliver to Bernard, Nov. 15, 1769, Hutchinson, *Diary*, 1:22. Mein's complaint: Mein, memorial, T 1/478. Hutchinson's account: Hutchinson to Hillsborough, Nov. 11, 1769, CO 5/758.

31. Mein as Sandemanian: Alden, "Mein," 577–579. Barrell: Adams, *Diary and Autobiography*, 2:26. Incident: Indictment of Colburn Barrell, Chamberlain Papers, although Barrell was apparently arraigned, P to P, April 24, 1770, Chalmers Papers, 3:76, the court files, minute books, and records do not show any disposition; the case may well have been nol-prossed. On Barrell generally: Edes, "Sandemanians," *passim*.

32. Hutchinson, *History*, 3:187; Dalrymple to Gage, Oct. 29, 1769, Gage Papers.

15. Seider the Martyr

1. Nonimportation: Narrative, n.d., Chalmers Papers, 3:56; Hutchinson, *History* 3:191–192. Shipbuilding: Narrative, n.d., Chalmers Papers, 3:56.

2. Ruddock and contract elsewhere: Narrative, n.d., Chalmers Papers, 3:56; Hutchinson to Hillsborough, Jan. 24, 1770, CO 5/759; see also Hulton, *Letters*, 26–27; it was said that some Boston merchants offered to order vessels built locally to make up the loss, *B. Gaz.*, March 5, 1770.

3. Hutchinson, *History*, 3:192; Narrative, n.d., Chalmers Papers, 3:56.

4. Events: Narrative, n.d., Chalmers Papers, 3:56; Brazen Head: *Legal Papers*, 3:318.

5. Narrative, n.d., Chalmers Papers, 3:56; William Jackson, deposition, Jan. 22, 1770, CO 5/759.

6. Events: Narrative, n.d., Chalmers Papers, 3:56. "Body": Rowe, *Diary*, 196. Quincy married: *B.E.P.*, Oct. 30, 1769; the wedding took place Oct. 26.

7. Hutchinson: Narrative, n.d., Chalmers Papers, 3:56; *Sibley-Shipton*, 3:185, quoting *Pennsylvania Chronicle*, March 5, 1770. Visits: Rowe, *Diary*, 196. Quiet: Nathaniel Rogers to Hutchinson, Jan. 19, 1770, Mass. Arch., 25:351. Lillie: George Mason to P, Jan. 24, 1770, Chalmers Papers, 3:63. Adjournment: Narrative, n.d., Chalmers Papers 3:56.

8. Tories: Narrative, n.d., Chalmers Papers, 3:56. Hutchinson and council: Minutes of Council Meeting, Jan. 18, 1770, CO 5/759. Freeze: Rowe, *Diary*, 196. Tory pressure: Hutchinson, *History*, 3:192.

9. Events: Narrative, n.d., Chalmers Papers, 3:56; see also "Cooper-Pownall," 314–316. Partridge: *Legal Papers*, 2:158–159; "Sons of Liberty—1769," 141.

10. Hutchinson's family and other merchants: Hutchinson to Hillsborough, Jan. 24, 1770, CO 5/759. Recommenders' resentment and Hutchinson's self-reproach:

Hutchinson, *History,* 3:192.

11. Protection: Hutchinson to Hillsborough, Jan. 24, 1770, CO 5/759. Advice to sue and response: Hutchinson to Thomas Pownall, May 28, 1770, Mass. Arch., 26:484. Molineux: Hutchinson to ?, n.d., *ibid.,* 27:280.

12. Council and Hutchinson: Hutchinson to Hillsborough, Jan. 24, 1770, CO 5/759. Jackson: Narrative, n.d., Chalmers Papers, 3:56.

13. "Illiberal," Hutchinson's tolerance, and need for "something more disorderly": Hutchinson to Hillsborough, Jan. 24, 1770, CO 5/759. Councilors and justices: Hutchinson, *History,* 3:192–193.

14. Attendance: Narrative, n.d., Chalmers Papers, 3:56. Phillips: Hutchinson to Hillsborough, Jan. 24, 1770, CO 5/759.

15. Dalrymple: Hutchinson to Hillsborough, Jan. 24, 1770, CO 5/759; see also Rowe, *Diary,* 196–197. Rogers: Hutchinson to Bernard?, Feb. 28, 1770, Mass. Arch., 26:450.

16. Hutchinson to Hillsborough, Jan. 24, 1770, CO 5/759; Hutchinson, *History,* 3:193; "Additions," 17.

17. Votes: Handbill, Chalmers Papers, 3:62. Restraint: Hutchinson to Hillsborough, Jan. 24, 1770, CO 5/759. Hutchinson's character: Narrative, n.d., Chalmers Papers, 3:56.

18. Sons of Liberty: Narrative, n.d., Chalmers Papers, 3:70. Analysis: Hutchinson to Hillsborough, Jan. 24, 1770, CO 5/759.

19. "Junius," Thursday routine, and events: Narrative, n.d., Chalmers Papers, 3:70; see also *B.N.-L.* Feb. 8, 1770. Town pump: Drake, *Boston Landmarks,* 84.

20. Events: Narrative, n.d., Chalmers Papers, 3:70. Tories: Hutchinson to Hood, Feb. 23, 1770, Mass. Arch., 26:444. Oliver: Oliver, *Origin,* 73.

21. Tea subscription: Narrative, n.d., Chalmers Papers, 3:70. Labradore and evasions: Oliver, *Origin,* 73–75; see also *B. Gaz.,* Feb. 26, 1770.

22. Tar: ? to ?, March 14, 1770, Chalmers Papers, 3:69. Hands: Narrative, n.d., Chalmers Papers, 3:70. Lillie: Hutchinson to Hood, Feb. 23, 1770, Mass. Arch., 26:444. Lillie's article: *B.N.-L.,* Jan. 11, 1770.

23. "Many hundreds" and blockade: Hutchinson to Hood, Feb. 23, 1770, Mass. Arch., 26:444; for smaller estimates, see the testimony at the subsequent trial, *Legal Papers,* 2:418–421, *passim.* Richardson's house: *B.E.P.,* Feb. 26, 1770. Richardson's history: see Chapter 4, test at nn. 14–16, above; see also *Legal Papers,* 2:396n. and sources there cited, and *B. Gaz.,* Jan. 23, 1769; Richardson, as a tidewaiter, several times informed his superiors of breaches of the Acts of Trade, Richardson, petition, Jan. 19, 1775, T 1/517; a friend referred to him as "an officer in the Coustoms," George Wilmot, petition, Jan. 19, 1775, T 1/517. "Abandoned wretch": John Adams to Dr. J. Morse, Jan. 5, 1816, Adams, *Works,* 10:210. Earlier remarks: *Legal Papers,* 2:416–417.

24. Radicals' suggestion: *B. Gaz.,* Feb. 26, 1770. "Care to improve" and "universally believed": Narrative, n.d., Chalmers Papers, 3:70. Reeve: *B. Gaz.,* March 5, 1770. Richardson's document: Richardson, petition, Jan. 14, 1775, T 1/517.

25. *B.E.P.,* Feb. 26, 1770.

26. Pelting: Hutchinson to Hood, Feb. 23, 1770, Mass. Arch., 26:444; the events, here and in subsequent paragraphs, unless otherwise indicated, are based upon the testimony at Richardson's trial, *Legal Papers,* 2:416–421. Matchett, Knox, and Procter as Sons of Liberty: "Sons of Liberty—1769," 141.

27. Wilmot at door: Richardson, petition, Jan. 19, 1775, T 1/517. Wilmot's career and itinerary: Wilmot, petition, Jan. 19, 1775, T 1/517. Petition and denial: *B. Gaz.,* March 5, 1770. Radicals' attempt to link: *ibid.,* Feb. 26, 1770.

28. The bystander was apparently referring to the ancient statutory rule, 13

Edw. 1, c. 2 (1285), that the locality bore fiscal responsibility for mob-caused damage. See Annotation, "Municipal Liability for Property Damage under Mob Violence Statutes," 26 A.L.R. 3d 1198 (1969), and authorities there cited. This point had been much mooted at the time of the Stamp Act disturbances in 1765.

29. Seider: Oliver, *Origin*, 84, says Seider was "crossing the Street" when shot. Doubt that Richardson would fire: ? to ?, March 14, 1770, Chalmers Papers, 3:70.

30. Shot and results, treatment and death: *B. N.-L.*, March 1, 1770; the indictment, SF #102009, says he died eight hours after being shot.

31. Bell: *B.E.P.*, Feb. 26, 1770; *B.N.-L.*, March 1, 1770; Hutchinson to Gage, Feb. 25, 1770, Mass. Arch., 26:448.

32. Noose and Molineux: Hutchinson to Gage, Feb. 25, 1770, Mass. Arch., 26:448. Molineux: Hutchinson to Hood, Feb. 23, 1770, *ibid.*, 26:445. Oliver: Oliver, *Origin*, 85.

33. Dragging: Narrative, n.d., Chalmers Papers, 3:70; Hutchinson to Hood, Feb. 23, 1770, Mass. Arch., 26:445; Hutchinson to Gage, Feb. 25, 1770, *ibid.*, 26:448. Examination: *B.N.-L.*, March 1, 1770. Dana: Dana, Pleas, Feb. 22, 1770, #13.

34. Second near-lynching: Narrative, n.d., Chalmers Papers, 3:76; see also *B.N.-L.*, March 1, 1770. Sheriff and justices: Hutchinson to Gage, Feb. 25, 1770, Mass. Arch., 448. Nonremovability of justices: Hutchinson to Bernard?, Feb. 28, 1770, *ibid.*, 26:451.

35. Autopsy: *B.N.-L.*, March 1, 1770. Coroner: SF #102009.

36. Hutchinson ill: Hutchinson to Bernard?, Feb. 28, 1770, Mass. Arch., 26:450. Effort with council: Hutchinson to Hood, Feb. 23, 1770, *ibid.*, 26:445. "Major part": Hutchinson to Gage, Feb. 25, 1770, *ibid.*, 26:448. Attacks and importers' response: Hutchinson to Bernard?, Feb. 28, 1770, *ibid.*, 26:450. Rogers, Hutchinson's nephew: *Sibley-Shipton*, 13:631.

37. Publicity: *B. Gaz.*, Feb. 26, 1770. "Largest" funeral: Hutchinson to Hillsborough, Feb. 28, 1770, CO 5/759. Snowstorm: Rowe, *Diary*, 197; *B.N.-L.*, March 1, 1770. Description of funeral: *B. Gaz.*, March 5, 1770. Length: Hutchinson to Bernard?, Feb. 28, 1770, Mass. Arch., 26:450. Adams: Adams, *Diary and Autobiography*, 1:349–350; see also Rowe, *Diary*, 197.

38. Nonresurrection: Hutchinson, Almanac. Council: Hutchinson to Hillsborough, Feb. 28, 1770, CO 5/759.

39. Allen similarity: Hutchinson, *History*, 3:194; Hutchinson also likened the Seider funeral to the burial of Sir Edmund Berry Godfrey in 1678, Hutchinson, Almanac. Allen: *Legal Papers*, 2:400n. and sources cited; *Va. Gaz.*, Aug. 18, 1768. Adams: *B. Gaz.*, Feb. 26, 1770. Omitted particulars: *ibid.*, March 5, 1770.

16. The Boston Massacre

1. Gage to Hillsborough, April 10, 1770, CO 5/88.

2. *Gazette: B. Gaz.*, Feb. 19, 1770. Adams: *Legal Papers*, 3:264. Resentment: Gordon, *History*, 1:281. Exultations: Hutchinson, *History*, 3:194.

3. Effectives: Hutchinson to Hillsborough, March 12, 1770, CO 5/759; Caldwell to Admiralty, March 14, 1770, ADM 1/1609. Adams: Adams, *Writings*, 2:94. Population: Frothingham: "Sam Adams Regiments," 702.

4. Frothingham, *Warren*, 127n.; Stephen, *Criminal Law*, 1:455.

5. Individual citation for each of the many facts described in this admittedly imperfect reconstruction would dizzy the reader without enlightening him; I have accordingly lumped at the head of each note, under the rubric "Facts," references to the main sources of this account, viz., *Short Narrative, Fair Account*, and

Legal Papers; citation to other sources will follow the usual form. Facts: *Short Narrative,* 3, 4, 5, 13; *Legal Papers,* 3:133–134, 141. Ropewalks: Drake, *Boston Landmarks,* 273. Samuel Gray: Narrative, n.d., Chalmers Papers, 3:70; Hutchinson, *History,* 3:196.

6. Facts: *Short Narrative,* 6–7; *Legal Papers,* 3:115, 135. Rodgers: Rodgers, deposition, July 28, 1770, Gay Transcripts, 12:111; Hutchinson, *History,* 3:195.

7. Facts: *Short Narrative,* 5; *Fair Account* (text), 12. Whereabouts: *B. Gaz.,* March 12, 1770, reported that he was found in a "House of Pleasure" on March 5.

8. Facts: *Short Narrative,* 7–9; *Fair Account* (text), 9. Eliot: Gordon, *History,* 1:282. Mrs. Welsteed: Hutchinson, "Additions," 18; Hutchinson, Almanac; *Sibley-Shipton,* 6:156. Frothingham, *Warren,* 123n. reports that the following hand-bill was posted: "Boston March ye 5, 1770. This is to Inform ye Rebellious People in Boston that ye Soldjers in ye 14th and 29th Regiments are determined to Joine together and defend themselves against all who shall Oppose them. Signd Ye Soldjers of ye 14th & 29th Regiments." I believe that in this instance Frothingham was misinformed; even if the poster was in fact stuck up, the inherent probabilities are against its having been produced by the troops.

9. Council: Hutchinson, Almanac; Hutchinson, *History,* 3:195. Parliament: *Annual Register, 1770,* 73.

10. Facts: *Short Narrative,* 14, 48, 53, 56, 58, 61; *Legal Papers,* 3:106, 117, 132, 210. Street lamps: Rowe, *Diary,* 264. Moon: Hutchinson, Almanac; Mr. John Carr, of Boston's Hayden Planetarium, was kind enough to calculate for me the moon's position in the sky.

11. Facts: *Legal Papers,* 3:9 and sources cited, 70n., 103, 108; *Fair Account,* 14. Basset: Everard, *Twenty-Ninth,* 72; Carr to Gage, June 25, 1769, Gage Papers.

12. Facts: *Legal Papers,* 3:opp. 68, 248. Green: Drake, *Boston Landmarks,* 98.

13. Facts: *Short Narrative,* 23; *Legal Papers,* 3:50, 108, 187. Inhabitants and soldiers: Hutchinson, *History,* 3:195.

14. Facts: *Short Narrative,* 23; *Legal Papers,* 3:50.

15. Facts: *Short Narrative,* 72–73. Mrs. Welsteed: Hutchinson, Almanac.

16. Facts: *Short Narrative,* 73; *Legal Papers,* 3:52, 102–103, 114, 117, 189, 195, 197, 198.

17. Facts (in this and the next three paragraphs): *Legal Papers,* 3:181–183, 211, 215, 216. Boylston's Alley: Drake, *Boston Landmarks,* 121. Mall: Everard, *Twenty-Ninth,* 72.

18. *Legal Papers,* 3:118n., 215–216.

19. *Ibid.,* 3:216.

20. *Ibid.,* 3:170, 171, 173, 176, 192, 209. Mitchelson: Alden, "Mein," 579; Edes, "Sandemanians," *passim.*

21. *Legal Papers* 3:172, 173, 176, 177.

22. Facts: *Short Narrative,* 7, 19, 57, 75; *Legal Papers,* 3:58, 77, 123, 174, 178–179, 202. Fire: Drake, *Boston Landmarks,* 272.

23. Palfrey: Palfrey to Wilkes, March 3, 1770, MHS, *Procs.* (1st Ser.), 6:480 (1863). Payne: *Legal Papers,* 3:222. Marshal: *ibid.,* 140.

24. *Legal Papers,* 3:133, 188; Sam Adams later claimed that until the bells rang, Gray "was at his own home the whole of the Evening, saving his going to a neighbour's home to borrow the News-Paper of the day and returning," Adams, *Writings,* 2:118.

25. Apprentice: *B. Gaz.,* March 12, 1770. Supper: Paine Papers; *Legal Papers,* 3:141. Elizabeth: Anderson, "Mackintosh," 46.

26. Johnson (later identified as Crispus Attucks): *Legal Papers,* 3:110, 118, 122, 209, 269; testimony of Thomas Symmonds in minutes of trial enclosed in

Hutchinson to Hillsborough, Dec. 5, 1770, CO 5/759; Samuel Condon, deposition, March 6, 1770, SF #101684; *NEHGR*, 13:300 (1859). Soldiers' heights: Everard, *Twenty-Ninth*, 73 (the figures are for 1773, but there is no reason to believe they were not valid for 1770).

27. Caldwell: Adams, *Writings*, 2:118. Paterson: *Short Narrative*, 55; *Legal Papers*, 3:127, 129.

28. *Legal Papers*, 3:69, 112, 134–136, 208, 212–213.

29. Facts: *Ibid.*, 3:59, 62, 77, 211; *Fair Account*, 15; Drake, *Boston Landmarks*, 71, says without support that Preston was at the Concert Hall (southeast corner of Queen (now Court) and Hanover streets, Rowe, "Diary," 46; Sergeant Hugh Broughton, deposition, July 24, 1770, Gay Transcripts, 12:112–113, says he (Broughton) brought the news to Basset, who then notified Preston. Hutchinson: *Legal Papers*, 3:81.

30. Facts: *Short Narrative*, 23, 62, 72–73, 74, 75–76; *Legal Papers*, 3:112–113, 132; *Wemms Trial*, 214–215.

31. Facts: *Legal Papers*, 3:196; *Fair Account*, 15. Gage: Gage to Dalrymple, April 28, 1770, Adams, *New Light*, 50.

32. "Case" of Captain Preston, most conveniently available in Matthews, "Preston," 6–10.

33. Facts: *Legal Papers*, 3:58, 125, 176, 196, 205; William Whitington, testimony, in minutes of trial, enclosed in Hutchinson to Hillsborough, Dec. 5, 1770, CO 5/759. Preston, in his "Case"; Basset, in an affidavit dated March 13; Daniel Calfe, who gave a deposition on March 21; and Ebenezer Bridgham, a witness at the men's subsequent trial, all say that the party contained twelve men, Matthews, "Preston," 8; *Fair Account*, 15; *Short Narrative*, 26; *Legal Papers*, 3:106. Yet the evidence is overwhelming that the group which formed in front of the Custom House contained not twelve soldiers, but eight. That the two officers most closely involved should both mistake the size of the force seems incredible. But no other available explanation suffices. Cato, black servant to Tuthill Hubbard, later swore that after the firing, he saw several soldiers go into the Custom House, *Short Narrative*, 56. Could these have been the missing four? No one else who testified by deposition or in court mentioned soldiers entering the Custom House.

34. Facts: *Legal Papers*, 3:52n., 56; also Oliver, *Origin*, 89. Caps: Everard, *Twenty-Ninth*, 60.

35. Facts: *Legal Papers*, 3:79, 111, 125, 128, 196, 211.

36. Facts: *Short Narrative*, 42; *Legal Papers*, 3:55, 196, 212; *Fair Account* (text), 19; see also Drake, *Boston Landmarks*, 85; Drake "Henry Knox," 347. Neck: *Short Narrative*, 67.

37. *Legal Papers*, 3:75, 76.

38. *Ibid.*, 3:78.

39. Facts: *ibid.*, 3:60, 69–70, 103, 104, 115–116, 135, 137.

40. Facts: *ibid.*, 3:55, 67, 69, 74, 77, 117, 198. Riot Act: *ibid.*, 3:70–71; see also discussion of the Riot Act in connection with the Malcom affair, Chapter 4, above. Although no Massachusetts civil officer would dare use his Riot Act powers, when the act expired on July 1, 1770, the radical-controlled legislature, in an excess of caution, refused to renew it, Adams, *Works*, 4:51.

41. Facts: *Legal Papers*, 3:71, 194, 199, 201. French: Jeremiah French, deposition, July 25, 1770, CO 5/88. Forrest: Adams, *Diary and Autobiography*, 3:292.

42. *Legal Papers*, 3:105, 135, 195, 212.

43. Gray: *ibid.*, 3:207; Paine Papers; Joseph Hinkley, testimony, in minutes of

trial enclosed in Hutchinson to Hillsborough, Dec. 5, 1770, CO 5/759. One life to lose: *Fair Account,* 20. Fallacy: Hulton, *Letters,* 29. Hutchinson: Hutchinson to Mackay, July 27, 1770, Mass. Arch., 26:525.

44. Facts: *Legal Papers,* 3:76, 78.

45. Facts: *ibid.,* 3:54–55, 66, 75, 118–119, 219; Matthews, "Preston," 8–9.

46. Facts: *Legal Papers,* 3:66–67, 75, 88, 109, 115, 117, 119–120, 125, 129–130.

47. Facts: *ibid.,* 3:52, 59, 60, 64, 67, 75, 76, 78, 79, 115, 125, 137, 179, 205.

48. *Ibid.,* 3:183.

49. Gray: *Short Narrative,* 30, 60; *Legal Papers,* 3:108; Inquest, March 6, 1770, Chamberlain Papers. Johnson: *Short Narrative,* 29, 58, 60. Advance: *Short Narrative,* 56. Caldwell: *Short Narrative,* 38; *Legal Papers,* 3:128; Inquest, March 5 [almost surely a misdate], 1770, Chamberlain Papers. Paterson: *Legal Papers,* 3:127. Carr: *ibid.,* 3:214; Charles Conner, deposition, March 15, 1770, Chamberlain Papers; Inquest, March 15, 1770, *ibid.* Maverick: *Legal Papers,* 3:185–186; Richard Hirons, testimony, in minutes of trial enclosed in Hutchinson to Hillsborough, Dec. 5, 1770, CO 5/759. Sumner says that Maverick, his cousin Joseph Mountfort, Peter C. Brooks, and Samuel and Thomas Car[e]y were playing marbles when the bells rang. They went to the scene. When the muskets fired, "Maverick cried out to his relative Mountfort, 'Joe! I am shot!' and ran down . . . Royal Exchange lane, to Dock Square, where he fell to the ground. . . ." I have rejected this version (although Sumner claimed to have obtained it from Mountfort's son) because: (a) it conflicts squarely with Jonathan Cary's contemporary testimony; (b) Peter C. Brooks was only three years old at the time, see *Legal Papers,* 1:xcviii; (c) it conflicts as to the place of Maverick's fall with Dr. Hirons's contemporary testimony. But the Sumner-Mountfort version, by suggesting that Maverick ran after being shot, rather than before, does explain how the bullet which felled Maverick—who collapsed while running away from the firing—could have entered from the front. See Sumner, *East Boston* 172.

50. Facts: *Short Narrative,* 60; *Legal Papers,* 3:78, 79, 112–113, 132.

51. Facts: *Short Narrative,* 29; *Legal Papers,* 3:56, 78, 132, 136.

52. *Short Narrative,* 62, 74.

53. Facts: *ibid.,* 40, 48; *Legal Papers,* 3:207, 214; Charles Connor, deposition, March 15, 1770, Chamberlain Papers; Joseph Petty, deposition, March 6, 1770, *ibid.* Maverick: Sumner, *East Boston,* 172.

54. Withdrawal: Matthews, "Preston," 9. Street firings: Tourtellot, *William Diamond's Drum,* 164.

55. Preston: Matthews, "Preston," 9; Sergeant Hugh Broughton, deposition, July 24, 1770, Gay Transcripts, 12:113. Bells: Hutchinson, Almanac.

56. Threat: *Short Narrative* (text), 22. Neck: Ensign Gilbert Carter, deposition, CO 5/88. Muskets: *Legal Papers,* 3:174. Reinforcements: Samuel Cooper to Thomas Pownall, March 26, 1770, "Cooper-Pownall," 317.

57. *Short Narrative,* 77.

58. Goldfinch: Private John Whitehouse, deposition, Aug. 25, 1770, Gay Transcripts, 12:84. French: Captain Jeremiah French, deposition, July 25, 1770, CO 5/88. Others: *Fair Account,* 16–19.

59. *Short Narrative,* 67.

60. Hutchinson to Gage, March 6, 1770, Adams, *New Light,* 14; Hutchinson, Almanac; *Legal Papers,* 3:80.

61. Joseph Belknap, deposition, n.d., Belknap Papers (at the foot is written in Belknap's hand, signed by him: "delivered in Cort at ye Triall of Capt Preston"; it is, however, much more circumstantial than Belknap's recorded testimony,

Legal Papers, 3:61); Hutchinson, Almanac.

62. Facts: Joseph Belknap, deposition, n.d., Belknap Papers; *Short Narrative,* 64–65; *Legal Papers,* 3:61, 81; Hutchinson, Almanac. "I'll do his business": Oliver, *Origin,* 90.

63. Belknap, deposition, n.d., Belknap Papers; Hutchinson, Almanac; Hutchinson, *History,* 3:196; Hutchinson, "Additions," 18.

64. Hutchinson's speech: Frothingham, *Warren,* 131. Response: ? to ?, March 14, 1770, Chalmers Papers, 3:70. Conference: Hutchinson, Almanac; Hutchinson, *History,* 3:196.

65. Adams, *Diary and Autobiography,* 3:291–292, 4:259.

66. Hearings: Tudor, *Diary,* 31; Hutchinson, *History,* 3:196–197; Hutchinson, Almanac. Witness called from home: *Short Narrative,* 66. Eustice: *Short Narrative,* 66–67; SF #101646.

67. Hutchinson, Almanac; Tudor, *Diary;* Matthews, "Preston," 10; *Legal Papers,* 3:87.

68. Hutchinson to Hillsborough, March 12, 1770, CO 5/759; see also ? to ?, March 14, 1770, Chalmers Papers, 3:70: "This affair from a Variety of Circumstances seems to have been preconcerted. The moment the bells were sett a ringing at Boston, the bells at Charlestown & Roxbury also began to Ring, and Numbers of people at both places gott under arms."

17. Preparation and Procrastination

1. Autopsy: *Short Narrative,* 69. Inquests: The inquests on Caldwell, Carr, and Gray are in the Chamberlain Papers; that on Johnson-Attucks is in the Bostonian Society, Old State House, Boston.

2. Crowd: Caldwell to Admiralty, March 14, 1770, ADM 1/1609; *B. Gaz.,* March 12, 1770. "Matchiavel": Hutchinson to ?, Sept. 4, 1774, quoted in Schlesinger, *Prelude,* 204.

3. Sources for the account of the council meetings: Hutchinson, Almanac; Hutchinson, *History,* 3:197–198; Andrew Oliver, affidavit, March 13, 1770, *Fair Account,* 25–27; affidavits enclosed in Hutchinson to Hillsborough, Oct. 30, 1770, CO 5/759; see also Boston Rec. Comm., *Reports,* 18:1–4; my version differs considerably from Frothingham, *Warren,* 137–149.

4. *B. Gaz.,* March 12, 1770.

5. Writing: Hutchinson to Gage, March 18, 1770, Gage Papers; Hutchinson to Dalrymple, March 6, 1770, Adams, *New Light,* 16–19. "Satisfaction": Rowe, *Diary,* 198. Blame: Dalrymple to Gage, March 7, 1770, Adams, *New Light,* 22; Hutchinson to Gage, March 18, 1770, *ibid.,* 30; Dalrymple to Gage, March 27, 1770, *ibid.,* 39.

6. Officers: Hutchinson, *History,* 3:198. Gage: Gage to Dalrymple, March 12, 1770, Adams, *New Light,* 27; Gage to Hutchinson, March 12, 1770, *ibid.,* 28. Adams: Hutchinson, *History,* 3:199. Molineux: John Adams to William Tudor, April 15, 1817, Adams, *Works,* 10:252.

7. Bar: Dexter, "Suffolk Bar," 148. Watch: ? to ?, March 14, 1770, Chalmers Papers, 3:70; Adams to Tudor, April 15, 1817, Adams, *Works,* 10:251–252. Militia: Hutchinson, "Additions," 18. "Caution": *B.N.-L.,* March 8, 1770. Activating order (dated March 13, 1770): Chamberlain Papers.

8. Gage: Gage to Dalrymple, March 12, 14, April 9, June 17, 1770, Adams, *New Light,* 27, 30, 45, 54–55. Copley: Boston Rec. Comm., *Reports,* 18:1. Committee: *ibid.* Hutchinson: Hutchinson, "Additions," 18–19. Notification: Samuel Adams to Paine, n.d., Paine Papers. Plan: see *Legal Papers,* 3:vii; Forbes, *Revere,*

159, 472. Engraving: Pelham to Revere, March 29, 1770, *Copley-Pelham*, 83.

9. Committee to Pownall, March 12, 1770, printed in *The Gentleman's Magazine* (London), April 1770; Hutchinson, Almanac, criticizes the letter extensively; see also Hutchinson, *History*, 3:199–200.

10. Horrid Massacre: John Wilkes had earlier applied the phrase to the shooting in St. George's Fields in 1768, *St. James's Chronicle*, Dec. 10, 1768, quoted in Gipson, *Empire*, 11:211. Andrews: *Short Narrative*, 72; James Murray to Elizabeth Smith, March 12, 1770, Murray, *Letters*, 165. Revere: Channing, *History*, 3:120n. "Banditti": *B. Gaz.*, March 12, 1770; see also *ibid.* March 19, 1770.

11. Evidence: *Short Narrative*, 44, 54; Hutchinson, "Additions," 19. Bourgatte and Manwaring: Gage to Hillsborough, April 10, 1770, CO 5/88; as to Manwaring, see also Hood, Log (June 17, 1769).

12. Hutchinson, Almanac; Hutchinson, *History*, 3:201; Hutchinson, "Additions," 20–21; ? to ?, n.d., Chalmers Papers, 3:73.

13. Robinson: Savage, Diary; Samuel Cooper to Thomas Pownall, March 26, 1770, "Cooper-Pownall," 318. Affidavits: Dalrymple to Hillsborough, March 13, 1770, CO 5/759. Bowdoin: Hutchinson to ?, Oct. 30, 1770, Mass. Arch., 27:45. Greenwood: *Short Narrative*, 75.

14. *Short Narrative*, 80; Hutchinson, *History*, 3:200.

15. Vote: Boston Rec. Comm., *Reports*, 18:20; see also William Whitwell to Samuel and William Vernon, April 10, 1770, MHS, *Procs.* (2d Ser.) 2:122 (1885). Distribution: see this chapter, text at n. 61, and Chapter 18, text at n. 13, below. English rule: *Rex v. Reason and Tranter*, 1 Str. 499, 93 Eng. Rep. 659 (K.B. 1722); Hutchinson, Almanac; Hutchinson, *History*, 3:201.

16. English: Hinkhouse, *Preliminaries, passim.* American: Schlesinger, *Prelude*, 117, 124, 126; Gage to Dalrymple, April 9, 1770, Adams, *New Light*, 45.

17. Impressment: *Rose*, Muster Book, ADM 36/7943; the man was John Fleming, twenty-one, of Greenock, Scotland, which may account for Boston's indifference. Hutchinson: Hutchinson to Gage, March 18, 1770, Adams, *New Light*, 31; Dalrymple to Gage, March 27, 1770, *ibid.*, 39.

18. Attucks: Fisher, "Attucks," 531–533 argues that Attucks was a Natick Indian (or at least part-black, part-Indian) from Framingham, a crewman off a Nantucket whaler. Byles: *Sibley-Shipton*, 7:481. First funeral and Carr: Rowe, *Diary*, 199.

19. Savil: *B.N.-L.*, March 29, 1770; see also Watkins, "Tarring and Feathering," 30; for subsequent developments, see Chapter 19, text at n. 2, below. Commissioners: Hulton, Paxton, Burch, and Robinson to Treasury, March 9, 1770, T 1/476; Commissioners, Minutes of Meetings, Bowdoin-Temple MSS, 7:62; Temple to Lord North, Nov. 6, 1770, T 1/478; Hulton, Account, 377; Hulton and Burch to Paxton, March 30, 1770, Bowdoin-Temple MSS, 7:63–64.

20. Attack: Hulton, Account, 377; Hulton, *Letters*, 22–24; *B.E.P.*, June 25, 1770. Reaction: Bowdoin to Hood, July 7, 1770, *Bowdoin-Temple*, 195; Hulton, Account, 377; Hulton, *Letters*, 39. Castle: Richard Reeve to Thomas Bradshaw, June 30, 1770, T 1/476.

21. Lathrop: Lathrop, *Innocent Blood*, 6, 11. Chauncy: Oliver, *Origin*, 91–92. "Porteous": ? to ?, March 14, 1770, Chalmers Papers, 3:70. "Card" and Gage reaction: *Legal Papers*, 3:9. Dalrymple's ignorance: Adams, *New Light*, 44. Scituate: *B. Gaz.*, March 19, 1770; Hutchinson, Almanac. Response: *B. Gaz.*, March 10, 1770. Pardon: Preston to Gage, March 19, 1770, Adams, *New Light*, 34.

22. *Legal Papers*, 3:46–47; the value of the lethal weapon echoed another

archaism of the law; technically, any such weapon was forfeited to the crown as "deodand."

23. *Short Narrative,* 58; Goddard, affidavit, March 6, 1770, Chamberlain Papers.

24. Judges ill: *B. Gaz.,* March 19, 1770. Grand jury: *Legal Papers,* 3:4–5; Zobel, "Newer Light," 128; the reverse of the indictment shows the warrants were issued March 26; Hutchinson to Gage, April 1, 1770, Adams, *New Light,* 242. Mall: Chamberlain Papers (in Samuel Quincy's hand).

25. Jailing: *Legal Papers,* 3:5. Bailing: *ibid.;* ? to ?, April 24, 1770, Chalmers Papers, 3:76; Dana, Writs (a record of the re-bailing that was necessary after the term ended).

26. "Petty Concerns": Savage, Diary. Sewall: Zobel, "Sewall," 123–126.

27. Quincy: *Legal Papers,* 3:7–8n. (Quincy must have been appointed by March 26, since Mall's indictment of that date is in his hand). Personality: Adams, *Diary and Autobiography,* 3:261; Adams, *Works,* 10:195. Paine's selection: *Legal Papers,* 3:8 and note. Marriage: Sibley-Shipton, 12:469 (Paine's first son was born two months later). Molineux: Molineux to Paine, March [April] 9, 1770, Paine Papers.

28. Auchmuty: Adams, *Diary and Autobiography,* 1:317. Refusals: *Legal Papers,* 3:6. Quincy: Adams to Abigail Adams, July 3, 1774, *Adams Family Correspondence,* 1:122. "Wilkes": *Sibley-Shipton,* 13:480; Hutchinson to Bernard, May 22, 1770, Mass. Arch., 26:491.

29. Adams, *Diary and Autobiography,* 3:292–293.

30. Forrest, memorial, AO 13/100.328 and Forrest file, AO 13/73.532ff; Hutchinson, Almanac, is similarly silent.

31. Quincy, *Quincy,* 26–28.

32. Hutchinson: Zobel, "Newer Light," 127. Committee: *Legal Papers,* 3:11. In addition to Auchmuty, Adams, and Quincy, Sampson Salter Blowers joined the defense legal staff, although it is not clear just when. "Short . . . thin," he had "untiring industry, vast legal knowledge, sound judgment, impartiality, and patience . . . little eloquence; no wit or imagination," Hutchinson, *Diary,* 1:342.

33. Special justices: Adams, *Writings,* 2:8. Bond to appear: see *Legal Papers,* 1:58. Demand: *ibid.,* 3:3–4 and note; Hutchinson, *History,* 3:205; John Robinson, testimony, June 26, 1770, *Acts, Privy Council (Col.),* 5:254; Hutchinson, Almanac. Resignation: Hutchinson to Hillsborough, March 27, 1770, CO 5/759.

34. For all pre-trial details and sources see *Legal Papers,* 2:401–403.

35. Complaint: Savage, Diary. Fitch: Boyle, "Journal," 263 (he was appointed advocate-general on March 4); see also Hutchinson to Hillsborough, Sept. 26, 1769, CO 5/758.

36. *Williams* v. *Ainslie:* Adams Papers; SF #101947; Lynde, *Diary,* 194. Adams quote: Sumner, *Memorandum Book.*

37. Letter: *B. Gaz.,* April 9, 1770. Gallows and watch: Sessions, Minute Book.

38. The events of the trial may conveniently be followed in *Legal Papers,* 2:411–424.

39. See generally, *ibid.,* 2:405. Oliver and the Richardson children: Ebenezer Bridgham, testimony, June 26, 1770, *Acts, Privy Council (Col.),* 5:251.

40. *Legal Papers,* 2:405–406.

41. Gage to Hutchinson, April 23, 1770, Mass. Arch., 25:389; Dalrymple to Gage, May 5, 1770, Adams, *New Light,* 52; "Eliot-Hollis," 45.

42. Repeal news: Dalrymple to Gage, April 20, 1770, Gage Papers; Rowe, *Diary,* 201. Fall: Hutchinson, "Additions," 20; Hutchinson, Almanac; *Legal Papers,* 3:12n. Adjournment: Lynde, *Diary,* 196. Fight: Hutchinson, *History,*

3:202; see also Rowe, *Diary*, 199. Meeting: ? to ?, April 24, 1770, Chalmers Papers, 3:76; see also Hutchinson to Hillsborough, April 21, 1770, CO 5/759.

43. Nonimportation pressure: ? to ?, April 24, 1770, Chalmers Papers, 3:76. Hutchinson effort: Gordon, *History*, 1:277. Rowe: Rowe, *Diary*, 201–207, *passim*. Hutchinson hopes: Hutchinson to Hillsborough, April 27, 1770, CO 5/759. Dissolution: Hutchinson, Almanac.

44. Otis: Rowe, *Diary*, 199, 201; Adams, *Diary and Autobiography*, 1:348–349; Hutchinson, "Additions," 24. Dalrymple: Dalrymple to Gage, April 24, 1770, Gage Papers; actually, Hutchinson's nephew Nathaniel Rogers was to be secretary; his commission was issued, but he died before it arrived; see Hutchinson to Hillsborough, Aug. 14, 1770, CO 5/759.

45. Warnings: SF #89545, #89546. Cartoon: *Legal Papers*, 3:96n.

46. Quarters: Gage to Hillsborough, Oct. 6, 1770, CO 5/88. Orders: Gage to Dalrymple, April 28, 1770, Gage Papers. Refusal: Gage to Hillsborough, June 2, 1770, CO 5/88. Departure: Boyle, "Journal," 265; Rowe, *Diary*, 202. New Jersey: *New Jersey Archives*, 27:162–163.

47. Hutchinson to Hillsborough, May 21, 1770, CO 5/759; Hutchinson to Bernard, May 22, 1770, Mass. Arch., 26:491; Hutchinson to ?, May 22, 1770, *ibid.*, 26:489.

48. Instructions: Boston Rec. Comm., *Reports*, 18:26; Hutchinson, *History*, 3:370. Uniforms: Hillsborough to Gage, Feb. 17 and Sept. 28, 1770, CO 5/88; Gage to Hutchinson, April 30, 1770, Gage Papers. *Vim vi:* Coke, *Littleton*, 162a.

49. This and the following paragraphs are based on: Richards and Woart, depositions, May 21, 1770, T 1/476; Hutchinson to Hillsborough, May 21, 1770, and July 2, 1770 (with enclosure), CO 5/759; Sheaffe and Robert Hallowell to Commissioners, May 21, 1770, T 1/476; Rowe, *Diary*, 202; *Richards* v. *Doble*, *Legal Papers*, 1:39–40; Adams Papers; SF #102288; *Richards* v. *Jones*, Adams Papers; *Richards* v. *Heakley*, SF #102127; Temple to Hulton, Burch, and Paxton, May 23, 1770, Bowdoin-Temple MSS, 7:75; Boyle, "Journal," 265; Watkins, "Tarring and Feathering," 36; Richards, petition, n.d., AO 13/75.350; Richards, petition, Oct. 22, 1783, AO 13/48.388. In T 1/476 are additional accounts of a similar but less outrageous occurrence at Providence on July 30, 1770, and the accosting of Comptroller-General Porter near King's Chapel, Boston, on June 6, 1770.

50. Sources cited in *Legal Papers*, 3:12; Hutchinson to Hillsborough, June 8, 1770, CO 5/759; Savage, Diary; Hutchinson, Almanac.

51. Sources cited, *Legal Papers*, 3:12; Wroth & Zobel, "Trials," *passim*.

52. Election: Adams, *Diary and Autobiography*, 1:350–351n. Loss of business: *ibid.*, 351. Beccaria: *ibid.*, 352.

53. Gordon, *History*, 1:279; Fleeming to Mein, July 1, 1770, Chalmers Papers, 4:5.

54. SF #152686; Fleeming to Mein, July 1, 1770, Chalmers Papers, 4:5; Cutler, memorial, Aug. 25, 1783, AO 13/50.219; Christian Barnes to Elizabeth Smith, June 29 and July 1, 1770, Murray, *Letters*, 178, 179; Adams, *Diary and Autobiography*, 2:8–9n.

55. Barnes: Christian Barnes to Elizabeth Smith, June ?, 1770, Murray, *Letters*, 175; for other interference with Barnes, see proclamation dated June 28, 1770, enclosed in Hutchinson to John Pownall, July 2, 1770, CO 5/759. McMasters: Petition of James, Patrick, and John McMasters, June 5, 1770, and petition of Patrick McMasters, June 27, 1770, enclosed in Hutchinson to John Pownall, Aug. 29, 1770, CO 5/759; *B.N.-L.*, June 21, 1770; Christian Barnes to Elizabeth Smith, June ?, 1770, Murray, *Letters*, 178; Hulton, *Letters*, 27; Fleeming to Mein,

July 1, 1770, Chalmers Papers, 4:5; Council minutes, June 21, 1770, enclosed in Hutchinson to John Pownall, July 2, 1770, CO 5/759.

56. Orders: Hillsborough to Hutchinson, April 26, 1770, CO 5/765, received about June 26, see Hutchinson to Hillsborough, June 26, 1770, CO 5/759. Rumor: "Eliot-Hollis," 451–452. Advice: Barlow Trecothick to Committee of the Town of Boston, May 16, 1770, *Bowdoin-Temple*, 183; Thomas Pownall to Committee, June ?, 1770, *ibid.*, 189; Hutchinson, Almanac; Preston to Gage, Aug. 6, 1770, Adams, *New Light*, 65; sources cited in *Legal Papers*, 3:13n. "Independence": Hutchinson to Hood, July 1, 1770, Mass. Arch., 26:517.

57. News of Parliament: Rowe, *Diary*, 204; Hutchinson, Almanac. Bernard: Morison, *Three Centuries*, 91. Young: Rowe, *Diary*, 205. Chauncy: Hutchinson, *History*, 3:237n.; *Sibley-Shipton*, 6:450. "Fair trial": Cooper to Pownall, July 2, 1770, "Cooper-Pownall," 320.

58. *Legal Papers*, 3:13–14, 15–16, and sources cited; Hillsborough to Gage, Oct. 3, 1770, Adams, *New Light*, 78.

59. The documents are printed in Matthews, "Preston."

60. Case of Captain Thomas Preston, enclosed in Dalrymple to Hillsborough, March 13, 1770, CO 5/759.

61. Cooper to Pownall, July 2, 1770, "Cooper-Pownall," 320. See Adams, *Independence*, a brilliant bibliographical study of the Revolutionary preliminaries. For the suggestion that Edes and Gill fabricated a "London" imprint, I am indebted to the typographical detective work of John E. Alden of the Boston Public Library.

62. Quincy: Hutchinson, Almanac. Sons on Preston: *Legal Papers*, 3:9. Clarke: Mass. Arch., 44:704; Clarke had pointed a loaded pistol at one Joseph Nowell on June 20, 1769; indicted at the Nov. 1769 sitting, he pleaded *nolo contendere* in March 1770; SF #101589; MB 91; Rec. 1770; fol. 28.

63. Opinion: Christian Barnes to Elizabeth Smith, June ?, 1770, Murray, *Letters*, 178. Lynch scare: *Legal Papers*, 3:12–13 and sources there collected.

64. Gage to Hillsborough, July 7, 1770, CO 5/88; *Legal Papers*, 3:12–13; Gage to Preston, Aug. 12, 1770, Adams, *New Light*, 69; Dalrymple to Gage, Aug. 12, 1770, *ibid.*, 67; Hood to Admiralty, June 29, 1770, CO 5/759; Hood to Admiralty, Sept. 25, 1770, ADM 1/483; Hood to Bowdoin, Sept. 7, 1770, *Bowdoin-Temple*, 211. Throughout the summer, Hood kept up a running battle with the customs service over the cashier's practice of turning a personal profit on public funds by using the cash to buy bills at a discount, then redeeming them at par, T 1/476, *passim*.

65. Arrival and sermon: Rowe, *Diary*, 205. Effect on Adams: Miller, *Sam Adams*, 85. Whitefield's health and spirit: *Britannica* (11th ed.), 28:604. Hutchinson: Hutchinson, Almanac

66. Whitefield's influence: Gage to Barrington, Oct. 6, 1770, Gage, *Correspondence*, 2:561. Orders: Hutchinson to Hillsborough, Sept. 12, 1770, CO 5/759.

67. Hutchinson to Hillsborough, Aug. 28 and Sept. 12, 1770, CO 5/759; Gage to Hillsborough, Oct. 6, 1770, CO 5/88. Hutchinson, *History*, 3:222–223; Rowe, *Diary*, 206; Bowdoin to Thomas Pownall, Oct. 22, 1770, *Bowdoin-Temple*, 215.

68. Hutchinson to Bernard, Aug. 28, 1770, Mass. Arch., 26:541; Lynde, *Diary*, 198.

69. *Legal Papers*, 2:406–407, 426–430. In 1772, Richardson finally won a pardon, *ibid.*, 410.

70. *Ibid.*, 3:14; Hutchinson to Gage, Sept. 11, 1770, CO 5/759.

71. Hutchinson, *History*, 3:222; Hutchinson to Hillsborough, Sept. 12, 1770, CO 5/759.

72. Fear: Hutchinson to Bernard, Oct. 16, 1770, Mass. Arch., 27:3. Fast: Hutchinson, *History*, 3:224; Rowe, *Diary*, 207.

73. Hutchinson to John Pownall, Aug. 29, 1770, CO 5/759; Cooper to Thomas Pownall, Nov. 5, 1770, "Cooper-Pownall," 320; Gipson, *Empire*, 11:271.

18. Rex v. Preston

1. Gage to Dalrymple, Aug. 19, 1770, Adams, *New Light*, 71.

2. Conflict: ABA, *Code*, Ethical Consideration 5–15; ABA, *Canons*, #6; see also *De Luna* v. *U.S.*, 308 F. 2d 140, 141 (5th Cir., 1962). Petition: Chamberlain Papers.

3. Palfrey to John Wilkes, Oct. ?, 1770, "Wilkes-Palfrey," 422.

4. Jury law: *Legal Papers*, 3:17–18n. (which details the procedure). Dalrymple: Dalrymple to Gage, Aug. 26, 1770, Adams, *New Light*, 73.

5. SF #101659; "Sons of Liberty—1769."

6. *Legal Papers*, 3:17, 48–49; SF #101659.

7. Events of the trial may be conveniently followed in *Legal Papers*, 3:48–98.

8. Thomas Preston, statement, n.d., AO 13/44.159.

9. Challenges: See *Legal Papers*, 3:19, 49n.; SF #101659; Samuel Adams to Stephen Sayre, Nov. 16, 1770, Adams, *Writings*, 2:59, says Preston challenged eighteen. Frobisher: Adams, *Diary and Autobiography*, 1:353; Winsor, *Boston*, 4:72; Henry Lloyd to Moses Lopez, March 30, 1765, Marcus, *American Jewry*, 333.

10. Inquest on Samuel Gray, March 6, 1770, Chamberlain Papers.

11. In addition to sources cited in *Legal Papers*, 3:19, see, for Deblois, Peter Oliver to Deblois, May 4, 1786, AO 13/44.130; for Wallis, will of Stephen Deblois (father of Gilbert and Sarah, who married Wallis), AO 13/44.112.

12. Statute: *Legal Papers*, 3:19–20n. Sam Adams: Adams, *Writings*, 2:60.

13. Pamphlet on counsel table: "Philanthrop" (Sewall) in *B.E.P.*, Jan. 28, 1771. Adams: *Legal Papers*, 3:87. Paine: Paine Papers. Hutchinson: Hutchinson to Hillsborough (private), Oct. 30, 1770, Mass. Arch., 27:46.

14. Description: *Legal Papers*, 1:xlviii; *ibid.*, 2:426; 3:65, 141, 197, 199; James Waddel, testimony, in summary of evidence, CO 5/759. Bystanders: Palfrey to Wilkes, Oct. 23–30, 1770, "Wilkes-Palfrey," 423, 426; Dalrymple to Gage, Oct. 25, 1770, Adams, *New Light*, 81.

15. Civil rate: *Legal Papers*, 1:xlix. Criminal: Quincy, *Reports*, 383n.

16. Record: Palfrey to Wilkes, Oct. ?, 1770, "Wilkes-Palfrey," 425–426; Adams to Jedidiah Morse, Jan. 5, 1816, Adams, *Works*, 10:201; Preston to Gage, Dec. 6, 1770, Adams, *New Light*, 95; *B. Gaz.*, March 25, 1771; *Legal Papers*, 3:67–68n.

17. Summary: Hutchinson to Hillsborough, Dec. 5, 1770, CO 5/759; Paine: *Legal Papers*, 3:50–80 notes, 87–88.

18. For definition of *surtout*, see *OED*.

19. Trowbridge: Hutchinson, Almanac. Need for beverages: Channing, *History*, 3:92. Provisions: Bill of jailkeeper Joseph Otis, in the office of the chief justice, Boston Municipal Court (photocopy in the Adams Papers); the bill suggests that the keepers did not bed with the jurors, although they ate and drank with them; see Adams, *Legal Papers*, 3:22n.

20. See Burdick's deposition, *Short Narrative*, 28–29.

21. Everard, *Twenty-Ninth*, 58–59.

22. Goddard: *Legal Papers*, 3:86. Deposition: *Short Narrative*, 57–58.

23. ABA, *Code*, Disciplinary Rule 5–101(B); see *ibid.*, Disciplinary Rule 5–101(A) note; ABA, *Canons*, #15, paragraph 3.

24. *Short Narrative,* 35–36.

25. Belknap's earlier statement: Belknap, deposition, n.d., Belknap Papers, MHS. Drowne: Hutchinson to ?, Oct. 30, 1770, Mass. Arch., 27:48.

26. On the development of the right against self-incrimination, see generally Levy, *Origins.*

27. *Short Narrative,* 59–60.

28. *Sibley-Shipton,* 13:367; *Legal Papers,* 1:51n.

29. Newton Prince, petitions, n.d., AO 13/75.282, 284; Gilbert Deblois, certificate, March 10, 1781, *ibid.,* 286.

30. *DNB.*

31. Gordon, *History,* 1:291; in his own copy, presently in the Boston Public Library, Adams wrote: "Adams' Motive is not here perceived. His Clients lives were hazarded by Quincy's too youthful ardour."

32. Peter Oliver to Hutchinson, Oct. 27, 1770, Mass. Arch., 25:414.

33. Verdict: *B. Gaz.,* Nov. 5, 1770. Palfrey: Palfrey to Wilkes, Oct. ?, 1770, "Wilkes-Palfrey," 424–425.

34. *Legal Papers,* 3:23.

35. Preston to Castle: see sources collected in *ibid.,* 3:24, and note. Letter to Auchmuty: Auchmuty to ?, Feb. 21, 1785, AO 13/43.256; Preston's letter itself has not survived.

19. *Rex* v. *Wemms et al.*

1. Margaret: Zobel, "Sewall," 133–135; *Legal Papers,* 2:50, 58–59. Eaton-Parker: Lynde, *Diary,* 200; MB 88; Rec., 1770, fol. 223–224.

2. SF #131971; MB 93; Rec., 1770, fol. 235–236; see also *B. Gaz.,* Nov. 19, 1770; Hutchinson to ?, Nov. 30, 1770, Mass. Arch. 27:61.

3. Blood: Cooper to Paine, Nov. 10, 1770, Boston Rec. Comm., *Reports,* 23:70. Blowers: Hutchinson to Gage, Nov. 26, 1770, Adams, *New Light,* 92; *Legal Papers,* 1:xcvii.

4. Juror: *Legal Papers,* 3:255. Catholicism: *B. Gaz.,* Nov. 19, 1770; see also Bailyn, *Origins,* 98 and note.

5. Jurors: Gage to Hutchinson, Nov. 12, 1770, Adams, *New Light,* 88; Lynde, *Diary,* 200; *Legal Papers,* 3:24. Argument: *Gridley* v. *Harraden,* Adams Papers; SF #132780. King: SF #102014; MB 91; Rec., 1770, fol. 55. Clergy and branding: see Chapter 11, n. 20, above.

6. Lynde, *Diary,* 200.

7. *Legal Papers,* 3:99n.

8. Audience: *ibid.,* 3:197; Benjamin Lee, testimony, Paine Papers. Accuracy: Adams, *Legal Papers,* 3:28 and note.

9. Mayo: Winsor, *Boston,* 2:336; Hutchinson to Bernard, Dec. 16, 1770, Mass. Arch., 27:72. Pierce: *Legal Papers,* 3:36 and note. Thayer: SF #101659. Davenport: Stark, *Loyalists,* 129, 130. Bass: Adams, *Diary and Autobiography,* 1:130. Adams on temperance: *ibid.,* 128–130. Dorr: Dorr Papers. Generally: *Legal Papers,* 3:99–100.

10. Sheppard: SF #101659. Generally: *Legal Papers,* 3:99–100. Adams: Adams, *Writings,* 2:83. Hutchinson: Hutchinson to Gage, Dec. 3, 1770, Mass. Arch., 27:63.

11. Adams, *Legal Papers,* 3:99n.

12. Adams, *Legal Papers,* 3:101, 283, 304; such practice is "not illegal," *Commonwealth* v. *Tucker,* 189 Mass. 457, 497 (1905); in most jurisdictions today it would be permitted, see Annotation, "Taking and Use of Trial Notes by Jury,"

14 A.L.R. 3d 831 (1967); Steckler, "Management of the Jury," 195; compare Moscowitz, "Trial of a Criminal Case," 382–384.

13. The narrative of the trial is chronological, *Legal Papers*, 3:101–314.

14. Zobel, "Newer Light," 126.

15. Adams: Adams, *Writings*, 2:89. Jury: *Legal Papers*, 3:111.

16. Apthorp and Greenleaf: Winsor, *Boston*, 2:545; *Sibley-Shipton*, 7:188.

17. Note in Hutchinson's hand opposite Simpson, testimony, in minutes enclosed in Hutchinson to Hillsborough, Dec. 5, 1770, CO 5/759; see also Paine's minute of Adams's argument, Paine Papers.

18. An anonymous letter in *B.N.-L.*, Dec. 12, 1770, says: "[T]he Person in a red Cloak declared by some of the Witnesses to have been very busy at the Beginning of the Tragedy will be ascertained, if Vindex [i.e., Sam Adams] and his Adherents desire it." Apparently they never did. For a sample of the speculation which has been going on ever since, see Forbes, *Revere*, 154.

19. Adams to Paine, n.d., Paine Papers; the letter has been arbitrarily docketed Dec. 2, but from its contents, I believe it was written Nov. 29. On Paine's disposition, see *Sibley-Shipton*, 12:468 and Adams, *Diary and Autobiography*, 1:59.

20. Zobel, "Newer Light," 126; see also the other sources collected in *ibid.*, 119–121.

21. *M. Spy*, March 7, 1771.

22. Adams, *Writings*, 2:132.

23. Testimony: see minutes enclosed in Hutchinson to Hillsborough, Dec. 5, 1770, CO 5/759. Objection and exclusion: Adams, *Writings*, 2:125.

24. Jeffries: *Legal Papers*, 3:213n.; Adams, *Writings*, 1:218–219. Aberdeen: *Sibley-Shipton*, 13:456–457.

25. Adams: Adams, *Writings*, 2:91. English judge: Lush, J., in *Reg.* v. *Osman*, 15 Cox C.C. 1, 3 (Eng. 1881).

26. Zobel, "Newer Light," 127.

27. *Ibid.*

28. "Trowbridge was . . . instead of a Judge, an advocate." Savage, Diary.

29. Zobel, "Newer Light," 125–126; see also Hutchinson to Bernard, Dec. 16, 1770, Mass. Arch., 27:72–73; *B. Gaz.*, Dec. 17, 1770.

20. The Flame Subsides

1. Hutchinson to Hillsborough, Dec. 5, 1770, CO 5/759; *B. Gaz.*, Dec. 10, 1770.

2. Samuel Quincy to Paine, Dec. 16, 1770, Paine Papers; Lynde, *Diary*, 201.

3. Samuel Quincy to Paine, Dec. 16, 1770, Paine Papers.

4. Jury: MB 91; SF #101659; *Legal Papers*, 3:99–100. Evidence: *Wemms Trial*, 211–212; the civilians' trial was reported in *ibid.*, 211–217, from which my description comes. Drowne an "idiot": Burch, Hulton, and Paxton to Treasury, Dec. 21, 1770, T 1/476.

5. Zobel, "Newer Light," 128.

6. Channing, *History* 3:119–120n.; Hallowell, Hulton, and Paxton to Treasury, June 10, 1771, T 1/482.212.

7. Committal: Hutchinson to Hillsborough, Dec. 12, 1770, CO 5/760. Subsequent events: *B. Gaz.*, March 18, March 25, April 1, 1771; MB 91; SF #101788 (the indictment); Chamberlain Papers (M.1.8.217) (the perjurious testimony, taken down by Clerk of Court Samuel Winthrop); Rowe, *Diary*, 213; *Sagittarius*, 106–107.

8. Hutchinson, "Additions," 33; Zobel, "Newer Light," 125; Adams in con-

versation (1822), Quincy, *Quincy*, 29n.; *B. Gaz.*, Dec. 17, 1770.

9. Frankfurter: *United States* v. *Morgan*, 313 U.S. 409, 421 (1941). "Vindex": Adams, *Writings*, 2:77–162, most conveniently collects the "Vindex" pieces.

10. "Philanthrop": *B.E.P.*, Jan. 14, 28, Feb. 4, 18, 1771. Hutchinson: Hutchinson to Hillsborough, Jan. 17, 1771, CO 5/760. Cooper: Cooper to Franklin, Jan. 11, 1771, Sparks, *Franklin*, 7:499–500.

11. Facts: Hutchinson, *History*, 3:237; Hutchinson, "Additions," 33; Hutchinson, *Almanac*; *B. Gaz.*, Dec. 17, 1770; Samuel Quincy to Paine, Dec. 16, 1770, Paine Papers. Otway: *Britannica* (11th ed.), 20:377.

12. Hutchinson to Israel Mauduit, Dec. ?, 1770, Mass. Arch., 27:70; Burch, Hulton, and Paxton to Treasury, Dec. 21, 1770, T 1/476; Hutchinson to Hillsborough, Dec. 22, 1770, CO 5/760; Hutchinson to Israel Williams, Dec. 10, 1770, Williams Papers; Hutchinson to Bernard, Dec. 16, 1770, Mass. Arch., 27:72, 73; Hutchinson to ?, Dec. 6, 1770, *ibid.*, 67.

13. Bad disposition: Dalrymple to Gage, Dec. 17, 1770, Adams, *New Light*, 97. Montgomery: Hutchinson, "Additions," 33.

14. Bookseller and Preston's anticipated pension: Isaac Smith, Jr., to Isaac Smith, Dec. 31, 1770, Smith-Carter Papers. Pension: *CHOP*, 3:638. Adams: *Adams Family Correspondence*, 1:75. Fees: *Legal Papers*, 3:32n.

15. Hutchinson to John Pownall, Dec. 5, 1770, Mass. Arch., 27:65; Hutchinson to Israel Mauduit, Dec. ?, 1770, *ibid.*, 69; *Legal Papers*, 3:27–28, 37–38; Hutchinson to Hillsborough, Dec. 5, 1770, Jan. 17, 1771, CO 5/759. The transcript was advertised as having been rendered "as accurate as possible, by comparing Mr. Hodgson's Copy with other Minutes taken at the Trial," *B.E.P.*, Jan. 21, 1771.

16. Assembly: Rowe, *Diary*, 211. Hutchinson: Hutchinson to Israel Mauduit, Dec. ?, 1770, Mass. Arch., 27:68.

17. Oratory: Bailyn, *Origins*, 7; for an oration in Newburyport, March 5, 1774, see *ibid.*, 247, 270. Adams: Adams, *Diary and Autobiography*, 2:74. Sam Adams: Hutchinson, "Additions," 34. Hutchinson: Hutchinson, *History*, 3:236.

18. Adams, *Diary and Autobiography*, 2:79; Quincy, *Quincy*, 29n.; Adams to James Lloyd, April 24, 1815, Adams, *Works*, 10:162.

19. Zobel, "Newer Light," 127.

20. Adams, *Diary and Autobiography*, 2:14–15; Quincy, *Reports*, 382–386.

21. Adams to Matthew Robinson, March 2, 1786, Adams, *Works*, 8:384; compare materials gathered in *Legal Papers*, 3:32 and note.

22. Quincy, *Quincy*, 29n.; see also *Legal Papers*, 3:34n.

23. See A. C. Goodell's account in the *Boston Daily Advertiser*, June 3, 1887, which also describes the dispute over the Massacre monument on Boston Common, a half-mile from the fatal scene.

INDEX

Abbot, Cornelius, 37
Abercromby, Gen. James, 27
Aberdeen, University of, 285
Adams, John: and Massacre trials, 3–4, 232, 241–43, 301, 302, 303; admitted to bar, 9, 10; conspiracy theory, 18, 111; as Town counsel for opening courts, 43–44; and radicals, 45, 67, 88, 152, 243; *Liberty* case, 76; prepares Instructions on grievances, 80; offered advocate-generalship, 106; and Corbet's case, 122, 124–131; Instructions on impressment, 124, 130; retained by customs commissioners, 131; on Massacre night, 204; sentry duty, 210; asked to defend Preston, 220, 221; and Williams's case, 223; elected to legislature, 231; defense, Rex v. Preston, 244, 254, 256, 260–264; disputes with J. Quincy, 259–260, 282–283; cases between trials, 267, 269; defense, Rex v. Wemms *et al.*, 268, 270, 272, 277, 280, 284, 288, 289–293; sentencing of Kilroy and Montgomery, 298; anniversary of Massacre, 301; mentioned, 15, 16, 81, 181, 186, 219, 266

    Comments: on Bernard, 7; on attorneys, 8; on law, justices, 9; on Hutchinson, 10–11, 31–32, 35, 47; on "Caucas Club," 27; on Oliver mob, 30; on Otis, 41, 147, 149, 340; on Stamp Act, 42, 46, 57; on celebrations, 48, 145; on Paxton, 50; on E. Richardson, 55; on Russell, 57; on dollars, 57; on Trowbridge, 64; on radical press, 88; on troops, 108;

on Seider funeral, 178; on *Short Narrative*, 246–247; on Hodgson's notes, 301
Adams, Mrs. John, 204
Adams, Samuel: Harvard *Quaestio*, 11; technique against adversaries, 18–19, 32, 35; and Boston mob, 28, 70–72, 76, 112; and radical organization, 28, 38, 49, 60, 145–146, 214; elected to legislature, 41; drive to open courts, 43, 44; chosen Clerk of House, 49; on E. Richardson, 55; activities after Malcom riot, 55–56; compensation issue, 56, 57, 59; on customs commissioners, 66; Massachusetts Circular Letter of 1768, 69; public indebtedness, 70–71, 285, 339; and nonimportation, 70, 146, 152–153, 154, 164–170 *passim*, 226–227; and petition against *Romney*, 78, 79; antimilitarism, 90, 91, 92, 99, 109–111, 139, 143, 181, 206–207, 208, 209, 211; and "Journal of Times," 109–110; on possibility of massacre, 110, 181; conspiracy theory, 111; resolves on laws, 133; and warrant for Mein, 158–159; and death of Seider, 178; and attempt to link Massacre to customs, 211–212; and Massacre victims' funeral, 214; preparation for Massacre trials, 219, 220–222; antigovernment policy, 234; and Preston's "Case," 235; at Rex v. Wemms *et al.*, 271, 272, 274, 281–287 *passim*; writes on trials as "Vindex," 298–299; anniversary of Massacre, 301; on S. Gray, 246;